Spirits
of the
Age

Scottish Self Portraits

Edited by

Paul Henderson Scott

THE SALTIRE SOCIETY

Spirits of the Age published 2005 by

The Saltire Society
9 Fountain Close,
22 High Street,
Edinburgh EH1 1TF

A catalogue record for this book is available
from the British Library.

ISBN 0 85411 087 9

 Scottish
Arts Council

The publisher is very grateful to the Scottish Arts Council
for financial assistance in the publication of this book

Cover Design by James Hutcheson

Printed and Bound in Scotland by Bell and Bain Limited

David Daiches

(1912-2005)

As this book was going to print we heard the sad news of the death of David Daiches, one of the 'spirits of the age', whose thoughts on his life and times are recorded here in an interview with Michael Lister. Like Robin Jenkins, who died earlier this year and who is also included in this collection, David made a remarkable contribution to Scottish life and letters. He was a past President and stalwart supporter of the Saltire Society and his passing will be keenly felt by all who love Scotland and its literature.

Spirits of the Age

A number of the essays appear in whole or in part in previous publications and the Saltire Society is grateful to the authors and publishers for permission to use them here.

Muriel Spark: 'What Images Return' from *The New Statesman*, 1961.

Edwin Morgan: 'Epilogue: Seven Decades' from *Collected Poems* (Carcanet Press, 1990) and 'At Eighty' from *Unknown is Best: A Celebration of Edwin Morgan at Eighty* (Mariscot Press and The Scottish Poetry Library) 2000.

Agnes Owens: 'A Hopeless Case' from *People Like That* (Bloomsbury) 1996.

Janice Galloway: 'Showing Off', from *A Scottish Childhood*, 1998.

Alan Riach: 'The View from the South Pacific', from *In Scotland*, 2001.

Inga Agusdottir: interview with Robin Jenkins from *In Scotland*, 1999.

Aonghas Macneacail: 'Meeting Ronald' from *Chapman*, 89-90, 1998.

Jackie Kay: Five poems from *Life Mask* (Bloodaxe Books) 2005.

The Saltire Society

The Saltire Society was established in 1936 to support and promote all aspects of Scottish culture. As well as publishing books the Society organises a series of awards for excellence in many fields including literature, civil engineering, housing design, historical and educational publication and science. Eleven of the contributors to this collection have won the Saltire Book of the Year Award and one the First Book of the Year. In addition five have received the Society's Andrew Fletcher of Saltoun Award for services to Scotland and two an award for Lifetime Achievement.

For further information contact the Administrator, The Saltire Society, 9 Fountain Close, 22 High Street, Edinburgh. EH1 1TF. Telephone 0131 556 1836. Email: saltire@saltiresociety.org.uk

Contents

Contents

Acknowledgements

Many people have assisted in the production of this book especially, of course, the contributors and those who have helped tell their stories when circumstances prevented a personal essay. I am most grateful to Michael Lister who interviewed David Daiches, to Robert Calder, who prepared the memorandum on George Elder Davie, to Douglas Gifford, who wrote the introduction to our reprint of Dr Inga Agusdottir's interview with Robin Jenkins and to Aonghas Macneacail, who allowed us to use his *Chapman* essay on Ronald Stevenson. This has ensured that these 'spirits of the age' took their rightful place at the head of this distinguished list. Several of the other essays have appeared in one form or another in previous publications and I thank the authors and publishers for permission to reproduce them here. Finally I would like to thank Ian Scott who has master-minded the transformation of the manuscripts into print and Angie Traynor in the Saltire office who handled with great efficiency the mass of correspondence involved.

P.H.S. July 2005

Introduction

In the 1980s, when I was Convener of the Publications Committee of the Saltire Society, I arranged for the publication of a series of pamphlets containing autobiographical essays by Hugh MacDiarmid, Naomi Mitchison, Sydney Goodsir Smith and Alasdair Gray. As I said at the time this was a conscious attempt to encourage a tradition established by Robert Burns, David Hume and Walter Scott all of whom wrote admirable essays of that kind. They show that it is possible for people to describe the major influences on themselves and their objectives in a short space and to convey also a sense of their personality more faithfully than any subsequent biographer can hope to achieve.

I still think that this was a good idea, but the pamphlet format was a mistake. They disappear too easily on the book shelves and for that reason, they are unpopular with the bookshops. So now, twenty years later, when I have again been charged with the responsibility of convening the Committee, I have returned again to the publication of autobiographical essays, but this time by more people and in a more substantial format.

The aim is to reflect and record the present cultural and intellectual climate in Scotland by accounts of their experiences by people who have made an important contribution to it. It does not, of course, profess to include everyone who has done so. Of the people I have invited, two have declined because of their agreements with their publishers, one because of other demanding commitments, and two without explanation. In any case, there are simply too many influential forces in this hot bed of genius to include them all in one book. I think that we shall need a second volume before too long which should include politicians, commentators on our affairs and scientists. Then there is the younger generation of highly talented people of all kinds, for whom we shall have to wait a few years before they can be expected to indulge in autobiographical reflections. I hope that my successors in the Saltire Committee will return to the idea every ten or twenty years or so.

Many of the contributors to this book have experience of living or working abroad, a familiar Scottish experience. It began centuries ago with travelling scholars, traders and soldiers of fortune. After the Union the Empire gave a new impulse to permanent emigration. Tom Nairn in his essay discusses the traumatic psychological consequences. of the Union and their effects on the attitudes of the emigrants. "Scottish intellectuals", he says, "dreamed up the modern world because they had lost their own". But he adds: "Devolution has at least opened new doors, and with its leaven of democracy made the return of real self-rule conceivable".

A strong sense of identity with Scotland and of affection for it emerges from many of these essays. Muriel Spark says: "Although I have lived abroad for many years I am always aware that I am Scottish both by birth and formation". Alexander McCall Smith's parents were Scottish, but was born and grew up in Africa. Later in his life he worked in Botswana, a country with which he had "a prolonged love affair". But he too felt that his roots were in Scotland. "I love this country and I am proud of it". Jackie Kay too has no doubt that her country is Scotland. Duncan Macmillan takes satisfaction from the fact that "Scottish art, from being a forgotten and neglected part of our history, has become in recent years a central part of the national consciousness and above all of national pride and self-esteem". David Daiches was not of Scottish descent but he went to school and university in Edinburgh. When he went to work in America, "he was very homesick for Scotland" and he feels "very committed to it". Alastair Reid has spent most of his life in Spain and in South America and the United States, but, as he says, he "never failed to return to Scotland". This I well know, because we had a mutual friend in Bert Davis and we both looked forward with pleasure to his more or less annual visits. Alastair, as is evident from his essay, has a deep understanding of Scotland and he identifies with it to the extent of feeling that it is, "the only place where I never feel the separation of being from somewhere else". Jamie Reid Baxter too has spent much of his life abroad, but he says: "Scotland has never ceased . . . to be the central focus". Allan Massie is sure that his novels reveal "a Scotch accent of the mind". Hugh Pennington is not Scottish either by birth or descent, being as he says modestly "only a Scot by domicile". But he too says that for him, "Scotland had become home".

To people familiar with Scotland this strength of feeling and commitment may seem perfectly natural; but after very nearly 300 years of the Union with England it is remarkable that Scotland has not been absorbed in its larger and more powerful neighbour. To a large extent Scotland lost its international identity and control over its own affairs in 1603 when James VI of Scotland succeeded also to the throne of England and flitted to London. When Scotland proposed in 1703 to escape from this subordination the English government made it clear that they would not tolerate it. England was engaged in a long war with France and could not risk an independent Scotland which might revert to its traditional policy of alliance with England's enemy. They insisted on an "incorporating" Union, intended to make Scotland part of a greater

England, to be called Great Britain. This, in the words of Linda Colley was "an invented nation, . . . forged above all by war"[1].

It was not complete incorporation however. In order to make the arrangement acceptable to the Scottish Parliament, the Treaty of Union and an associated Act, provided for the continuing separate existence of the Scottish Church and legal system and therefore of local government and education, and for about a hundred years these had far more influence on Scottish life, attitudes and habits than a distant Parliament in London which took little interest in Scottish internal affairs. As Sir Walter Scott said; Scotland was "left . . . under the guardianship of her own institutions, to win her silent way to national wealth and consequence". But Scott goes on to say that this ceased early in the 19th century when Westminster started to interfere in Scottish affairs and he protested vigorously against it.[2]

Michael Hechter, the American sociologist in his book, *Internal Colonialism: the Celtic Fringe in British National Development* (London, 1975) argues that "a defining characteristic of imperial expansion is that the centre must disparage the indigenous culture of peripheral groups". By imperial expansion he means the process by which England over several centuries asserted control over Wales, Scotland and Ireland. He adds that "one of the consequences of the denigration of indigenous culture is to undermine the natives' will to resist" and that "conversely, the renaissance of indigenous culture implies a serious threat to colonial domination"[3].

I think it is unlikely that any English statesmen ever consciously and deliberately formulated policy in these terms. There is, however, plenty of evidence in this book and elsewhere that this "denigration of indigenous culture" was indeed the consequence of the Union. In a sense, England did not have to take any special measures to achieve this result. The mere fact that London became the centre of the royal court (when that still mattered), of political power, of wealth, fashion and the publishing industry meant that English language and culture became the model to which people of any sort of aspiration felt obliged to do their best to adjust. Even Scottish schools and Universities, proud as they may have been of Scottish traditions, had to ape English ways if their students were to be able to make their way in careers dominated by English tastes. This book is full of examples.

Aonghas Macneacail recalls "being in a (small) class of native Gaelic speakers who were taught by a native Gaelic speaker, through the medium of English". And, of course, a similar process went on for decades outside the Gaeltach where native Scots speakers were taught by a native Scots speaker, again through the medium of English. The consequence after about three centuries of this is that the use of both Gaelic and Scots has been greatly reduced. That they have survived at all, after this systematic and prolonged effort to eradicate them, is a proof of their power and vitality. That is why both of them are the vehicles of great poetry and song. As Alastair Reid says in his essay, your mood and personality changes when you switch from one language to another. A language "imposes its own attitudes, its own sense of the world". To the extent that the Scots have been educated to abandon their native speech, they tend to become less Scottish and become a pale imitation of something else.

Fortunately, Gaelic and Scots are fighting back. Two of the contributors to this book, Derick Thomson and Aonghas Macneacail, are among the poets who have given a new impulse to Gaelic. Edwin Morgan, Sheena Blackhall, James Robertson and Jamie Reid Baxter are among those who are doing the same for Scots. In his essay Robertson says that the need which many writers feel to write in Scots "against all the pressures to write only in English" proves "that Scots is not just a spoken language but a living, developing and essential literary language too".

Discrimination has not only been against language. In most countries, it is assumed that some knowledge of their own literature, history and music is an essential part of education, This has not been the general practice in Scotland. Janice Galloway says of the books read in her secondary school: "no women and not much that was Scottish save Burns". James Robertson says much the same: "Scottish literature, except for a bit of Burns, didn't exist". Joy Hendry speaks of her determination "to do everything in her power to ensure that future generations would not be so cheated of their own inheritance".

This sort of disapproval of everything Scottish and a tendency to look at everything through English eyes, has been evident too in the Universities, although less so in recent years than previously. George Davie says: "Given the excessively conciliatory habits of mind long current in Britain, Scottish ideas could too easily be deemed strange or indigestible, or ditched . . . Even within Scotland, Scottish ideas short of visible pedigree are always liable to be mistaken for superstitions, outdated dogmas of a backward territory. Seen in terms of an English tradition . . . the older Scottish perspective can be incomprehensible". Davie's important book, *The Democratic Intellect*, is a study of the process by which the Scottish universities were gradually forced into conformity with the English model, which he says was intended to "prepare the way for the cultural subordination of Scotland to England parallel to its political subordination" [4].

In these essays there are other examples of similar pressures. Jamie Reid Baxter gives several examples and concludes: "The old lies about the cultural poverty of mediaeval and Renaissance Scotland really are lies". Duncan Macmillan describes the resistance which he encountered in establishing that Scottish art was important, distinctive and influential in the rest of Europe. "To claim something was Scottish and was of value was fine so long as it was also clearly subordinate to the English view of history" When Alan Riach introduced the study of Scottish literature into the University of Waikato in New Zealand he found opposition from the "po-faced, long-bearded, blue-stockinged, shrill-minded, so called traditionalists (so often, alas, Oxbridge-impaired)". I think that he is right to identify Oxbridge, that is the Universities of Oxford and Cambridge, as the frequent source of what Walter Scott calls the "supercilious disdain of the English". [5]

As a consequence of all these pressures, Scottish culture since the Union of 1707 has more than once appeared to be threatened with extinction, but has been saved by a counter-attack, such as the revival of vernacular poetry in the eighteenth century by Ramsay, Fergusson and Burns. George Davie in *The Democratic Intellect* describes an "alternation between catastrophe and renaissance, in which the distinctive national inheritance was more than once brought to the very brink of ruin only to be saved at the last minute by a sudden burst of reviving energy" [6].

Once such brink of destruction was in the 1920s and 30s. Several books at that time reported the situation in Scotland in terms of despair. Edwin Muir in *Scottish Journey* (1935), for example:

> My main impression . . . is that Scotland is gradually being emptied of its population, its spirit, its wealth, industry, art, intellect and innate character . . . (It) is now falling to pieces, for there is no visible and effective power to hold it together [7].

Colin Walkinshaw (a pseudonym for J. M. Reid) said in *The Scots Tragedy* (1935): "our generation must see either the end of Scotland or a new beginning" [8].

There were several reasons for these gloomy predictions: the cumulative effects of the anti-Scottish pressures; the consequences of the First World war in which a disproportionate large number of Scots were killed; the world economic depression. J. M. Reid, under his own name, in his book *Scotland Past and Present* (1959) mentions another factor which was both a symptom and a further cause:

When regular broadcasting began in 1922, Scottish self-confidence was at its lowest ebb. It is impossible to believe that, at any other time, a people who had long had most other cultural media in their own hands – Church, schools, newspapers – would have accepted a monopoly in a new form of communication over which Scotsmen had no sort of control. [9]

Broadcasting, and particularly, when it arrived, television, has filled Scottish homes with a dominantly English view of the world which takes little or no account of Scottish conditions, institutions or ideas. The historian Geoffrey Barrow has said that this London domination of broadcasting is the most destructive blow which has ever been inflicted on Scottish distinctiveness. [10] It is therefore deplorable that broadcasting remained a subject reserved to Westminster when the Scottish Parliament was restored in 1997. Westminster presumably thought, like Michael Hechter, that a renaissance of Scottish culture implied a serious threat to their domination.

Even while the gloomy books about Scotland's future were being written, "a sudden burst of reviving energy" in George Davie's phrase was already making itself felt, the 20th century Scottish Renaissance largely inspired by Hugh MacDiarmid. In their essays in this book, Jamie Reid Baxter describes MacDiarmid as a living force in his life and James Robertson says that "MacDiarmid started a revolution in my head". Many other people, including myself, would say the same. MacDiarmid campaigned for Scottish independence and for Scotland's own distinct cultural and literary traditions, including the Scots and Gaelic languages. He was not the first or the only campaigner for these causes, but the most clamorous and insistent.

MacDiarmid's slogan, "back to Dunbar", was a call for Scotland to re-establish contact with its own rich mediaeval and renaissance culture and in particular with the poetry of Dunbar, Henryson and Gavin Douglas. Not only the poets, but the scholars have responded enthusiastically. To this Jamie Reid Baxter, a poet as well as a scholar, has made a powerful contribution. He mentions the importance of Frank Dunlop's inclusion of Saltire Society programmes in the Edinburgh International Festival. At the time I was a member both of the Festival Council and of the Saltire Festival Committee and was therefore able to introduce Frank to the Saltire programmes. His response was immediate and enthusiastic. It is unfortunate that the Saltire Society no longer takes part in either the Festival or the Fringe. It is a serious loss.

In MacDiarmid's time, much of the blame for the break in tradition, and for the loss of Scotland's close involvement with the rest of Europe, was attributed to the Reformation and to John Knox in particular. Edwin Muir wrote a highly disapproving biography of him. [11] Modern scholarship has taken a more favourable view of Knox's contribution to democratic and egalitarian ideas and respect for education, [12] and there is also a more positive view of the cultural consequences of the Reformation. Duncan Macmillan, for example, says in his essay: "The Reformation was a product of this Scottish Renaissance [that is the one of the 15th century] not its antithesis; nor indeed were its leaders fundamentally hostile to art". James Robertson says: "Whatever kind of agnostic or atheist I may be, I am first and foremost a Presbyterian one. The democratic and egalitarian aspects of Presbyterianism also, without question, informed my political views". I think that is true of many of us. The Church of Scotland was democratic in structure and egalitarian in its values, at least three centuries before the Parliaments of Scotland, England or Britain. Even in this secular age, these Presbyterian values still colour much of Scottish life.

David Murison, shortly after MacDiarmid's death made an unlikely comparison between him and John Knox: "After Macdiarmid, as after Knox, Scotland will never be the same place again". [13] Murison was right. Since MacDiarmid died in 1978 the political and cultural climate of Scotland has changed radically. The Scottish Parliament has been restored, even if its powers are still drastically restricted, and in achieving it the pressure has come more from the writers than from the politicians. We are living in one of the liveliest periods of Scottish literature. UNESCO has recognised Edinburgh as the first World City of Literature More books on Scottish history have been published in the last fifty years or so than ever before. The schools still have to catch up, but Scottish literature and Scottish history are now actively studied in Universities, and not only in Scotland.

It is widely recognised that one of the strengths of Europe is the richness and diversity of its distinct national traditions. The value and the international influence of the Scottish contribution is now more internationally appreciated than ever before. In this the Edinburgh Festival has played a significant part. So has one of our contributors, Richard Demarco, a man of tireless energy and inexhaustible ideas, who has radically enlivened our involvement in the cultural life of contemporary Europe.

Much remains to be done, particularly in the schools, which have so far failed to respond adequately to the progress made in the Universities. In the 1990s the Consultative Council on the Curriculum, an official government appointed body, set up a review group to consider the reform of the treatment of Scottish culture and history in the schools. In May 1998 they drew up a report, with detailed recommendations. The Council itself, apparently because of political pressure from the Government, did not publish this report, but instead a feeble and emasculated version of it. It seems that Hechter's warning of the effects of cultural renaissance had found a new response.

The report of the Cultural Commission headed by James Boyle may stimulate a new response in the schools and elsewhere. The press on 22nd March 2005 reported a speech in which he said that Scottish history and literature should be taught systematically in the schools and that Scottish public libraries should be required to buy Scottish books. These self-evident points are precisely among those which the Saltire Society made in its submission to the Cultural Commission. In such matters as these, official Scotland still has to respond to the resurgent Scotland of the 'spirits of the age'.

P. H. S.

July 2005

References

1   Linda Colley, *Britons; Forging the Nation, 1707-1837* (Yale, 1992) p.5

2   Sir Walter Scott, *The Letters of Malachi Malagrowther*, edited by
     P.H.Scott (Edinburgh, 1981) p.10

3   Michael Hechter, op. cit., pp. 64,73

4   George Davie, op. cit. (Edinburgh, 1961) p.58

5   Sir Walter Scott, *The Heart of Midlothian*, Chapter XXXV

6   George Davie, op. cit., p. XVI

7   Edwin Muir, op. cit., pp. 3,25

8   Colin Walkinshaw, op. cit., p.167

9   J.M.Reid, op. cit. p.167

10   Geoffrey Barrow, in an address to the Saltire Society.

11   Edwin Muir, *John Knox: Portrait of a Calvinist* (1929)

12   Rosalind K. Marshall, *John Knox* (Edinburgh, 2000); Roderick
     Graham, *John Knox, Democrat* (London, 2001)

13   *Lines Review*, December 1978.

George Elder Davie

Born Dundee, 18th March 1912

PHILOSOPHER

Andrew Fletcher of Saltoun Award 1999

The Democratic Intellect : *A Memorandum*

Prepared by Robert R Calder

Any memoir of George Davie must deal with ideas and with Scotland together, and by no means entirely retrospectively. Retrospection can however, like travel, afford significant contrasts of perspective on what currently is or isn't happening, a lesson from a Scottish Eighteenth Century whose study George Davie pioneered. Compare past Scottish institutions with English ones of the same period, and you're more likely to find evidence of England's very distinctive history than any otherwise instructive equivalences. Draw comparisons with institutions across the water in Europe, and there is evidence that the older Scotland was more than a collection of backward regional anomalies.

Some years ago an American scholar applied the term 'The Scottish Renaissance' to what's now casually called the Scottish Enlightenment (but when, George Davie asks, did Scots ever fancy they needed enlightening?). 'The Scottish Renaissance' is of course too confusingly close to a term C.M. Grieve coined, much at the same time as he coined the name Hugh MacDiarmid. For convenience he'll mostly be called MacDiarmid here — and to essay what Thomas Reid called a 'due mean' between an over-familiar 'George' and forensic sounding use of his surname George Elder Davie will be called G.E.D.

He is especially aware of the actual Scottish *Renaissance*, the Latinist and Humanist cultural development of the immediate Reformation period, associated with the towering figure of George Buchanan. G.E.D. has been concerned with questions of Scottish renaissance since an undergraduate, and it's now clear that Buchanan remained a presence during the now more widely recognised renascence of the eighteenth century. In *The Democratic Intellect* G.E.D. drew attention to a distinctive Scottish classicism extending from then into the nineteenth century, a sense of culture rather than academic research. J.S. Blackie sought a cultural renascence then, as did J.F. Ferrier, possibly the major figure in that book, in Scottish philosophy and in the understanding of the Presbyterian polity. John Burnet's subsequent work for a renascence in Scottish education was continuous with these earlier ventures. Like Ferrier's it had a fate well enough imaged, G.E.D. has written, by the sort of bathetic flop recurringly dramatised in MacDiarmid's *A Drunk Man Looks at the Thistle*. The intellectual quality as well as the heroism of these men remains an inspiring challenge.

Dundee

George Elder Davie was born in Baxter Park Terrace, Dundee on March 18th, 1912. His grandfather Peter and great-uncle Andrew Davie were partners in a painting and decorating firm. His father, George Sr., was a pharmacist with a shop in the Hilltown district, a dapper, good-humoured man who used his professional expertise to stay out of the 1914 war. George Sr. died in 1939 after a long illness.

The family of G.E.D's mother, Isabella Elder, of Angus farming stock, had a bakery in the Lochee district. Like her sister Alice, Isabella had trained as a schoolteacher. Somewhat formidable, she'd rather her son had found a profession with more obvious public cachet, in the Kirk, say, or Law. Publication of *The Democratic Intellect* in 1961 did give her the satisfaction of being congratulated by an acquaintance that G.E.D. had written a very welcome and necessary vindication of Scottish teaching.

The young George's interest in the Elders' migration to Dundee drew him to a story in A.H. Millar's *Haunted Dundee* (Dundee, Malcolm MacLeod, 1923). An 1827 broadsheet reports:

> MARY ELDER or SMITH, wife of David Smith, Farmer at Denside, Parish of Monikie, and county of Forfar ... tried at Edinburgh, an Monday the 19th February 1827, for the wilful Murder of Margaret Warden, her young Servant maid, by administering poison to her, on the 5th September last, in consequence of which she Died the third day after; but the libel was found Not Proven.

Mrs. Smith had given Margaret a milky liquid as 'medicine'. Margaret was 25 years old, and pregnant, she had told friends, by Mary Elder's son. The Lord Justice Clerk presided, the Lord Advocate represented the Crown, Francis Jeffrey defended. G.E.D. recalls a contemporary ballad, according to which Mary 'poisoned her servant/ to keep up her pride':

Oh, Jeffrey, Jeffrey,
ye haena done fair,
ye hae robbed the gallows
o its proper heir,

If it hadna been for your guineas
sae frank and sae free
she'd hae hung like a troot
in Bonny Dundee.

In G.E.D's time at Dundee High School the teaching of poetry conformed discouragingly to the Preface to *The English Parnassus*. Living poets weren't favoured, and Burns was a 'peasant poet'. The modern poet George Bruce remembered arriving at Dundee High as a teacher of English not long after G.E.D. had left. He found no place for his enthusiasm for Ezra Pound. As for Shakespeare, shortly before Bruce joined the BBC he was able to explain to an inspector of schools why his class had done better in one specific year's Leaving Certificate examination. As an experiment that year, he'd tried to teach not Shakespeare, but the orthodoxy of A.C. Bradley's commentaries on Shakespeare. For G.E.D., Latin and Greek poetry filled an interest poorly served by the *English Parnassus*. His academic performance did draw head-hunters from Oxford, but he wasn't interested.

John 'Moses' McLennan was a headmaster nicknamed for his Old Testament visage and his wonted rhetoric about the promised land beyond the Canaan of study. From 'Moses' G.E.D. first heard of John Burnet, whose assistant 'Moses' had been for a couple of years in the Greek dept at St. Andrews University. G.E.D's one poem, collected here for a first time, was inspired by the High School's mock election in 1929:

What! Has The School so spiritless become,
That, when the traitors roar, the patriot's dumb?
Does no good Tory list to Maxwell's call
When fluent Robbies rant and Potters call?
Britannia, rise! And don thy war attire,
Thy foes with fear, thy sons with sense inspire!

Blast with thy bolts and wither with thy fire!
Till that foul crime called Communism cease,
Till Comrade Potter howls and begs for peace,
Till Liberal hope in Robbie droops and fails,
And love of Country through the school prevails.
 Why round the Pillars roars the raging pack?
Is Bell Street forced? Has West Green's door blown slack?
Or does the School rejoice in drunken cheer,
Full flown with insolence and Robbie's beer?
Who's that thin lunatic that yells and howls
And groans and roars and sweats and swears and growls?
With bright red badge, with voice like creaking tin,
With forward stoop, with maniacal grin
Jim Potter speaks and makes his pledges rash,
Spouting out specious fibs and senseless trash.
Yes trash! But yet the multitude still cheers,
Applauding and believing all it hears,
As if that frenzied figure, strange and odd,
Were not a demagogue but demigod.
What though he lacks Burke's charm and Chatham's fire,
Disraeli's wit, or Gladstone's righteous ire?
Potter the Great will soon collect a crowd,
Merely by talking rot and shouting loud;
Excess of voice makes up for want of wit
And bawling hides the senses' deficit.
'This is not true!' Potter once only spoke;
In doing so, his cause he almost broke.
Tell! Who cares? Let him quake in his shoes!
And rouse his party on to jeers and boos!
Potter's a coward! Coward is my taunt!
Afraid last week in School to show his front;
Afraid to let two Tory speakers speak,
Showing in all he does the yellow streak;
Afraid last lunch to talk before the School,
Lest he should show us what he is — a fool.
And as a cobra waits before it bite,
Potter waits last before he speaks tonight,
Proposing Government OF, BY, FOR all,
At least, I think thus ran his crimson bawl.
A miserable policy; you'll see
For under Communism — credit me —
Each puling little infant of class three

Will with the noble ninth class equalled be.
You foul attacker of the British throne,
You friend of every country but your own,
Destroyer of our army and our fleet,
Not caring if in battle we are beat.
In the last war the Reds tried to rebel,
And their own country's cause to foes to sell.
Four years ago, the General Strike they made
To ruin this land and Russia's cause to aid.
Potter! Oh Potter! Are you not ashamed
To count yourself among a pack so blamed?
Enough of Potter! Subject now too vile
To raise up laughter or evoke a smile.
Consider well! Ye lovers of your land,
Ye Scotsmen true, ye patriotic band —
Think ere you vote and think of my advice —
Shall Communistic cads or Lib'ral lice
Triumph through Venom, Villainy and Vice?
Shall William Maxwell fail to top the poll?
Perish the thought! Or perish else the School!

On G.E.D's later appointment as a philosophy lecturer his former maths teacher, a Mr. Meiklejohn, wrote with congratulations, remembering that though no high-flier with special mathematical aptitude, G.E.D. had always displayed exceptional interest in the detail of mathematical proofs. The family minister had reminisced to the schoolboy G.E.D. about his own time at Glasgow University. The Logic professor John Veitch, poet, patriotic scholar of literature and Scottish philosophy, had been so affronted by the Hegelian Edward Caird's appointment in Moral Philosophy he denounced Caird's teaching in a lecture series (published as *Knowing and Being*, 1889 — with limited grasp, reviewers said, of the doctrines he was attacking). Veitch was a very minor figure *qua* philosopher, but G.E.D. remembers being told of his defiant declaration, 'Pure Being, gentlemen, is pure nonsense!'

University

In Autumn 1930 G.E.D. matriculated in an Edinburgh University very different even from the institution to which he returned as Lecturer in Philosophy thirty years later.

With or without belief or doctrinal assent, intellectually active undergraduates attended the Kirk on Sundays, and discussed sermons with the sort of interest in theology G.E.D's teacher and later colleague Angus Sinclair took to be part of philosophy (*An Introduction to Philosophy*, 1944). Incidentally, G.E.D. suspects that MacDiarmid didn't grow up in a household where the only books were the Bible and Burns, but one without the Burns. At the soiree where *de luxe* copies of MacDiarmid's 1978 *Complete Poems* were presented to friends and subscribers (unsigned, the poet had died hardly more than weeks before) the poet's widow Valda told G.E.D. she'd been reading through her advance copy, and, 'Christ! For an atheist Chris wrote a Hell of a lot about God!'

G.E.D. graduated with First Class Honours in Classics in 1935 and has vivid recall of the 'thrilling' teaching of A.F. Giles, Lecturer and subsequently Reader in Ancient History, on (1) the wars between Athens and Sparta and (2) the transition from Republican to Imperial Rome. They were held in 'a lovely little circular lecture room' on the top floor of the Old Quad in the same North East corner as the Philosophy Department. Students not enrolled in the smaller second-year class sat in simply to hear Giles, whose style in lectures was informal, and not interrupted by specific scholarly references. All in all a great man, Giles was a first-rate academic administrator who believed the Scottish universities ought to maintain their distinctive character. Among his more behind the scenes work he ensured the results of innovations, good *and* bad, were duly chronicled.

W.M. Calder, Professor of Greek, editor of the *Classical Review*, had studied at Oxford, in Paris and with Wilamowitz-Moellendorf in Berlin. He'd taken his first degree within the University of Aberdeen Greek dept. whose abolition after three centuries seemed ominous in the 1980s. G.E.D. recoiled at the Professor's response to John Burnet's view that Plato had given an accurate account of the person and teachings of his friend and mentor Socrates. Burnet was 'a sentimentalist!' G.E.D. wasn't the sole Scottish opponent of that view. He read a great deal of Greek, retaining powerful admiration of the tragedies of Aeschylus, but published only reference book entries in the field.

His reading in Latin, customarily called 'Humanity', extended among the Scottish Humanists, and he provided MacDiarmid's *Golden Treasury of Scottish Poetry* with translations of Buchanan and Arthur Johnstone.

A colleague in Classics was John MacLean, whose remarkable family was further distinguished by his brothers Sorley, the great Gaelic poet, and Calum, pioneering Scottish folklorist. Sons of a Gaelic-speaking crofter-tailor, they demonstrated a great tradition of respect for learning. Sorley already as a schoolboy was intellectually very active, for all his later shared amusement that his first experience of any train was boarding the one at Plockton which took him to Edinburgh and university. Later the translator of Homer's *Odyssey* into Gaelic verse, as a postgraduate in Vienna John found himself at home with the Viennese sense of humour. Latterly Headmaster of Oban High School and an inspiring teacher of Classics, he'd resigned from H.M. Inspectorate of Schools in disgust at the examination board's adjudication of a case he had referred.

G.E.D's closest undergraduate friend was the greatly gifted W.R. Aitken, whose precocious independent reading informed several contemporaries. After a career in libraries, Bill Aitken retired as Reader in Librarianship Studies at Strathclyde University. Beside his bibliography of 20th Century Scottish Literature and a historical study of the public libraries in Scotland, he's remembered as co-editor of MacDiarmid's 1978 *Complete Poems* with the poet's son, Michael Grieve.

William Soutar's own appointee as his literary executor, Bill Aitken edited a long overdue properly inclusive *Poems of William Soutar: A New Selection* (1988). Earlier he'd responded to the resentful accusations of one scholar whose work he'd scooped, pointing out that if he'd stolen the man's unpublished work it was surely a case of burglary, and shouldn't the police be called in?

G.E.D. long kept in touch with Stuart Hood, pre-war lyric poet in Scots and fellow teacher with Sorley MacLean at Boroughmuir Secondary School. Hood's *Carlino* is an account of his time as an escaped POW with the wartime Italian resistance. He became an important presence in the BBC and media generally, a major literary translator (Ernst Jünger, Erich Fried, Dario Fo) novelist and author. Only later did G.E.D. meet Hood's Montrose schoolfellow R.S. Silver, technologist, poet, playwright, author of an autobiography G.E.D. thinks important. Only an extract from that book has ever been published, in the *Edinburgh Review* when G.E.D's pupil Peter Kravitz was editor. A lengthy interview with Hood was also printed in the journal, beside several items relatable to *The Crisis of the Democratic Intellect*.

James B. Caird's gifts, 'which were considerable', never found realisation. Another major undergraduate discussant, he wasn't the only man to find postgraduate studies in France didn't serve as a recommendation for academic preferment in Scotland. A longtime HM Inspector of Schools, he was restricted by the requirement to secure official approval of anything written for publication. Caird compartmentalised his respective undergraduate activities, which included courting. G.E.D. never got to know that well Caird's wife Janet, a versatile writer and critic whose later verse G.E.D. admires a lot.

He esteems Robert Garioch highly, notably Garioch's prose memoir of Prisoner of War experience *Two Men and A Blanket*, which the admirable Robin Lorimer eventually saw into print. G.E.D. rates it beside Garioch's verse, an important expression of Garioch's Weltanschauung, which could be called 'Christian', though Garioch himself probably wouldn't himself have used that term. In response to a lecture by the nuclear physicist Oppenheimer, Garioch's long poem 'The Muir' opts for 'Jehovah', preferring the Old Testament to a science whose course, painstakingly traced in extended verse argument, seems to dissolve every consideration in infinity. Garioch also produced the then considerable novelty of translations of George Buchanan's Latin tragedies (*Jephtha* and *The Baptist*) into vital language, classical Scots like Fergusson's. His rendering of a Buchanan poem, 'The Humanists' Trauchles in Paris' is as modern as Garioch's own schoolteaching experience. 'Garioch's Ripone til Buchanan' and his sonnet on being haunted by recollection of two censorious old teachers presage his later dedication to formally strict renderings of the more bitingly satiric Romanesco sonnets of Giuseppe Belli.

Hugh MacDiarmid

In print, G.E.D. first encountered MacDiarmid, Grieve, in copies of *The Scottish Educational Journal* his Aunt Alice passed on to him. Other things in the journal interested him too, but the 1925-'27 *Contemporary Scottish Studies* brought into his ken a wide ambit of cultural concerns, beside the rejoinders of conventional-minded readers. Beyond the persona of the drunk cosmopolitan intellectual looking at the thistle in the earlier 1920s, who at the time knew pretty well 'bugger all' about Scotland, MacDiarmid went on to enact a precept later articulated by James Bulloch, co-author of a *History of the Scottish Church*. G.E.D. commends: the best way to learn about anything is to *write* a book about it.

One statement of G.E.D's *must* be quoted in bold:

MacDiarmid didn't get his philosophy from me. He already had his own philosophy long before we ever met.

G.E.D. remembers admiring such demonstrations of the capabilities of Scots as in the following, from 1931, uncollected before 1978:

Your bike-wheels ga'en like bees-wings doon the road,
Or, your face scarlet frae the icy wind,
Openin your big broon bag and showin' in'd

Cakes, apples, oranges, a wondrous load ,
Frae hogmanayin' . . .

Or 'mang your books, as queer a lot to me
As ony library frae Mars might be,
Or voicin' Trade Union and Co-operative views
Or some religious line, as 'twere the crude
Beginnin's o' my ain deep interests there,
Or gien me glimpses, fleetin, unaware,
O' feelin's that noo I micht ha'e understood,
Or jokin' mither (a ploy you aye were at),
Then suddenly deid, wha'd never ailed afore . . .

The blackly ironic tabloid headline title is 'Fatherless in Boyhood' (*Complete Poems*, 1978, p.1250). Reflecting on a preoccupation with Scotland, 'The Dog Pool' (ibid., p.1252) is cited in *The Crisis of the Democratic Intellect*. Its only previous appearance was in the *Scottish Educational Journal* in 1931.

G.E.D's first sighting of MacDiarmid was of a man walking across the Meadows in Edinburgh with the air of having a mission in life. Caird had made the poet's acquaintance, and introduced G.E.D. to him one evening in 1933 in Rutherford's bar on Drummond Street, near Old College. They 'got on like a house on fire', and talked till the pub closed. Next day, G.E.D. returned to his digs after the hair of the dog to find his mother had arrived on a visit from Dundee. She disapproved further of his later spending a month on the Shetland island of Whalsay, where MacDiarmid lived from 1933 until wartime. She disapproved of MacDiarmid.

Like the Clydeside socialist John Maclean, MacDiarmid had been converted to Scottish nationalism by the Hon. Ruaraidh Erskine of Mar. G.E.D. shared their concern for a renascence of Scotland whose concerns were inseparably the revival of the despoiled intellectual and artistic culture and the remedy of the then heinous material deprivation during the Depression.

G.E.D. and MacDiarmid admired Wyndham Lewis's 1929 *Paleface* for its critique of shallow trendy enthusiasms for the exotic, on the part of people who never investigated their own native European culture. G.E.D's current rejection of the postcolonialist template is grounded in a critique of intellectual globalisation, ignoring not merely the scale of the Scottish intellectual but its substance, the tradition of a distinctive philosophy generated by address to specific national, local concerns. Sheerly 'international' philosophy is a criticism of standards, but is liable to be blinkered, dealing.with the specifics of a local situation from a limited perspective. It is also liable to be blinkered as regards its own standards and prospects, which historically have been dependent on the infusion of fresh considerations raised within the 'national' contexts. G.E.D. has repeatedly expressed concern about habits of looking at Scottish philosophy and other intellectual concerns with the limited perspective of the historian.

A major achievement of MacDiarmid's was in demanding and furthering recognition of Scottish things as Scottish, in contrast with David Masson's Victorian project of 'internal Scotticism'. All very well to introduce good ideas *qua* good ideas into Great Britain under plain cover, but for want of easily discerned profile and visible intellectual pedigree such ideas can come to seem aberrances from rather than criticisms of dominant tendencies. Given the excessively conciliatory habits of mind long current in Britain, Scottish ideas could too easily be deemed strange or indigestible, and ditched. The Robbins report on higher education assumed that the merits of Scottish university models would be visible and influential on a unified British system. That was a mistake. Even within Scotland, Scottish ideas short of visible pedigree are always liable to be mistaken for superstitions, outdated dogmas of a backward territory. Seen in terms of an English tradition of rules of thumb which facilitate slick performance, the older Scottish perspective can be incomprehensible. Such rules of thumb of course have their own severe limits, fostering inability to appreciate anything different, and serious slowness on the uptake with anything 'foreign'.

G.E.D. underlines the importance of A.R. Orage's journal *The New Age* (1907-1922) as a vivifier of European intellectual standards in Britain, fostering MacDiarmid, Edwin Muir and some contemporary Scottish philosophers including John Anderson. Orage came from the Yorkshire outback opened up by Victorian education, and his journal also published Ezra Pound, T.E. Hulme and Wyndham Lewis, the preface to whose 1927 *Time and Western Man* insists on the need to seek and question the general principles underlying obvious surface concerns.

G.E.D. admires Lewis's considerable philosophic competence, his gift like MacDiarmid's for telling quotations such as exposed T.H. Green's puritan evangelical imperialism, and phrases such as 'revolutionary simpleton', which is integral to G.E.D's own thought and language. There was also in Lewis's novel *The Revenge for Love* (1937) the acuity to set in anglosaxony many of the questions of Dostoevsky's *Devils*, itself perhaps the greatest novel G.E.D. has read.

Lewis in 1927 was concerned with a development of habits of expression which just fell in with the new, notably with the philosophy and science of the day and its false prestige. Influenced by post-Einstein physics, philosophers had been 'taking time seriously', to the exclusion of taking other considerations seriously enough. Beside time and change there is space, as real as a mountain range, and what is defiant of time: works of art, ideas, Classics, and such contested distinguishable entities as Scotland.

G.E.D. respects greatly some philosophers Lewis criticises, Bergson, Samuel Alexander (whose *Space, Time and Deity* has much to give to future philosophy) and A.N. Whitehead, for having opened up dialogue with earlier philosophers. With the dominance of a conciliatory mind-set and progressivist assumptions an emphasis on attention to time and change can degenerate into an uncritical, very superstitious *go with the flow*. With no delight, G.E.D. sees in MacDiarmid's *Lucky Poet* an abandonment to progressivist rhetoric like Bergson's in *L'Évolution Créatrice*. *Lucky Poet* is swept along in a tide of journalistic paraphrase, and promises that the new mathematics will finally achieve the Benthamite project of universal progress, with new 'scientific' techniques of universal education.

That sets aside Scotch or other metaphysical considerations of human or even Scottish nature, such as were raised by T.E. Hulme and by G.E.D's teacher Kemp Smith, recognising — 'original sin' or 'secular calvinism' — human limitedness and dependency on culture and tradition and its criticism. In his 1981 Dow Lecture, G.E.D. contrasted the profundity of the allegedly refractory and not forward-looking Scots with both the old Benthamite project and the new English and Jacobin inspiration of the new wave of 'economic' historians latterly arrived on the scene. These historians did stir prospects of reviving debate, with their fresh but not entirely new and also restricted perspectives on Scotland. Their attack on the *lad o pairts* legend of Scottish nineteenth century education, from an excessively globalising perspective, could be a fair enough criticism of some versions of the American Dream. The ability of some individuals to ascend to positions far above their beginnings at the socio-economic bottom establishes no case, in the Scottish context, against wider provision of opportunity. To attack nineteenth century Scots for maintaining their intellectual traditions rather than pursue an absolute egalitarianism is, as Kemp Smith makes clear, unhistorical. G.E.D. diagnoses it as bad geography forby.

As against educationalists who wrote of Victorian Scotland's educational system as designed to train personnel to run the British Empire, John Burnet's concern was with the need to equip Scots to govern Scotland, aware of the country's institutions and their functions. Burnet foresaw the danger of a situation in which technocrats, other empire-builders and buffoons, presided as another kind of foreign ruler over a serfdom of ignorance.

With MacDiarmid's later 1930s conversion to Stalinism *Lucky Poet* was a *saltus in absurdum* from amid those earlier ostensibly contradictory considerations which G.E.D. and Caird discussed at length. Contradictions fortunately survived, hence MacDiarmid's abiding if diminished worth in later years as a valuable stirrer. His *persona* as the Great Poet and returning unconciliatory presence seemed a huge achievement when it was supposed the poetry had pretty nearly dried up. Only later did it become clear that he'd pretty well deliberately written himself out before leaving Whalsay — to do war work as a manual labourer in Clydeside engineering works.

MacDiarmid had the remarkable gift, helpful alike to pedagogue and journalist and not to be forgotten elsewhere, of the quotation or coinage telling in being both memorable and an encapsulation of something worth saying. This is rhetoric in the high sense, finding a hold on ideas to enable their communication or criticism. His rare power of material rather than formal organisation operated (for instances) on linguistic or ('On a Raised Beach') geological surveys, or versifying in Scots a prose paragraph from Valery's *M. Teste*.

G.E.D. shared MacDiarmid's enthusiasm for John Davidson's wresting of 'unpoetic' and scientific subject-matter and language into poetry, in opposition to a one-sided aestheticism. An admirer of Ian Bowman's Scots prose rendering of some biographical minutiae of Davidson, G.E.D's concern for Scots was close to an interest, shared with MacDiarmid and makars of his own generation, in Charles Doughty. G.E.D. and his Scottish generation admired Doughty's studies in etymology and old grammars and rhetoric books, and his effort to revive old words in the cause of intellectual advance. Burnet had insisted that revival of concern with Greek rhetoric was an essential prerequisite to scientific advance during the Renaissance, and the bringing into being of a culture threatened by a new Middle Ages. G.E.D. sees in MacDiarmid's 1920s work in Scots no mere pursuit of 'poetic' effects, but an attack on moribund English and Whistlebinkie Scots, moribund culture and society, attacking megalopolitan globalised English, Auden, Day Lewis, Spender & co.; but not in the cause of any mere linguistic variety.

MacDiarmid connected people. G.E.D. was one of several introduced to the great poet's former teacher and longtime friend the composer Francis George Scott. F.G. had wide interests, but was so literary a man he'd argue what he saw as the badness of a Schubert song by demonstrating at the piano that the music did something other than underline the text. He told G.E.D. the proto-*Phantom of the Opera* tale of his trip to collect the score of an orchestral work the then Scottish Orchestra had decided against. He'd gone into the former St. Andrew's Halls in Glasgow, and without encountering a soul had found his score on a desk in a basement office, retrieved it and left. One evening F.G. induced G.E.D. to expand on his ideas about Scottish education, heard him through and said that if that was written down he'd see it into print. The encouragement had been invaluable in organising the ideas, publication took longer.

Among G.E.D's numerous enthusiasms for different MacDiarmid poems, perhaps 'Prayer for a Second Flood' doesn't get its due.

> There'd hae to be nae warnin, times hae changed,
> And Noahs are owre numerous nouadays . . .

G.E.D. wonders what wider effect might have followed if MacDiarmid had been able to organise and publish *The Muckle Toon*, his autobiographical long poem in Scots set in Langholm. The question isn't secondary to *The Muckle Toun*'s place within an even larger poetic structure, but G.E.D. did share the interest that led to Bill Aitken's eventual essay on MacDiarmid's planned but unfinished or unwritten books. *The Muckle Toon* presumably included 'Fatherless in Boyhood' and such long hibernated items as 'Whuchulls', found in ms. and first published in the 1960s.

To Circumjack Cencrastus remained a fascination, despite MacDiarmid's unreasonable disappointment at its failure to attain the impossible. Unable at one time to find his own copy, G.E.D. borrowed one from James Caird, and for various reasons didn't get round to returning it for years. When he said he felt especially guilty, seeing that the book had been inscribed to Caird, Caird said he needn't have worried. Over the years MacDiarmid had inscribed and given him another two. G.E.D. appreciated Andrew Noble's reference to MacDiarmid's 'confessional' poetry, the vein of *A Drunk Man* and *Muckle Toon* and lots of *Cencrastus*. G.E.D. and Caird were especially interested in *Cencrastus* for its out-of-the-way and Scottish matter, and thought well of it generally.

Far from MacDiarmid's philosophically and otherwise distinguished early lyrics and *A Drunk Man*, there is however 'Tam o the Wilds', with regular stanzas in orthodox standard Scots, and dead like something Stalinist-inhuman. Forby more things, the fulsome doggerel tribute to Willie Gallacher, sometime lone Communist MP and often blamed for legends of John Maclean's mental incapacity, is maybe bad enough to suggest MacDiarmid actually disliked Gallacher, the man there credited with the gift of 'always being right'!

Later in the 1930s G.E.D. met Douglas Young, and George Campbell Hay, whom he took to greatly. With Young he visited Edwin Muir in St. Andrews.

Young's penchant for clowning and self-deprecation disguised a serious, valuably enterprising man. G.E.D. wasn't surprised that in Young quickly became an authority on local history in his brief time in South Carolina; or that he was mourned there years after his sudden death at his desk after the morning's jogging.

Beside translations from the Gaelic poet which represent an entirely novel sensibility in Scots, Young's maybe least known achievement was the invention of Sorley MacLean: which is to say that he induced MacLean to use an English transliteration of his Gaelic name, rather than 'Samuel', the routine substitution for Somhairle established by a Victorian registrar of births. One happy by-product of recent scholarship has been recognition of Young's voluntary labours as combined secretary and agent for MacLean and Hay when they were in the army overseas.

Philosophy

G.E.D's most important academic teacher was Norman Kemp Smith, Professor of Logic and Metaphysics, whose former student, Angus Sinclair, had returned from postgraduate studies in Oxford and the USA just before G.E.D. graduated in Classics. Sinclair was a splendid lecturer, working from drafts later worked into *The Conditions of Knowing* (1951) in a large, ledger-like book. Sinclair's wartime broadcast series *The Voice of the Nazi* impressed G.E.D. deeply.

The young A.C. Lloyd (1916-1994) arrived from Oxford as a teaching assistant, with amusing word of Kemp Smith's dark reputation down there. The physically small and personally unconventional Lloyd characteristically read works nobody else knew. A lifelong friend, at Edinburgh he was important to G.E.D's work in opening a perspective on Berkeley's philosophy very different from Kemp Smith's.

The Professor of Moral Philosophy, A.E. Taylor, had less effect on G.E.D.. No less rigorous in argument than Kemp Smith, he carried less conviction. A prodigious scholar, his *An Introduction to Metaphysics* is in effect a commentary on F.H. Bradley, to whom Taylor was unusually close at Oxford. Taylor rather warned students off that book.   During his tenure of the St. Andrews Moral Philosophy chair, with G.F. Stout and Burnet as colleagues, he had come to espouse a version of the philosophical Realism implicit in Burnet. Bradley's Absolute Idealist philosophy could not accommodate problematic new scientific questions, and Bertrand Russell's new philosophy modelled on the mathematical sciences was with his shallow individualist *Principles of Social Reconstruction* yet worse.

Burnet had found common ground between philosophy and poetry and the sciences in his exposition of Early Greek science, Pre-Socratic philosophy. Taylor's massive *Plato, the Man and His Work* followed Burnet, but with the excesses of a convert. It rather courted the charge of sentimentality. For G.E.D., Taylor's Plato book is needlessly difficult because Taylor absent-mindedly assumed that every reader would have his own command of mathematics.

Kemp Smith was perhaps the major philosophical scholar writing in English in his lifetime, though less prolific and promiscuous in topics than Taylor. Born in Dundee, he grew up in Cupar following his father's business failure, the youngest of the family. G.E.D. gathered he'd not been happy at home.

His *Studies in the Cartesian Philosophy* (1903) had already been influential when Kemp Smith in 1906 went as Professor to Princeton, N.J. His monumental *A Commentary on Kant's Critique of Pure Reason* (1919) is actually a critique of Kant, which fact as much as any difference in their respective interpretations much displeased H.J. Paton, who in his time was both student and professor at both Glasgow and Oxford. G.E.D. got on well enough with him. Paton's Kant's *Metaphysic of Experience* (1936) is a well-respected strictly expository account of Kant's aforementioned *Critique*, with outbursts against Kemp Smith's affrontery in having challenged 'the founder of the Critical Philosophy'. The consequent state of war caused between Edinburgh and Glasgow over Kant, G.E.D. discovered after publication of *The Democratic Intellect*, had been outdone by a contemporary one in the respective universities' mathematics departments.

Much as G.E.D. regrets Kemp Smith's disdain of Thomas Reid, he grants Kemp Smith's genuine difficulty in recognising philosophers below his own very high level. Kemp Smith was also better on Kant in the classroom than in the *Commentary*. Dedicated to his mentor Robert Adamson, as the book an untimely death had prevented Adamson from writing, the *Commentary* might well have suffered unduly from wariness of going beyond what Adamson might have endorsed.

Variously known to friends as Hamish or Bertie, Herbert James Paton finally retired as White's Professor of Moral Philosophy at Oxford, and living near Crieff wrote *The Claim of Scotland* (1968), well-received north of the border. G.E.D. observes that it shocked former Oxford colleagues who'd always supposed Paton might have liked them.

Kemp Smith took such a scunner at writing academic articles that he wrote his last in 1927, on Universals. He was genuinely pleased to hear G.E.D's high opinion of them. His one book not ostensibly a commentary, *Prolegomena to an Idealist Theory of Knowledge* (1924), enraged the by that time elderly destroyer of Associationist psychology, James Ward. Its extent of reference to neurophysiology puzzled readers, but apparently Kemp Smith was trying to relate the new science to those psychological insights for which he esteemed John Calvin, whom he believed deserved no less recognition qua psychologist than was currently allowed Nietzsche. The *Prolegomena* had the acknowledged assistance of Kemp Smith's sometime Logic lecturer John Anderson, who following emigration to Sydney, NSW in 1927 came to be known as the 'Father of Australian Philosophy'. Postgraduates and others sustained Anderson's reputation in Edinburgh through the 1930s, G.E.D. recalls.

Kemp Smith left only an outline, in essays, of his important views on the Middle Ages, the Renaissance, Romanticism and the Modern Mind; and the secular import of Calvin. G.E.D. regrets that John Passmore, the self-styled Australian 'Andersonian', who died in 2004, didn't take up the Kemp Smith/ T.E. Hulme secular doctrine of original sin as human limitedness in his *The Perfectibility of Man*. Passmore's notion of kindliness was a weak alternative. G.E.D. remembers a very affable young Passmore's first British visit, wearing a broad-brimmed bush hat, over fifty years ago.

Beside personal reserve, restraint and self-imposed high standards, Kemp Smith had the sense of humour G.E.D's daughter Anne remembers, teasing her as a child. When a customer in the late lamented Thin's bookshop had requested a copy of the Scottish Hegelian R.B. Haldane's *The Pathway to Reality*, as 'Haldane's *Half-way to Reality*', Kemp Smith was hugely amused. He'd himself have said '*only* half-way'.

Kemp Smith is for G.E.D. an internationalist in philosophy, unconcerned with that detail and distinctiveness of Scottish philosophy which G.E.D. has explored as important. Although he contemplated writing a book on each of them, Kemp Smith published only essays on A.N. Whitehead and on John Locke, the former bridging between modern and earlier philosophy, the latter doing for Locke what Kemp Smith's 1954 book on Descartes did for that thinker. Each of these men was a pioneer, identifiable as a great philosopher by dint of his holding the centre ground. Each one could be misleadingly accused of holding extreme views, if his statements weren't considered in proper context. The claim as to David Hume's real greatness must begin with the hypothesis that he too maintained the intellectual centre ground, as against vanity, silliness, confusions, and the construction of shams.

The Philosophy of David Hume (1941), Kemp Smith's masterwork, was perhaps inspired, G.E.D. speculates, by reading the mss. of the Gifford lectures his close friend Baron Friedrich von Hügel didn't live to deliver. Hume was no merely clever intellectual mischief-maker, for all that his narrow upbringing had kindled a hostility to Christianity that no other major eighteenth century Scottish thinker manifested. There might be more authentic Calvin in Hume than in the rigid legalistic circumscriptions of Hume's childhood. The Hume book let Kemp Smith discuss philosophical issues he had previously thought to address otherwise. His perspectives on Hume had been influenced by the German discussions of Hume by Meinong and Husserl, and the latter's pupils including the Englishman C.V. Salmon. Kemp Smith's book liberated Hume's text from two centuries' hearsay. Until T.H. Green and T.H. Grose produced their edition of the *Philosophical Works of David Hume* (1874-'75) the *Treatise* had been a rare book, Green's introduction to the edition had been dominated by widespread assumptions as to the gist of Hume's philosophy. The same account of Hume was maintained by Betrand Russell's followers, who unlike Green were enthusiastic about what they thought was Hume. Demonstrating that Hume was not what either party supposed, Kemp Smith in 1941 initiated recognition and study of a serious and very major philosopher.

Shortly after the *Treatise* 'fell dead-born from the press' Hume suppressed its Book I. Where legend spoke of Hume having done so for reasons like political correctness, Kemp Smith observed Hume's general disdain of political correctness. Hume had come to appreciate the errors in Book I, and already by Book III he was arguing views counter to the Associationist doctrine on which Book I relied. (Associationism is not the same thing as the 'association of ideas').

Book I is a work of genius, whose investigations are of the greatest worth; they founder on the false assumption of Associationism, that mental operations reduce to mere physics or chemistry, a combining of atomic entities. The child's responses to its mother, learning and the development of morality, are operations of more complex entities, as Hume recognises. There are operations Hume's Scottish contemporaries, and Nicholas Malebranche, attributed to Divine Providence, operations which Hume agrees occur. He offers an alternative, and he believed superior account, with reference rather to the operations of Nature, and human motives. One difficulty G.E.D. has drawn attention to is the lack of awareness of Hume's ambivalence on a number of issues, for instance Isaiah Berlin's paper on Hume and Hume's influence on German religious thought.

G.E.D's discovery of the Swedish philosopher Torgny Segerstedt's *The Problem of Knowledge in Scottish Philosophy: Reid, Stewart, Hamilton, Ferrier* (Lund: Gleerup, 1935) was something of a breakthrough when that book was new.

The phrase 'The Scottish Philosophy' has been applied widely, whether to the teaching curriculum compiled from Thomas Reid and Adam Smith at the end of the eighteenth century, and to the philosophy of Sir William Hamilton. The international reputation of both was badly damaged by J.S. Mill's *Examination* of Hamilton's Philosophy, 'using good arguments and bad.' In G.E.D's closely historical analysis Hamilton's philosophy (quite apart from false contemporary claims as to his greatness) was continuous with the discussion of a cluster of core philosophic questions whose beginnings were in the pioneering activity of *undergraduates* in earlier eighteenth century Scotland. Those gifted students who met in Ranken's tavern in Edinburgh took an assiduous interest in Newton's and Boyle's innovations in scientific method, and the philosophy of Bishop Berkeley, exchanging correspondence with Berkeley. In important respects, Hume's *Treatise* continued the Rankenian discussions of such as Thomas Reid's later teacher George Turnbull, although Hume towers above those able individuals.

Hume's *Treatise* prompted Reid's working out of his Common Sense philosophy, but for all. Reid's achievement he lacks the depth which commends Adam Smith to G.E.D., not least for his subsequent development of philosophy as comparison of perspectives.

Berkeley's breakthrough was in recognising that the everyday seeing of things depends on co-operation between different senses. The visual sense can't construe distances without formative experiences of moving about, and touching, in co-ordination with the operation of the eyes. Roundness isn't seen directly, it is cognised by interpretation of what the senses deliver. The infant's command of space, physical orientation and efficient movement is a trial and error business.

Not overrating human capacities, Hume presented a case G.E.D. restates in the two 'primitives' flung in a river, staying afloat clinging to a log. The effort which gets them to the shore follows from a period of floundering. It terminates with the discovery made when each man's independent floundering chances to reinforce the other's in attaining to a shoreward motion. Co-operation, and indeed the operations of society, follow from origins in trial and error and accident.

Smith's account of the origins of conscience (inspiration of Burns's 'see oursels as ithers see us') locates the child among its elders, performing imitatively and reactively amid their respective approvals and disapprovals. Among elders and others, the child begins a differentiation of right and wrong. The young boy's first account of his own movements is in the third person, 'Peter's walking'. The German philosopher Fichte is said to have held a party to celebrate his son's first use of the first person singular, I (*Ich bin ein ich*). Smith gives an account of the coming into being of the impartial spectator in the human breast following experience of external spectators.

Smith is further distinguished by having learned from his teacher Hutcheson, *and* from Mandeville and other theorists and observers, just quite how various human motivation is, altruism and self-concern co-existing. Smith's account of the social origins of conscience, of knowing, of the inefficiency of slavery as a stifling of initiatives, presaged the 'master and slave' argument of Hegel. The master is the slave of his slave's limitations, and of his own restricted perspective. If it occurred to him to work in the kitchen, both he himself and his slave who cannot cook might both eat better.

Smith's anticipations of, or influence on Hegel or Fichte, were important in J.F, Ferrier's naturalisation within Scottish philosophy of what he had learned from German reading and studies in Germany. Ferrier (1808-1864) is central to G.E.D's account of what he calls (adapting an English term of pejoration) *The Scotch Metaphysics*.

The cluster of philosophic topics brought under discussion by the Rankenian pioneers was the vortex of the Scottish intellectualism of university philosophy through Ferrier's heyday. In early articles for *Blackwood's Magazine*, where complex philosophic articles held their place within a context of general culture — the early Blackwood's of the *Noctes Ambrosianae* is for G.E.D. an admirable model of cultural discussion — Ferrier's real greatness was displayed.

Ferrier, trained in Law, had anticipated the crisis in the Kirk which precipitated as the 1843 Disruption, and in his pamphlet *Church and State* expounded the constitution of the Christian commonwealth as worked out in the age of Knox and Buchanan. The failure of this initiative to manage the dispute was the worse because the seceders' avowed position was in Ferrier's reasoned account contrary to ecclesiastical law; Ferrier's point of law (Ferrier was in fact an Episcopalian) was misinterpreted by them as a factional or party viewpoint.

This cost Ferrier the Edinburgh professorship which was his by right of distinction. Free Kirk factionalism expressed itself in Scottish chauvinist propaganda accusing Ferrier of imposing German philosophy, whereas he sought a renaissance of the Scottish philosophy, informed by continental dialogue. His public questioning of the first principles involved in the pre-1843 Kirk dispute cost Scotland and philosophy dear. Academia suffered from successive appointments on party lines, philosophy from a German-inspired globalisation where the native philosophy had declined.

As a further twist, disgust at the 1843 debacle had precipitated Ferrier's composition of the *Institutes of Metaphysic*, a seriously misguided magnum opus which distracted attention from his best work.

Important for Kemp Smith, Husserl's extension of German interest in the Scottish philosophy and Hume initiated the Phenomenological movement whose work Ferrier has now been seen as anticipating. Phenomenology has been important to G.E.D's concern with Scottish philosophy as European without ceasing to be Scottish.

In the later 1930s G.E.D., mentioning his admiration of German philosophy to some German students in Edinburgh, was shocked to be told that Hegel and Kant belonged to an old, bad Germany, which the new Germany of Hitler would wipe away. He recalls a seminar led by Richard Kroner, a distinguished exile and Gifford lecturer whose classes in Kiel members of the Hitler Jugend had disrupted very violently, and Kemp Smith's old friend G.F. Stout. A greatly distinguished psychologist and philosopher, G.E.D. thought Stout as capable of getting things as nearly right as is possible in philosophy, while making the result somehow uninteresting. Stout manifested awesome powers of understatement by responding to Kroner's 'a case of 'the identity of opposites' by suggesting it was rather one of 'the likeness of differents'. To the chairman's 'perhaps Herr Kroner favours a more Romantic form of expression Kroner replied, 'perhaps we live in a Romantic Universe!'

Belfast

Beginning military service in 1941, G.E.D. explored Burns Country on foot in uniform. In Albert Camus' native Algiers he purchased copies of books by Shestòv, MacDiarmid's 'favourite philosopher'. Stationed behind the D-Day landing he also followed up the bloody assault on Monte Cassino, where Benedetto Croce's library had been lodged in vain for safe-keeping. In 1944 George Campbell Hay wrote congratulating G.E.D, on his marriage to Elspeth Dryer, whose pre-war journal describes the younger G.E.D. Elspeth Davie became a highly respected and, unusual for Scotland, modernist rather than mainstream author of shorter fiction and novels. Her memoir of Anne Scott-Moncrieff, wife of 'Scomo', George Scott-Moncrieff, recalls not only a greatly gifted writer who died tragically early, but forgotten times. The Davies moved to Belfast in 1945, where after demob G.E.D. found a post as Lecturer in Philosophy at Queen's University.

G.E.D. retains great respect for Alexander Macbeath, Gaelic speaker from Applecross and Professor of Logic and Philosophy at Queen's, 1925-1954.

Glasgow University classmate of Macmurray and John Anderson, lecturer at Glasgow after demob in 1918, Macbeath completed the ailing Robert Latta's *The Elements of Logic* (1929) a detailed, very readable general work on sound reasoning which G.E.D. esteems greatly. For all G.E.D's regard for Angus Sinclair, he regrets that Sincalir's *The Traditional Formal Logic* (1937) proved so attractive a textbook it restricted circulation of Latta and Macbeath.

Macbeath reminisced about A.D. Lindsay, Glasgow Professor of Moral Philosophy (1922-24), subsequently the distinguished controversial Master of Balliol and dominant presence in a commission to reorganise postwar German education whose plans scandalously weren't carried through. After 1945 Lindsay set to founding the 'new university' at Keele.

G.E.D. approved the acute criticism of Kemp Smith Lindsay produced like a rabbit from a hat in the middle of a popularising account of Kant. A practitioner of internal Scotticism, Lindsay wrote about Church and State and impressed G.E.D. with his account of the Putney debates in *The Essentials of Democracy* (1932). A Glasgow graduate and bane of the Oxford establishment, Lindsay disdained ivory tower and other bad habits of modern academia. Macbeath remembered reflecting disconsolately at Glasgow in 1924 that he now seemed unlikely to get the Belfast chair; his main competitor had just produced a second book in as few years. The new book, Lindsay retorted, was in fact a good omen. Nobody that productive could possibly be any good!

Lindsay's Keele scheme drew on Scottish experience and longtime involvement with the Workers' Educational Association. Like Kemp Smith at the same time in Edinburgh, Lindsay taught a Glasgow WEA course against the influence of a current 'scientific' millenarian revolutionary Marxism. Immediate compassion for the suffering poor had been declared wrong, as possibly obstructing arrival of the inevitable Revolution. In the 1930s G.E.D. heard the same 'scientific' millenarianism preached from soapboxes in Edinburgh, with spurious citation of John Maclean, and dismissal of the Spanish Civil War as a mere blip pending the imminent final collapse of late Capitalism.

Glasgow experience presumably informed Macbeath in Ulster in time of other civil war. As university administrator he ensured that Queen's dealt not with the Stormont parliament, but with Westminster: to forestall any appearance or risk of Queen's being an enclave Catholics could feel excluded from. When an aunt of G.E.D's visited Belfast, her plans to visit Catholic friends of Dundee friends caused some alarm. Yet she went blithely into Roman Catholic arondissements and got on very well there. The pervasive effects of the Protestant-Catholic divide on twentieth century Scottish culture are a huge question.

Macbeath's force of character also showed when in delivering a paper to an Aristotelean Society meeting in the 1930s he was confronted with the impassioned heckling of the Cambridge professor G.E. Moore. Moore's habitual interruptions, often cavils over minutiae of verbal expression, had on one occasion apparently required physical restraint of both him and his former teacher Stout. Immune to Moore's noise and prestige, Macbeath addressed the chairman with a repeated, 'do I have the floor? Do I have the floor?' until order was established and he could continue. Alasdair MacIntyre cites Macbeath's one big book among the most distinguished series of Gifford Lectures. *Experiments in Living* (1952) was perhaps the most easily available representation of the sort of anthropology taught within Kemp Smith's Scots contemporaries' lecture courses. Unlike in Frazer, whose viewpoint Kemp Smith demolished in an early paper, but as in Robertson Smith, no superiority is granted to the civilised's in contrast with the primitive's powers of reasoning. Each reasons in terms of the questions he or she has learned to ask, including about differences between right and wrong. In contrast with excessively abstract contemporary versions of moral theory, Macbeath wanted concrete exemplification of what morality is. It appears to be social, a matter of informed feeling.

The first major event during the Davies' time in Belfast was the birth of their daughter Anne. Teaching in Belfast was more satisfying than in Edinburgh, Belfast undergraduates seemed more concerned with their native place. Although Edinburgh did have a more cosmopolitan student body, specific interest in Scottish philosophy there seemed stronger among English or non-Scottish students..

Over his first seven years at Queen's G.E.D. worked on *The Scotch Metaphysics*. Philip Larkin, then librarian at Queens, seemed intrigued by G.E.D's 'take' on the Scottish works he borrowed. Larkin later helped in the dealings necessary to secure a publisher's provisional acceptance to meet Edinburgh's requirements for award of the D.Litt. An admirer of Elspeth's work, Larkin remained in contact until his death. The D.Litt. was awarded in 1953.

Scotland

In 1956 the Davies settled in Edinburgh, G.E.D. returning to Belfast for the teaching terms, waiting for the vacant teaching post which appeared in 1960. He relinquished a promoted post in Belfast to take up the appointment as Lecturer in Philosophy at Edinburgh.

The Professor of Logic and Metaphysics, A.D. Ritchie, was a congenial colleague, whose book on Berkeley G.E.D. completed during Ritchie's last illness (1987). H.B. Acton was a subsequent congenial associate, of broad culture, Professor of Moral Philosophy, a scholar whose seminar on the history of philosophy made considerable contribution to Scottish Enlightenment studies.

Publication of *The Scotch Metaphysics* had been conditional on the provision of an introductory chapter on the historical and cultural setting of the philosophical work discussed. The mass of material uncovered in service of that requirement soon staked its own claim to a priority beyond that of a mere preface. G.E.D. became very conscious of information learned informally from numerous teachers and seniors which had never been presented as documented research in print. .

When Edinburgh University Press published *The Democratic Intellect* in 1961 it was greeted not warmly but with heat by the Principal, the sometime Nobel laureate in Physics, Sir Edward Appleton. He disapproved strongly of the book's account of the contest for the Edinburgh chair of Mathematics. There were threats to engage an established senior mathematician to denounce the book, on questions of the foundations of mathematics which G.E.D's friend Joseph J. Russell raised in his book *Analysis and Dialectic* (cf. *The Crisis of the Democratic Intellect*).

The Principal could hardly have been pleased by the book's considerable unconciliatory attention to questions of academic politics. That topic was further exposed with attention to John Burnet in the twentieth century, in *The Crisis of the Democratic Intellect*. Simply stated, the issue is between the respective priorities of humanistic and democratic education, and those of the universities as discharging other functions measurable in quantitative terms. Writing as a Glasgow undergraduate, John Anderson had foreseen the inevitability of State funding and consequent threats to intellectual autonomy. Decades later, G.E.D. pinpointed linked threats active within institutions. Whatever qualified function academic competition might have between respective specialist departments of technological or medical research, proposals to establish certain universities as 'Centres of Excellence' on an American Ivy League model generally involve too much silence on too many wider topics.

In *Higher Education and the War* (1915) John Burnet discussed the Prussian system's polarisation between a research-centred professorate in ivory tower isolation, lacking in worldly wisdom, and an inadequately informed public, likely prey to superstitions or charlatanism. Education for democracy or a democratic intellect had low, if any priority.

A proposed chapter on Burnet was omitted from *The Democratic Intellect*, a book marked throughout by Burnet's 1915 chapter on 'Research' (Burnet's book was the text of a 1913 series of lectures inspired by a recent *Times* article from A.D. Lindsay) rather than Burnet's attack on Prussian obsessions with paper qualifications. Burnet's contrast between 'research' and both educational priorities *and* scholarship bears relation to the present (2005) *Research Assessment Exercise* in British universities. The quality and inter-disciplinary awareness of current *publish or perish* products has been questioned. The disbandment some years back of the philosophy section at the University of Strathclyde, whose members published little, disallowed both the claim that it was a 'teaching department', and graduates' testimonials.

In *The Democratic Intellect* G.E.D. contrasts the ivory tower precisian and research focus of traditional Oxbridge Classics teaching, a long-standing case, with the Scottish concern to treat Greek and Latin texts as contributions to participation in general culture. Enthusiasm for Greek or Latin poetry ought not to be stifled, nor any reading of literary texts postponed, pending command of the detail of grammar, and techniques of textual study, well beyond the needs of humane understanding.

There's also the wide issue of the philosophic foundations of mathematics and the physical sciences, and their reciprocal relation to general culture. That issue is discussed in detail in J.J. Russell's *Analysis and Dialectic*, whose relation to Husserl G.E.D. discusses in his 1986 *The Crisis of the Democratic Intellect*. The false prestige of one or another physical science was canvassed in advance by Francis Jeffrey in the then Edinburgh Review in the early nineteenth century, a very important reference in *The Democratic Intellect*. Jeffrey foreshadowed much that has happened since with his claim that the rise of science justified abandonment of metaphysical or dialectical discussions, and moral philosophy. Jeffrey supposed such always provisional discussions could be abandoned pending the development of science to provide easily accessed, secure answers to every possible question.

Appleton's disapproval of *The Democratic Intellect* was consigned to a publicity-conscious silence by C.P. Snow's glowing review of the book. Snow was plain about the book's relation to his own question of the Two Cultures. Unfortunately, Snow's challenge had stirred F.R. Leavis to a response which George Steiner, in what was otherwise a tribute to Leavis, later deplored as pretty well hysterical. A man Snow had praised highly became an object of suspicion to members of a very much Leavisite English Literature department, and the amicable co-operative relations G.E.D. had hoped to maintain with the Edinburgh dept. became far less feasible. He was also dismayed by the range of disagreements between other individuals which resurfaced with publication of his 1961 magnum opus.

The turn of the 1960s into the 1970s was marked for G.E.D. by health problems, including serious eye trouble, but in 1977 he took up the invitation to Australia on a Fellowship, and accompanied by Elspeth went there for a year. That brought him into close contact with the work of John Anderson, whom he never met but had known of for over forty years. He formed a very high opinion of Anderson's last writings, responding after ten years to Gilbert Ryle's article 'Logic and Professor Anderson' and to the Russellian mathematical Logic it took for granted; and challenging proposed changes in Australian education.

The extent of reference to Burnet in Anderson's writings on education, 'Socrates as Educator' and 'Classicism', brought home to G.E.D. the importance of Anderson's first-hand witness of the debates on Scottish education in which Burnet was so active, with considerable sacrifice of his own scholarly work. Anderson had been a student and then university teacher over the period, and as sometime student teacher and then journalist MacDiarmid had also been very much there. At least implicitly, elements of that national discussion surely informed and were a context of the latter's work in prose and verse. Anderson's late explicit references to Burnet identify a recrudescence of old illusions on old issues,

G.E.D. retired from teaching in 1982. His subsequent survey of the voluminous unresearched Burnet correspondence in Register House contributed much hitherto forgotten detail to *The Crisis of the Democratic Intellect*.

Beginning with questions about educational policy, that book proceeds to consider the question of a general intellectual cultural life in Scotland, sustained sometime or in part by the universities, and then by autodidacts associated with the journal *The New Age*. The parallels between the *Noctes Ambrosianae* and MacDiarmid's publications are preliminaries to asking what, latterly, sustained anything of the once metaphysical Scotland.

Education policy and university politics had proved important, beside that near-disappearance of the traditional Scottish MA degree which G.E.D. chronicled in an *Edinburgh Review* essay. Originally a prerequisite to further study for an Honours degree, which took an extra year, the Ordinary MA was shaped around philosophy's function in comparison of perspectives between the humanities, the sciences and the ordinary common life. The degree's decline may be related to the import of sorts of philosophy conceived without any such function, and of developments of specialisms in the other two academic areas quite distinct from the educative comparisons of perspective intrinsic to the Scotch Metaphysics. Also, some dominance has been accorded to the superstition current in early Victorian Oxbridge, identifying education with the special expertise in one subject attained by the modern Honours degree. Specialisation was deemed to bestow whatever intellectual virtues the old Ordinary degree might have, without caring to explore what they were, or what were the *raisons d'être* of the old degree. The Ordinary degree and the case for it faded away as, for various reasons independent of investigating its longstanding rationale, its curriculum was progressively attenuated. By the methods of self-fulfilling prophecy it was allowed to decline, with no necessity, into a sort of regional anomaly.

David Daiches

Born Sunderland, 2nd September 1912

LITERARY CRITIC AND HISTORIAN

Andrew Fletcher of Saltoun Award 1989
Saltire Book of the Year, God and the Poets, *1984*

Committed to Scotland

Interviewed by Michael Lister

Over the course of the past seventy years almost, you have written over eighty books and more than two hundred research papers. How did it all begin?

When I was young I thought I was going to be a great poet — I was passionate about poetry, and words always fascinated me, words always mattered to me. And I began writing poems when I was about 7. And so there was never any doubt that I would study literature. I was always very interested in literature.

My father always had a romantic vision of Scotland, long before he came here — when he was in Germany he wrote his doctoral thesis on the relationship between Hume's history and philosophy and that gave him the feeling that Scotland was the home of philosophy. When he got a call to come to Edinburgh to be rabbi, he felt this was the fulfilment of his great ambition. He was very happy to be here and became passionately Scottish in his feeling. And I remember how excited my mother was when we were about to move to Scotland from Sunderland, where I was born. I remember how my mother got a book of Scottish songs out of the library and sang them to us at the piano — she loved music and was a very good pianist. Song is a very important part of Scottish culture. You know the famous remark by Fletcher of Saltoun, who said that if he were permitted to make all the ballads, he need not care who should make the laws of a nation.

My love of Scottish literature began with Stevenson, before I went to school. *A Child's Garden of Verses.* I was given this as a birthday present as a small boy. It spoke to me very directly. I always felt a curious affinity with Stevenson. I identified with him — we both came from Edinburgh and we had a similar relationship with our fathers and so it was something very personal, and I was very involved with Stevenson.

Literature was always my passion. There never was any question of anything else — well, perhaps history, because history is bound up with literature in a very special way. In fact in my first year at Edinburgh University the classes I took were English and History and Latin. And I came first in all three. Later, the Professor of History invited me to dinner in order to persuade me to do honours History and not honours English. But literature was always what I wanted. History was involved of course, it is so intimately related to literature, and the study of literature came to me so easily.

You read Stevenson at a very early age. And I wonder if you also came into contact with any of the writings of the 'Kailyard' and sentimental poetry of that ilk which had abounded in Scotland, or were such things outlawed from your home?

No, they were not banned. I did come across them and I did read them.

The Kailyard was a peculiarly Scottish phenomenon. Was it perhaps something of a 'necessary' phenomenon?

Well, 'necessary' is a tricky word, because in a sense whatever happens is necessary. The Kailyard happened during an interesting period in Scottish culture. It expressed some aspects of the Scottish *Geist*, and there is a core of deep sentimentality in Scotland. And Scotland had always had a great love for lost causes, because in a sense Scotland was a lost cause. Though it makes me happy to see the Scottish Parliament restored, as this may help undo a lot of that sense of that loss. Whether the Parliament justifies itself remains to be seen. But it is a good thing. And it is encouraging that Edwin Morgan has been appointed Scotland's Makar. It is a very good gesture.

You have said before that you are not a specialist but a generalist?

Yes, that's right, though I did specialise in particular periods at different times. I did concentrate for a time on contemporary literature — Joyce and Eliot and Woolf. And I was always fascinated by Hugh MacDiarmid, of course. MacDiarmid was *sui generis*. He never wrote anything to beat his early lyrics, though I don't think he realised that himself. Some of his early lyrics are quite wonderful. The longer poems, the epic poems, I think were a bit misguided. I don't think that is where his real genius lay. He overloaded them with erudition, with fake erudition, cribbing things from books he had read without understanding. He even once quoted some Hebrew in *In Memoriam James Joyce*, but printed it upside-down. But I don't think MacDiarmid ever produced anything finer than his early lyrics.

What was it that made you decide to specialise in Scottish literature?

When I was in America, I was very homesick for Scotland. I had always had an emotional relationship with this country and when I went to America, Scotland's appeal rose to an extraordinary level. 'Distance lends enchantment to the view' and this intensified my romantic feelings for Scotland. I felt a sort of obligation to write about Scotland and its writers. I felt I owed something to Scotland and to Edinburgh in particular. Scotland had been very kind to my family and I felt very committed to Scotland. My father always said that Scotland was the only country in Europe that never persecuted Jews, but of course one of the reasons for that was there weren't any Jews here in the first place.

But it has been said that the Presbyterian Scots did — and perhaps still do — greatly respect the 'People of the Book'.

Yes, my father found this to be true. He felt that very deeply. I think my father must be the only person in the world who was invited to a Burns' Supper where they had a special kosher haggis for him. He even has a street named after him, here in Edinburgh.

Yes, indeed, Daiches Braes. The beautiful conjunction of the Jewish and the Scottish — not street, not road, not place, but Braes.

When I first wrote about Stevenson, I tried to rescue him from those who regarded him as a children's entertainer and bring him back into the mainstream of Scottish culture and establish him as a writer worthy of critical attention. I identified very closely with Stevenson and I was very involved with him.

With Burns, though, this required a much more objective approach. He came from a milieu of which I had no personal experience. Though his poetry also spoke to me very directly, Burns came from a different world. And I had to learn about that world through reading and empathy rather than through personal experience. I tried to take him out of the sentimental Burns' Supper tradition. While DeLancey Ferguson in America had written very well about Burns, he was more of a biographer than a critic. And so my work on Burns was pioneering in many ways. And with Scott too, I like to think my work was instrumental in reinstating his reputation. Scott had fallen into total disrepute and no-one seemed to read him anymore, so I thought I would try to revive his reputation and I think I succeeded. Scott was of course an 'unread landmark' and was regarded as a writer of historical romances. It is amazing what Scott did for Scotland. He created the modern historical novel. And this put Scotland back on the cultural map of Europe. Scott was very well-aware of his place in history. And when he built Abbotsford, that was to signify his place in history too.

Where earlier Scottish writers are concerned, I would have liked to have written more about Dunbar who is a fascinating writer, and about the other so-called 'Scots-Chaucerians' — in particular Henryson who is a very remarkable poet — though the term 'Scots-Chaucerians' is a stupid term.

Of course, Scottish literature as such was not taught then, at least not as a subject in its own right when I studied at Edinburgh University in the early 1930s. It was taught, when at all, as a kind of minor aspect of English literature. We did read Dunbar and Henryson and the mediaeval Scottish poets, but approached them through the English Language course, which was rather daft, really. And no-one ever thought of Dunbar as a poet worthy of studying in the Literature course. Burns did come in as part of the Eng. Lit. course in Grierson's classes. And Stevenson was certainly not regarded as a suitable subject for academic discourse. It was felt that being Scottish was being provincial, you know. Like Boswell trying to shed his Scotticisms in his speech, it wasn't 'genteel' being Scottish. 'Yes, I do come from Scotland, but I can't help it.'

At university you were a contemporary of Norman MacCaig, Sorley MacLean, Robert Garioch.

Yes, though they were a bit ahead of me at university. But I did know them all. They were an extraordinary bunch.

Those must have been extraordinary times. What a remarkable period to have been young in. These brilliant young people who were to go on to have astonishingly productive lives as poets and writers.

Yes, indeed. But we thought of that period as something absolutely normal, not something extraordinary at all.

Robin Jenkins

Born Flemington, Cambuslang, 11th September 1912

NOVELIST

Andrew Fletcher of Saltoun Award 2001
Lifetime Achievement Award 2003

A Lost Autobiography

Introduction by Douglas Gifford

Robin Jenkins is recognised as one of Britain's greatest novelists, with almost thirty volumes since *So Gaily sings the Lark* in 1950. With his deeply ironic outlook on human frailty, its confused morality, and its muddled spiritual beliefs, he has been described as Scotland's 'Thomas Hardy'. He has mercilessly anatomised social hypocrisy and the ambiguities of 'goodness' and idealism in his novels; yet despite his scepticism his work insists on a subtext which yearns for 'some kind of grace' (the title of one of his novels) which will redeem fallen humanity.

Jenkins had agreed to contributing a record of his intriguing and far-travelled life for this volume. At ninety-one, typing was becoming difficult for him, and so he agreed that I should tape-record his memories. Sadly, this was not possible, since he became ill quite suddenly early this year, and soon he died. In the absence of his own record, it was decided to include a very brief statement outlining his achievement together with an extended interview with him in recent years by Dr Inga Agusdottir (reprinted from *In Scotland* with kind permission from Conrad Wilson).

Robin Jenkins was a very private man; his entry in the Scottish *Who's Who* typically lists only his work, without any fanfare regarding his private life, interests, or other achievements. His relationship with Scotland was equivocal; he both loved and deprecated his country, rooted as he was in its landscape, yet deeply concerned about its post-war industrial decline, its ambiguous morality which derived from Calvinism, and the profound gap between its romantic iconography presented to the outside word, so undercut by its harsh lowland realities. He often expressed his sometimes controversial view that Scottish literature and culture had little to boast of, and his public appearances were marked by his uncompromising but always perceptive comments on Scottish culture and society. Yet anyone who read his fiction, whether Scottish or post-colonial, realises the immense humanity and empathy of his feelings about ordinary people, and the depth of his existential concern with the human condition.

A full biography of this singular man will be a difficult task, given his preference for privacy, and his almost reclusive withdrawal to his windswept house high on the hill overlooking his beloved river Clyde at Toward Point. All that can be given here now is the briefest of indications of his huge achievement in the hope that the interview with Dr Agusdottir brings back his voice, with its ironic tones and its range of comment.

The Achievement

After the Second World War, Scottish literature lost the drive towards cultural Renaissance which had been led by writers like MacDiarmid, Gunn and Gibbon. Jenkins led the counter movement in the 'fifties against romanticising views of Scotland as timelessly rural — and in novels like *Happy for the Child* and *The Thistle and the Grail* he presented pessimistic but all too credible accounts of dreary lives alleviated by drink and football in dismal Lowland Scottish towns. *The Cone-Gatherers* and *Guests of War* looked to the countryside — but hardly for escape or optimism, as in both novels moral innocence is destroyed by grotesque evil. And the darkest of Jenkins's novels so far came in 1958 with *The Changeling*, and its harrowing account of well-intentioned but ill-thought-out idealism, in which a well-meaning Glasgow schoolteacher takes a slum boy with his own family on holiday down the Clyde — only to find that naïve idealism can bring about appalling tragedy.

Given his disillusioned view of Scotland, it comes as no surprise to find Jenkins leaving Scotland in 1957 until 1968, to teach in Afghanistan, Spain and Borneo, and producing some of the earliest and best of post-colonial fiction. *Some Kind of Grace* gave an unusually sympathetic picture of dignified and graceful Afghan tribal leaders. *Dust on the Paw* is one of the most understanding portraits of Afghanistan. These and the later Borneo novels mock British imperialism with its snobbish embassies and corrupt officials, patronising natives and their simmering religious tensions, as in the *Holy*

Tree. The title symbolises ambivalently; the tree is at once the tree of Western knowledge and Oxford scholarship which native Michael Eking yearns to attain; but it is also the holy tree of his people, beneath which he is sacrificed for what they perceive as his betrayal of his race and gods.

A third phase, of deepening moral ambiguities, began with his return to Scotland in the mid-seventies, as in *A Would-Be-Saint*. In an industrial Lowland town young Gavin Hamilton seems to be that rarest of creatures, a genuine Christian. He is brilliantly talented, at school and in football — but he gives up football, seeing it as Scotland's corrupt religion, and his motives in sheltering a prostitute are of course misunderstood, as is his conscientious objection to the war. Can such apparent goodness be genuine? Jenkins leaves it to the reader to decide ...

Thereafter Jenkins became even more enigmatic. *Fergus Lamont* portrays an almost McGonagall-like protagonist, full of pathetic pride and self deceptions and false prides. Later protagonists range from a vainglorious minister at the time of the Disruption of the Church of Scotland in 1843; a boy who wages war on social hypocrisy, only to destroy himself through his ruthless crusade; a humble Glasgow hospital porter who finds no trace of God in the Arizona deserts (although, too late, he finds the crucial value of his human love for his dying wife); while his latest, *Lady Magdalene* reverses conventional historical views of the valiant Montrose of the Covenanting wars, by seeing him from the point of view of his saintly wife as a pompous and glory-seeking ass.

At ninety-one, Jenkins was the last bar Glasgow's Edwin Morgan, of that wonderful group of post-war Scottish writers which include Naomi Mitchison, Norman MacCaig, Iain Crichton Smith, Sorley Maclean, and George Mackay Brown. In recognition of his achievement the Saltire Society in May 2002 awarded him the Andrew Fletcher of Saltoun Award for notable service to Scotland. The President of the Society, Paul Scott, and the Chairman of the Council, Ian Arnott, went to Jenkin's remote and isolated house at Toward to present him with his portrait by Sandy Moffat. It is pleasing to remember that in November 2003 he and Edwin Morgan jointly received Scotland's first ever Lifetime Achievement Award for Literature from the Scottish Arts Council and the Saltire Society, and that just before he died, Sir William Kerr Fraser, Chancellor of Glasgow University, led a small group down the Clyde to his home to confer upon him the degree of Doctor of Letters — which experience, with typical reduction, he described as being less unpleasant than expected. Such recognition was long overdue.

The Interview: *A Truthful Scot*

Could you name a few of your favourite authors and tell me why you like them?

The modern novelist that I like best — not as a person, mind you, but as a writer — is Evelyn Waugh. I think that his prose style is just perfect for a novelist. And you don't find him showing off. And Robert Louis Stevenson is somebody that I've got great affection for. Particularly *The Beach of Falesá* and *Weir of Hermiston*, and of course *Treasure Island* and *Kidnapped* — these two because they bring back my childhood. When I was a boy — I must have read an awful lot — a favourite of mine was Zane Gray — *Riders of the Purple Sage*, *Delight of Wisdom Stars*. Some titles, aren't they? I used to love these. He was writing about the Wild West and was trying to make a kind of poetry out of it. When I was in Afghanistan, the college where I taught was a big building, but my God, there was no heating in it. Well, there was some heating in the corridors, but in the library, or where we called the library, it was freezing cold. You had to have your overcoat on, your scarf and everything else. Once I was waiting to take a class, and I was looking around at the books and there was Zane Gray — *Riders of the Purple Sage*! Now, I hadn't seen it for fifty or sixty years, so I took it down, and oh what a sad disappointment. It really was, it seemed so amateurish, so like throwing away a wonderful opportunity that he had.

As for contemporary writers, I could tell you the ones I don't like more than those I do, I don't like Iris Murdoch, I don't like Muriel Spark. The reason why I dislike them is that I do not understand their characters. They are the kind of people I would never meet, and never want to meet. Particularly the characters of Iris Murdoch. Muriel Spark's *The Prime of Miss Jean Brodie* was set in Scotland. Mind you, she was brought up in Scotland, but then she left and never wrote about Scotland again. And you'll find it very difficult to get any real Scots person accepting her as a Scottish writer. I know the English do. They think she is a wonderful Scottish writer, on the strength of Miss Jean Brodie. But all the other novels, they're set in Venice, they're set in London, particularly. I just don't get it, I can't understand how I, as a Scottish writer, could be content to stay in London, and write about the English. Never! Never! And I don't know if there were any really good Scottish novels ever written by anybody in those circumstances. However, she would probably say she's not interested in writing a Scottish novel, she's just interested in writing a novel. In *The Ballad of Peckham Rye*, now and again she drops in a wee hint that she knows Scotland, but I don't think her heart is in Scotland. She reminds me a bit of Lord Byron, who was Scottish in the same way. Well, who else? Ah, one of my favourite books is Melville's *Moby Dick*. I like that and appreciate it. And of course Hardy. *The Mayor of Casterbridge* sort of suits me in some of my more lugubrious moods. And he ends up by writing a sort of testament; 'let no man remember me'. It's awfully self-piteous, isn't it?

I just cannot think that anybody ever influenced me. There are so few Scottish writers who could do that, and I wouldn't allow an English writer to influence me. I have mentioned Stevenson but who are the modern Scottish writers? Alasdair Gray, James Kelman; I've met them. And William McIlvanney. Well, I can tell you, I can take credit for *Docherty*, to some extent. He and I were addressing a group of teachers in Jordanhill. And I was on my favourite theme, that a writer should write about the people he knows well, that is to say, the people he was born amongst and brought up amongst. That's something I do believe. And then when it was McIlvanney's turn, he said he didn't agree with me; he thought I myself was a contradiction to what I had said, because of course I had written books about all sorts of places. Nonetheless, it occurred to me afterwards that he went off and wrote *Docherty*, which is about the people he was brought up with. His father was a miner. I have attempted to write about other people, but, I tell you, I'm uneasy, even when writing about English people. Writing about Americans, you never feel sure you've got the dialogue right. Whereas with Scots I wouldn't put a foot wrong. Kingsley Amis, if he put an American in a book, used to get his dialogue checked by a native American.

I don't see myself as part of any tradition of any kind. I just write because I enjoy writing. My daughters used to say it was a disease, I had to be doing it, and to some extent that was true. And it came easily to me, perhaps too easily. I never found it very difficult to find a theme. My wife used to say: 'I don't understand how you can write all these books — you go nowhere and you meet nobody!' That's a wee bit of an exaggeration, but there's a great deal of truth in it. She was a much more gregarious, sociable character than me. And I would often say: 'Och, no, I'm not going to this or I'm not going to that'. Yet I have to admit she had a point. Where did I gather all this information if I didn't go and meet people? However, I would say you don't need to know people well, you just need to sneak a glance at them, just hear a sentence spoken by them, and that's enough, if you have the ability. Now, I have to say this, it sounds conceited, but you have to have certain abilities to be a novelist.

Though I've pointed out the wealth of subject matter within the Scottish scene, and have used Milton's words, 'In my own country, where I most desire' as a motto, I've also explained, in the foreword to *Lunderston Tales*, that Scotland's a dull wee place. Because, damn it all, there are no presidents being assassinated, and so forth. Everybody is living very amicably together, and that's fine, that's good, that's civilised, but it's not very exciting for the novelist. And that's why in *Lunderston Tales* I decided to challenge myself, to see if in ordinary people, ordinary circumstances, you could find something worth writing about. Whether I did so is something I would have to leave to readers. I don't really think I am a short story writer. I am apt to be too long-winded. Well, maybe that's unfair, but I need time to develop characters, and in a short story you can't do that.

But I've produced twenty-five novels, and I used to say that once I'd written thirty, that would be it. Nobody should want to write more than that, because you're going to have said everything worth saying. But in fact I've now got up to thirty; I've got five in the drawer and I've twenty-five already published. As a matter a fact, I think there are thirty-one, which is me breaking my own rule.

In Willie Hogg *you seemed to make a deliberate point of linking the issue of the American Indians with that of the Scottish situation. Do you see a solution to the apparent dilemma of Scottish national identity, and is it perhaps reflected in the Indian dilemma examined in* Willie Hogg *that the only solution for the Indians would be to become American?*

That's right. That is what I thought. I knew it was impossible for some of them, quite impossible. But some did come into the main body, and they were always under a big handicap. The Scots are too able a race, somehow, for that to happen. They think they're more able than the English, you know. Yet spoken from the point of view of literature, our literature still gets ignored, it's shoved under a carpet, whereas Irish literature, the whole world knows about Irish literature. They don't know about the Scottish literature, and it's simply because we're smothered by the English. And that's one reason why I certainly vote for SNP. In any case, I don't know if I would have the courage to vote for Labour. I've voted Labour all my life, but I'm not happy with it at the present moment. I don't see any point in having a Labour Party unless it's there to ensure the social justice, that this gap between rich and poor narrows; that's the only purpose, as far as I can see. The social gap has widened under the Tories, and looks as though it will continue under Mr Blair. So if I didn't have the Scottish Nationalists to vote for, I don't know.

Here, of course, we've got a Liberal Democrat as an MP. And I think she was speaking sense about the Union Jack, and they didn't seem to understand what she was saying.

I don't know if you've read about her saying that the Union Jack should be done away with as a flag — oh, yes, she's in trouble for having said that. But take a rugby match; the national anthems are sung before the game. The Scots sing that dreary little dirge, 'The Flower of Scotland', which is awful; the Welsh lift up my heart with 'Land of My Fathers', it's marvellous; the Irish play, I think, 'Londonderry Air'; the English — the National Anthem! As if it was theirs! It's not an English anthem, it's the British anthem. But the English sing that! The same with the flag, they're waving the Union Jack. We wave the Saltire, the Welsh wave their Welsh dragon, but the English assume that the flag is theirs! In other words, the rest of us don't matter, that's what the Liberal Democrat MP was trying to say. And I think what she said made sense. But the leaders of her party think her a vote-loser, so panicking tell her to shut up.

Don't do anything original, don't do anything bold, or you'll frighten away the voters. Terrible. I once, at a public meeting, said my regret was that I hadn't, when I was younger, taken part in Scottish policies, on behalf of the SNP. Three or four days later I was bombarded with stuff from the SNP, trying to get me to join them. But I've not been a joiner; I don't think that I've ever been a participator. I'm a spectator. I'm not saying that proudly, but I think it's true. When you see a football match, and the crowds are in ecstasy, a team scores a goal — my God, it is as if the millennium was here, their hearts and soul are into it — you can see me standing there, as quiet as can be, watching. And that was me as a boy, too; I wrote *The Thistle and the Grail* from my remembrance of Cambuslang Rangers when I was a boy. I used to stand in the crowd being quite fascinated by their ecstasies. It's even more so now.

Go to all the churches in Scotland on Sunday and you'll not see any fervour or ecstasy the way you do in a football match. And, when you come to think of it, it is a pretty trivial thing, the football. Their whole heart and soul poured out on this triviality — oh, dear, But to get back to this, I think most writers have to be observers rather than participators. And, you know, I'm not a conscious observer, I think it's done subconsciously, and I think that is why a writer finds it very difficult to explain his work, because most of it is instinctive. Somebody will say to me: 'Now, why did you think of that?' I'll say: I have no idea, it just came into my mind'.

I'm sceptical of organised religion, and 'churchy' religion; but I'm not stupid and I realise there are marvels in the universe here. I like to say: in my hand

I've got two seeds, one will be a rose, one will be a daffodil; well, that's actually marvellous it's a miracle. And I'm well aware of that, and I would say yes I'm religious in that sense. But it's when that gentleman at the crematorium [two days before the interview Jenkins went to his sister's funeral; he is referring to that here] talked about my sister already being in a happier land, I think it's awfully naïve. It embarrasses you a wee bit. You want religion to be a grander thing than that.

I come from a family where nobody ever went to church, and I made no effort whatsoever to influence my own family. None of them go to church. My two daughters would never go to church, my wife never went to church although she had an uncle who was a minister — so religion has been something that just did not come into our ken. Although when I was a boy, at thirteen, fourteen, I went out to all the churches, I even was a member at one time of the Episcopal Church. In fact, I can remember that I used to go and pump the organ for the lady organist. This was me trying to find out just where my spiritual home was, but I had finally to decide that it wasn't in any church. Yet if you are at all a thinking Scot, you are bound to think about religion. This is Montrose [he picks up a book from the sofa-table], and, oh my goodness, religion, religion, religion, the whole book is steeped in it — Covenanting, Calvinism, and so forth. So I couldn't avoid that, I have to admit. Maybe it's a pity, it'd be better to be free of it. But if you're a Scot, you're not going to be free of it.

My book [unpublished at the time of the interview] *Matthew and Sheila* starts off with Matthew going a walk across the machair in the Hebrides with his grandfather, who is a minister of the Wee Free Kirk, who are the narrowest of narrowest, and the old man is more or less just talking to himself. He's embittered that he has spent all his life trying to obey the Lord, and yet he feels the Lord has not rewarded him by making him one of the Elect. And the wee boy is listening to this all the time, and he gets it into his head that he would like to be one of the Elect, and he asks his grandfather questions about it. And he wonders why shouldn't he be the one. And then there's a snag: the Devil! Where does he come in? The boy asks: 'Grandfather, is the Devil stronger than God?' Says the grandfather: 'It would seem so, considering the evil that triumphs in the world'. That's the opening of the book, so you see it's utterly and absolutely Scottish. And this wee boy — he's a nice wee boy — I'm trying to portray goodness in him: hard job. I'm portraying evil in the girl: easy, dead easy. But goodness is very hard indeed. I'm sure I succeed with Matthew; I don't know about Sheila, she is a mysterious character, but one likes to create mysterious characters. I myself am not sure of what her motives are. And right to the end I leave Matthew in doubt as to whether Sheila did the things she says or not. That sounds quite promising as a theme, doesn't it? I make her very talented. She's a great singer, a very handsome looking girl, and indeed I have an epilogue — twenty years later, and she has become a famous operatic singer. Anyway, that might be the next book to come out. Either that or Montrose's wife [*Lady Magdalen*].

You once said that A Toast to the Lord *was a gauntlet to Christianity. Could this apply to other novels of yours? I'm thinking of* The Missionaries, Some Kind of Grace, *and* Just Duffy.

Well, *A Toast to the Lord* was an attempt I made to test the faith of someone who absolutely believed in God, who believed that everything that happened to you happened because God meant it to happen. So *A Toast to the Lord* involves this poor girl in every damn mishap and miserable situation there could be. She bolts up at the end, still intact. I have to mention that Edwin Morgan reviewed this book, and said he couldn't accept that all these things could happen, and could be described without irony. Without irony! I mean, the thing's overflowing with irony. Now, *Just Duffy*: I was really displeased with the reception of *Just Duffy*, although Margery McCulloch lifted my heart a wee bit by understanding it — although I noticed there were certain things she didn't understand. Even she didn't realise the irony in the title: *JustDuffy*. I didn't mean only I am just Duffy, you don't need to heed me; he was setting himself up as a judge, and I was suggesting, was he a just judge? I think I made a mistake in deciding not to have Scots — they speak in English — I had hoped that this was going to have a universal appeal, and therefore I'd better not have them say wouldnae and didnae and all that sort of thing.

That's another thing you might be interested in: what does a Scottish writer do when the Scots people are speaking all kinds of dialogue? Now, take Kelman. The English think he has given us an authentic Scottish, Glasgow vernacular. He's done nothing of the kind. He has characters like Sam [in *How late it was, how late*] saying above, not abin, down instead of doon — through the whole book it's like that. And he has had to make a decision what he's going to use as Scots and what he's not going to use, but it's not genuine Glasgow vernacular, I can tell you that. He thinks the only genuine thing is the swear words; that amused me. I can remember there was a time when if he'd had one swear word, one fuck through three hundred pages — ah, horror, horror! Now he's got about thirty in a page, somebody tried to count them, there were three thousand in one of his books.

Speaking of my own work, *The Missionaries* is a peculiar book. I don't understand *The Missionaries* myself. What I think I was trying to do was to create a place, like an island, where you might expect miracles to take place. Some think the setting was Iona. I don't understand why I wrote it. It is quite an unlikely book for me to have written, I think. I regard myself as a realist, maybe too much so. Take Tolkien, I couldn't possibly read Tolkien, with his Hobbits and everything else. You have to suspend your disbelief and I can't suspend it to that extent. Would you take *The Missionaries* seriously in the sense that it's a book worth reading? It's a book that I sort of nervously tiptoe away from.

I'm trying to think, now, in the book I have still to publish — where does religion come in? I hope it doesn't. Have I ever managed to create a book without religion? Maybe one of those in the drawer, which is called *Poor Angus*. It's about a painter, an artist, living in Islay. I think this would make a very good film, to tell you the truth. I mentioned that to someone and he wants to see it — he is the fellow who was trying to make *Willie Hogg* into a film. I got a phone call from him, and he was a wee bit sad, they sort of pushed him out of the thing. They wanted a director who has already got a reputation, whereas he hasn't, you see. He's just done episodes on TV like *The Bill* or something like that. But I was telling him about *Poor Angus*, and that it would make quite a good film. Angus has been teaching art in a teacher's training college in, let's say, Borneo, and he's just not very nice towards women. And he keeps saying, after he's discarded one, that if ever they're in any trouble they should look him up. And he doesn't mean this, oh my God no. But one Philippine lady and an Australian one take him at his word, while he is in Islay, and the Philippine is already married, and her husband comes to the scene. It's nice and concentrated, and there is another lady on the island itself, a real Celtic type, who say's she's got second sight, and she bothers Angus too. So he's surrounded by ladies. And in the end he has his come-uppances, rather terrifyingly. One of the things he has brought back is a blowpipe — these blow-pipes had a spear attached to them — and he had it on the wall, and the last scene is where Fidelia, that's the Philippine lady, is in the room with him, along with her husband, and Angus is not taking her part at all, and she suddenly springs up, grabs the blowpipe, and he's sitting thinking it's her husband who's going to get it, and it's Angus who gets it, ha! So I give you his last dying gurgles, ha, ha!

What about the narrative perspective — is there any particular reason why you change the third person narrative constantly in most of your work?

One of the advantages of the third person is that you do go from character to character. Although one of them may be your main character, you still are able to go to another character, although I find most writers don't do that very much; you're apt to keep to the main characters, aren't you?

But sometimes you suddenly push aside a character that's been in the centre, like Agnes in A Toast to the Lord.

Yes, well, you see, I have to say that I didn't take the book very seriously; it's one of my later works. But surely all novelists jump from one character to another.

Yes, but I find it a bit different in your case; sometimes your characters are blocked off and a person that was at the centre is suddenly pushed aside and you don't see any more of that person — in most of your work, except in Willie Hogg, *where you stay with one person only.*

Really the only other person would be Mrs Hogg and she wasn't a very interesting person. She's so ordinary — mind you, I'm not running down ordinariness but I made a decision that I would change her, have her change, because characters don't often change in a book, do they? And I decided that Maggie would have to change a wee bit maybe I went too far.

In *Matthew and Sheila* I came up against the fact that the Scots — we were talking about their attitude to religion, they never mention the word love. They would say, as Matthew says, that he 'likes' Mrs McDonald; really, he loves her, but nobody ever says it. I don't know why — look at the Americans, they're in a big telephone conversation: 'love you', and she says 'me too'. That's the other extreme. Maybe we should be a little less afraid to use the word.

It seems to me that you are very fond of taking things to extremes in your work.

Is that right? Tell me now, give me an example.

The Cone-Gatherers, *for example, the end goes to extremes a bit, doesn't it?*

Well, it's a tragedy, you know. The extreme is the death of a leading character. I thought I was a wee bit cautious about that. The one thing one hopes to preserve is credibility.

What about Just Duffy? *You take Duffy to the extremes in that novel.*

Oh, he definitely takes the whole thing to extremes. He is more or less calling everybody's bluff, isn't he? He thinks he is standing up for what's good and just and honest, and all round about him he's surrounded by the very opposite. And he tries to shock people into realising. And yet at the same time, I always have thought of *Just Duffy* as one of my most optimistic books, because he makes a discovery that there is something quite beautiful in the dependence of people on one another. And I say — I think somebody contradicted me not very long ago — that you can only see that if you're an outcast. If you're one of the crowd, you don't notice it. For instance, when he's watching the people playing badminton; it never enters their head how much they depend on each other, but he sees the beauty of it. It's so necessary, so beautiful, and he can't partake of it. And at the end, when he sees the people outside the church, all chatting away, he sees it again.

I cheated myself out of a real sensational ending there, didn't I? Did you think he was going to kill himself? You see, I don't go to the extremes all the time. I used to think, what the hell happened to Duffy afterwards? What kind of future did he have? He had too much sensitiveness for a person in his position, I suppose. I quite liked his girlfriend [Cooley], though, she's the kind of person I like, with all sorts of odds stacked against her, but it's never going to get her down. She doesn't emerge, I suppose, as an awfully attractive character, but I like people like her. I don't suppose I'm like that at all; I'd be a cringing feartie out of the road and so forth, but she didn't. She stands up for herself,

They keep on saying that *The Cone-Gatherers* is an allegory or fable, though I don't know I'd say so; I think I try to tell a fairly plain story. What happens to my characters when the book ends, particularly in the case of *A Would-Be Saint*, Gavin; how did Gavin do with this minister's sister? I think I could have made quite a good love story out of that. But I've always resolutely resisted having a sequence. It's better to leave the characters in the reader's mind. Mind you, this is a criticism of my books that I've heard many times, that my endings are not satisfactory.

I don't rule two lines at the end of a book, I'm sure. It used to be in the old days: the hero and heroine marrying, and that was it. Or dying: but now we're inclined to just leave them to get on with their lives.

If the characters have been really created well enough, given life, then the reader could carry it on in his own mind, just what did happen to them. But endings are hard, just where do you end a book?

Are you ever conscious of using symbolism in your work?

No, I'm not, although I've been accused of it quite a bit. I would just leave it to other people; I do not try to stick in symbolism. To tell the truth, I am a wee bit surprised that people find so much in my books, because I think I'm a fairly straightforward, simple kind of chap.

And your books are very ambiguous, even elusive, and sometimes savage in their depiction of human behaviour. Do you think that this could perhaps contribute to the fact that your work hasn't been recognised as much as it deserves?

I was telling you about Neil Gunn [before the interview itself took place]; Gunn's last years were a bit soured because he felt he hadn't been given his due. But see, my attitude is this: none of us is any good, really. By us I mean writers. If you take, say, *The Guardian* or *The Observer*, every week novels are reviewed that seem to be — well, somebody saying: 'it's as good as Tolstoy, at least, wonderful!' — but within two weeks they're completely forgotten. And that's why I keep on trying to compare myself with the writers of the past. That's why I think I'm on the right lines, not Candia McWilliam with her 'cat's paws like little white strawberries' [a sentence in that author's book which strikes Jenkins as too ornate, as 'showing off']. Because I think that the writers that matter of the past — George Eliot, Jane Austen, and so forth — they didn't go in for something like that. Could you think of a single Jane Austen book where she would talk about the cat with paws like white strawberries? No, never in a million years! Therefore I think I'm on the right lines. What did Austen and Eliot go in for? They go in for the story, they go in for the characters, and the relationship of characters. And that's what I go in for too, I think.

What about the women in your work — would you say that they sometimes symbolise strength, for example Bell McShelvie in Guests of War?

I'm always quite impressed by certain working-class women who show a surprising strength. I don't know who in my relatives influenced me. I had an aunt called Rachel, long since dead; she symbolised strength, I suppose. I'm sure I've met quite a number of these ladies. I think that they shame the men, because they carry heavy burdens, but the men don't. Mrs Curdie in *The Changeling* is a bit of a harridan, is she not? I was invited to go and address the pupils of the sixth form of Moffat Academy. The sixth formers had to read *The Changeling* at school, and some had been rather shocked at the ending.

But, you see, it was the only possible conclusion, surely. Nowadays, of course, that won't bother pupils; they can accept that ending quite easily. I mean, they see slaughter and murder all over the place.

Where can the boy go? The Forbes are not going to take him, they can't, that's out of the question. He's not going to go back to where he came from, so where does he go? Very sad, really. Charles Forbes.... I was talking about addressing these people with McIlvanney. You know who was introducing us? The Chief Inspector of Schools, whose name was Charles Forbes, ha, ha! I was slightly embarrassed. I assured him I didn't mean him. Most of the audience understood this. They must have read the book. It did interest Scottish teachers, Glasgow teachers, that book, when it came out, because, after all, it is about Glasgow schools and I was thinking of Riverside School when I wrote it. It was quite a coincidence I had called him Charles Forbes, I had no idea the Chief Inspector was called that. You've to be careful with these things, you know.

In fact, I was quite worried about *Lunderston Tales*. In it, there's a story about a bloke who goes to prison because he cheats the social security. You know, in Dunoon there is somebody as like him as could be, who was married twice, who's got ten children, who's a Catholic, and I thought, my God, if he hears this, he'll sue me. But of course my defence was that I make him a heroic character, and he's good with his children— if you're good with kids you're a bit of a saint, aren't you? And you've to be careful that you don't make yourself open to that.

When *Dust on the Paw* was published I couldn't call it Afghanistan, the publisher wouldn't allow that, because, you see, I had named all sorts of people. But it was published in America with Putnam and they just said it's Afghanistan and that's it! What are we going to insure us for?' And I thought that was great because it made a big difference to call it Afghanistan.

I don't know if you've ever read a book called *Some Kind of Grace*? A publishing company called B & W Publishing are reprinting *Guests of War*, which puzzles me because it has been reprinted before. However, they asked if there was anything else that I thought should be printed, and I suggested to them: why not *Some Kind of Grace*? And I'll wait and see what they say — there are improbabilities in it — but it's quite a good story as far as I remember. My idea was a thriller, because, my goodness gracious me, if there ever was a country where you can set thrilling stories, it was Afghanistan.

Some people have had the damned cheek to criticise me because, although I set my story in a far-off place, I have cast Scottish characters! What else should I have?

Do you think that there is any specific or conscious message or lesson you want to get through to your readers?

Oh, absolutely not. I'm not a preacher. I wouldn't know what advice to give anybody. I don't think as a person I worry too much about morality. I can't see that most people who know me would think that I was besotted with morality.

Something I come up against is the limitation of being human. One of the poems I've been writing is about, not so much the limitations of being human, but the burden of being human. I often go on walks here and see all the animals and so forth, and I sometimes stop and wait, and imagine what it would be like to be one of these — a bird, a mole, a rabbit — to lay down, even for a minute, the burden of being human. And how could you do it? Could you do it with the moles, could you do it with the rabbits, or with the deer? — only if you were as humble as they. And that is not possible.

And another of my poems is about a buzzard that perches on a pole in my garden. It comes quite often and last summer they were two, and I watched them going up the sky — they're great soarers, up and up and up and up. And now I can hear it hallooing — what's happened to its companion? I don't know, I'm sure something has happened to it. There are usually two of them together. Your attention is attracted to them not by seeing them, but by hearing them. They make a meowing noise like cats and their coming from high up there fascinated me. I stood watching them for at least half an hour. And then this one comes and perches on the pole there. That's what I'm now doing, writing poems of that sort, you see.

Muriel Spark

Born, Edinburgh, 1st February 1918

NOVELIST

Saltire Book of the Year, Collected Stories, 1987

Nevertheless

From The New Statesman, 1961

A few years ago I was obliged to spend some weeks in the North British Hotel in Edinburgh, isolated and saddened by many things, while my father's last illness ran its course in the Royal Infirmary. It was necessary for me to be within call. I do not like the public rooms and plushy lounges of hotels anywhere in the world, I do not sit in them; and least of all in one's native city is it spiritually becoming to sit in the lounges of big hotels.

I spent most of my time in my room waiting for the hours of visiting my father to come round. I think at such times in one's life one tends to look out of the window oftener and longer than usual. I left my work and my books and spent my time at the window. It was a high, wide window, with an inside ledge, broad and long enough for me to sit in comfortably with my legs stretched out. The days before Easter were suddenly warm and sunny. From where I sat propped in the open window frame, I could look straight onto Arthur's Seat and the Salisbury Crags, its girdle. When I sat the other way round I could see part of the Old City, the east corner of Princes Street Gardens, and the black Castle Rock. In those days I experienced an in-pouring of love for the place of my birth, Which I am aware was psychologically connected with my love for my father and with the exiled sensation of occupying a hotel room which was really meant for strangers.

Edinburgh is the place that I, a constitutional exile, am essentially exiled from. I spent the first 18 years of my life, during the I 920s and 1930s there. It was Edinburgh that bred within me the conditions of exiledom; and what have I been doing since then but moving from exile into exile? It has ceased to be a fate, it has become a calling.

My frequent visits to Edinburgh for a few weeks at a time throughout the years have been the visits of an exile in heart and mind — cautious, affectionate, critical. It is a place where I could not hope to be understood. The only sons and daughters of Edinburgh with whom I can find a common understanding are exiles like myself. By exiles I do not mean Edinburgh-born members of Caledonian Societies. I do not consort in fellowship with the Edinburgh natives abroad merely on the Edinburgh basis. It is precisely the Caledonian Society aspect of Edinburgh which cannot accommodate me as an adult person.

Nevertheless, it is the place where I was first understood. James Gillespie's Girls' School, set in solid state among the green meadows, showed an energetic faith in my literary life. I was the school's Poet and Dreamer, with appropriate perquisites and concessions. I took this for granted, and have never since quite accustomed myself to the world's indifference to art and the process of art, and to the special needs of the artist.

I have started the preceding paragraph with the word 'nevertheless' and am reminded how my whole education, in and out of school, seemed even then to pivot around this word. I was aware of its frequent use. My teachers used it a great deal. All grades of society constructed sentences bridged by 'nevertheless'. It would need a scientific study to ascertain whether the word was truly employed more frequently in Edinburgh at the time than anywhere else. It is my own instinct to associate the word, as the core of a thought-pattern, with Edinburgh particularly. I can see the lips of tough elderly women in musquash coats taking tea at MacVittie's, enunciating this word of final justification, I can see the exact gesture of head and chin and gleam of the eye that accompanied it. The sound was roughly 'niverthelace' and the emphasis was a heartfelt one. I believe myself to be fairly indoctrinated by the habit of thought which calls for this word. In fact I approve of the ceremonious accumulation of weather forecasts and barometer-readings that pronounce for a fine day, before letting rip on the statement: 'Nevertheless, it's raining.' I find that much of my literary composition is based on the nevertheless idea. I act upon it. It was on the nevertheless principle that I turned Catholic.

It is impossible to know how much one gets from one's early environment by way of a distinctive character, or whether for better or worse. I think the puritanical strain of the Edinburgh ethos is inescapable, but this is not necessarily a bad thing. In the south of England the puritanical virtues tend to be regarded as quaint eccentricities — industriousness, for instance, or a horror of debt. A polite reticence about sex is often mistaken for repressions. On the other hand, spiritual joy does not come in an easy consistent flow to the puritanically-nurtured soul. Myself, I have had to put up a psychological fight for my spiritual joy.

Most Edinburgh-born people, of my generation at least, must have been brought up with a sense of civic superiority. We were definitely given to understand that we were citizens of no mean city. In time, and with experience of other cities, one would have discovered the beautiful uniqueness of Edinburgh for oneself as the visitors do. But the physical features of the place surely had an effect as special as themselves on the outlook of the people. The Castle Rock is something, rising up as it does from prehistory between the formal grace of the New Town and the noble network of the Old. To have a great primitive black crag rising up in the middle of populated streets of commerce, stately squares and winding closes, is like the statement of an unmitigated fact preceded by 'nevertheless'. In my time the society existing around it generally regarded the government and bureaucracy of Whitehall as just a bit ridiculous. The influence of a place varies according to the individual. I imbibed, through no particular mentor, but just by breathing the informed air of the place, its haughty and remote anarchism. I can never now suffer from a shattered faith in politics and politicians, because I never had any.

When the shrill telephone in my hotel room woke me at four in the morning, and a nurse told me that my father was dead, I noticed, with that particular disconnected concentration of the fuddled mind, that the rock and its castle loomed as usual in the early light. I noted this, as if one might have expected otherwise.

POSTSCRIPT
August 2004

I wrote the above piece for the *New Statesman* shortly after the death of my father in 1961. It describes an authentic experience and reaction to his death. I loved my father very much.

On looking through this piece at a much later date I have been struck by the fact that time has put a different shading on my feelings about "exiledom".

I no longer feel an exile.   The world has become a more international place over the four decades since I wrote the piece.   I have lived in Italy for over thirty years, with many travels in Europe, Asia, America. I feel at home on this more integrated planet, now. What has helped to induce this definite feeling of territorial security has of course been the fact that many more of my books have been written, published and translated throughout the literate world. Wherever my books are read I feel I belong, although the lovely City of Edinburgh is in fact and in memory always in a special sense my home.

I am always very happy to return to Edinburgh. Not only is it my native city but my father, too, was born and spent his life here. My grandparents lived here most of their lives. My brother was born and brought up with me in Edinburgh and my mother spent all her married years here with us. I am a truly Edinburgh product, both in historical fact and in my deepest feelings.

To me, Edinburgh is the seat of Enlightenment, the home of law and reason. This city has always been harmonious in its designs, far-reaching in its outlook, with the imperative of Freedom informing the whole of its civil life. Long may it remain so.

I owe to my Edinburgh education a formative experience which has influenced the whole of my work. First of all, the savage-sweet Border Ballads, the spirit of which I think is often reflected in my writings. They truly entered my life-blood as a child. Without a knowledge of those Border Ballads nobody could understand my work. Although I have lived abroad for many years I am always well aware that I am Scottish both by birth and formation.

Edwin Morgan

Born Glasgow, 27th April 1920

POET, CRITIC, TRANSLATOR

FIRST SCOTS MAKAR

Saltire Book of the Year, Poems of Thirty Years, *1983*
Lifetime Achievement Award, 2003

I Want it Bright

I offer these two poems instead of an essay, which I feel unable to write. A good deal of my poetry has been autobiographical, especially in recent years, and my sense of having put so much of myself into poetry drains the impetus out of my attempt to re-tell the story in prose.

In *Cathures* (Carcanet, 2002) and *Love and a Life* (Mariscat, 2003) I have been open about loves old and new, the Glasgow Laureateship, contemporary events, my house and environment, old age, cancer — it is all there, my friends are named, my house is named, and I am 'I'. This does not mean that masks are not to be found, but any biographer worth his salt would relish working out how much of me, and what aspects of me, are to be unearthed in *Pelagius*. (Pelagius whose real name was Morgan!) or in the unnamed Demon whose adventures and thoughts and feelings certainly give me a shock of recognition. If you want something more political, you can read *New Times* the poem I wrote on being appointed Scots Makar, and the longer poem I provided for the opening of the new Scottish Parliament building in October 2004. When you turn the kaleidoscope, different Morgans may appear; but isn't that true of any writer who has lived for a long time and (as the late Marlon Brando might have said) covered the waterfront.

Epilogue: Seven Decades

At ten I read Mayakovsky had died,
learned my first word of Russian, *lyublyu;*
watched my English teacher poke his earwax
with a well-chewed HB and get the class
to join his easy mocking of my essay
where I'd used *verdant herbage* for *green grass.*
So he was right?   So I hated him!
And he was not really right, the ass.
A writer knows what he needs,
as came to pass.

At twenty I got marching orders, kitbag,
farewell to love, not arms (though our sole arms
were stretchers), a freezing Glentress winter
where I was coaxing sticks at six to get
a stove hot for the cooks, found myself picked
quartermaster's clerk – 'this one seems a bit
less gormless than the bloody others' – did
gas drill in the stinging tent, met
Tam McSherry who farted at will
a musical set.

At thirty I thought life had passed me by,
translated *Beowulf* for want of love.
And one night stands in city centre lanes –
they were dark in those days – were wild but bleak.
Sydney Graham in London said 'you know
I always thought so', kissed me on the cheek.
And I translated Rilke's *Loneliness*
is like a rain, and week after week after week
strained to unbind myself,
sweated to speak.

At forty I woke up, saw it was day,
found there was love, heard a new beat, heard Beats,
sent airmail solidarity to Saõ
Paulo's poetic-concrete revolution,
knew Glasgow – what? – knew Glasgow new – somehow –

new with me, with John, with cranes, diffusion
of another concrete revolution, not bad,
not good, but new.   And new was no illusion:
a spring of words, a sloughing,
an ablution.

At fifty I began to have bad dreams
of Palestine, and saw bad things to come,
began to write my long unwritten war.
I was a hundred-handed Sindbad then,
rolled and unrolled carpets of blood and love,
raised tents of pain, made the dust into men
and laid the dust with men. I supervised
a thesis on Doughty, that great Englishman
who brought all Arabia back
in his hard pen.

At sixty I was standing by a grave.
The winds of Lanarkshire were loud and high.
I knew what I had lost, what I had had.
The East had schooled me about fate, but still
it was the hardest time, oh more, it was
the worst of times in self-reproach, the will
that failed to act, the mass of good not done.
Forgiveness must be like the springs that fill
deserted furrows if they wait
until – until –

At seventy I thought I had come through,
like parting a bead curtain in port Said,
to something that was shadowy before,
figures and voices of late times that might
be surprising yet. The beads clash faintly
behind me as I go forward. No candle-light
please, keep that for Europe. Switch the whole thing
right on. When I go in I want it bright,
I want to catch whatever is there
in full sight

From *Collected Poems*, Edwin Morgan (Carcanet Press, 1990)

At Eighty

Push the boat out, companeros,
Push the boat out, whatever the sea.
Who says we cannot guide ourselves
through the boiling reefs, black as they are,
the enemy of us all makes sure of it!
Mariners, keep good watch always
for that last passage of blue water
we have heard of and long to reach
(no matter if we cannot, no matter!)
in our eighty-year-old timbers
leaky and patched as they are but sweet,
well seasoned with the scent of woods
long perished, serviceable still
in unarrested pungency
of salt and blistering sunlight. Out,
push it all out into the unknown!
Unknown is best, it beckons best,
like distant ships in mist, or bells
clanging ruthless from stormy buoys.

From *Unknown is Best: A Celebration of Edwin Morgan at Eighty* Eds. Robyn Marsach and Hamish Whyte (Mariscat Press & Scottish Poetry Library), 2000

Derick S. Thomson

Born Isle of Lewis, 5th August 1921

ACADEMIC AND POET

Saltire Book of the Year, Creachadh na Clàrsaich, *1983*

Some Recollections

Genes, family and the locality in which we spend our early years have strong and lasting influence on each individual's life, and perhaps a special impact on the work of a creative writer. So it may be appropriate to begin an autobiographical story with some such personal details.

I was born on 5th August in Stornoway, the younger son of James and Christina Thomson. My elder brother, James, was born in 1917, and since my father was still on war service his first years were spent in Keose, the village where my mother was brought up. So his first language was Gaelic. By the time I arrived the family was living in Stornoway, and my first language was English, although my father was by then head of the Gaelic department in the Nicolson Institute. But in 1922 he was appointed headmaster of Bayble School, seven miles out of Stornoway.

Bayble at that time had a population of about 1000, and Garrabost, its neighbouring village, had about 500. Of that joint total of 1500 only two or three were not Gaelic speakers, and there were still a few Gaelic monoglots around. The local nurse, from the Borders, had to rustle up a few Gaelic words when dealing with monolingual patients.

Our family was soon to become very bilingual. Gaelic was my parents' original language, and both were deeply involved in it, my mother having inherited an impressive repertory of Gaelic song, and my father becoming more and more involved in promoting and writing Gaelic. Before she married, my mother had been an Infant Teacher at Luerbost School, in Lochs, so she was well aware of the intricacies of combining Gaelic and English in a changing environment.

When I started school in Bayble, in 1926, I was the only member of my class to be reasonably fluent in English so I had to adjust quickly to the Gaelic environment in the playground. I do not recall any great problems though it must have taken some time.

Another curiosity was that my paternal grandmother was a Campbell, of Harris origin and my maternal grandmother a MacDonald who had family connections with Applecross. It was much later that I got to know of the ancient rivalries between Campbells and MacDonalds, and the more jocular rivalries between Harris and Lewis. To add to the ancestral complications, one of my father's ancestors was also a James Thomson, who came to Lewis in the late 1720's or early 1730's, as a teacher. He was a Gaelic speaker, with Perthshire origins, and finally settled in Ness. There are still Thomsons in Ness, though my branch of the family settled in the Back and Tong areas of Lewis, and produced a number of headmasters in the twentieth century.

My paternal grandfather was a fisherman, and my maternal grandfather a carpenter who expanded his activities into becoming an undertaker, a post-office keeper and small shop-keeper, and one of the earliest bus-owners in Lewis. My mother was one of a family of thirteen, and my paternal grandfather had a family of twelve, my father being part of the second marriage, after the death of grandfather's first wife. A complicated and interesting family background.

The gradual invasion of English into Gaelic territory had some amusing aspects to it. The school cleaner at Bayble was a lady called Murdina Maciver. Her Gaelic name was Murdag, and presumably very early in our stay at Bayble I christened her Mucka. She sometimes acted as baby-sitter when my parents were away at communions and other activities. She had also worked as a fish-gutter, in Stornoway and in England so she had acquired a variety of English which we found enticing. Years later, about 1935, after my father had bought his first car, he taught me to drive, using the large school playground as I was only about fourteen then. Once I took Mucka on a trip round the playground, and she later reported the incident as follows : " We are be walking and walking through the playground until a luaithrean (English dizziness) are come into our ceann (English head)". Mucka's sister was called Cotrìona Mhòr (i.e. Big Catherine or Catherine the Elder), and although she had done some fish-gutting she was not keen to speak English. I often visited the two sisters at their Bayble home, and heard many stories, especially from Cotrìona Mhòr. The two sisters feature in some of my poems from decades later.

My interest in writing began to develop fairly early. By the end of the 1920s I had founded a newspaper called the *Bayble Herald*. The readership was limited to four, my parents and brother and my mother's sister Nan who lived with us at that time. This paper included features in both English and Gaelic, and cartoons of Cotrìona Mhòr.   After a few years I tried to move from journalism to poetry, and wrote poems in both Gaelic and English. No doubt all these activities were influenced by my father's work. He was the first person to be awarded the Bardic Crown by the National Mod (in 1923), and I could observe his activities with an ancient typewriter.   His writing involved editing a collection of Lewis songs, and much later the publication of a collection of his own poems, *Fasgnadh,* and later still the editorship of An Comunn's magazine.

Another life-long interest, or obsession, began to surface in the mid 1930's. With a general election in 1935, our history teacher at the Nicolson Institute organised a mini-election in our third-year class, and we elected a Nationalist. A fellow class-mate was Donald Stewart, who after some years as a Labour supporter, and Provost of Stornoway, became a Nationalist MP for the Western Isles, and led the party at Westminster for a number of years. My Auntie Nan, who became Ann Urquhart after marrying the head of Maths at the Nicolson, served two terms as Provost of Stornoway, so politics seemed to run in the family.

In 1934 I enrolled in Class Two at the Nicolson Institute, and in many respects this was a move into a new world, making acquaintances and friends from other areas of Lewis: the West Side, Bernera, Ness, Uig, Lochs, and of course Stornoway. This involved getting the wide range of dialects of Gaelic, and the rivalries between different districts. And also the English dialect of Stornoway, as there were many coves and bloans from the town in my class. It was a stimulating experience, which has stayed with me throughout my life. We had a number of inspiring teachers. Without listing all of them, I was greatly influenced by our history teacher Albert Nicol, our English teacher James Barber, and our Gaelic teacher Alex Urquhart.   Eventually I followed in my brother's footsteps by becoming dux of the school in 1939.

The middle years of the 1920's began to open windows to other areas of Scotland.   We had a family holiday in Aberdeen, my father's University town, and one in Glasgow, were his brother Donald was a minister.   Donald's manse was in Elmbank Gardens, where I first learnt to ride a bike, and about thirty years later was head of the Celtic Department, a few doors along from the manse.   And about 1935 we began a series of holidays in Killin, where Donald had become minister, and lived in the manse where the first Gaelic translation of the New Testament had taken shape in the 1760s. These visits to Killin kindled a lasting attachment to Perthshire, with boating on Loch Tay and climbing the mountains, including Ben Lawers, followed by many visits over the years. My uncle was also a councilor in Perthshire, and always ready to debate political issues with me.

In 1939 it was time to go to University. I had sat exams in Inverness for an Aberdeen University bursary, and got £50 per annum. Together with another bursary for £30, this was enough to fund my expense for the University year, with payments of 25 shillings a week for board and lodging, and a few spare pennies for the odd beer on Friday or Saturday.

The new environment was interesting in many ways, from the city's landscape to the North-east dialect, and of course the many new acquaintances made at University. Several of my Nicolson classmates were fellow students, so old friendships continued and new ones were made. In my first year I took, somewhat unusually, four subjects (Latin, Maths, Celtic and English), and in my second year another three (Higher Celtic, Higher English and Moral Philosophy). To my surprise I came top of the Philosophy class, and still have as part of the prize a book by John Laird who was Professor then. Laird asked me to consider continuing to Honours Philosophy, but I had already decided to opt for Celtic and English. So the third year began with Honours classes in these two subjects, but as war service was looming I decided to drop out after the first term, thinking that if I returned after the war it would be better to do the two final years of Honours. In the event it was not until early summer in 1942 that I was called up. Another fellow-student who left in that first term of 1941-1942 was Alex Scott, and our friendship was to last for many years. Alex was later to be closely involved in developing the separate Department of Scottish Literature at Glasgow, and he published widely collections of his own poetry, anthologies, and the diaries of William Soutar, to name only some of his books. When we came back to University in 1945 our English class had a large contingent of ex-service people, and in 1947 six of us got first-class Honours degrees, a very unusual total for these days.

My three years of war service (1942-45) were in the RAF. After some brief training in Arbroath I opted for a course as a radar mechanic, beginning with a general course at Bradford, where ironically I first learnt to swim, followed by a course in radar at Cranwell, and then postings to Rodel in Harris and Point in Lewis. At some point, in England, I was interviewed about the possibility of applying for officer training. Asked about my foreign travel, I said it included only England, and as to foreign languages I had to cite English again. I don't think that gained me any points. My radar expertise was only slightly better than my command of French or German. I must confess it was a relief to leave the RAF and return to University.

The head of the Celtic Department, and its only member of staff, was John MacDonald, known as Celtic John, and he was both an inspiration and a kind friend to me over many years. He had been a student both at Aberdeen and at Emmanuel College in Cambridge, and he persuaded me to apply to Emmanuel when I graduated.

The Professor of English, Geoffrey Bickersteth, was an interesting teacher and character. I remember going to his home for several tutorials, and he would frequently nip over to his bookshelves to look at a literary quotation. Another personal memory I have of him involved standing at the door waiting to enter one of his lectures, when he stopped to say that he had enjoyed a poem of mine that had just appeared in a student magazine.

I was deeply involved in activities with the student Celtic Society, and with the Aberdeen Branch of An Comunn Gaidhealach. And as a member of the student Nationalist society I was involved in founding and editing a magazine which we called *Alba Mater*, playing with the title of the student magazine *Alma Mater*. I managed to sell a copy of the first edition to the then Principal, as he was entering the grounds of the University, and I remember his wry smile as he read the title of the magazine.

The move to Cambridge took place in October 1947, and this brought yet another new world to explore. The course I chose was a demanding one, studying Anglo-Saxon, Archaeology, Old Irish and Welsh, with a fifth paper on the work of James Macpherson and Ossian. The head of the department was Professor Bruce Dickins, and the lecturer in Welsh was Rachel Bromwich, who was to become a long-lasting friend and colleague. My interest in Macpherson had been triggered by Celtic John at Aberdeen, and was to become a long-lasting preoccupation. My Cambridge paper was expanded and resulted in the publication of *The Gaelic Sources of Macpherson's Ossian* in 1952, and a succession of papers over several decades. Since I already had a degree, and because of war service, I was allowed to complete the course in one year instead of the normal two, and this meant a hard slog. My Anglo-Saxon and Archaeology were less than brilliant, but I was awarded a First, and this no doubt made it easier to be appointed as an Assistant in Celtic at Edinburgh University in 1948.

The head of the Celtic Department there was the distinguished Irish scholar Myles Dillon, and it was a privilege to have his guidance during my brief spell at Edinburgh, and his friendship for many years. The city has a lengthy and distinguished literary reputation, and it was being further enhanced in the mid 20th century.   I had a useful contact with the literati, through acquaintance with Hector Maciver, head of English at the Royal High School. Hector was a Lewisman, and I first met him at the 1945 General Election. Prominent literary figures in Edinburgh at that time were Norman MacCaig, Sydney Goodsir Smith and Sorley Maclean, and among the students at that time was John Macinnes.

My stay in Edinburgh was enjoyable but short, as Glasgow University decided in 1949 to establish a lectureship in Welsh, and I was called to an interview, and given the job.   During the interview I said that if I were appointed it would be desirable to spend some time in Wales, improving my knowledge, and this was quickly agreed. So in autumn 1949 I moved to Glasgow, and got closely involved with the then head of the department, Angus Matheson, and began to plan Welsh input into the Celtic Honours courses. The secondment to Wales ran from January to July 1950, attending many classes at Bangor, and finding new friends, especially Caerwyn Williams.

Since the Welsh input was confined to the Honours courses I was also much involved in teaching Scottish Gaelic and Irish, so the years at Glasgow gave many opportunities to broaden my teaching experience.   Other doors began to open more widely also, with involvement in Gaelic radio programmes, and the Gaelic life of the city.   In these days you could hear people talking Gaelic on Byres Road and Partick, and Gaelic song was hugely popular in the city.   Predictably my interest in Gaelic writing continued, and grew more intense.   In 1951 my first collection of poems, with some English translations, appeared.

1951 was also the year when preparations began for the launch of a Gaelic quarterly.   In 1948 An Comunn Gaidhealach has started a Gaelic periodical, *Alba*, jointly edited by Tom Murchison, but for lack of funding it appeared only once.   It seemed urgent that the gap should be filled, and I suggested to Finlay J MacDonald, by then involved in the Gaelic Department of the BBC, that we should found a Gaelic quarterly. We spent the first year gathering funds, from a wide range of supporters, and in 1952 *Gairm* was launched. We had raised close to £1000, and since the first edition cost less than £300 to print, it seemed a safe start. *Gairm* lasted for fifty years and two hundred editions, and did much to enliven and revolutionise Gaelic writing.   The magazine had a mixture of fiction, verse, history, biography, politics, photographs, reviews and whatever turned up, and built up a good readership in Scotland and overseas.   Finlay and I edited it for the first twelve years, and when he decided to stop I carried on until 2002. *Gairm* Publications developed a wide range of Gaelic books: more about that later.

During my short time in Edinburgh plans were beginning to be made for what would later become the School of Scottish Studies, and I was recruited after moving to Glasgow to go on collecting expeditions, gathering especially songs from traditional sources. This involved summer expeditions to Skye, Lewis, Harris, the Uists and Benbecula, and also to Kintyre. These trips produced a valuable cache of traditional song from individuals who clearly inherited long-lasting traditions, and these recordings became a valuable part of the School's archive.

1952 was another memorable year for me. In that year I married Carol Galbraith, already widely known as a Mod Gold Medallist, and a popular singer in many parts of Scotland as well as her native Campbeltown. She had been a student of mine a little earlier. Our family began in 1954 with the birth of Donald, and another five were to follow over the years. Carol had qualified as a teacher, and taught Maths in various Glasgow schools, as well as some Gaelic later in Perthshire.

In 1956 my old mentor Celtic John retired, and I was appointed to succeed him as Reader in Celtic at Aberdeen. We soon settled into living there, a new experience for Carol, and a renewal of memories for me. Our first house faced King's College, and there were a good number of old friends within reach. Over a busy seven years we were involved in many activities, and I had to find time to write some poems and essays, and in 1961 produce an edition of *Branwen Uerch Lyr*, the second of four branches of the Mabinogi, one of the most famous productions of Medieval Wales. I was encouraged to produce this book by Myles Dillon, and it was published by the Dublin Institute for Advanced Studies.

In 1963 my old colleague at Glasgow, Angus Matheson, died, and I was appointed to the Chair of Celtic at Glasgow. After seven years at Aberdeen I was quite ready to return to the Green Place, and to get involved again in the varied activities there: academic, social, literary, political and so on. With good support from above it became possible to build our teaching resources and expand the range of studies in the Department. We soon had an academic staff of five, and expanded the curriculum, especially for the Honours Degree, but also introducing special courses for learners of Gaelic. The staff included a Welshman, Donald Howells, an Irishman, James Gleasure, and three Gaelic Scots, Kenneth MacDonald, Donald J. MacLeod and myself.

I had begun to publish some Gaelic books from the Department at Aberdeen, and did the same at Glasgow. But the most significant development in this sphere came later in the 1960's, with the establishment of the Gaelic Books Council in 1968. A similar organisation had already been set up in Wales, and seemed the right model for Gaelic Scotland also. I had two meetings with Willie Ross, then Scottish Secretary, and he quite quickly agreed to provide funding. Glasgow University also joined in, providing accommodation and some funding. When I approached our Principal, Sir Charles Wilson, my recollection is that he first looked rather surprised, and asked why Ross had agreed. I suggested that Winnie Ewing's Hamilton victory in 1967 may have been a factor, and he nodded agreement. Later the funding was provided by the Scottish Arts Council and continues to the present, although the Books Council no longer has close ties with the University.

The Council, with its provision of funding to Gaelic publishers, made a huge difference. A wide range of books came on stream, with Gairm Publications one of the main operators, joined later by Acair and some smaller publishers. The flow of fiction, poetry, children's books, translations etc. increased greatly. I chaired the Council until I retired in 1991, and had much pleasure in working with colleagues, and especially the long-lasting Director, Ian MacDonald, who is still in post.

Our growing family settled into a spacious house and garden in Pollockshields. By 1974 there were six children, some of them just passing their teens and developing a range of interests and careers. Donald was studying art at Aberdeen, and Daniel was later to take a degree in English at Edinburgh University and then quickly switch back to piano playing as a life career. Cairistìona (known as Tia) took a degree at Glasgow, and became a competent piano player, Ranald, who died at the age of thirty-seven, was also interested in playing music and writing, Roderick is a football journalist and Calum is a chef. There are some parental influences in these developments, and a fair degree of independence.

Politics began to play a greater role in my life from the late 1960's, and I was active in the Pollockshields area in particular, working with George Leslie, D'arcy Conyers, Gordon Wilson and others. Gordon Wilson rang me shortly after midnight to tell me that Donald Stewart had just won the Western Isles seat for the SNP. The 1970's saw a significant upsurge in SNP support, both in Glasgow City Council and in the country generally. I remember climbing lamp-posts in Pollockshields with Malcolm Slessor to place posters, and canvassing for Margo MacDonald in Govan. At one point Winnie Ewing and Billy Wolfe called to ask me to stand for the SNP, but I had the sense to decline thinking I could make a better contribution to Scottish life as an academic. The decade was to end with the unseemly

Westminster activities at 1979, and we had to wait almost twenty years for a significant revival.   Nationalist leanings were not much of a credential at Glasgow University, but that did not make me change my mind.

Academic activities, despite political work, continued to dominate much of my time, and produced a fair number of books and articles, including *An Introduction to Gaelic Poetry* in 1974 (with a fresh edition in 1989), the *New English-Gaelic Dictionary* in 1981, and the *Companion to Gaelic Scotland* in 1983, with an updated edition in 1994.   Work began on an Historical Dictionary of Scottish Gaelic in the late 1960's.   This was a Celtic Department project and a sizeable quantity of work was built up, but it has not yet been finished.

Committees work expanded outwith the University, with long associations with the Scottish Gaelic Texts Society, the McCaig Trust, and the Gaelic Society of Glasgow, and in the early 1970's a spell in the Scottish Arts Council.

I had a long history of moving addresses, going back to student days at Aberdeen.   Then in 1977 we decided to move out of Glasgow, and finally settled in Aberfeldy, going via Comrie.   Perthshire always attracted me since the 1930's and we stayed in Aberfeldy for seven years.   It meant a lot of road travel for me as I normally went to Glasgow about five days a week.   Carol became involved as Secretary with the local branch of An Comunn, and took up Gaelic teaching part-time.   The Rector of the local high school was a fellow Lewsiman, Willie Morrison, who lived a few doors away from us. Roderick and Calum got involved in golf, and some of the other boys spent part of the summer planting trees.   And we often visited Pitlochry and Perth, and explored the Perthshire countryside.

I was granted a six-month sabbatical soon after moving to Perthshire, and devoted a good deal of time to preparing the *New English-Gaelic Dictionary*. That was followed later by the more complicated work of organizing the *Companion to Gaelic Scotland*, with a wide range of contributors.   And after seven years we decided to return to Glasgow.   A new raft of activities had begun to emerge before we moved.   In 1983 I shared with Edwin Morgan the Saltire Book of the Year Award, for my collected poems, and the following year was asked to join the panel that decided the awards.   This was a most interesting, at times exacting experience, as we had a great variety of books to read.   Our meetings were lively, sometimes controversial, but it was a great experience to work with such a diverse group.   At first it was chaired by Paul H Scott, and later by Ian Campbell and Douglas Gifford.   I enjoyed the company as much as the books, and was glad to serve for twelve years or so.   I also did a shorter spell on the panel for the MacVittie Prize.   These prizes helped greatly in raising the profile of Scottish writing.

The involvements in academic work, family activities, committees and so on were fairly demanding, but lifelong interest in writing poetry kept on resurfacing.   This obsession was known to my family.   On one famous occasion I had evidently been saying something that my daughter Tia, then in her early teens, disapproved of, and she said "Away and write a poem". I'm not sure if I obeyed, but it often happened.   Tia herself has also taken to writing poems.

My interests in writing poetry had begun to develop very early, with family influences an important factor.   At the Nicolson I made one or two contributions to the school magazine, but at Aberdeen the world of poetry began to open and expand, with growing acquaintance with modern trends in English and Scottish Poetry, deepening interest in the work of Gaelic poets which as William Ross and Alasdair Mac Mhaighstir Alasdair, and the work of Hugh MacDiarmid, T S Eliot and W B Yeats.   Student contacts at Aberdeen helped also, especially the friendship with Alex Scott, and marginal contacts with Douglas Young, then a lecturer in Greek at Aberdeen, and still a Nationalist.   I had my first, and perhaps last, taste of absinth at his flat when he was looking for a little advice on Gaelic.   On moving to Cambridge in 1947 I decided to make Gaelic my first choice for writing poetry, with the concession of making translations of my own verse from time to time, as it was clear that this allowed Gaelic verse to reach a wider public.   Edinburgh contacts also opened the doorway to that wider public, and Hector Maciver was influential in finding a publisher for my first collection, *An Dealbh Briste*, which appeared in 1951.   By this time I was using traditional styles and also developing free verse.   Free verse was not popular in traditional Gaelic circles, but its development was part of the movement into the wider poetic world, and this movement was to go on growing in the succeeding decades.

In addition to the personal concerns that inspired some of the poetry, I thought it was very important to record the indigenous Gaelic society in which I grew up in Lewis, and which was already beginning to be eroded by the mid-century.   This involved capturing and recording attitudes and life-styles that were perhaps beginning to disappear, the characters that embodied these, and the intrinsic language that they used.   These preoccupations continued to influence my work in the 1950's and 1960's including poems such as 'Cotrìona Mhòr', 'Clann-nighean an Sgadain / The Herring Girls', 'Cisteachan-laighe/ Coffins' and many others.

Sequences of poems became one of my favoured approaches from the 1960's onwards.   My collection of 1970, *An Rathad Cian*, was an extended example, focused closely on Lewis. This was published by Gairm Publications, in Gaelic only, and in 1971 English translations of the sequence were published under the title *The Far Road* by Lines Review and New Rivers Press, New York. This was of course Callum MacDonald's initiative. Eleven years later Callum was to publish my collected poems *Creachadh na Clàrsaich/ Plundering the Harp* and our friendship was to last until his death. Callum had a crucial influence on poetry publishing in Scotland.

I had published *Saorsa agus an Iolaire/ Freedom and the Eagle* in 1977. This collection contained a good number of political poems, and some sequences. Only twenty of the poems had translations added. Two other collections were to follow: *Smeur an Dòchais/ Bramble of Hope*, published by Canongate in 1991, and *Meall Garbh/ The Rugged Mountain*, published by Gairm in 1995.

That fairly long trail of poetry publications led to a good many poetry readings over the years. This involved readings in Stornoway, South Uist, Inverness, Glasgow, Dumfries and other places, but the liveliest location for poetry readings was Edinburgh. *The Heretics* provided one of the earliest and most varied series of readings, and later the Book Festival and the Poetry Library were to become prominent players. One of the largest gatherings was to celebrate Norman MacCaig's eighty-fifth birthday. In the early 1970's a series of poetry exchanges between Scotland and Ireland began, and I greatly enjoyed visits to Ireland, its large audiences in Dublin and Cork in particular. There were occasional forays into England (London, Sheffield and Kent), some visits to Wales, a fascinating visit to Nova Scotia in the early 1980's, and short visits to Germany, Italy and Austria. Some of these trips were accompanied by translations, including many into Welsh by John Stoddart, and some into German by Heidi Prüger. As a kind of reciprocal gesture Gairm Publications issued in 1990 an anthology of translations of British and European poetry into Gaelic: *Bàrdachd na Roinn-Eòrpa an Gàidhlig*. Gairm Publications had been building up a wide range of books from the late 1950's, and this grew significantly in the last three decades of the twentieth century, including the take-over of Alexander MacLaren's publications, and the development of a wide range of books: dictionaries, language books, fiction, poetry, children's books etc.

The twentieth century saw a fairly remarkable renaissance of Gaelic Poetry, in terms both of volume and diversity. I had close relations with a number of the poets. Iain Crichton Smith was a fellow-villager and early acquaintance. His main poetic output was in English, but he wrote a fair amount of Gaelic poetry, and some very accomplished Gaelic novels and short stories, while his translations of Sorley MacLean's poems were very influential.   Donald MacAulay was an old friend, and he greatly raised the profile of the 'Famous Five' Gaelic Poets with his anthology *Nua-Bhàrdachd Ghàidhlig/Modern Scottish Gaelic Poems* (1976).   George Campbell Hay corresponded with me over the years, though I only met him once.   Willie Neill was another long-term correspondent, and an enthusiastic convert to Gaelic.   Younger poets such as Myles Campbell, Meg Bateman and Anne Frater have been making significant contributions to Gaelic poetry over recent decades.   A number of these poets were dedicated Nationalists, notably Campbell Hay and Neill, and also Myles Campbell and Anne Frater.

Academic activities produced another raft of trips in Britain and abroad. I was external examiner at a number of universities, including Aberdeen, Cambridge, Oxford and Leeds.   The Oxford and Cambridge assignments were spread over a good many years, especially during Ellis Evans' tenure as Professor of Celtic at Jesus College, Oxford.   Academic conferences over the years involved visits to Norway, Finland, Germany, France and Spain, together with England, Wales and Ireland.   Sometimes these visits could be combined with family holidays.   But from 1971 onwards we began to have regular European family holidays, with France becoming the favorite.   Our first family holiday in France involved stays in Brittany and Normandy, and an introduction to French cuisine on its home territory.   Later trips took in Paris, Chinon, Bordeaux and trips to the far south.   In the late 1990's our son Roderick married a French girl, Stephanie, and their daughter is fluent in French and English, with two or three words of Gaelic added.   Visits to Germany were partly triggered by the award of the Ossian Prize in 1974, and this later involved visits to Hamburg and Lubeck, and a lasting fascination with the fiction of Thomas Mann.   But France provided the most lasting European fascination.

Retirement has been a gradual process, punctuated with bursts of activity. The late Colin Matthews asked me to contribute to the New Dictionary of National Biography, a project which he set in motion but did not survive to see its publication in 2004.   I wrote a good number of articles for this and *Gairm* continued as a weekly activity for another eleven years after I retired from University, allowing me occasional forays into political commentary as part of the magazine's range.   There was also some involvement in TV, with Finlay MacLeod initiating a detailed programme on my poetry.   This led to recordings in Glasgow, Perthshire and of course Lewis, and I greatly enjoyed the experience.   A few years later Scotsoun produced a cassette of my poems, with some commentary by John Macinnes and much help from Ian MacDonald.

Politics continued to fascinate me, and this, among other interests, led to something of an obsession with reading newspapers. The creation of the Scottish Parliament added greatly to this obsession, with some annoyance over the media's prejudices, although one could appreciate some of these. This fragile but meaningful step towards independence could do with more positive reporting, and it is fair to say that there are a few positive journalists operating.

Family activities were the other dominant ones, with very regular contacts maintained. In our frequent gatherings literature often surfaced, while Carol often shared her musical and culinary interests with some members of the family, while I shared my political and football interests with some.

Finally, I still look forward to sensing a tremor in the brain that says "Away and write a poem".

Alastair Reid

Born Whithorn, 22nd March 1926

POET, TRANSLATOR

Travelling Correspondent of New Yorker *for 40 years*

On Not Living in Scotland

I have spent two thirds of my life living outside Scotland, although I have never failed to return to it, at irregular intervals, nor have I ever contemplated taking another nationality. Scotland, however has always remained for me as a measure of change — change in me, change in it.

One thing I count as a piece of early luck — I grew up in Galloway with next to no awareness of money. It never entered my day-to-day existence. My father, a country minister, would once a month go ceremoniously to the bank and then settle accounts with the butcher, the baker, and the grocer. My mother was a doctor, and often stood in for the local doctors. She did not believe in sending bills, so we regularly received bounty in the form of eggs, potatoes, rabbits, game. I first heard of money at school, but I had trouble connecting it with the pennies we were handed for church collections. Once I asked my father if I could see a pound. He went to his bookcase, fingered a volume, and took out a single pound note. I read it, both sides, and gave it back to him, back to the bookshelf. I took that as a norm; and to this day, I think of money much as motorists think of petrol — only when necessary, and not all that often.

What I have carried over most from my beginnings has been my earliest astonishments and perplexities over language. I have recently watched my two small grandchidren starting the ascent of language, from gurgles to words, from speaking to naming, from questions to stories, and, finally, to reading. I remember that breakthrough, the sudden empowerment of reading; and I have never got over my astonishment at the mysterious act of putting-into-words.

My father was a classicist; and when he saw that I could read and write, he decided to teach me Latin and Greek grammar, not at all strenuously, for he had great patience, and a constant, quiet humour. I loved these lessons, and learned the grammar to please him. It stood me in good stead later. This was my first taste of different languages, different ways of saying, different worlds. But I was discovering the same thing at school. In the playground among friends, we had a separate conversational world, we spoke our local language easily; but I can clearly recall going from playground to classroom and crossing not just a threshold of space but also one of language. In class, we were taught, and spoke, in English. A Scots word used in class was an intruder, sure to bring a snigger from someone. Knowledge may have come to us in English; but we wore it in our own tongue.

As I grew, these differences widened. We came in for a fair share of obligatory church-going. In the pulpit, my father wore a gravity that I seldom saw at home; but he had a transfixing voice, and I listened to the wording of the King James Version that was even further from my wordings at the time. On Sundays, I waited for him to come home, robeless and reassuringly familiar, his own voice back.

At school, I always felt a tacit assumption that English was the language of the Master Race, and it was somehow up to us to learn to use it as well, if not better, than they did. With my friends, I spoke Border, at home, we spoke Family (most families develop a Housespeak over time), and in speaking to any kind of authority, we spoke English, or Proper, as we called it. I was realising then that there was not simply one language, but many; and that even within one language there were different registers, depending on who was speaking. I listened a lot; and I still do.

Like those of my generation, my life was divided, drastically, by the war. Before it lay my childhood and my growing. Then, with the war, normal time stopped and became wartime. I spent the last two years of the war on a small naval ship working in the Indian Ocean and later the Persian Gulf. Languages multiplied; and I also experienced the desperate isolation of being surrounded by a language I could not understand. When I got back to Scotland, to the bleak postwar years, I had realised that languages were all varying ways of giving order, like maps or sets of rules, but that these rules varied from climate to climate, from country to country, from language to language, and also that different languages reflected varying solutions to the same essential problem — how to live. Rather than settling back into my own language, I chose what turned out to be a travelling existence.

I went first to the United States, to New York in particular, where I have lived for different spells over the last 50 years, and which still feels warm and familiar to me. To live in a place is to learn its language, and in the United States, English has been substantially modified to fit different human wavelengths, shifting and changing. For a spell, I taught at a small college; but I had begun to write then, although I had little idea how to survive as a writer. I decided to try, however, and I left my job, and moved to Spain, where I could live simply, and where my time was my own.

I had gone to Spain for the first time the previous year, almost by accident, knowing little about the country and nothing of the language. Something about Spain drew me in at once — the Mediterranean light felt to me like the antidote to the flinty Scotland I had left behind me. I did not sense it then, but it was an immersion that made a vast difference to my ongoing life.

Spain at the time had been left behind by the rest of Europe. Isolated by its own Civil War in 1936, followed by World War II, it had become disconnected under Franco's dictatorship, and it was changing before its own eyes, ready to liberate itself from the horrors of the immediate past. By coming to live there, I took it on myself to get to know the country, and — the first essential step — the language.

By this time, I had begun to write. I had published a number of poems in the New Yorker magazine, and had read it with enthusiasm. From Spain, I wrote my first chronicle for the magazine, and soon after I joined the staff as a travelling correspondent. Over the years I covered all kinds of improbable happenings — the World Cup, on five occasions, Scottish nationalism, interpreters in the United Nations — under a remarkable editor who cared only for good, clear writing, whatever the subject. He left me free to follow my nose, and I moved often, sometimes from the demand of events, sometimes from curiosity alone. In retrospect, I think I became a writer because of a fierce determination to own my own time.

What consumed me then, however, was the experience of entering another language. It happens on various levels — the essential ones of listening and understanding, the others of speaking and responding. Add to these the extra skills, of reading and writing, and eventually their coming together, in living in the language. I also went through the barrier that keeps most people from new languages — the inevitable stage of entering conversations as a semi-idiot, groping for intelligibility. With time, it comes. Entering another language, however, to the point of fluency, brings with it certain unforeseen changes. It is not so much that we learn to speak another language as that we are instead spoken by the language. It imposes its own attitudes, its own sense of the world. Speaking Spanish, to this day I feel a change coming over me, a loosening, a different way of being. Entering Spanish felt like growing another self.

Even as I grew comfortable using the language, I grew aware of my ignorance of things Spanish; and I had read almost nothing of its literature. In Barcelona, I had a close friend, an adventurous publisher, who decided to supervise my education, and who plied me with books. Over a couple of years, I did little else but read, and learn Spain. He was just then receiving the first manuscripts from the generation of Latin American writers whose writings were translated enthusiastically during the 60s and 70s. I had never thought much about the South American continent, but now, through what I read, it began to loom large in my imagination. I read all I could of Borges, and I discovered the poetry of Pablo Neruda. Although I had no inkling of it at the time, I would much later translate a large part of the poetry of both of these writers, and enjoy long friendships with them both.

Mario Vargas Llosa came to Barcelona; and in the course of a long conversation, he urged me to go to Latin America. "You have to know how it feels, how it smells" he told me. I took him seriously; and in 1964 I made a four-month-long pilgrimage through the southern continent, making many stops on the way. In every sense, it was a New World to me – its extraordinary landscapes, its highly-coloured history, but most of all, its people. Mario had put me in touch with various writers, and they would pass me on to others at my next destination. Some of them remain friends to this day. What fascinated me endlessly was how the fairly formal Spanish I had learned in Spain broke up into many different variations and vocabularies in the countries of Latin America. The language loosened and became more playful. What has taken me back there time after time is the high value placed there on human conversation. Come down anywhere, and you are likely to fall into conversations that are part-entertainment, part-sporting event, and part-high art. Back in Spain, I felt that my world had doubled in size.

I had never thought of translating seriously, although at times during my reading, I would occasionally translate a few striking lines from a poem out of curiosity, to see if it could be recreated in English. Besides that, in learning the language, I had at first done a good bit of translating in my head. So translating became part of my writing life, and I have always had at hand some work waiting for its English version. I got in the habit of translating for a spell to start the day, and then moving to my own writing. I have been lucky enough to know well most of the writers I have translated, and to have the sound of their voices in my head, as a kind of touchstone. I have chosen to translate mostly poetry, which is more challenging than prose, in that the original poem has to be matched by its version in English. But since I have spent a large part of my life living in Spanish and writing in English, translating feels at times like a two-sided conversation with myself.

With all this moving it might seem that Scotland has receded in my attention; but while I feel at home in a number of different cultures and languages, Scotland is the only place where I never feel the separation of being from Somewhere Else, the state of being a foreigner that I have worn for a long time. In Scotland, besides, my childhood is enclosed as in a glass bubble, along with the language of my beginnings, which has stayed with me as a secret vocabulary. In pieces I wrote for The New Yorker, I would often use a Scots word deliberately, which would always bring on an editorial query. I would argue strenuously, and I managed to get the adjectives "douce" and "thrawn" into circulation, and the verb "to swither", which the English language badly needs. My son used to tease me by speaking Spanish to me in an exaggerated Scots accent. For examples of brilliant, cross-cultural translation, however, I would often turn to W. L. Lorimer's New Testament in Scots, where the phrase "Hold thy peace!" from the King James' Version becomes, unforgettably, "Wheesht!"

I think that working across languages has made me hyper-conscious of the gap between what is going on in our heads, and whatever language we choose to put it into. As Borges reminds us constantly, verbal reality is very different from lived reality. Once put into language, reality takes on certain shades and forms that depend on the language that is used to contain or explain it. Similarly, I have often had occasion to remember an observation from Lawrence Durrell's Alexandria Quartet, which has proved incontrovertibly true for me:

> Our view of reality is conditioned by our position in space and time — not by our personalities as we like to think. Thus every interpretation of reality is based upon a unique position. Two paces east or west and the whole picture is changed.

Although I take great pleasure in human conversation, talking is quite different from writing. In talking, we are able to use not just words but voice-tones, facial expressions, hand-gestures, emphases, whereas, in writing, we have no such extra aids. It must all be there in the words alone, stemming from the language alone, from the always-mysterious act of putting-into-words. Yet sometimes, in both reading and writing, we find those astonishing moments that reverse the process of creation, in which the words on the page dissolve and turn back into real feelings, real perceptions, some living realisation. Writing is a constant search for the right words and, sometimes, being lucky enough to find them.

I still spend a lot of my time listening and reading, since I believe that people exist most completely in their voices, written and spoken; and I also spend a lot of my own time swithering.

Agnes Owens

Born Milngavie, 24th May 1926

NOVELIST

A Hopeless Case

I was born on 24th May, 1926 in a one room dwelling within a row of cottages in a place called Milngavie outside Glasgow. It was the time of very high employment and so in those days most people were poor, but I never noticed the misery it caused. As a child I was fairly happy, even although my father stood less chance of getting a job than other men had, since he'd lost a leg in the first world war and was considered unfit to work. Years later he got a job in the local paper mill and being unfit never came into it. Unemployment had came down and conditions in general had improved. This allowed us to go holidays to places like Troon, Ayr and Girvan. My mother was the first to have a washing machine in our bright, new council house kitchenette. It was about this time my brother was born which made him seven years younger than myself and had to watch him when my parents were out bowling. By this time they had became keen bowlers. I don't know if that was anything to do with it but I began to do badly in school. In my report card it went from 'does well in all subjects' to 'easily distracted.' By the time I reached the 'big school' I was deemed by one of the teachers as 'a hopeless case.' This cancelled out any notion of me either going to college or more ambitiously university. When I told my parents that in any case I'd rather work in the paper mill, my father said that no child of his would work in the paper mill. I pointed out that he did; he declared that was because he never had a chance, unlike some he knew. When I did leave school I began work as a filing clerk in an office where I mainly made the tea and was sent messages. At least it's a start said my mother, and was horrified when I threw it up to work in a cosmetic factory. Our job was to fill small jars with expensive rejuvenating cream and do as many as possible in a short space of time. 'Piece work' it was called but I didn't have any aptitude for the job. I kept getting the cream all over my fingers and dropping the jar. I left before they could give me the sack. It was then my mother decided to send me to a college where I would learn shorthand and typing. That costs money I said, dismayed she should have to go to such lengths. She explained she had been paying an insurance policy for just such an eventuality, so I went to college and became quite proficient as a shorthand typist. I might have been somebody's private secretary if I hadn't met and married a man who returned from the second world war shattered in spirit if not in body. He couldn't stand fireworks or any loud noise, although he did his best to hide it in case I would laugh. I would never have laughed at him because I didn't take it too seriously and anyway the hospital said he would get over it in time. Yet he never did.

Our baby daughter was barely eight weeks old when my husband said we would have to leave the city to find a place to stay. Work wasn't the problem any more; it was accommodation. Nothing had been built during the war. At present we were staying with his brother who in a weak moment had agreed to give us a room, but now there was a baby, he wanted us out. But since there was no accommodation to be had for love nor money we didn't know what way to turn, that is until we read an article in a newspaper that gave us hope and prompted us to collect our belongings together before we stealthily crept out of the brother's room to avoid paying any rent as we needed all the money we could get.

In June 1949 my first husband, baby daughter of two months, and myself set forth for the north of Scotland. This venture was prompted by an article in a paper saying that people were wanted to work land in the Highlands, with accommodation provided. I was not keen on marching into the unknown, but it was a case of squaw follows Indian brave and asks no questions. So with £11, our baby, our clothing, a two-man tent and pram we took the train from Glasgow to a station beyond Inverness called Garve. It dawned on me then that we had no idea where we were going, apart from a vague intention to reach a place called Scoraig situated on the Little Minch.

I remember we obtained a lift from a tradesman going in the direction of Scoraig, but he had heard nothing about work and accommodation. We arrived at Scoraig and the only sign of habitation was a single house staring from a high point towards the Atlantic sea. We might as well have been in the Sahara. We spied a small brick building, possibly a shelter for animals, and inside this we huddled, hating each other, while I attempted to feed the baby. However a woman came down from the house and took us in and gave us a room to sleep. She must have thought us mad, but accepted our story and for a week we camped in her garden. Her husband, who worked on the road, told us it was the only work available. The only payment we could give her, though she wanted none, was a carton of Epsom salts. She was as grateful as if we had given her a magnificent gift. We promised to write when we were in better circumstances. Sadly, we never did.

We set off back through this mountainous region, possibly beautiful if you were a tourist, but to me desolate and harsh, gushing rivers and jagged rocks.

We came to an inn stuck in the middle of nowhere and, overjoyed at this bit of civilization, set up our tent beside it. The buxom woman who owned the place sold us food, even offering my husband a job. She took a fancy to him but not to me.

After two days of camping and happiness for my husband, mainly because of his access to beer, I took the initiative and unpegged the tent, wrapped it up, and we set off again in silence. I can't remember how long it took us to reach the town of Beauly but by the end of the journey we were both covered in cleg bites. The baby in her pram was protected by wet nappies hanging over the hood. The money was nearly done. In Beauly I located what nowadays would be called a Social Security office and managed to obtain fourteen shillings by genuinely sobbing my heart out and holding the baby who cried too. This allowed us to buy food and walk to Inverness.

We reached Inverness and put up the tent in a place called, I think, The Black Park Camping Site, for a few shillings weekly. We stayed here for quite a while, since my husband got a job to do with erecting pylons. It couldn't have been much fun for him going to work from a tent but I had problems too, walking every day from the site to the town for a few herrings or whatever was cheap, and making food on the primus stove which was difficult to light. I remember one occasion when my husband complained about his meal and I threw the semolina for the baby round the tent in a fit of temper. On another I nearly set the tent on fire in the night while heating milk for the baby.

And yet there were occasions when I was happy pushing the pram along the canal bank or sitting by the river. It was summer and the place was lovely. This situation continued until late September when the weather became colder and the days shorter.

About this time I decided I could not carry on living in a tent with an infant a few months old and the winter approaching. One Saturday evening I packed and, pushing the pram, headed for Inverness railway station to return home to my mother. I left my husband in the tent drinking whisky.

I had to wait some time for the Glasgow train and, before it came, I turned about and pushed the pram back to the tent and that was that. We both decided to leave. We now had some money from my husband's work so a few days later we assembled our belongings and we left Inverness on a train for Keith, another destination unknown to us. Anywhere, we thought then, was better than returning to Glasgow.

We arrived in Keith in the dark, came to a field and pulled our tent round about us. We marched through the town the next morning, not a big place then as I remember it. We purchased some groceries from a shop in the town square owned by man called McGillviray who asked us questions — why and where and what were we doing. We answered shamefacedly. "There's a man lives here, originally from Glasgow," he said. "I'm sure he'll let you put your tent up in his back garden.   It's a good size."

This man called Alec Simpson did just that and his wife washed our grimy clothes and the baby's nappies. Alec was pleased with us because my husband came from Glasgow and I had worked there. For a fortnight we camped in his back garden, burning fires at night, hanging our clothes to dry over the fence. The townsfolk called us the squatters. Before October ended we moved to a broken-down old building.

We lived there for a year. We were comfortable. We had coal, paraffin light, and my husband got a job with the English Electric Company. My second child, a boy, was born in Keith hospital. We might have lived in Keith forever but the woman who owned the condemned building told us regretfully that it was being knocked down and we must leave. It was then my husband and I parted for a time. I returned to my home town and he went on working with English Electric. I've often wished to go back to Keith and see it all again, but no doubt everything would be unrecognizable now.

This adventure was judged by a councillor in my home town as "irresponsible" — I was desperately applying to him for one of the available prefabricated houses. We got the prefab after waiting another year and a half and my husband and I, plus another three children making four in all, lived not particularly happily ever after until he died at the age of forty-three.

I suppose you could say my life was a struggle, as it is with most men and women of the working class even in years of good employment. I always worked when possible at anything I could find, i.e. in shop, office and factory. That was in the good old days when work brought satisfaction even if it was a hassle. Work was money and security and if I was not exactly happy with my lot I could relax with a drink at the weekend while watching the telly.

Any disagreement which arose under the influence was forgotten when facing work on Monday. Yet I suppose there was always a hankering to do something better.

So many years ago I began writing fiction, prompted by the fact that I had joined a writing class in Alexandria. Glasgow University sent tutors who were enthusiastic about what I wrote. When they stopped attending the class I simply carried on writing and periodically some of them got in touch as if to prod me on with that lonely business. Sometimes it was the last thing I wanted to do, especially after cleaning somebody's house, which was now the only job I could get. The years of unemployment had set in once again.

Then my novel *Gentlemen of the West* was published and some short stories in a book, shared with two other authors, called *Lean Tales*. This was great but didn't pay the rent. I continued to clean houses and, with the assistance of a grant from the Scottish Arts Council, wrote another short novel called *Like Birds in the Wilderness*. It wasn't a success though some people liked it.

Eight years later Bloomsbury published *A Working Mother* and then I completed a collection of stories. Since the depression of the past decade took the security of steady work away from my present husband Patrick, from myself and from countless others I was thankful to still be in the business of writing. At least I can tell my grandchildren (if they are interested, that is) that not only did I publish a few books in my time but I once was "irresponsible" enough to set off with my first husband and child into the unknown wilds of the Scottish Highlands where we wandered about with scarcely a penny in our pockets.

My first husband was forty three when he died of a thrombosis. My mother died ten years later. A sad time for us all. She was a good woman and never did anything wrong that I knew of apart from being a bit of a gambler. She liked a bet on the horses and was obsessed with the bingo, but I had always been a disappointment to her. She never liked anything I wrote, especially *Gentlemen of the West* which to her way of thinking had a lot of swearing in it. I thought she might have given me some credit for writing at all. Then a terrible thing happened that drove everything else out of my mind My youngest son was stabbed to death outside his home a week before Christmas 1987. He was only nineteen and we were all devastated. I didn't think I could ever be bothered writing again. Two or three years passed and I managed to write *For the Love of Willie*. It was published and I got writer of the year award, narrowly missing a bigger Stakis Prize. This put me back on track again, and eventually *Bad Attitudes* was published in 2003.

I haven't written anything since, apart from two short stories I've put aside to revise since I don't think they're good enough.   Perhaps I'm being too critical but I've never had publishers clamouring for my work. My novels are too short they say, but I've always had good reviews, and the publishers know that, so maybe that's why they publish me.

I got married again and had another three children to my present husband, two girls and a boy, making seven children in all, and fourteen grandchildren, three of whom are French.

When people ask me what made me start to write I just say it was a fluke. I had joined a writing group to get away from the house, although I was writing some bad poetry then. But when I wrote about a brickie and his drunken mates, Jim Kelman, a writer himself and the tutor, told me to forget about the poetry and concentrate on the brickie, I did that.

And you know the rest.

This is an expanded version of an article from
People Like That, published by Bloomsbury, 1996.

Ronald Stevenson

Born Blackburn, Lancashire, 6th March 1928

COMPOSER

Andrew Fletcher of Saltoun Award 2002

Meeting Ronald

Introduction by Aonghas MacNeacail

Reprinted from *Chapman* 89-90, Winter 1998

Years before I met Ronald Stevenson in person, I had met him through the pages of *The Listener*, that distinguished and now much lamented house journal of the serious radio listener, when there were only three wavelengths to listen to; the Home Service, the Light Programme and the Third Programme. Ronald contributed regular articles on the kind of music then heard primarily on the Third Programme in an auto-didactic quest for understanding of the widest possible range of musics.

I can't pretend to remember the specific subject-matter of any of Ronald's essays. What I do recall is that his columns were always required reading. His fluent, vivid style gave a strictly non-musically-literate reader, such as I was (and remain), a sense of the shape of the pieces he described, so that what had previously seemed altogether remote became more accessible. He took a delight in making pictures in words, as, I would later discover, he also did in his own music.

My first encounter with Ronald Stevenson in person was entirely accidental – if such moments ever can be entirely anything. I'd gone along to a local hotel with a friend who was collecting stocks for the bar at a wedding ceilidh at the Gaelic College in Skye where I was Writer in Residence. I'd no intention of going to the event. I'd only made this lunchtime trip with Davie to help him load his van with crates of drink. Because it was lunchtime, and midweek, the bar was empty, apart from a lively group at one table who were obviously in party mood. Trying not to eavesdrop, but eavesdropping, I heard fragments of an anecdote in which Ronald's name came up on more than one occasion. When, eventually, a dapper gent with a fine head of grey hair came up to the bar to replenish his friends' glasses, I diffidently asked whether he might be Ronald Stevenson.

Quickly recovering from his surprise at being recognised at such an hour in such a place, he set about finding out who I was. A Gaelic poet? I must meet his daughter who was at that moment in Portree, being witness at her best friend's wedding. Gerda, he informed me, was an actress with a deep interest in poetry and in Gaelic. He'd introduce us at the wedding ceilidh later that evening. I hadn't planned to go to the wedding ceilidh, but curiosity about this ebullient man's daughter persuaded me.

My next meeting with Ronald was at his and Marjorie's home in West Linton, when some time later Gerda took me to meet her parents properly. My abiding memory of that occasion, and many subsequent visits, is that I was inundated with books from Ronald's extensive library which he insisted would be of essential or compelling interest to me. As yet another book descended on my lap before I'd proceeded beyond the fly-leaf of the one previous, I was soon overwhelmed, physically and emotionally. While books slid off the growing literary mountain on my lap, I had to deal with feelings of guilt that I had not the speed-reading capacity to offer informed comment on their contents. Meanwhile some aspect of our conversation had sent Ronald off in search of another key text.

I later discovered that I was not the only victim of his enthusiasm for sharing knowledge, and that his propensity to bury guests under Gutenberg mountains was shared by a dear friend and former colleague of his, Charlie King. When I first met Charlie, he was the English Adviser in the Education Department at Grampian Regional Council, but many years before he taught English at Broughton Senior Secondary School in Edinburgh where one of his colleagues in the music department was Ronald Stevenson. As Charlie's great passion was music, while Ronald's was literature, with each at times finding it hard to separate personal enthusiasm from professional obligation, it's hardly surprising that they should have become such close friends. I have often imagined a scenario where pupils discovered their music in the English class, while learning all about literature in the music room. One contemporary Scottish writer, and in his time a very reluctant scholar, Alan Bold, certainly credits Ronald's literary enthusiasms with firing his own interest in writing.

By the time I met Ronald he had long since parted company with the formal education system, although the pedagogic impetus remained strong. He still gives regular piano lessons to children from the West Linton area, including his own grandson, while older students from various corners of the world make frequent pilgrimages to obtain personal tutorials from a master. And such is his passion for ideas that few can have left his study without some item of knowledge that may have little obvious connection with music, but which fits into the totality of life as Ronald lives it.

I have inevitably had many discussions with him about music, and I am sure I'm much wiser on the subject than before, although the only specific musical fact that I can acknowledge learning from him is that the precentor-led Presbyterian Gaelic form of psalm singing, with its wonderfully wild improvisatory qualities, is known as heterophony. Such an admission implies no failure on his part, but on mine. The languages of music and mathematics are as accessible to me as ancient Sumerian.

I did learn from him that my own interest in the folk song of the Gael as a potential motor for cultural revival was paralleled by the instincts which led composers like Kodaly and Bartok to collect the folk songs of their native Hungary. Their perception that song was central to the soul of a culture led them to recognise the importance of the language in which the songs were sung. This in turn brought them to play a central part in the revival of the national language of Hungary, Magyar, which, in their time had become a very fragile language indeed, having languished under the homogenising Teutonic pressures of the Austro-Hungarian Empire.

Another cultural territory I had tentatively begun to explore was that of the Native American peoples. Dee Brown's *Bury My Heart at Wounded Knee* made me aware of a number of striking echoes between the experiences and attitudes of American Indians and my own people. Removal from their lands was one factor: their feelings for the lands they inhabited, their sense of belonging to it rather than it to them, inevitably struck a chord. Ronald drew my attention to chords, in a more literal sense, when he showed me Natalie Curtis's collection of traditional songs of the North American Indian. It was a short step from that to her brother Edward's extensive collection of photographs which spanned life-styles, linguistic families and generations of Native American communities. Farmers, fishers and hunter-gatherers, wise ones and warriors, are all portrayed. It quickly became clear to me from the Curtis family's work and the wide range of summaries and studies I now sought out, that those people I had previously only seen representations of as destructive savages were actually a heterogeneous social medley of great cultural and linguistic diversity. Their histories I would probably have sought out anyway: Ronald's particular enthusiasms steered me naturally toward the deeper and more essential aspects of their nature, to seek out what they sang, and how, and why.

Among other visitors to any conversation with Ronald, one is liable to encounter Keats, Goethe, Whitman, Marx, Morgenstern or Dante Alighieri, in quotation or biographical anecdote. He had a long correspondence with the noted theatre designer, Gordon Craig, whose work he greatly admires. Ronald likes to make an annual pilgrimage to the Scottish National Gallery's Turner exhibition which can only be brought to the surface in the weak light of January. Other artists, particularly the great Italian Renaissance masters, are tremendously important to him. This concern for the verbal and the visual may offer a significant key to the way he approaches his own music. He frequently talks about his compositions in terms of narrative and a sense of almost visible physical structures.

Having maintained contact with his former pupil Alan Bold long after Broughton school was a memory to both, he would meet and befriend artist friends of Alan's including John Bellany and Sandy Moffat. Many years earlier a chance meeting with the great thistle head of Scottish poetry, on the last evening bus from Edinburgh to Biggar (which passes through West Linton) began a friendship with Hugh MacDiarmid which would endure till the end of the older man's life. Through MacDiarmid he met Sidney Goodsir Smith, whom he remembers with great warmth, Norman MacCaig and Sorley MacLean, among other denizens of Edinburgh's literary howffs.

My own bridge to that legendary coterie was MacLean, which is not to suggest that I thought less of the others, as poets or as people. But with Sorley I had direct kinship in terms both of language and of history. That Ronald recognised on our first meeting, and the understanding remains an important part of our relationship as artists, as members of the same family and as friends. I remember that the works of John Lorne Campbell and Francis Collinson on Gaelic music and song were among the books that descended like a volcanic lava of knowledge into my lap in those early days. F G Scott has also mattered to him, as an adopted Borderer perhaps, because of the MacDiarmid connection certainly, but particularly because of what Scott had done with and for Scotland's own music.

If I suggested that Ronald taught me little about music, it should be clear that that is only true within the realms of possibility and at the level of technicalities, the finer nuances of which will remain forever beyond my comprehension. I have gained much knowledge and appreciation of his own music and of many others', particularly of the composers that have mattered most to himself such as Shostakovich, Busoni, Percy Grainger, Paderewski (who was both pianist and head of state), all the MacCrimmons and the innumerable makers of songs whose only identifying characteristic was the melody which endured and defined their urge to sing.

My earliest experience of that urge manifesting itself in Ronald occurred one Christmas day – it was either the first or second I spent among the Stevenson family. I'd given Gerda a copy of Flora MacNeil's album *Craobh nan Ubhal* (The Apple Tree) for Christmas. When all gifts had been exchanged, the album was played and listened to with obvious pleasure. Later, I heard Ronald at his piano. There was something familiar, yet not fully formed, about what he was playing. Before evening a new work had taken shape. Ronald had been particularly taken by Flora's singing of 'A Bhradag Dhubh', the Barra version of a musical duel between two women from neighbouring islands. She described it as a "boasting song": inevitably, in her version, the Barra woman has the edge over her Uist rival. In Ronald's piece, which he called the "Barra Flyting Toccata", right hand and left take the place of the opposing voices in the song, in a wonderfully exuberant piano transposition which remains totally respectful of the tradition, while being new and different.

And that's how meetings with Ronald continue to be, even if a succession of illnesses has drained something of his natural ebullience. Ideas, in their historical place, in their present relevance, and in their potential to make the world new and different, still remain an animating factor in his personal and creative life. Then when the circumstances are right, and the company congenial, he can be observed forgetting how well he's supposed not to be, as the old ebullience spreads through his bones and overflows into great gusts of laughter and music.

In the short piece that follows, Ronald Stevenson refects on the links between his music and Scottish verse, particularly the work of Sir Walter Scott.

The influence of Walter Scott's poetry on my music

Scott's poetry is not generally studied in schools today. Neither was it in the mid-20th Century. I found it from my own reading. About 15 I had begun to compose music. I searched for poems to make songs. At 15 I made my own verse anthology. Scott's was the first I included. His poems were ideal for music, having rich vowels, just enough to leave space for music; and no obtrusive consonants to halt melodic flow.

In Edinburgh in the 1960s I knew four Scottish poets: MacDiarmid (C. M. Grieve), MacCaig, Goodsir Smith and Sorley MacLean and set to music verse by each of them. As background to what Scott's poetry may mean in the 21st Century, consider the views of Sir Walter by each of those four poets.

In 1926 Grieve refers to Scott on nine pages of his Contemporary Scottish Studies: 1st Series. MacCaig told me he found Scott's poetry shared terseness with Scarlatti's harpsichord sonatas. Goodsir Smith's *Under the Eildon Tree* identified with the hills of the Scott country. He also admired Scott's Lallans in his *Lament of the Border Widow*:

Wi ae lock of his yellow hair
I'll chain his heart for ever mair

Sorley MacLean pointed out to me that Scott's descriptions of the Scottish bens made the Swiss aware that their Alps could be tourist attractions. By ten, Scott had collected a library of ballads. Today an enthusiastic school-teacher could encourage students to emulate Scott by making their own ballad collections from a reference library copy.

Burns was musically literate. His correspondence with his publishers is informed with the technique of music notation. Burns was a pioneer folk-song collector. The first stanza of the majority of his lyric poems are verbatim quotations from folk texts. The remaining stanzas are Burns's development of the lyric in his own words. His complete collection of songs, printed with the melodies for which they were written, was first edited by James C Dick in 1903. This includes a total of 359 songs with music-type. Thus, Burns's importance in that connection is as a folklorist.

Scott's *Minstrelsy of the Scottish Borders* also belongs to the same genre of folksong collection. But Scott's own collection of poems are not folklore but original verse. The Minstrelsy was first published in two volumes in 1802 and volume 3 in 1803. The ethos of that collection was the *fond et origo* of *The Lay of the Last Minstrel*

Richard Demarco

Born Edinburgh, 9th July 1930

ARTIST AND STIMULATOR
OF THE ARTS

"Too Rough to go Slow"

On the Road to Meikle Seggie

Sir Maxwell Macleod, the son of Lord Macleod of Fiunary, the Founder of
The Iona Community, and restorer of Iona Abbey, suggested that the title of
my autobiography should be the one his father chose for the account of his
own life which he never managed to write.

The title came from George Macleod's experience of one of his many
missionary journeys in Africa. He was warned that if he wanted to visit a
certain tribe of would-be Christians, he had to travel to a remote and
inaccessible region involving a long journey by a sturdy motor vehicle. All
was possible for the first few hundred miles, until there would appear a
signpost, with hand written information upon it, indicating the last fifty
miles of the journey over what appeared to be a rock-strewn terrain. The
words on that signpost were good advice and a warning. They were "Too
Rough to go Slow".

Max Macleod gave me this as a present on behalf of his father. I regard
them both as dear and close friends who knew the nature of the road I have to
travel through this life. The title of my autobiography is a precious gift from
two souls wishing to help me on my way. It is an act of friendship. It reminds
me that any worthwhile journey is liable to get harder as it reaches its end.

The Road to Meikle Seggie

I recognise that road.   I have given it a name.   It is 'The Road to Meikle Seggie' and I dedicate this autobiography to all those friends who have dared to accompany me on that road, on even a small part of the way.   It is the road taken by the Celtic saints and scholars who travelled from Iona into the heartland of Europe, and before them, the Roman Legionaries who endeavoured to make Scotland the North Western frontier of the Roman Empire.

I am thinking of my family on that road, my father, born in Scotland, my mother, born in Northern Ireland, my paternal grandparents, born in Italy and their journey from Italy via France to Scotland.   My maternal great-grandmother was a Dubliner.   She was a widow with six daughters.   Her name was Elizabeth Guinness.   My great-grandfather, Giovanni Fusco, found lodging in her Dublin boardinghouse, married her, gave her a son, my grandfather who I knew as John Fusco.   My great-grandfather had fought against Garibaldi's Redshirts for the Papal Army.   John Fusco met and married my grandmother, Maria Bratisani, whose family originated from a Tuscan mountain village.   St. Patrick's Church in Edinburgh's Cowgate was within walking distance from where they lived.   It was in that church that they married.   As I write, I am thinking, not only of their descendants, my brothers, Michael and Louis, but also my cousins Cristina and Norma, my uncles and aunts representing the families of both my father and mother: the Demarcos and Fuscos.

I am also thinking of my wife, Anne, and her Northumbrian family and their antecedents.   She and her family helped me develop a sense of belonging to the cultural heritage of England as well as Scotland.   Her insights as an artist and art teacher have proved invaluable to me in the process of making difficult decisions involving inherent risk-taking.

I am thinking, too, of my teachers at St. John's Primary School in Portobello, the Ursuline nuns: Mother Vincent and Sisters Aloysius and Campion, and at Holy Cross Academy, Hugh Toner, my English teacher who taught me to love the English language, and at, Edinburgh College of Art, all the artists and students who taught me to respect the history of ideas through the process of drawing and painting, and my fellow soldiers in The King's Own Scottish Borderers and The Royal Army Education Corps, and those who became patrons of my career as a watercolourist.   All of them helped me to recognise 'The Road to Meikle Seggie.' Nowadays, it is the name of a Kinross-shire farm; but not that long ago, it was a village. It represents all the lost villages and their communities whose names have slipped off the maps of modern Europe. It symbolises all the historic roads and bye-ways which have been used by cattledrovers, shepherds, travelling folk and their fellow tellers of tales, the Scottish bards who identified Scotland as the Land of Fingal and his son, Ossian.

It is the road I used to introduce Joseph Beuys to Perthshire, Arygyll, Inverness-shire and the Kingdom of Fife when I revealed to him Loch Awe and the Moor of Rannoch and a Hebridean sunset viewed from the harbour of Oban. It is the road I walked with my 'Edinburgh Arts' Summer School students so that they would meet Lord Macleod on Iona and listen to Sorley Maclean reading his Gaelic Poetry whilst sailing towards his beloved Island of Raasay — it is the road that led to the Orcadian world expressed through George Mackay Brown's writings and through Margaret Tait's film-making. It is the road that leads to Margaret Gardiner's art collection at the Pier Arts Centre and to The Ring of Brodgar and the Cathedral of St. Magnus. Most meaningfully to me it leads to the Chapel built by Italian prisoners of war. Southwards, it leads to Tuscany, and Barga, the hilltop town from which my mother's forebears originate, and to the Monastery of St. Benedict at Monte Cassino near to Picinisco, the village from which my father's forebears began their long journey to Scotland. It delineates the pilgrimage route taken by Scottish Monarchs on their way to Rome and Jerusalem via St. Andrews.

It is the road which awakens long forgotten memories and intermingles them with hopes and plans beyond the limitations of the immediate future. It leads to those viewpoints where land and sea and sky are inseparable. It is the road on which you travel with those you respect and love, not as fellow tourists, but as fellow explorers and adventurers, of both time and space.

I do believe that artistic endeavour originates in that moment every human being must experience which Gaston Bachelard, the French phenomenologist, defined as the 'edge of reverie', the point which lies not in full wakefulness, nor in deep sleep where dreams slip away into unconsciousness, but in that precise moment found in what the English-speaking people know as 'day dreaming'. Art comes into being right there, always catching the human mind unawares. It is part of a gift which comes to us when we are not content to look at the horizon but far beyond that into what intrepid sailors or fisherfolk know as 'the offing'. This is the space, which is unobservable to the human eye but must be taken into account when a plan or strategy is being formulated to make a work of art. It is the space discoverable only through a sixth sense, which comes when fears are cast momentarily aside. It is the space I have come to know on 'The Road to Meikle Seggie'.

Sometimes an art work cannot come into being through the efforts of one person alone. A combined effort must be made to bring about a climate of change. My life has been committed to such a 'combined effort' and to sharing the experiences of being on 'the edge of reverie'.

Such combined efforts gave Europe its medieval cathedrals and later the the Italian Renaissance. Such efforts brought about a climate of change which extended over a prolonged period, to reach 18th century Scotland in the form of The Enlightenment. This brought together in Edinburgh an extraordinary gathering of creative scientists, politicians, artists and philosophers. Undoubtedly, they must have travelled on roads with the characteristics of that which leads to Meikle Seggie.

I see this autobiographical essay as the introduction to a full-scale autobiography in which I can fully consider the history of Europe as Christendom and the fact that the Sea of Faith has receded over the eight decades of my lifetime. Whatever I write must be with reference to those parts of the road which still provide me with evidence that Europe's cultural heritage remains essentially Christo-centric, embedded in the principles laid down in The Magna Carta and the Declaration of Arbroath.

My Roman Catholic upbringing taught me to take seriously The Communion of Souls. I am, therefore, looking back over a period of seventy-five years to a vast almost incomprehensible array of the living and the dead representing those human beings I was privileged to meet and with whom I have shared the experience of life upon this blessed planet. They are my fellow adventurers and explorers on 'The Road to Meikle Seggie'. Most of them will have their own name for that Road which the Celts recognise as the road to "T'Ir N'An Og" (The Land of the Ever Young). It lies for them beyond the rim of the Hebridean horizon where time stands still and eternity can be felt as a physical reality and when, in midsummer, the experience of sunset is inextricably linked to that of sunrise.

Many of them began their lives in the 19th century; some of them, like my parents, were born at the very beginning of the 20th century

I do earnestly believe that enduring and meaningful art can not originate around a committee meeting involving the functionaries and bureaucrats who nowadays initiate and control the cultural strategy which has linked art with the overwhelmingly powerful combined of forces of consumerism, leisure and entertainment.

Enduring art cannot come into being in the period we now regard as leisure or holiday time. It can only happen when human beings know they must continue moving towards unexplored territory, and forego the easy and obvious paths towards those which have to be taken in order to ascend the mountain of truth. They do so either on their own or with the help of friends who share their hopes, aspirations and their dreams in the building and maintenance of a just society. Such a society can endure when blessed with a cultural identity which transforms the basic rules and conditions laid down by politicians and economists into a working order where truth and beauty are interwoven and human beings can fully utilize the energies released through friendship.

Friendship is an aspect of love, and Joseph Beuys regarded love as the necessary ingredient in the making of art, a love for every blessed thing in creation: expressed in the mineral, plant, animal and human kingdoms, and in the very elemental forces of fire, air and water. His view of this world was akin to that of St. Francis. That is one of the reasons why he is regarded, twenty years after his death, as one of the most memorable and influential artists of the 20th century.

So my autobiographical essay abounds with the lists of names of some of those friends who I can just begin to see clearly from my long lifetime's experience. Each name is deserving of a pen portrait and, indeed, many of them deserve a whole book devoted to their achievements, and not all of them are artists in the strict sense of being a painter, writer, actor, musician or whatever. They are simply creative human beings and their lives provide ample proof that Joseph Beuys had every right to say that everyone had the potential to be creative through their life's work; that, indeed, 'every one is an artist'. Joseph Beuys regarded teaching as a form of making art. He helped me question deeply the modern art word all too rigorously controlled by market forces expressive of an all-pervading spirit of materialism.

It was my good friend, Patrick Reyntiens, arguably the most important living stained-glass artist, who made it clear to me that friendship is the necessary ingredient in the process of making enduring art. He defined this fact in an essay he contributed to The Demarco Gallery's 1975 'Edinburgh Arts' exhibition catalogue. The essential truth expressed in this essay is encapsulated in a short sentence written by his friend, Cecil Collins, the English painter and his fellow teacher at The Central School of Art. This sentence should be place above the entrance to any art gallery. It states simply that "Art originates in the meeting of friends and in their shared dreams and ideals."

'Edinburgh Arts'

I had always believed that from my earliest childhood, and from my schooldays at Holy Cross Academy and from my student days at Edinburgh College of Art. So this introduction to my autobiography attempts to explain how my friends contributed greatly, and continue to contribute to my work, whatever it may be, as I play the roles of artist, teacher, university professor, promoter of exhibitions and performances of theatre, dance and music. Perhaps the most important aspect of my work as a teacher is expressed through 'Edinburgh Arts'. This was my name for a highly experimental school which integrated both the performing and visual arts with the history of ideas and a physical exploration of Scotland in relation to Europe. It came into being in collaboration first of all in 1972 with Edinburgh University's Schools of Extra-Mural and Scottish Studies.

It developed throughout the seventies and eighties in collaboration with American and Canadian universities and art councils, including the Universities of Toronto, York and Guelph, and The Rhode Island School of Design, Minneapolis College of Art and the Art Institutes of Baltimore, Chicago and Kansas City, as well as in Europe, The National Art School of Ireland and Sheffield School of Art, and then in 1992 with Kingston University through my work as a Kingston University Picker Fellow and then as Professor of European Cultural Studies through which I benefited from the patronage of Professor David Youlton.

I wanted 'Edinburgh Arts' to help university and art school students focus on the European cultural heritage of Scotland which made sense of my own life and my family as part of a community recognisable as Italo-Scots.

Wartime Childhood in Portobello and Largs

I was born on 9th July 1930 in a private nursing home, in Grosvenor Street in Edinburgh's West End. My mother was born Elizabeth Valentina Fusco. She married my father, Carmine Demarco in 1929 in St. John's Roman Catholic Church, Portobello. They had moved from Portobello to Edinburgh in 1930, not anticipating The Wall Street Crash which swiftly brought disaster to their business: a 'state of the art' café and 'The Dansant' on Princes Street which they called 'The Trocadero'. This was an Edinburgh version of 'Maison Demarco' on Portobello Promenade, a popular meeting place for all those citizens of Edinburgh who wished to experience the atmosphere of a Parisian café, serving real coffee with a spacious interior of dark walnut wood, art nouveau stained glass window and light fittings, with marble-topped tables and a central dais around which musicians in dinner jackets would gather beside a grand piano amidst potted palms.

'Maison Demaro' was the very model I had in the back of my mind when I first dreamt of The Traverse Theatre and The Demarco Gallery, as places where all the arts could be enjoyed in a convivial atmosphere of good food and drink with more than a touch of the Continental way of life.

The very name, 'Maison Demarco', sharpens my memory of the physical presence of all those who found themselves at home there: not only my uncle and aunt, Gabriel and Cristina Demarco who were the owners, but my father who was Cristina's younger brother, 22 years her junior. She employed him as manager of her expanding business world. This included an adjoining ice cream factory, a thriving catering service and a summer theatre programme starring the Scottish Music Hall favourites of the Twenties and Thirties. Chic Murray and Donald Pears were names associated with this theatre, housed in a circus tent within walking distance from Portobello Promenade.

My mother was the second oldest child of a family of twelve children, born to Giovanni and Maria Fusco. They were the owners of The Marine Café, a single-storey wooden building situated on Portobello Promenade, a quarter of a mile from Maison Demarco and wedged between two other wooden buildings housing the two Portobello amateur rowing clubs. The war shattered Maison Demarco and The Marine Cafe as thriving businesses as effectively as the Wall Street Crash had shattered my father's business venture on Princes Street.

My childhood was blighted by my personal experiences of the Second World War, and in particular my experience of the agonising moment of knowing I had placed myself with my little brother, Louis, on the front line of this global conflict as early as September 1939. It was on a fateful day of Indian summer weather when Portobello Beach became a battleground. The German Luftwaffe had set their sights on the Forth Rail Bridge for the very first target in their initial plans for the Battle of Britain. The hail of fire from a Spitfire's machine guns was aimed at the Heinkel Bomber which flew with one engine on fire, 100 feet above my head. The Spitfire's pilot could not have seen the figures of two little boys on the water's edge by the turning tide. I gathered the bullets which were embedded in the sand about my feet. They were still warm as I put them into my pockets to give them to my distressed mother, who, like every adult in Portobello, had known the terror of the first air raid of the war.

The Second World War brought insecurity and violence into the lives of Scotland's Italian community and the pain of bereavement for all those grandfathers, brothers and sons who were drowned when 'The Arandora Star' taking them to internment in Canada was torpedoed within sight of The Hebrides. The War tested me to the breaking point, but it gave me the opportunity as an evacuee to experience the delights of the Clyde Coast around Largs, a world of paddle steamers voyaging to the islands of Bute, Great Cumbrae, Arran and to the Argyllshire fishing ports and coastlines, leading to the Hebridean world of Fingal on Staffa and St. Columba on Iona. My father was the manager of a building well known to Glaswegians as 'The Moorings', an art deco masterpiece, housing a ballroom, restaurant and shops – and dwarfing its rival, the nearby Café Nardini. Both were the work of John Houston, a Scottish architect par excellance.

Education at Holy Cross, Art College and on National Service

The 1940s, like the 30s, were clouded by the madness of World War Two. But despite this, I was encouraged to study art by Teresa Clarke, the art mistress at Holy Cross Academy, and Isobel Henderson Blyth, one of my French teachers and the wife of Robert Henderson Blyth, one of Scotland's leading painters, and Betty Maxton, the Scottish artist who painted my portrait as a thirteen year old schoolboy. It was she who persuaded my aunt Cristina not to put pressure on my parents to end my education at primary school level, but allow me to go on to Holy Cross Academy and Edinburgh College of Art.

At the College, I was to become life-long friends with John Martin and Douglas Soeder, the founders of Scotland's first commercial art studio. This was Forth Studios. Without their expertise and business acumen, there would not have been the Traverse Theatre, or indeed the Demarco Gallery.

My real education, taking into account all the arts, came in 1947 when, along with my classmates at Holy Cross Academy, I was given the opportunity to attend a performance of an Edinburgh Festival production performed, not in English but in French. It was The Comedie Francais' production of Moliere's *L'Ecole des Femmes* starring the great French actor, Louis Jouvet. Despite my failure to pass a French exam, it caused me to fall in love with French culture and provided me with the experience of the first-ever Edinburgh Festival establishing its credentials as promoter of the highest imaginable world theatre.

In 1948 through my summer holidays, I worked as manager of The Camera Obscura in the Outlook Tower on Castle Hill. The Tower had a café which was used by actors rehearsing next door in the Assembly Hall of the Church of Scotland. This led me to become a friend of one of the actors, Duncan Macrae, who invited me to attend the rehearsals of *The Thrie Estaites*. This production was a masterpiece and changed the course of theatre history and theatre architecture. It was the world's first manifestation of openstage theatre because the Assembly Hall had no proscenium stage. It was directed by Tyrone Guthrie who had founded the Festival together with Rudolph Byng, Lord and Lady Rosebery, James Bridie and Harvey Wood.

In my last year at school, in 1949 on my first visit to Europe and the Continent, I was enraptured by Les Ballets des Champs Elysees' production of *Carmen* at the Theatre Marigny in Paris. I was stage-struck by the elegant beauty of the theatre itself and by ballet as a full-blown work of avant garde theatre. Within a month, I was able to enjoy this splendid company again when they brought the production to the Edinburgh Festival at the Empire Theatre as well as their production *The Sphinx* which launched the career of 16 year-old Lesley Caron.

Thankfully, a significant number of teachers and students at Edinburgh College of Art shared my interest in the performing arts, and they were given the opportunity to design the extravagant setting for the College Revels; Edinburgh's equivalent of The Chelsea Arts Ball. Also, the College had a theatre to the delight of John Arden, a budding playwright heavily disguised as a student architect.

Members of College staff were willing to speak of their War experiences. Leonard Rosoman, had been a fire fighter during the Blitz before he taught me mural painting, and John Kingsley Cook sailed with the Merchant Navy's Atlantic convoys before he taught book illustration and print making. His sketch books of life at sea led me to develop an interest in the art of the War Artists, Edward Bawden and Eric Ravillious, and, indeed, in all the War Artists and to take a special interest in the student work of George Mackie who had survived the War as a bomber pilot with a well-earned Distinguished Flying Cross. He became chief designer of The Edinburgh University Press and Head of Design at Aberdeen College of Art.

John Houston, Liz Blackadder, Barbara Balmer, Frances Walker, David Michie and Alistair Park were among my student contemporaries whose paintings I admired when I was responsible for organising The College Sketch Club exhibitions in 1953 and '54. I can now see that it was in these years that I began my career as a director of exhibitions.

The Edinburgh Festival continued to be a source of inspiration when I found myself working behind the reception desk of The Caledonian Hotel in the summers of 1950, and 1952 when I was the only male receptionist.   I found myself endeavouring to explain to some of the American guests that the hotel had only nine rooms with private bathrooms.   Inevitably, I was welcoming to Edinburgh the likes of T.S.Eliot, Thorton Wilder, Richard Burton, Claire Bloom, Audrey Hepburn, Joan Bennett and Mel Ferrer.   Harold Clurman, the theatre impresario, commented that he could not 'swing a cat' in the room he had been allocated.   I had to explain to him that the only hotel with vacancies was 'Gleneagles' but that involved a three-hour journey by road and ferry-crossing at South Queensferry.

The Fifties was the decade when I experienced National Service and army life in The King's Own Scottish Borderers at their historic barracks in Berwick-upon-Tweed, where I did my square bashing.   It was a test of my powers of mental and physical stamina; thankfully, it led to my becoming a sergeant instructor in The Royal Army Education Corps stationed at the headquarters of The Royal Army Ordnance Corps in Bicester.

Bicester is fifteen miles from Oxford and its University.   It was the perfect setting in which to meet John Thomson, the psychiatrist and philanthropist. He had travelled on a very long arduous road from his schooldays at Fettes College, via the devastated cityscapes of post-war Europe, to the Radcliffe Infirmary in Oxford.   John Thomson worked with patients in his psychiatric clinic.   He believed he could cure them with the help of young artists such as I was, as a recent graduate of Edinburgh College of Art.   He commissioned me to paint images of normal and abnormal living environments for his patients to identify.   Thus, he was my first serious patron.

He took upon himself the responsibility of adopting six German orphans during the time he worked in Germany as one of the founders of UNESCO. Two of these adopted sons became medical students at his 'alma mater', Edinburgh University, and I was pleased to introduce them to my friends. They personified my hopes for Germany's recovery from the devastation it had suffered.   They are now both deceased; they were my good friends Sebastian Littman and Matthias Leber.

John Thomson taught me the invaluable lesson that the worlds of the medical scientist and the artist were but two aspects of the same world and that through art and education, the wounds of war could be healed.

School Teaching with Gallery and Theatre Directing

On demobilization, I added to my experience of teaching in the Army by beginning my ten years as Art Master of Duns Scotus Academy. I benefited greatly from this by working alongside Arthur Oldham, the Academy music master who was also choirmaster of St. Mary's Roman Catholic Cathedral and later to be chorus master of The Edinburgh Festival Chorus and The Paris Conservatoire — as well as Miles Baster and his fellow members of The Edinburgh Quartet. With such teachers, the boys of Scotus Academy proved to me that every single one of them could be considered as a creative soul despite the fact that most of them were ill-suited to academic life.

The Fifties were a gestation period for the birth of the Traverse Theatre. This period began with my first meeting with Jim Haynes at a performance of an Oxford University's Dramatic Society's production of Ugo Betti's "Corruption in the Palace of Justice" at the 1957 Edinburgh Festival Fringe.

It was the year Jim Haynes befriended myself and my wife, Anne. We introduced him to our Edinburgh Friends at the parties we gave in our top floor flat at 29 Frederick Street. He introduced us to his American friends who were enjoying their Junior Year Abroad as 'Ivy League' American University students at Edinburgh University. The university was Jim Haynes natural milieu in which he thrived and made his presence felt in Edinburgh as a force for good, whilst he was stationed at the American Air Force radar station at Kirknewton on the outskirts of Edinburgh. He was, to most of his friends, a fellow student. Few of his friends saw him in the uniform of an American National Serviceman.

In 1959, Anne and I visited the United States and Jim Haynes' beloved New Orleans and experienced the full impact of racial discrimination. Jim was as dismayed as we were so he was easily encouraged to return to Edinburgh. He sold his Volkswagen 'Beetle' and bought a run-down antique shop in Charles Street, within sight of Edinburgh University's Students Union. With the help of his friends, he converted it into Britain's first 'Paperback Bookshop'.

I introduced him to Tom Mitchell, the Cumbrian farmer, property developer, and rugby enthusiast, who had purchased a dilapidated tenement on The Royal Mile, part of James Court. Jim introduced me to John Calder, the publisher of Samuel Beckett and the French "Nouvelle Vague" writers. John Calder had been attracted to the Paperback as a outlet for his Calder and Boyers publications,and as an Edinburgh base where he could spread the good news that he had established a small-scale version of Glyndebourne, at Ledlanet, his family estate high in the Ochil Hills, near to Milnathort. Jim Haynes and I and all our friends were introduced to the world of opera in this Arcadian setting. Almost a decade later, I was to discover that it was the threshold leading to The Road to Meikle Seggie.

Establishing a career as an Artist

The Sixties constituted a period of almost violent change and risk-taking. It was a time when the Off-Off Broadway movement began changing the American world of contemporary theatre. It was the decade when I became professionally recognised as an artist and exhibited as The Royal Academy, The Royal Scottish Academy and The Royal Scottish Society of Painters in Watercolours. I had my first ever one-man exhibition at The Douglas and Foulis Gallery during the 1962 Edinburgh Festival, the Festival made notable by The Writers' Conference. John Calder and Jim Haynes set this conference close to The Paperback in the University's McEwan Hall. It involved Hugh MacDiarmid in a violent argument with Alexander Trocchi and introduced the likes of Mary McCarthy, William Burroughs, Lawrence Durrell, Norman Mailer and Henry Miller to Scotland with the invaluable help of Sonia Orwell.

The Conference led Henry Miller to see my exhibition at The Douglas and Foulis Gallery and although I wanted to talk about his life in Paris writing 'The Air-conditioned Nightmare', I was astonished that he wanted my advice on how to apply gouache paint to paper as he was then focussed on his own career as a watercolourist rather than as a novelist.

Richard Buckle was in Edinburgh as the ballet critic of *The Sunday Times*. He was a legendary figure to me as the creator of the two great Edinburgh Festival exhibitions — that of Epstein's sculpture at The Waverley Market in 1959, and the Diaghalev Exhibition in 1953 at Edinburgh College of Art. He visited my exhibition at Douglas and Foulis, and as a direct result, I found myself being commissioned by him to make an oil painting on a 16ft by 10ft canvas, specially made in Holland, on the subject of 'The Spirit of Repertory descending upon the City of Dundee' for The Dundee Repertory Theatre. He himself had been commissioned by the Scottish Arts Council to refurbish this historic theatre housed then in a converted cinema. He was my first major patron, because, in 1964 in the four hundredth anniversary year of Shakespeare's birth, he also chose to place my work alongside artists such as Oscar Kokoscha, Sydney Nolan, Peter Blake, Jean Hugo, David Hockney, Astrid Zydower and Keith Vaughan. Richard Buckle had again commissioned me to make a painting.   He asked me to consider as its subject one of Shakespeare's plays: *Much Ado About Nothing.*

Seeing it in Stratford-Upon-Avon, and afterwards in Edinburgh at the 1964 Festival, I was inspired to paint with greater conviction and enthusiasm. My career developed as an illustrator when I was commissioned to illustrate the booklets published by BBC Radio Scotland for their 'History for Schools' programmes.   It certainly helped focus my attention on Scottish history.

In 1962, my friend, Patrick Prenter telephoned me from Cambridge to inform me that some of his fellow undergraduates wished to find a different venue from that of the Cambridge Footlights for the Festival.   I contacted Tom Mitchell who agreed with me that a space on the two lower floors of his James Court tenement would be ideal for their revue.   They called the space 'The Sphinx Club'.   Patrick Prenter's fellow undergraduates included John Cleese, Tim Brooke Taylor and Ian Lang who was later to become Secretary of State in Scotland.   In 1963, on a cold January evening, The Sphinx Club was re-opened as The Traverse Theatre Club, and I dealt with the press and the guests who appeared in evening dress on the Opening Night, in my capacity as Vice-Chairman of the committee which founded the club.   The Honorary Patron was Lord Kilbrandon; the Honorary President was Tom Mitchell, who charged the Traverse Theatre Club a peppercorn rent of one pound per annum.   Sadly, Jim Haynes was travelling abroad because of family obligations, so he missed this historic occasion.   I assured a BBC television crew that, despite the fact that The Church of Scotland's Gateway Theatre had been obliged to close its doors through lack of an enthusiastic audience, The Traverse Theatre Club would depend on an entirely new audience of 'friends' who had joined a club dedicated to showing the avant-garde aspects of world theatre.

From the Traverse to the Demarco Gallery

As Vice-Chairman of The Traverse Committee of Management, I made it my responsibility to re-assure those prepared to become Traverse Club members that I would personally refund their membership fee if, after the first three productions, they were dissatisfied.

I also founded and directed The Traverse Art Gallery, located above the Theatre, so that there would be extra income from sales.   I managed to sell around twenty thousand pounds worth of paintings and sculptures over a two-year period — of art works from Spain, USA, Australia, Iceland, Poland,

France, Ireland, and, of course, England and Scotland. The artists all became friends, particularly the Catalan artists, Santiago Pericot, Jorge Pericot and Xavier Corbero, as well as Bill Wright, the Australian painter. There were also Bill Crozier and Mark Boyle, two Scots expatriate painters who had established themselves in London, and Martin Bradley, the English painter who had an enviable reputation in Paris, and the American artist, Abraham Rattner, who inspired Henry Miller to write "The Air-conditioned Nightmare".

As the doyenne of the Scottish art world, Anne Redpath helped enormously by supporting my idea of a gallery and was delighted that her elder son, Alistair Michie, should be the first Traverse Gallery artist to have a one-man exhibition of his paintings. Alan Harrison, the Newcastle-based art collector, helped by exhibiting his collection introducing major English artists.

In 1963, John Calder and Jim Haynes presented what was to be the infamous 'Drama Conference' as a follow-up to 'The Writers' Conference'. It ended in confusion with Scotland's first experience of 'a happening', created by Alan Kaprow, Mark Boyle, Charles Marowitz and Ken Dewey. It involved a half-nude woman momentarily appearing on a balcony in the McEwan Hall. The spirit of the avant-garde 'Fluxus' and 'Dada' movements had finally reached Scotland. Even Kenneth Tynan, David Frost and Bernard Levin, three of the supporters of the Conference, were surprised by the impact of the shock-waves suffered by Edinburgh Festival-goers. Sadly, this caused Lord Harewood to resign from his position of Festival Director. He had proved to be an enthusiastic supporter of The Traverse.

Among The Traverse Theatre's contributions to the Festival Fringe programme was 'Comedy, Irony, Satire and Deeper Meaning' by Dieter Sebastian Grabbe, a 19th century German playwright who died tragically young, aged 24. I noted that most of the playwrights attending The Drama Conference were in the first-night audience, including J.B. Priestly, Lillian Hellman, Edward Albee, Alan Snyder and the New York impresario, Harold Clurman, as well as London's leading critics, Ken Tynan and Harold Hobson. From that day, I knew that the Traverse Theatre had achieved its purpose.

If I have managed to achieve anything worthwhile in the world of the visual arts, it is due to the likes of David Baxandall in his capacity as Director of the National Galleries of Scotland and George and Cordelia Oliver, the artists who were his friends. It was they who recommended me to him and it was he who introduced me to Roland Penrose. He became a friend and patron and helped me realise my dream of a Scottish equivalent of Liverpool's

John Moore's Competition and Exhibition in time for the 1967 Edinburgh Festival in the form of an exhibition entitled 'The Edinburgh 100'. The Demarco Gallery soon became infused with the spirit of Roland Penrose's Institute of Contemporary Art in London's Dover Street.

I needed the support of all those who shared my enthusiasm of what was made manifest through The Traverse Theatre and the Demarco Gallery. I now know that nothing I achieved would have been possible without the friendship and support of John Martin and his wife, Dorrie. It was Dorrie who suggested that The Traverse Gallery should establish itself in Edinburgh's New Town, in Melville Crescent, in a Georgian-style town house. It had provided a temporary exhibition space for artists who had exhibited at the 1965 Ledlanet Festival. They were organized by Alex MacNeish. John Martin, together with Andy Elliott and Jimmy Walker were the original board members of both the Traverse Theatre and Demarco Gallery.

It was born out of the commitment to it from St. Ives-based artists such as Bill Featherston, Patrick Heron, Bryan Wynter, Alan Wood and Michael Tyzack. Within its first year, it was linked to the world of Ellen Stewart's Off-Off Broadway 'La Mama' Theatre.

August 1966 saw the Gallery open its doors with an exhibition which expressed its commitment to bringing the world of Bond Street and Cork Street galleries to Scotland. John Martin, Andy Elliott and Jimmy Walker transferred their allegiance to the Demarco Gallery after a disagreement with Jim Haynes. The Demarco Gallery was intended to release the Traverse Gallery from its cramped space in James Court. Jim Haynes chose Nicky Fairburn as the new Traverse Chairman. He refused to give the gallery the use of the Traverse name, so the name finally chosen was that of myself as director with the full weight of responsibility to sell international contemporary art to an untested market.

Within the first year of opening, I shared my fears for the Demarco Gallery's future with Ellen Stewart. She encouraged me to dispel any such fears because she could feel strongly that the Gallery like her own "La Mama" theatre in New York, had "lots of love in it", and that's all you need, she insisted. I have ample evidence that this was good advice.

The Gallery was originally located on three floors of its New Town house. It also provided a perfect domestic setting for small-scale theatre productions, music recitals and lectures, organised by the Association of The Friends of The Demarco Gallery. Thus, the Gallery took on the aspect of the Traverse Theatre as a club. The Association's first two chairmen were Lord Haig and Douglas Hall.

Clive James, Tony Buffery, Nancy Cole, Richard Stilgoe, Nancy Meckler's Freehold Theatre Company, Roger McGough and The Scaffold poets all performed there, as well as Joseph Szajna's Polish Theatre Company and Lindsay Kemp's Dance Theatre. On one memorable evening, Laurence Olivier and Frank Dunlop were among the audience enjoying Clive James perform in a revue he had written as a Cambridge University undergraduate along with Tony Buffery and Pete Atkin.

Arthur Boyd, Patrick Heron, William Scott, Trevor Bell, John Piper, Jorge Castillo and Alan Davie all had major one-man exhibitions. The Gallery's restaurant catered for large numbers at lunchtime, attracted by the high standard of food and the bistro ambience. Among the many visitors was the Duke of Edinburgh, who came to see the exhibition of Polish Art in 1968, as well as David Hockney and actors such as Ian McLellan, Derek Jacobi, Timothy West, Julian Glover, Zoe Wannamaker, Pepe Wilton, Frances de la Tour and Virginia McKenna when the Gallery became the studio for the 1970 Scottish Television Festival Programmes.

It was not big enough, however, for Official Edinburgh Festival Exhibitions such as the 'Edinburgh Open 100' and the 'Canada 101'. Both these exhibitions caused me to seek sponsorship outside Scotland. I was indebted to David Silcox, the Director of the Canada Council, for the generous support he gave to enable the Demarco Gallery to collaborate with the Art Galleries of Ontario, Vancouver and Montreal. Housed in Edinburgh University's Appleton Tower, and Edinburgh College of Art, these exhibitions widened my horizons and emboldened me to develop the Demarco Gallery's international dialogues, and so it seemed perfectly natural that I should accept invitations to visit both Poland and Romania.

Alexander Schouvaloff, the Assistant Director of The Edinburgh International Festival, initiated the meeting I had with Peter Diamand which resulted in my being given the task of directing the Festival's Exhibitions of Contemporary Art with one priviso — I would have to bear the burden of the cost involved which added up to a few million pounds, from 1967 to 1994.

The exhibition of Dusseldorf artists in 1970 was housed in Edinburgh College of Art — a well-nigh perfect setting for the avant-gardist spirit encapsulated in the exhibitions palendromic title 'Strategy: Get Arts'. It introduced the genius of Joseph Beuys to Britain. The controversial and challenging nature of this exhibition and those that followed in the next three years introduced the European artists to Scotland from both sides of the Iron Curtain from Romania in 1971, from Poland in 1972, from France, Austria and Yugoslavia in 1973. At the 1973 Edinburgh Festival in my house in Frederick Street, I introduced Joseph Beuys to Tadeusz Kantor. I regarded them as the very personification of the much-needed cultural dialogue between Germany and Poland.

In 1972, I was appointed the first Director of Sean Connery's Scottish International Education Trust (SIET). The Trust's office was in the two upper floors of the Melville Crescent house. The Demarco Gallery's 1972 Edinburgh Festival exhibition of Polish art received financial support from the Trust. Sean Connery took a personal interest in the work of those Polish artists who were teachers at Poland's world famous film school in Lodz.

I felt morally bound to strengthen the cultural links between East and West Europe and between Europe and North America. It involved me in many visits behind The Iron Curtain — 97 in all between 1968 and the fall of the Berlin Wall, and countless lecture tours of American and Canadian galleries, universities and art schools during the same period. The process of transforming the Gallery into a place of education imposed enormous strains upon myself, the Gallery staff and Board members. I knew I was dealing with some of the most important artists in the world and that it was wise to invest in their work before they became world famous. The Arts Council was not programmed to support international initiatives which would link Scottish artists to their contemporaries worldwide. The Gallery Board decided to pay off debts of six thousand pounds by selling the Melville Crescent building. In 1973, the property fetched a good price – eighty-four thousand pounds. Considering that it had cost fifteen thousand, five hundred pounds to buy in 1966, it had been a good investment.

Thankfully, with the support of those members of the Board who wished the Gallery to continue its work of helping to internationalise the Scottish art world, the Gallery moved to temporary office accommodation in Great King Street. These Board members included Michael Spens, the publisher of 'Studio International', and Bert Davis, who had retired from his role as Director of The British Council in Scotland, and Rory McEwen, the Scottish artist and his brother, the art critic, John Sebastian McEwen, and Duncan Macfarlane, a leading architect and art patron as well as James Dougdal and James Ferguson. This led to the Gallery finding a new home in Monteith House in The Royal Mile, under the chairmanship of Lady Polwarth who took over this position from Sir Robin McEwen in 1975. It was too small for large-scale theatre, but Ruby Wax made her Edinburgh theatre debut there, directing and performing in Genet's 'The Three Maids', and Joan Bakewell performed there her one-woman play on Charlotte Bronte, and Jim Sheridan directed his Dublin-based theatre company in a production of W.B. Yeats's play 'On Baille Strand'.   It was there, too, that Louis le Broquy, the doyen of Ireland's painters, presented his 1977 Edinburgh Festival exhibition of portraits of W.B.Yeats.

'Edinburgh Arts' developed to extend its journeys to Italy, Malta and Yugoslavia in collaboration with Gabriella Cardazzo's Galleria del Cavallino, The National Gallery of Malta, and The National Gallery of Yugoslavia. Joseph Beuys continued to inspire as a teacher under the aegis of Edinburgh Arts.   He taught together with Jack Burnham, the acknowledged authority on Marcel Duchamp, and George Melly, the redoubtable patron of the Surrealist Movement, the Polish sculptor, Magdalena Abakanowicz, the Director of the Berkeley Museum, Peter Selz, and the British art historian, Norbert Lynton.   The 'Edinburgh Arts' faculty also included Tadeusz Kantor, Paul Neagu, Buckminster Fuller, Patrick Reyntiens, Lord Ritchie Calder, David Daiches, as well as Gary Kennedy and Gerry Ferguson.   The Kennedy-Ferguson collaboration as co-directors of Nova Scotia College signalled to the art world's luminaries that an art school could become a "total art work". They all gave me hope that 'Edinburgh Arts' was developing to become a worthy successor to Black Mountain College.   Among the 'Edinburgh Arts' student participants were Sandy Nairne, Charles Stephens, Tina Brown and Mark Francis, all of them Oxford undergraduates.

In the seventies my parents died: my father in 1975 and my mother in 1979.   Their deaths marked an end of an era in the history of my family's contribution to the Italo-Scottish cultural heritage and strengthened my resolve to concentrate my energies as an artist on expressing myself through the medium of photography as well as that of watercolour.   My paintings continued to be of townscapes and landscapes experienced on the Road to Meikle Seggie.   My photographs had as their subject matter the meetings I was privileged to have with artists, writers, musicians, actors, teachers and their students in the spaces in which they spent their working life and in which they found inspiration. As I write, I have fond memories of the studios in Scotland of Lord Haig, Jon Schueler, Archie Sutter Watt, Margot Sandeman and Mary MacIver, Dawson and Liz Murray, Chris Wood, George Wyllie, as well as Victor Pasmore in Malta, David Nash in Wales, and, of course, of the studios of Gunther Uecker, Joseph Beuys and Gerhard Richter in Dusseldorf, and the theatre of Tadeusz Kantor in Krakow and that of Oskaras Korsunavas in Vilnius, and Mladen Materic in Sarajevo.

The photographs I took of such meetings and encounters were simply an attempt to acknowledge their importance of meetings marking nodal points on 'the Road to Meikle Seggie'.   In this way, I was not only observing key moments in the history of the development of European culture, but the ways in which they advanced modernist ideas originated from age-old cultural traditions.

That is why the 'Edinburgh Arts' were integrated with and validified by Edinburgh University's School of Scottish Studies and the teaching and research activities of its Director, Professor John McQueen, together with his colleagues, Hamish Henderson, Alie Munro and John MacInnes. 'Edinburgh Arts' also collaborated with the School of Extra Mural Studies and the programme of its Director, the art historian, Basil Skinner.

In Scotland, it was inevitable that Ian Hamilton Finlay's Garden Temple was an all-important part of my concept of a creative journey. With every visit, I became more and more aware of the vast psychological distance between the urban spaces where most artists dwelt and worked, and the windswept Lanarkshire hillscape of Stonypath Farm.

In England, I sought out the farm buildings which Winifred Nicholson had given to Li Yuan Chia which enabled him to set up the LYC Museum, his unique studio and visual art centre. It was in the world that had inspired Kurt Schwitters to create his masterpiece, the Merzbarn, in a small Cumbrian barn, vulnerable to wind and weather.

This Cumbrian world was that which gave inspiration to John Ruskin and led me to re-read the favourite books of my youth, particularly the writings of G.K.Chesterton, and Hilaire Belloc. From them, I saw clearly the importance of 'the rolling English road' and 'The Path to Rome'. I read Henry Thoreau, and Goethe's account of his journey to Italy and Lewis Grassic Gibbon's 'Sunset Song'. All this made me more and more convinced that the history of the Demarco Gallery should not be governed only by its programmes of art exhibitions and theatre productions. I wanted it to be defined by the chance encounters which all journeys bring into being. 'New beginnings are in the offing' is the title Joseph Beuys gave to the masterpiece he made as a result of his teaching under the aegis of 'Edinburgh Arts'. The title of this work rings true when those who journey have their eyes not fixed to any quantifiable or measurable destination observable on even the furthest horizon, but on that which lies beyond, bringing to bear the challenge of the unknown where risk-taking is all important.

The Scottish Arts Council found it difficult to accept the Gallery's commitment to 'Edinburgh Arts' as an experimental summer school, particularly when the journey included a three-week voyage of exploration onboard the replica of Charles Darwin's 'Beagle'. It began on the Pembrokeshire Coast in Tenby Harbour and a voyage to the Cistercian

Monastery on Caldey Island, and then to St. David's Cathedral. It proceeded to the National Library of Wales in Aberystwyth, then to Cork and on to the Scilly Isles and the pre-historic monuments of Brittany in the Gulf of Morbihan.

This was the prelude to a 76 day circumnavigation of the British Isles in 1980 which began in the St.Ives' studios of Patrick Heron, Wilhelmina Barns Graham, Dennis Mitchell and John Wells. At one stage, it involved a voyage across The Irish Sea from Anglesey to Dublin to the James Joyce Tower at Sandymount. Michael Scott, who had rescued The Tower from dereliction and misuse, was waiting at Sandymount along with the poets of The Joyce Society. They had gathered to meet the 'Edinburgh Arts' voyagers and welcome them to the Dublin world of Leopold Bloom. Among the 'Edinburgh Arts' participants who had sailed from Wales were two special friends of mine who happened to be friends of Samuel Beckett. They were Tony Cronin, who had been Beckett's secretary, and Robert O'Driscoll, who was Professor of Celtic Studies at the University of Toronto and a world-expert on W.B. Yeats. The voyage continued towards Belfast, to the Ulster Museum, where there was a warm welcome given by Ted Hickey, the exhibitions curator, Brian Ferran, Director of the Arts Council, and Alastair MacLellan and other Belfast artists. From there, the voyage took the 'Edinburgh Arts' participants to meet the artists of Glasgow, led by Chris Carrell, Director of The Third Eye Centre. They were waiting on the Island of Arran. This was in preparation for the voyage via the world of Colin Lindsay MacDougall, the Laird of Lunga and the Correyvreckan whirlpool towards Iona, where Lord MacLeod was ready to give a warm welcome in the form of a service of prayer and his conducted tour of St. Columba's Monastery. From thence, the voyage continued to Iain Noble's Gaelic College on Skye and onwards to the Pier Arts Centre at Stromness where George Mackay Brown embarked on that part of the voyage which was the first for sixty years of a ship sailing a ship through the perilous waters of The Sound of Eynhallow, in order to view the prehistoric and Viking settlements on the western shoreline of the Island of Rousay. This was part of what I regarded as 'the long way round, over land and sea, to the Edinburgh Festival'.

It had nothing whatsoever to do with the Scottish Arts Council's idea that a Scottish gallery, to be considered worthy of an Arts Council grant, existed simply to put on an annual programme of art exhibitions.

Victor MacDougall was for many years the Secretary of The Institute of Chartered Accountants of Scotland. He fought valiantly for the Gallery's interests during the six year period of 1975 to 1980 that it was operating within the confined spaces of Monteith House. He was an Oxford-educated lawyer, well able to cope with the burgeoning bureaucracy of the Scottish Arts Council.

In 1976, Tadeusz Kantor's reputation was such that his Cricot Theatre's production of *The Dead Class* could not be accommodated in The Forresthill Poorhouse. It was presented, therefore, at Edinburgh College of Art, in the ideal setting of the Sculpture Court. I was indebted to David Gothard, who acted as my assistant with the special responsibility for the Cricot's contribution to the Festival and to Matilda O'Brien who provided accommodation and a warm welcome for the Cricot Company in her house in Peebles. David Gothard became involved in the conversion of Riverside Studios in London and so it seemed entirely appropriate that *The Dead Class* should transfer to London to receive its rightful acclaim from the London theatre world.

The link with London was strengthened when important and loyal members of the Demarco Gallery staff followed David Gothard to London. I was sad to see them go but happy to think that their experience in Edinburgh had prepared them well for the work they found. Clare Street became an invaluable press officer for the Royal Opera House and Jane Chisholm and Erica Bolton helped David establish himself at Riverside, working with Peter Gill as Director.

From Monteith House via Jeffrey Street to Blackfriars Church
With the help of Joseph Beuys and 1,000 Friends

The eighties began with the Scottish Arts Council making the decision to end the Demarco Gallery's role as recipient of their highest annual grant of forty thousand pounds a year. This was a direct result of the Gallery's preparedness to support Joseph Beuys and his contribution to the official Edinburgh Festival programme. This involved Joseph Beuys making a major artwork entitled 'Jimmy Boyle Days' in the form of a diptych of two blackboards. The Gallery was condemned as unworthy of receiving public funding because it "had brought dishonour to the meaning of art in Scotland, and to the meaning of the Demarco Gallery". This decision was the Council's re-action to Beuys' decision to go on hunger strike in defence of Jimmy Boyle's right as an inmate of The Special Unit to be considered as an artist as well as Beuys' decision to take a court action against The Secretary of State in protest against the inhuman conditions existing in Scotland's prison service.

The Gallery was rendered homeless and obliged to raise funds in the form of donations equal to the Arts Council'a annual grant, together with statements of support from 1,000 of its Friends and supporters, Dawson Murray and George Wyllie, the Scottish artists who helped Beuys make another major sculpture out of the doors of The Poorhouse.   Beuys contributed 18,000 pounds to the Appeal as a result of the sale of 'The Poorhouse Doors' to the Moechengladbach Museum.   Among the most inspiring statements were those from Helen Mirren, Lord Harewood and Lord Balfour of Burleigh, George Mackay Brown, Sorely Maclean, Norman MacCaig, and Frank Ashton Gwatkin, the English poet, President of The Arthurian Society and the architect of The Ministry of Economic Warfare. This was a decade when the Gallery was tested to the breaking point, when I depended on the loyalty and understanding of Jane MacAllister as my deputy, Arthur Watson, artist and founder of Aberdeen's Peacock Printmakers, Murray and Barbara Grigor, as filmmakers and initiators of The Scottish Sculpture Trust, and Jeremy Isaacs and Justin Dukes, the architects of Channel Four.   This was the period when the Gallery's public face moved towards the world of Art Fairs in Bath, in London at Islington, Olympia, as well as in York, Edinburgh, Budapest and Los Angeles, and art auctions in Dublin, Glasgow, London and Edinburgh.   Through the patronage of Lord Gowrie as Chairman of Sothebys, paintings from the Demarco Archive were auctioned to help with the running costs and development of Blackfriars Church.

The 'Edinburgh Arts' journeys now concentrated on exploration of Eastern Europe, mainly to Poland, Romania and the former Yugoslavia. In collaboration with Peacock Printmakers and the Scottish Sculpture Trust, an exhibition was presented of 44 artists in Sarajevo for the city's Winter Festival.

It is difficult to believe that a few months after this splendid example of cultural dialogue between Scotland and Eastern Europe, the war in Yugoslavia began and the streets of Sarajevo with their Christian churches, Jewish synagogues and Muslim mosques were to be devastated by an interminable siege.

This was the decade when the Chernobyl disaster reminded all Europeans that the misuse of atomic energy can wreck havoc in the environment of Europe.   This was the disaster that made me more determined than ever to lead 'Edinburgh Arts' expeditions to Belarus, Lithuania Latvia, Estonia, as well as Poland, and all the countries which constituted the former Yugoslavia.

These journeys were developed in relation to the programme of conferences and symposia I presented in both Edinburgh and Dublin on the theme of Art and the Human Environment.   I used Edinburgh University for

The Edinburgh Conference and The Irish National Gallery for the Dublin Conference which was entitled 'Contemporaire'. The driving force behind this Irish conference was Mike Murphy, the Irish radio and television journalist and art patron. He helped me continue the cultural dialogue I had developed since 1967 with Ireland through my good friend, the Irish architect, Michael Scott. These conferences were really versions of Edinburgh Arts and they enabled me to invite art world luminaries to the Celtic world — the likes of Rudi Fuchs, Count Panza di Biumo, Giuliano Gori, Arthur Sackler, Mrs. De Menil, Jean de Loisy, Sir Hugh Casson. In Dublin, they were able to meet Michael Scott, Declan McGonagle, Dorothy Walker, Sean and Rosemary Mulcahy, and Anthony Burgess, as well as the Irish Taosoich, Garrett Fitzgerald and his political opponent, Charles Haughey. In Edinburgh, they met Ian Hamilton Finlay in his Garden Temple of Little Sparta, a world-renowned expression of 'concrete poetry', as well as Barry Gasson, the architect of The Burrell Museum.

In 1984, I was invited to Australia and New Zealand under the aegis of their respective arts councils, as well as to Japan by The Japanese Arts Council. This led me to focus on Australasia and present an art exhibition which introduced, for the first time, the avant-garde artists of both Australia and New Zealand in relation to a 12-day Conference which enabled Australia and New Zealand museum curators to consider the question of 'Housing the Arts in the 21st Century'. I was indebted to Nick Waterlow, in Australia, and Ian Hunter, in New Zealand, Nobuo Nokamura and Fumio Nango in Japan.

The resultant exhibition was entitled 'Anzart' and it was very much 'at home' in Edinburgh College of Art alongside an international conference and an art fair, entitled 'Demarcation'. For the Fair, I invited galleries from London, Houston (Texas) and Venice. The Robert Fraser Gallery was represented with Keith Haring and Jean-Michel Basquiat and the Bruton Gallery with sculptures by Rodin and Bourdelle.

Over a period of four years from 1981 to 1984, Arthur Sackler, as patron of The Demarco Gallery, presented major exhibitions at the Edinburgh City Art Centre. In 1982, there were The Piranese Etchings, 'Art of the Andes' (pre-Colombian Ceramics), and Chinese Watercolours, all from his collections. The largest, and fifth exhibition, was presented at The National Museum of Scotland. It celebrated the 200th anniversary of the founding of The Smithsonian Museum and it included such treasures as the Buggy from America's first Moon Landing, and modern masterworks from the Smithsonian Art Collections. The dinner celebrating the anniversary was held, appropriately, in Prestonfield House which at one time had welcomed Benjamin Franklin, Dr. Johnson and James Boswell. All four Demarco Gallery exhibitions were presented as a gift worth millions of pounds to the Edinburgh Festival through Arthur Sackler's generosity.

I was indebted to Lord Binning as a member of the Gallery's Board of Directors who welcomed Arthur Sackler and his wife, Jill, and their legal advisor, Michael Sonnenreich, to the world of Mellerstain House, arguably the most impressive Robert Adam mansion in Scotland.

Arthur Sackler bought *Studio International* from Michael Spens and appointed him Editor; I was appointed Contributing Editor and, in this capacity, interviewed Pontus Hulten as Director of MOCA in Los Angeles, James Turrell at his Roden Crater sculpture in the Arizona Desert, and Joseph Beuys at Brookes Club on his 7,000 Oak Tree Sculpture, planned for the Seventh Documenta, as well as Sam Francis in his Los Angeles studio.

Four 'Edinburgh Arts' Expeditions were made in the spirit of pilgrimage to the world of Dom Hans van der Laan, the Benedictine monk. He was the architect of the modern development of the Monastery of St. Benedictusburg at Vaals, my favourite example of 20th century architecture. I was advised to make these expeditions by Rudi Fuchs. Vaals is just three miles from the German border and Charlemangne's Temple at Aachen, the heart and centre of the Holy Roman Empire. Mies van der Rohe was born in Aachen, and therefore I identify it with the spirit of Modernism and with his beloved Bauhaus. Hans van der Laan was his kindred spirit, and, for me, of equal importance because of his concept of architecture and the sublime beauty of his masterpiece, the modern extension of the St. Benedictusberg Monastery in which he lived most of his life in a world in which architecture, made of concrete and glass, ascended to the condition of prayer.

It was in the eighties that George Riches, as Chairman of Phaidon Press, celebrated the Gallery's work with a dinner at which the three speakers were Lord Palumbo, Sandy Nairne and the Italian Ambassador, Boris Biancheri. I was indebted to Sally Dunsmore, Phaidon's Press Officer, who arranged this dinner with impeccable efficiency in the perfect setting of The Signet Library in Edinburgh. I was indebted, too, to her subsequent work as a participant on Edinburgh Arts expeditions to Poland, Romania, Hungary and Italy.

John David Mooney made it possible for me to maintain close links with the American art world through his Chicago-based foundation and I was delighted to propose the toast to The Immortal Memory to The Chicago Burns Society in his splendid studio space in West Kenzie Street, in the very heart of Chicago.

Countdown towards the Third Millennium
From Blackfriars Street via St. Mary's School, to New Parliament House

It was in the nineties that I received the last of seven invitations to take part in Scottish university Rectorial elections. Five generations of Edinburgh University students invited me to consider being their representative on the University's Governing Board, beginning in 1978. Two generations of St. Andrews students did so as well. Thrice, I was runner-up, and each time, I knew I had the disadvantage of not being in the world of entertainment.

The 1990s were a countdown towards my seventieth year. In that period, the Demarco Gallery was obliged to sell part of its Archive — the part which ended in 1995 — to The Scottish National Gallery of Modern Art in order to fund its annual running costs and cope with the need to terminate the annual programmes of visual and performing arts in the building which housed the gallery known as Blackfriars Church. These programmes were continued under the aegis of The Demarco European Art Foundation which had come into being in 1991 in order to facilitate the donation of Bryan Montgomery's international collection of contemporary art, worth approximately one million pounds, to The National Gallery of Hungary.

1990 marked the 20th Anniversary of 'Strategy: Get Arts'. This led to a major Edinburgh Festival exhibition entitled 'Pictland Garden' because I invited Gunther Uecker to explore 'The Road to Meikle Seggie' with particular reference to the Land of the Picts. He did so by making an exhibition of new art works from his direct experience of Scotland's cultural heritage. In 1995, Henning Christiansen and his wife, Ursula Reuter, helped mark the 25th anniversary of 'Strategy: Get Arts' with an expedition to the Moor of Rannoch in collaboration with George Wyllie. They also contributed to the exhibition programme at Edinburgh College of Art which evoked memories of 'Strategy: Get Arts' with an 'action' in the same life-room in which Henning Christiansen had collaborated with Joseph Beuys to perform 'Celtic (Kinloch Rannoch): The Scottish Symphony'.

John Latham is a British artist who had been in close and fruitful dialogue with Joseph Beuys. Together with his wife, Barbara Steveni, John had been committed to questioning the role of the artist in modern society. He had also collaborated with The Scottish Office to create the concept of a gigantic 'land art' sculpture in West Lothian in an ambitious effort to reconsider disused shale-oil bings as large-scale sculptures. For this reason, I presented an exhibition of John Latham's work as an avant gardiste at The Edinburgh College of Art in relation to the 25th anniversary of 'Strategy: Get Arts'!

The Gallery sold Blackfriars Church to the Italian Ministry of Foreign Affairs. This obliged the Gallery to seek a new building which could house its archive. This building had been known to generations of parishioners of Edinburgh's Roman Catholic Cathedral as St. Mary's Cathedral Primary School. This move coincided with the beginning of my work with Kingston University. Sadly, it also coincided with the deaths of three of the Gallery's key supporters who were member's of the Gallery's Board of Directors. They were Dik Mehta, an outstanding member of Edinburgh's Indian community. He and his wife, Elizabeth and his daughter, Nina, contributed greatly to the Gallery's capacity to welcome artists to Scotland and strengthen the Italo-Scottish cultural dialogue. Dione Pattullo funded the award-winning theatre productions of Sarajevo'a Obala Theatre under the direction of Mladen Materic. Bert Davis was the third long-serving member of the Demarco Gallery's Board of Directors who died at this time. He contributed greatly to the programmes I devised to link the visual and literary arts.

St. Mary's provided more space for the Demarco Archives. I was reassured by this, and by the fact that with the support of Martin Kemp as Professor of Art History at St. Andrew's University, the Foundation was awarded a grant of nearly 60,000 pounds from The Leverhulme Foundation. This enabled Steve Robb, as an art history graduate from St. Andrew's University to work on the photographic element of The Demarco Archive, a vital part which had not been acquired by The National Gallery of Modern Art.

My involvement in the 1990s in the life of Kingston Polytechnic and its highly respected School of Art and Design was entirely due to Ainslie Yule, the Scottish artist who was appointed Head of Kingston's School of Sculpture. It was he, together with the Vice-Chancellor, Dr. Robert Smith, and the Pro-Vice Chancellor, Dr. Robert Godfrey, who made me feel that together we could help Kingston Polytechnic identify itself with the academic and cultural life of Budapest, as Hungary strove to unshackle itself from the bonds of Communism. I was honoured to receive a 'Picker Fellowship' from the Polytechnic. When Kingston Polytechnic was granted university status, I was given the title of Professor of European Cultural Studies. I was then able to lead Kingston University art students to Venice and Varese to the art and artists associated with Gabriella Cardazzo in Venice and Count Panza di Biumo in Milan and Varese. Also, I identified Kingston University with the 1992 Venice Biennale with a conference involving Dr. Robert Godfrey, Bryan Montgomery, John Calder, Richard Calvocoressi, and Lorand Hegyi, Director of the Gallery of Modern Art in Vienna, related to an exhibition of Ainslie Yule's sculpture and another by artists of Hungary, Austria and Italy.

This led to a large-scale exhibition and theatre programme at the 1992 Edinburgh Festival presented by the University of Kingston which brought the Medici Quartet together with the Royal Shakespeare Company led by Dorothy Tutin to perform in St. Mary's Episcopal Cathedral.

In 1991 at Kingston University, I organised an international symposium with the title of 'Pentagonale Plus' in collaboration with the Italian Ministry of Foreign Affairs and the Polish, Romanian, Bulgarian and Hungarian Embassies in London at which Lord Palumbo gave the Key Address. Other major contributions were by the Romanian and Bulgarian Ambassadors, the Director of The Polish Cultural Institute, and Timothy Clifford, Director of The National Galleries of Scotland. I then presented 'Pentagonale Plus' for the Edinburgh Festival and the key address was delivered by Gianni di Michaelis, the Foreign Minister of Italy. My Professorial Chair in my last three years at Kingston University was under the patronage of David Youlton, an extraordinary businessman and a good friend who directed his business affairs with the instinct of an artist unafraid to take risks.

During this period, I was invited to Atlanta to receive an Honorary Doctorate from The Atlanta College of Art and act as arts advisor to Bettina Carr-Allinson's European Youth Parliament in relation to its parliamentary sessions at Oxford University, at the Reichstag in Berlin and in Strasbourg and Ghent, the last two sessions in collaboration with Kingston University and Peacock Printmakers, resulting in major exhibitions of prints made by those members of The European Youth Parliament who were art school students in Lithuania, Croatia, Hungary, Poland, France, Scotland, England and Wales. The nineties ended with my mind focused on Malta, as advisor to The Maltese Ministry of Environment, and The Ministry of Education, I was invited to help with the transformation of the 16th century bastion known as St. James Cavaliere into a 'state of the art' museum, gallery and theatre, built to the architectural plans of Richard England.

In collaboration with Marijan Susovski, Chief Curator of the City Gallery of Zagreb and the Festivals of Dubrovnik, I led an expedition of 25 international artists to make site-specific art works in support of Dubrovnik's Otok Gallery and the work of the European Youth Parliament in Croatia. This was made possible with the support of the British Ambassador in Croatia and The British Council.

The 90s provided all the proof I needed that 'the Road to Meikle Seggie' is "too rough to go slow", and I was grateful for the invaluable support I received from Mary James, the Headmistress of St. Leonard's School in St. Andrews, and her husband, the historian Lawrence James. Mary James worked in collaboration with Derek Huckle, the Director of Fife College, in helping me establish the Foundation's presence in Fife for the 1994 Edinburgh Festival with an international Edinburgh Festival theatre programme located in Kirkcaldy. The main event was the Belarus State Theatre's outdoor production of *Macbeth* at Ravenscraig Castle, made possible by the generous British Council support orgranized by Hannah Horowitz. Her commitment to the cultural dialogue between Britain and Eastern Europe made it possible for me to support the avant-garde theatre of, not only Belarus, but Poland, Bulgaria and The Baltic States.

Both Eric and Anne Wishart provided essential support as the Foundation's accountants. They committed themselves to supporting the world of the visual arts in Scotland. I was also indebted to Bill and Maggie Williams. Their Northern Books publication *A Life in Pictures* gave me the opportunity to express my thoughts on art and education. BBC 2 made a one-hour documentary, directed by Andrea Miller, which included my 'Edinburgh Arts' expedition from Budapest to Timisoara, and an 'Edinburgh Arts' expedition to the 1990 Venice Biennale focussed on the Scottish Pavilion, in which Arthur Watson, David Mach and Kate Whiteford made their presence felt at the entrance to the 'Giardini' within sight of The British and Italian pavilions, under the aegis of The Scottish Sculpture Trust in collaboration with The Demarco Foundation.

In 1994, I was invited to Morocco by Alain Bourdon, Director of The French Cultural Institute, in Casablanca. This led to an exhibition of Moroccan artists at the 1995 Edinburgh Festival, shown along with an exhibition of Lithuanian art presented with the support of The Soros Foundation and the Gallery of Modern Art in Vilnius.

With the support of Mary James, I was able to lead an expedition to Lithuania and persuade Oscar Korsunovos to present his production of three plays by Erofefev, the Russian writer of avant garde theatre. This was the highlight of two successive Edinburgh Festival programmes which the Foundation presented in Dundee in collaboration with Hamish Glen, Director of Dundee Repertory Theatre with generous support from Tayside Enterprise.

1998 was a year in which the Foundation relied heavily on the generosity of its friends. Those who gave financial support in order to help the Foundation pay the 30,000 pounds rent charged by the Edinburgh City Council for the use of New Parliament House as an Edinburgh Festival Venue were Michael McLaughlin, Tom McLaughlin, John Martin, Andrew Elliott, Douglas Soeder, Mary James, The Lady Leigh, Terry Ann Newman, Andrea Tana and Mary MacIver.

The 1990s culminated in the Foundation presenting an exhibition of international significance in Malta at The National Maritime Museum of Malta, in collaboration with the University of Malta. All the participants were invited to consider the cultural heritage of Malta and, in particular, its maritime history. Among the Maltese artists were Richard England, John Borg Manduca and Norbet Attard, exhibiting along with Alfred Graf from Vienna, and Geert Bisschop from Brussels and Shelley Horton-Trippe from New Mexico, and John David Mooney, a veteran of 'Edinburgh Arts', representing the United States.

This encouraged the Maltese Ministry of Culture to commission John David Mooney to transform the massive castle known as The St. James Cavaliere into a total art work as the centre piece of Malta's Millennium celebrations. I was invited to collaborate with Richard England in the process of conversion of The St. James Caveliere as a semi-derelict part of Valletta's historic system of defence into an highly sophisticated National Arts Centre.

This Millennium celebration was a culmination of the cultural dialogue which began in Edinburgh at the 1999 Edinburgh Festival with an exhibition and conference presented in collaboration with the Schools of Architecture and Music of Edinburgh University at the University's Matthew Gallery and in the Lecture Theatre of The Royal College of Physicians. The Conference took place considering "The Arts and Science of Peace and the Prevention of Conflict". Among the speakers were Dr. Louis Galea, Minister of Education and Culture of Malta, and Professor Neil MacCormack, as a Member of the European Parliament, and Richard Muscat, one of Malta's most senior diplomats who was to become Malta's first Ambassador to Ireland. There followed an ecumenical service focussed on Christo-Islamic harmony at St. Giles Cathedral. This included a recital by Maltese opera soprano, Lydia Caruana, and culminated in a Civic Reception in Edinburgh City Chambers. Ros Lambert was commissioned to make a film for Scottish Television focussed on the Foundation's cultural dialogue with Malta, a dialogue which began in the 1960's which brought the first exhibitions of Maltese artists to Scotland and led to two 'Edinburgh Arts' expeditions to Malta in 1998 and 1999, in collaboration with the National Gallery of Malta.

Journeying From a Seventieth to a Seventy-Fifth Birthday
Towards Skateraw and a Safe Haven for a Living Archive

Via Belarus, The Baltic States, Ireland, Italy, France,
Georgia, Germany, Poland, and Slovakia

In the first year of the New Millennium, The University of Kingston honoured my seven years as Professor of European Cultural Studies with an exhibition and related programme of lectures and symposia entitled '70/2000 on the Road to Meikle Seggie'. This was also was a celebration of my 70th birthday and enabled me to exhibit a significant part of the Demarco Archives. The Edinburgh City Gallery presented an enlarged version of this exhibition in collaboration with Kingston University as part of their Edinburgh Festival Millennium exhibition programme. Thereafter it was presented at The Ruskin Museum at Brantwood, then over a period of 18 months at The Richard Hamilton Gallery at Oxford Brookes University, and The National Gallery of Lithuania, as well as in The Oakham School Art Centre and The Glebe National Gallery of Ireland in Donegal.

2004 was the year in which the Foundation ended a prolonged and, in the end, futile six year battle with Edinburgh City Council in contesting the Council's determination to demand monthly rent at a commercial rate for the Council's office accommodation provided at New Parliament House, despite the fact that the Foundation is a non-profit distributing charity and the Council gives generous support to other charities using New Parliament House.

I was indebted to Michael Borland, owner of The Lady Glenorchy Church, for his transformation of this church into an arts centre so that it could provide four theatre spaces and become an important Festival Fringe Venue. The Foundation was able, in collaboration with Rocket Productions, a major American Festival Fringe promoter of theatre programmes, to present over 200 theatre productions during the 2002, 2003 and 2004 Festival. Among the companies represented were The National Theatres of Siberia and Belarus, and theatre companies from the United States, Poland, Italy, Germany, France, Montenegro, Serbia, and Bosnia. Xela Batchelder, the Director of Rocket Productions has over the past four years become an invaluable friend and collaborator. Her office is in Ohio but, in the age of the computer, there is no problem in creating highly complex international theatre programmes.

My friendship with Brigadier Allan Alstead has enabled me to collaborate with him as Chairman of Mercy Corps (Aid International). This collaboration resulted in an exhibition 'Beyond Conflict' which was presented in Edinburgh in collaboration with The National Museum of Scotland and Apex Hotels with financial support from The Russell Trust and at the Manchester Commonwealth Games where it was opened by the Countess of Wessex. The exhibition catalogue had a foreword by Nelson Mandela and there was a letter of support from Her Majesty The Queen. The exhibition consisted of paintings by twenty-four Scottish artists who were invited to seek inspiration from their experience of the treasures in the Museums of Scotland, expressing both the Islamic and Christo-Judaic cultural heritage and how there were countless points of interface to give hope for a world without conflict. Finally, it was exhibited at The European Parliament in Brussels and gave extra meaning to the address I had made to the European Parliament's Session in Edinburgh in the summer of 2002. I was invited to do so by Struan Stevenson one of Scotland's most active Members of the European Parliament.

In collaboration with The Waterways Trust Scotland, an exhibitions inspired by the landscape of Scottish canals was held with support from Miller Developments at Edinburgh Quay. In collaboration with Terry Smith, Director of Property for Forth Ports plc, the Foundation presented two symposia related to two exhibitions in The Forum Gallery of Ocean Terminal, in Leith Docks. In collaboration with the organisers of 'The Festival of the Sea', the Foundation presented an exhibition celebrating the British tradition of maritime art.

The Foundation's life was transformed by the impact of computerization on the art world. I became advisor to two 'Online' galleries; one in London which had the esoteric name 'Unit 26' and the other BlinkRed.com based in Leith.

2004 was an impossibly busy year. I conducted two Master Classes, one at Pitlochry Theatre inspired by their newly established hillside garden dedicated to Scottish plant collectors, and the other at The Burren College of Art in Co. Clare. It was the year I was invited by The University of Dundee to deliver 'The Discovery Lecture' on the theme of '"The Artist as Explorer'. John Haldane, as Professor of Moral Philosophy at St. Andrew's University invited me to be part of a five-part lecture series. I spoke on the subject of art and religion suggesting that The Incarnation must be regarded as an incomparable 'art work' of sublime significance.

As an Honorary Fellow of The Institute of Contemporary Scotland, I was invited by Kenneth Roy, the Institute's Founder and Director, to speak at the Institute's conference in Kilmarnock. It attracted an extraordinarily impressive group of young people from every part of Scotland. They provided proof that in their hands Scotland has a future full of 'new beginnings'. I also spoke at two conferences celebrating the enlargement of The European Union — one at the University of Paisley, invited by Professor George Blasyck, and the other at the University of Wroclaw invited by Professor Zbigniew Makarewicz. At my lecture at Wroclaw Academy of Art and Design, I was informed that I would be the recipient of an Honorary Doctorate from the Academy.

The year 2004 ended with the knowledge that Dundee University has been awarded a Grade A listed grant from The British Universities' Arts and Humanities Research Board. It is valued at just over 312,000 pounds. It will enable Dundee University students to begin the process of digitisation which will make The Demarco Archive a resource for galleries, museums, art schools and universities in a global context.

Then, to add to this, there came an offer made by Johnny and Sandra Watson to have The Demarco Archive housed on their East Lothian farm at Skateraw in a new building with over 9,000 square feet of floor space and a 40 foot high ceiling. This will help Dundee University with their work on the Archive (that part of it not in the Collection of The Scottish National Gallery of Modern Art). It is the part that has been housed and developed by The Demarco European Art Foundation in St. Mary's School (1993-1998) and in Building Two of New Parliament House, involving the Foundation in payment of rent to Edinburgh City Council of well over 150,000 pounds. The total investment in the Archive is at least ten times that, an investment well worth the cost because the Archive encapsulates the history of countless numbers of human beings who have contributed significantly to the cultural life of Scotland over the course of my lifetime. Without their preparedness to focus their creative energies upon Scotland, my life's work would not have materialised and 'The Road to Meikle Seggie' would have lost its true significance over the past thirty years.

I am forever indebted to those who offered storage space for The Demarco Archive in the 80s, particularly Lord and Lady Rosebery, and Nick and Limme Groves Raines, my favourite restorers of Scotland's architectural heritage. I must not forget in the history of The Demarco Foundation the whole-hearted support I received from Eric Milligan whilst he was chairman of Lothian Regional Council and Lord Provost of Edinburgh, and his colleague, Councillor Elizabeth McGinnis, in her role as chairman of the Education Committee responsible for Edinburgh's schools. The Foundation depended on the unswerving loyalty of its board members and on its friends such as Willie and Charlotte Macnair, and, most recently, David Mabbs who has helped me establish a base for the Foundation's work in the form of his

Rockcliffe Gallery on the enchanting Galloway coastline of the Solway Firth.

2004 was the year in which Tom Craig died. His name was synonymous with John Calder's world of music and books and with The Demarco Gallery. He helped create ASCENT, the Association linking Science, Engineering and all the Arts. He introduced me to Colin Sanderson, who took on the mantle of the Director of ASCENT. Together, we organised innumerable symposia and conference on 'Art and Science' — at Dundee, Abertay and Kingston Universities — involving the likes of George Steiner, John Latham, Vytautis Landsbergis, Lord Sutherland, Bishop Vincent Logan, George Wyllie, Dr. Alan Flowers and Dr. Alexander Lutzko, the founder of The Zakarov University, and Dom Aidan Bellenger OSB, as Headmaster of Downside Abbey School. At the interface of Art and Science, you cannot ignore Theology and Philosophy. I am thinking, therefore, how much I owe to John Haldane, as an artist and Professor of Moral Philosophy at St. Andrews University with regard to my work relating art to religion. 2004 was a year in which many friends died. Most important among those who were artists were Paul Neagu, and Wilhelmina Barns Graham. I placed alongside their names that of Peter Arden as I saw him as an artist for the highly creative ways in which he played the key role of administrator of The Demarco Gallery during the years in which it was obliged to sell many art works in its Archives, as well as make profitable exhibitions by Maggi Hambling, Paula Rego, Mario Merz, Mimmo Rotella, Gerard Gasiorowski, and Paul Neagu, and a memorial exhibition in honour of Joseph Beuys, in collaboration with Caroline Tisdall and The Arnolfini Gallery. An exhibition of French artists was made possible by the commitment to the idea of these artists exploring 'the Road to Meikle Seggie' by Caroline Davie, Director of the Fondation Regional D'Arte Contemporaine Pas de Calais and Alain Bourdon. This exhibition was in three parts, not only in the Demarco Gallery, but also in The Scottish National Gallery of Modern Art and in the French Institute. As well, in close collaboration with Jane MacAllister, he administered the conversion of The Demarco Gallery's premises, built as Blackfriars Church so that it had not only a suite of galleries but also theatre spaces which could enable it to be one of the key venues for the Edinburgh Festival Fringe. Peter Arden and Jane MacAllister also dealt with the complexities of the sale of the building to The Italian Ministry of Foreign Affairs who regarded it as ideal to house The Italian Cultural Institute in Scotland and Northern Ireland. Peter Arden spent a profitable and adventurous life in Africa as a pilot flying to remote corners of the domain of wild animals which he loved. He had a meticulous way of working without the aid of computerisation. All his reports and account had the mark of authenticity that only the handwritten statement can provide.

In 2005 already I have reason to mourn the passing of friends who contributed to the creative energy of The Demarco Gallery over the years – Harald Szeemann, the supreme example of an exhibition director who directed both the Venice Biennale and Documenta; Margaret Gardiner helped me pay homage to Thomas Merton, the Cistercian monk and writer; Miles Baster, as leader of The Edinburgh Quartet enhanced the Gallery's programmes of classical music; Norman Adams provided an exhibition of paintings inspired by his love of the Hebrides; Nigel Greenwood, who as one of London's gallery directors, helped me present the sculpture of Edgar Negret in London in 1968. I cannot forget the wisdom and support David Daiches bestowed upon his fellow members of The Demarco Gallery Board in the 1980s.

2005 marks the 20th anniversary of my association with Oakham School and The White Cube Project which enable me to collaborate with Martin Minshall, Oakham's Art Master, to provide proof that the school teacher's role is akin to that of the artist and that each and every schoolchild is capable of being uniquely creative. In collaboration with Joe Spence, the Headmaster of Oakham, I hope to provide further proof of this — at this year's Edinburgh Festival. 2005 also marks the year when the Demarco Foundation's Archive will be exhibited for the first time in its entirety in a brand-new building with 9,000 square feet of floor space at Skateraw Farm, on the East Lothian coastline. John Muir, the father of environmentalism, learned to love the beauty of nature on this coastline, and James Hutton, the father of Geology, saw, in its rock forms, the evidence he needed to calculate the age of our planet, not in thousands, but in many millions of years.

Joseph Beuys personified the 'artist as environmentalist' and therefore 'the artist as scientist'. He would have regarded Skateraw as a space for artists to consider as an alternative to the urban space which constitutes the vast majority of art galleries and museums. Skateraw is a farm. So, too, is Ian Hamilton Finlay's 'Little Sparta' at Stonypath Farm, and so, too, is my favourite place for site-specific sculpture in Italy. This is 'La Fattoria di Celle' (literally 'the farm of Celle') where Giuliano Gori has invited some of the world's leading artists to be inspired by the quintessential beauty of Tuscan landscape. This is, in essence, the classical European farmscape of the vineyard and olive grove. Skateraw is the Scottish equivalent of this. It is the Northern European farmscape where Grade 'A' farmland produces the high quality grain essential to the making of Scots whisky — the 'water of life'.

Skateraw is farmed by Johnny and Sandra Watson; they represent the kind of art patronage which is very much needed in Scotland. They share my belief that Scotland's landscape is beautiful to a great extent because of the way it is farmed, and in particular, the rich farmlands of the Lothians. They were inspired by their experience of Giuliano Gori's Tuscan Fattoria. I am indebted to them and to the deputy director of the Demarco Foundation, Terry Ann Newman, who shares their profound respect and understanding for the world of the farmer facing the challenge of globalisation. They share my belief that the Demarco Archive provides proof positive that the worlds of the farmer and the artist throughout history have been inextricably interwoven. Now, the symbol of such an interweaving must be, for me, 'the Road to Meikle Seggie' leading to Skateraw.

Ever since my 70th birthday, I have had the feeling that I am playing the game of life in extra-time, indeed, in penalty shoot-out time. For the sake of all the dear friends who have helped me play the incomparable game of life in the arts, I cannot afford to ease up on my efforts to play as well as I can, right up until the time when I am obliged to leave the field. I find myself with new team-mates such as James Thomson who has helped me extend the playing field to encompass his beloved Prestonfield House with its magical parkland in the heart of Edinburgh, and my fellow members of The Royal Scottish Academy.

They know, as I do, that the language of art is a dangerous and difficult one, when it can be so easily misunderstood and abused. However, they know, too, that despite human failings, as is evidenced in the life of Van Gogh and his friend, Gauguin, great art inevitably ascends to the condition of prayer. I have always had the feeling that the Rule of St. Benedict can also apply to artists when I consider the achievements of Joseph Beuys. He personified the role of an artist whose values are deeply rooted in the Christo-Judaic cultural heritage of Europe.

For this reason, whilst preparing my contribution to the Tate lecture programme related to the recent Beuys exhibition at Tate Modern, I found it necessary to re-read the autobiography of Thomas Merton who exemplified the life of a 20th century artist chosing to live it as a Cistercian priest, forsaking the success offered all too readily in the world of contemporary culture. I believe it was Robert Rauschenberg who gave this uncompromising answer to a question put to him by an aspiring young artist on how to succeed in the art world: "You must be prepared to give up everything for the truth you wish to express through your art, particularly any idea that you have of becoming a successful artist".

From Rauschenberg's experience of the game artists choose to play, success lies not in winning the goal but in simply facing the challenge of playing according to the rules laid down by the anonymous artists who gave us the wall paintings of Lascaux. They were ignored for thousands of years but they provided the foundation for what must be considered as the history of art. They were made by hunter-gathers before our forebears became farmers. St. Benedict's Rule demands of those who dare to follow it, a commitment to the life of the farmer, as well as the life of prayer and scholarship. There is much food for thought in contemplating the points of interface linking the life and work of the farmer, the priest and the scholar with that of the artist.

Europe's medieval abbeys and the libraries inspired the concept of universities on the lines of Oxford, Cambridge, St. Andrews and Aberdeen. Whether they realise it or not, today's art schools are judged initially as an extension of such a concept.

When my friend, Dom Aidan Bellenger, was headmaster of Downside Abbey School, he showed me the Abbey's library, housing a quarter of a million books and precious manuscripts. I thought then that every art gallery and art institution dedicated to presenting art should have such a resource. It set a standard for me when I contemplated the future of the Archive which has come into existence through the energy expressed in the ideals and aspirations of many friends and collaborators who share my belief that art is all important to the making and maintaining of a civilised society.

Elizabeth Violet Blackadder

Born Falkirk, 24th September 1931

PAINTER AND PRINTMAKER

Early Beginnings

Although Blackadder is a border name, my family had been settled in Falkirk for several generations, probably coming to central Scotland around the time Carron Company and other iron foundries were starting up. Most of my forbears, indeed most of my immediate family were engineers and my grandfather, Thomas Blackadder, and one of his brothers had established a family engineering works by the time I was born in 1931.

My early upbringing was happy and secure and revolved around family and school. During this period my grandfather escaped the Scottish winters by travelling from November to May, to Southern Europe and often further afield and I remember the excitement when he returned home with tales of his travels and, to my eyes, wonderful and exotic presents. Perhaps these travellers' tales whetted my appetite for foreign travel and I certainly inherited his passion for collecting objects of all kinds which I now call my 'source material'. Many members of my mother's family also travelled widely, some as marine engineers eventually settling in Australia and New Zealand.

However, the end of the 1930s brought many changes. My grandfather never returned from his last trip to Nice and was buried in the cemetery there above the town. With the outbreak of war and then my father's final illness I was sent off to stay with my grandmother Scott and my mother's sister who were living in Kilmun on the Holy Loch. The first school I attended there was the two teacher village school in Strone, 3 miles or so from Kilmun; penny for the bus, if lucky, one way and walk the other. I was fascinated by the things I found on the walk to or from school along the shore, stones, pieces of pottery, bits of coloured glass or bones all worn smooth by the sea, dead seagulls, jelly fish and on the hillside, grass snakes, wild flowers and sometimes an adder.   I did draw the boats in the loch, the puffers which came to the pier to bring coal to the village and also the paddle steamer, 'The Marchioness of Lorne,' which daily made several stops at all the piers, from Gourock across to Blairmore then round to Dunoon.   To satisfy my brother Tom's critical eye these early artworks had to be rendered as accurately as possible.   Tom, five years my senior joined me later at Kilmun and we both went to Dunoon Grammar School for a time.

On the whole an uneventful childhood, plenty of time to look at things. Pleasures were simple, an old rowing boat, fishing at the end of the pier and lots of books to read.   I read avidly and quite indiscriminately.   Scott, Dumas, Dickens etc. and The Peoples' Friend, as well as all the other magazines displayed on the counter of the village Post Office.   Towards the end of the war I returned to Falkirk and to Falkirk High School again.   My mother became the strongest influence on my life; she had a wide range of views, a love of books and poetry and also of music, with a strong sense of duty and a belief in hard work.   She encouraged both my brother and myself to look further afield than our immediate surroundings.

I left Falkirk High School in 1949.   At that time under the wise and kindly rule of the Rector, A C Mackenzie, the curriculum was typically Scottish with a range of subjects which have continued to be a source of interest and pleasure to me, from botany to literature and history.   By that time I was set on applying to Edinburgh College of Art and the University of Edinburgh for the comparatively new combined course of MA Honours Fine Art.   Once there I came into contact with a group of people who were to have a profound influence on my life and, for the first time I met professional painters and I began to understand what it meant to be a painter and just what it entailed. At the College of Art the influence and example of William Gillies, Penelope Beaton, Robert Henderson Blyth, Robin Philipson, William MacTaggart and later, meeting Anne Redpath and Joan Eardley, all were an inspiration to me. Likewise, at the University Professors David Talbot Rice and Giles Robertson opened up whole areas of art history – early Italian Art, Romanesque, Byzantine Art and Architecture as well as Islamic Art, all have been enduring sources of interest to me as a painter and I am grateful to them both.

However, the best thing that happened to me in my later years as a student was to meet fellow student, John Houston.   We married shortly after graduating and since then have been able to work together, encourage and support each other, travelling in Europe, the USA and Japan to visit galleries and to get inspiration from these various countries.   We both taught in the Drawing and Painting School at Edinburgh College of Art, John becoming depute head of the School, until we retired in the 1980s. We are fortunate that we have been able to remain in touch with some of our fellow students such as David Michie, Frances Walker, Robert Steedman, James Morris and other and, as members of various artists' societies such as the Royal Scottish Academy, The Royal Academy of Arts and the Royal Scottish Society of Painters in Water Colour we meet up not only with our contemporaries but with the new generation of young painters, sculptors, architects and printmakers. For a number of years now I have been working in various print studios and my long association with the Glasgow Print Studios has introduced me to many new and exciting techniques of print making and has also allowed me to meet and learn from experts in their own fields. I feel that I have been extremely fortunate and lucky in my chosen career.

Tom Nairn

Born Freuchie, Fife, 2nd June 1932

PHILOSOPHER AND ESSAYIST

Saltire Book of the Year, The Enchanted Glass, *1988*

Finishing the Story: reflections at a distance

> Let the images go bright and fast
> and the concepts be extravagant
> (wild host to extravagant guest)
> thats the only way
> to say the coast
>
> all the irregular reality
> of the rocky sea-washed West
>
> Pelagian discourse
> atlantic poetics
> from first to last

'Scotia Deserta', Kenneth White, from *The Bird Path, collected longer poems*, 1989

Exile in the Blood

I recall clearly the departure of my great-uncle Charlie for Canada, during my teen years. He did the rounds of all the relatives to say 'good-bye', rather cheerfully, explaining he was going to live with his daughter Katherine (who had emigrated some years before, married and set up home in Alberta). I remember thinking how incredibly old he seemed (he must have been in his 'fifties); and also, how everyone took for granted this was the natural thing to do. We never saw him again, which was also normal. Every family we knew had some part of it somewhere else: Durban, Sydney, Auckland, the USA or (of course) London or Birmingham, England. About eighteen months later, my father (a school headmaster) set about applying for a job in the Education Service of Barbados, in the British West Indies. He didn't go through with it, to general disappointment and my mother's annoyance, deciding instead to work out his time until retirement in Fife.

The point is: being elsewhere, or having important kinship ties elsewhere, was more than taken for granted. It partly defined us. Had father succeeded, then — like Charlie in Canada — he would have devoted himself to Barbadian matters. We know now that 'becoming Barbadian' would in fact have posed problems, but at that time, unblessed by hindsight wisdom, people didn't appreciate this. Father didn't doubt that Scots should go on serving the Empire, or that devotion to the interests of Barbados would be part of the same thing. It was assumed that the system would go on forever, or at least for a very long time. That system included natural dispersal, not to be confused with what was later often called 'diaspora'. With few exceptions, this dispersed retained a primarily sentimental emotive link to their source, invariably seen as a sacred past only dimly related to any present (and actually, curiously similar to the feelings of the stay-at-homes). In the early 1950s a traditional pattern remained set in its ways; and it was a lot older and more deeply rooted than they understood.

His other son, my elder brother David, had made an abortive move in a similar direction some years earlier. When I was seven, he finished his High School studies and decided to go and work on a stock-breeding farm in Galloway, South-West Scotland. To this day I vividly recall our father's stern comments on the disgrace. He summoned me to his study, and urged me to be sure and 'keep the flag flying' — by going to University, like all right-thinking Scots of our class. But I learnt almost simultaneously that David was actually signing up for the Galloway branch of a much grander enterprise elsewhere. The owner of the Whithorn farm regularly sent employees as well as pedigree bulls off to service his much bigger estates in Argentina. Which caused our mother to take a quite different attitude to the turn of events. She saw it as an adventure, leading possibly to prosperous exile and romance. As an obsessive reader of *Wide World*, a popular illustrated magazine of travellers' tales and exotic places, she saw Scots as denizens of this wider realm.[1] While nodding solemnly at the paternal strictures, I of course really agreed with her, dreamt of gauchos, tangos and Buenos Aires, and looked forward keenly to learning Spanish.

Alas, it was 1939, and the Second World War intervened. My brother was called up into the Royal Naval Air Service, and never returned to farming. I guess that, had Father Nairn's own later escape-bid succeeded, he would have tried to be like the Scots where I am living now, in the state of Victoria, Australia. Southern Victoria may have started off as 'Caledonia Australis', but went on to become a loyal element in 20th century all-Australian institutions and identity. [2] A Scottish accent often remains, with or without some addiction to what Tom Devine has called 'Highlandism' – tartan displays, music, games and so on.[3] But there is almost no collective presence comparable to that of the Irish, the Croats and Serbs, the Greeks or the Chinese. By and large the Scots are (as SNP fund-raisers have consistently found) unconcerned about the political fate of their land of origin. Sometimes it is thought this is because most of them had not been victims of preceding colonization or oppression. I have my doubts about that. Nothing like it applies, for instance, to the modern Irish, the Greeks, the Chinese, the Indians or Indonesians of Melbourne: mixtures of voluntary and involuntary, most retaining a vocally political concern with homeland affairs and culture. I have attended meetings of Plaid Cymru here, which combine cultural displays with Welsh homeland politics. It's true such communal interest here is usually conservative, and often quite out of touch; none the less, it maintains a strong sense of active community, which seems to interact with their function in Australian multi-culturalism.

Scots don't think that way, most likely because they never did. One revealing aspect of this is how easily unconcern tends towards hostility. In *Stone Voices* Neal Ascherson recounts amusingly an experience of going out to Malaya with the army, and shyly showing a tin-mine manager there his copy of the post-WWII Scottish Covenant petition for Home Rule. 'Laddie, if you know what's good for you, you'll just put that piece of nonsense away and we'll hear no more of it . . .' (p.232) One might also say: the representatives of a 'disbanded' nation are unlike those of one that has maintained its identity – whether as victimized or as victimizer. 'Identity' is often misunderstood as a kind of narcissistic choice, deciding which mirror-image to adopt. Comparative analysis has shown it to be far more fundamental than this. In the spectrum of modernity it voices an inherited deep grammar of boundary – that is, what has been made from kinship on a wider scale, in a world where *metaphorical* communities have become dominant. 'Metaphorical' means here much the same as Ben Anderson's 'Imagined Communities'. The identity-process invariably ties such external frontiers to individual sensibility, fostering the cohesion or 'common interest' that such communities depend on. Though of course historically constructed, such attitudes come to be felt as natural, and transmitted accordingly from infancy onwards (which for a long time was conceived as meaning 'in the blood').

However, these dispositions can also be *de*-constructed, abandoned or reformed. Conservatives like to think they're permanent, but they function only via a certain malleability and change. Parts of them — their 'relics', as it were — can then be passed down in similar fashion. I suspect this is what happened in the Scottish case. To put it in a different way: intermittent long periods of exile, interspersed with returns to Scotland, has made me feel that a quite peculiar past may also still be haunting us, from long before colonies and clearances: song-lines of summoning distance and out-goingness, a dream-time of departure as nature, and of the horizon as hidden — or God-disclosed — arrival.

Nor is the point just poetical (or in Kenneth White's sense, 'geopoetical'). Nostalgia is a vital ingredient of Devine's Highlandism: Scotland became 'Auld Lang Syne' country for a reason. But what the social DNA of this compensatory trend voices is a kind of disablement. It voices exaggerated attachment to close kinship, as a compensation for failure, at that metaphorical or abstract level upon which modernity depends. And one reason for its force and persistence is its intimate association with an engrained and all too practical culture. Such blue remembered hills appear romantic; yet they also resemble a set of old clothes, simultaneously comforting *and* demeaning. People feel naked without them; yet they also feel compelled to cover them up, and render the mixture more presentable with bag-pipes and poetry.

George MacDonald Fraser put it well in his memoir *The Light's on at the Signpost* (2002): 'My feeling is a nostalgic one, for a time when Scotland was the junior but never the lesser partner in a Britain that mattered in the world' (p.123). 'Mattered'? The Scots chose to share in such mattering — which actually meant domination, or 'lands we harriet', as Hamish Henderson bluntly put it[4]. In doing so they deluded themselves they were never lesser, a trick accomplished partly by a special form of over-assertiveness, usually including 'knowing what was good for them'.

This entailed *over*-identification with the superior (and apparently non-ethnic) forms of Britishness. An ideology of that sort has then to be defended and serviced. It feels threatened by any young fool turning up with ideas about turning the clock back. Nationalist ideologies are disconcertingly convertible: the passions they mobilize can be 'transferred' from one sacrosanct object to another, surprisingly easily. And the components of a disbanded (or de-politicized) identity like the Scottish one seem to be especially liberated, and disposable. Once translated into *someone else's* 'New Sang' — British-imperial, Australian, Canadian or whatever — the re-cycled idea-structure becomes the source of legitimacy and equality, and is naturally fought for. The effect of such transference is a heightened passion, rather than the reverse — as if something has all the time to be proved, or validated. So a serious return to the older song-lines turns into a threat: those things *must* be kept in the show-case.

From Migration to Haemorrhage

In the greatest of all Scottish memoirs, George Lockhart of Carnwath wrote that:

> For tho' Scotland is not the best, yet neither is it the worst country in Europe; and God has blessed it with all things fit for human use, either produced in the country itself, or imported from foreign countries, by barter with its product.

Hence the English had plenty of good reasons for wanting to control it, and had finally succeeded with the 1707 Treaty. He went on to underline one attribute of the inhabitants: they had always ventured abroad, far more than their southern neighbours:

> Those of rank (as they still do) travelled abroad into foreign countries for their improvement; and this won't seem strange, for the English themselves allow the Scots to be a wise and ingenious people, for they say, to a proverb, They 'never knew a Scotsman to be a fool' and vast numbers, when their country at home did not require their service, went into that of foreign princes, from whence they returned home. Whereas 'tis well known that it is but of late that any inclination to travel has seized the English (tho' not near to such a degree as in Scotland) . . .[5]

Lockhart could not know what would become of these contrasting attitudes, following the Union that he so strongly opposed. The numbers were to grow enormously, fewer and fewer returning home, while the new English 'inclination' would swell into an empire at once profitable and fatal to both old kingdoms. In the short run the Scots had more to gain, relatively speaking. But in the longer run, they also had more to lose. 'Long run' here means, the inevitable era of that empire's decline and abandonment. Their participation had been possible only via what one can call *self-colonization* — a strategy that reconfigured and fixed the homeland social culture, encouraging certain traits, like emigration, commerce and militarism, but repressing others, like popular tumult and religious zealotry (Lockhart himself, as an Episcopalian, interpreted the Union as Divine punishment for Scottish revolutionary excesses of the preceding century).[6]

The long-term difficulty of self-colonization is that, if the surrogate faith-object itself fails, there's no going back. Transcendence seems to lack a reverse gear. And yet, even if choosing re-confinement is hard, there really is no alternative. Human nature may be 'species-being' — in the societal genes rather than the blood — but such traits remain ineluctable. We need more diversity, even as we evolve into the 'global village' (I'll come back to the point later). The point of cultivating your garden is that it is *yours*: that is, the precondition of individuality (and individualism) in this or that actual environment — and hence of those features held in common, the general or 'universal'. With all its agonies and bloodshed, liberation from old imperial colonization remained philosophically straightforward; but emerging from the cocoon of *self*-subordination brings more of an existential dilemma. Independence from the former could be 'declared'; exit from the latter needs a phased and double-edged struggle, of which (we can now see) devolution is only one phase.

The point of the situation Lockhart so regretted wasn't just that the door was locked: the political key had to be thrown away *for good* . In this strange extremity, certain factors of identity were not wounded or suppressed, but shut up in a museum case. Which meant that, if and when the broader circumstances of Scottish imperial allegiance altered, they could no nothing about it. Economics is fickle; states (and the personalized meanings linked to them) are made of more enduring stuff. And it was this that entailed an analogous persistence of the deeper levels of the common culture and the 'public dimension' — of that overall calculus of present-day loss which Ascherson has expressed in *Stone Voices*, and Carol Craig in her recent study *The Crisis of Scots Confidence (2002)*.

I suspect the answer to both the obsession with stones and the absence of self-confidence lies at this level: on the interred plane of a foresworn state, and of those outer boundaries which Craig now mistakenly dismisses as secondary, or optional. Such identity-loss probably arose out of a decisive trauma immediately before the Treaty of Union: the total failure of the attempt at an independent Scottish empire, in the years 1697-1700. As many accounts have shown, the Darien Expedition was far more than a bit of failed trading-company business. In the words of its leader William Paterson: 'The Company . . . is calculat for the general interest of Our Nation . . . Our Nobility and gentry who are Landed men will get their rents better paid and raised; our Tenants and Labouring people better employed . . . the Poor will hereby find Work and Food'.[7] It is said to have called on about half the available capital of Scotland, and occurred in an economic context (the 'seven ill years') in which five percent of the Scottish population are believed to have *starved to death*.

The Project was to seize the isthmus joining North to South America, establish a Scottish trading company on the annexed territory, and exploit the East-West commerce that Paterson assumed would flourish in the 18th century. It was an attempt to make Scotland a serious player in the growing empire business, one that would count alongside the Netherlands, England, France and the other colonists of the time. The 'general interest' lay in the continuing independence of a state, in other words: the 'final gamble' (in Neal Ascherson's words) of chronically impoverished outlanders. Already habituated to emigration, they made a realistic assessment that, without overseas investment of their own, they would stand small chance of retaining any real autonomy. 'The mystery (Ascherson continues) is why Scots so seldom mention it . . .' I suspect the answer here does not lie in tragedy and failure alone. There are, after all, many examples of myths employing disasters for the purposes of a later nationalism (e.g. Australia's Anzac Day).

This *occlusion* of failure may have been because it could never fit in with the romantic reinterpretations that subsequently imposed themselves. Above all following 1745-6, suppression fitted best with vigorously expanding exile culture – the new migratory torrent of the British Empire. Devine's 'Highlandism' was an identity of exile comfort – the contrary of irredentism or redemption. For those carried off, or influenced, by the new modes of exile (i.e. almost everybody) there could be no real point in harking back to the lost gamble. By contrast, 1745-6 and Jacobitism proved relatively digestible, in the required ideological sense.

Liberals of the present day often say Scots didn't know about being occupied or colonized. But this was not true *then*. Paterson's (and Lockhart's) generation knew all too well what it was like. Only forty years before they had undergone an authentic, if short-lived, colonial occupation, and 'integration' into Oliver Cromwell's southern rule. They had seen the 'memory' of the Scots (the mediaeval court and state papers) seized and carried off to London (they were later lost at sea). The prolonged struggle of earlier centuries to avert English conquest was abruptly ended. And though the episode itself ceased with Charles II's return in 1660, its meaning as omen remained: it had shown how easily a determined England could impose its will, possibly for good. But the causes of the catastrophic failure at Darien (under-investment, ignorance, English sabotage, Spanish attacks) are not so important for the argument. It's the transcended results (and benefits) that became decisive, and deserve to be stressed here. The 'surrender' of statehood in 1707 was in truth a self-colonization charter, and the deal included some recompense for those who had lost their fortunes trying to stay independent nine years previously.

This was a political failure unique in the annals of Atlantic statehood — and with effects equally singular, and permanent. Farther defeat and colonization were then judiciously evaded by self-colonization: or in the terms used earlier, by identity-reconfiguration. By contrast, the Basques had also been determined emigrants and mercenaries, but in the 18th and 19th centuries they were able to 'stand aside' (as many commentaries put it) under the circumstances of a shrinking imperial domain. The Scots, on the other hand, could not avoid being borne forward by a ferociously expanding commercial and territorial one. An external or emigrant mind-set had been checked by state failure — to be then strongly reanimated by almost immediate incorporation into a much larger outward-directed enterprise: the British Empire. So the latter's effect was to transform an already existing tendency into something more dramatic : in effect a multi-generational *haemorrhage*. The original domestic society was re-constituted by ever mounting external pressures and opportunities. Modern, imperially-governed migration took over from the older kind, but with added impetus and great new incentives.

Logics of Loss

Seneca the Younger made some thoughtful remarks on migration two thousand years ago, in his essay *On the Shortness of Life*. In a letter to his mother Helvia, he comments how 'the word "exile" itself now enters the ear more harshly through a sort of conviction and popular belief, and strikes the listener as something gloomy and detestable'. Yet he recommends her to disregard such notions. People say 'it is unbearable to be deprived of your country' (he goes on) *but* —

> Come now, look at this mass of people whom the buildings of huge Rome can scarcely hold: most of that crowd are deprived of their country. They have flocked together from their towns and colonies, in fact from the whole world, some brought by ambition, some by the obligation of public office, some by the duties of an envoy, some by self-indulgence seeking a place conveniently rich in vice, some by a love of liberal studies, some by the public shows . . . Absolutely every type of person has hastened into the city which offers high rewards for both virtues and vices . . .

The mass of people in 1st century Rome, like that in 21st century Melbourne, Los Angeles, or London, show no signs of this being unbearable. Nor (he rubs the point in) does one get different signals from the countries of which they have been deprived. Reflecting on his own Iberia and the fate of Sicily, Seneca adds —

> In a word, you will hardly find a single country still inhabited by its original natives: everywhere the people are of mixed and imported stock. One group has followed another: one longed for what another scorned; one was driven out from where he had expelled others . . . there can be no place of exile within the world since nothing within the world is alien to men. [8]

His conclusion is rhetorical and over-wrought. But of course, the point behind it is genuine. Exile and migration have indeed been integral parts of history, from pre-history to the present, and assumed an equally great variety of shapes and consequences. The nexuses of communal identity are necessary, but also shifting, and malleable — another way of saying they're deep-cultural, rather than genetic, or in the blood-stream. In Karl Marx's sense, 'species-being' is nomadic *and* home-fixated: it identifies with Heimat so strongly — as in laments of deprivation and nostalgias of loss — because it is not instinctually forced to. Which is only another way of saying that human nature remains societal, rather than cloned, or birth-coded. The nexus of its 'second nature' may represent the Bible's 'coat of many colours', but no one should perceive these as fixed, immutable patches. The colours have always been flowing, partly and repeatedly interwoven and re-woven, a kaleidoscope rather than a stained-glass retrospect of past time.

In this perspective the Scots' communal destiny appears as comparable to that of the Greeks, the Jews and the Arabs: chronically impoverished margin-dwellers who were forced, by a mixture of geographic terrain and climate into outward-directed projects. For such edgeland societies, emigration was a long-term, formative fate. It came originally with sky, stone and deserts — wholly unlike the short-term opportunism of more recent imperial or colonizing states, in the 18th century and after. The latter expanded because of relatively sudden advantages, using the leverage furnished by industrial development and trade, and (later) military superiority. But in the Scottish case these two kinds of emigration came to be fused together, one on the back of the other. And the result was an inherited 'way of life' — a distinct and heritable identity-structure — assuming to this day many different forms, military, political, economic and cultural.

In *The Scottish Nation*, Tom Devine contends that Scotland emerges clearly as 'the emigration capital of Europe' in the later 19th and early 20th centuries (rather than Ireland or Norway, the other contenders). He goes on to echo the writer Edwin Muir's telling summary of what that entailed. This enormous haemorrhage of people from a small country 'meant it was gradually emptied of its population, its spirit, wealth, industry, art, intellect and innate character. If a country exports its most enterprising spirits and best minds year after year, for fifty or a hundred, or two hundred years, some result will inevitably follow.'

Today, Scotland lives with that result. For the haemorrhage is continuing, if not increasing. While most other European Union countries have immigrant problems, the Scots have an emigrant one: far from attracting a new population, their native one is fleeing faster than ever. [9] Some estimates have suggested the total population may drop well below its present five million. Devolved government has done nothing to alter these parameters, and may even have aggravated them. The same report on young Scots quoted below contained indications of their attitude towards the new politics: 'The research results contain devastating findings for politicians: 48% of 17 to 25s and 40% of 11 to 16s said politicians were among the people they trusted and respected least. Only one in six thought voting was an important aspect of citizenship'.

Ascherson notes how, when Boswell and Dr Johnson toured Scotland in 1773, 'they found the chiefs struggling to hold back a wave of enthusiasm to leave the country'. The famous Highland dance 'America' showed how 'emigration catches till all are set afloat', an allegory for what Johnson called 'the epidemical fury of emigration' (p.201). Were they to tour again today, would it be so different? Except that clan chiefs have been replaced by a worried Scottish Executive, still not quite happy calling itself 'Scottish Government'?

The Britannic Identity

Another similarity is bound to strike anyone, within this broader comparative perspective: homeland-exporters have often run into serious long-term problems with *the* homeland itself — that is, the inadequate turf-patch out of which they originally moved. Other societies also show how prolonged haemorrhage can end up not just by affecting but in a sense formed, or re-forming the source-land. The great Baltic emigration wave of mediaeval times suffered less from turf-problems: their countries were neither colonized, nor self-colonized like those in the British orbit. Norway, Sweden and Denmark emerged in later, nation-state times, and have undergone startling rebirths in the 20th century. Post-Hellenic Greece and post-Islamic Arabia, on the other hand, became important and often intractable 'national questions' over the last two hundred years. The second, of course, remains a series of unresolved 21st century dilemmas, from Iraq to Algeria. The same region has also been grievously complicated by the most extreme of all such 're-constituted homeland' problems: the literal 'reconstitution' of a Jewish state in Palestine, after a millenium of forced exodus and diaspora.

The reconstitution of a Scottish state is sometimes thought to have become unnecessary because of the vitality of Scotland's 'civil society' — a self-supporting social order, as it were, for which state politics has become redundant, or secondary. Delusions of this sort have been encouraged by the appearance of Arthur Herman's celebrated analysis, *How the Scots Invented the Modern World: the True Story of How Western Europe's Poorest Nation Created Our World and Everything in It* (2001). Herman suggested that the Edinburgh Enlightenment of Adam Smith, David Hume and the others accomplished a miracle. A politically dependent society managed to set modernity going, by civil self-motivation liberated from interference and regulation from above.

However, the perspective sketched out above allows an alternative view. The 'miracle' took place via a ruling class dispossessed of its previous powers, as a cultural compensation for loss. One might also say: as a continuation of outward migration by other means. An imperialism of the intellect replaced the one foiled at Darien, and then 'renegotiated' through the Treaty of Union. Scottish intellectuals dreamed up 'the modern world' *because* they had lost their own — and this was no less true of those who welcomed the 1707 Union. That loss was recent, and traumatic (unlike analogous failures or retreats suffered by the Greeks, the Jews and the Arabs). But it also took place in a significant window — on the very edge of 'modernity', as enabled by 17th century developments in science and applied science. The Enlightenment itself was not unprecedented: Hellenism and late-mediaeval pan-Arabism were precursors, as (more obviously) was the cultural manifestation of Jewish displacement in early-modern Europe. But no other episode was to be so favoured — practically immortalized— by the historical conjuncture that followed.[10]

As Herman describes it, the Scottish dream-projection was hugely successful. But he tends to view it the wrong way round— as part of a single Progress-tale culminating in the Neo-liberal, American-crowned triumph of the post-Cold War times. In reality, it was (in contemporary jargon) a 'comparative advantage' due to the accident of Scottish failure, followed by recovery within a rapidly developing British imperial project. The English didn't make the Edinburgh Enlightenment; but they undoubtedly provided the vehicle for its successful global export and impact. And emigration was the *Leitmotiv* carried forward from one phase into the next — the global expansiveness of that 'Britain' made fully possible by 1707, and then confirmed by military successes against the French *ancien régime* later in the century.

In her *Self Confidence* book Craig comments very perceptively on the 'extraverted' traits of much Scottish culture, and also upon a tendency to set curiously detached or abstract fantasies over against glum and greyly confining reality. But these can also be read as symbolic expressions of this long-term structural deformation. Among Scots, 'modernization' had produced a society not so much opened up as turned inside out — 'evacuated' at every level by successive waves of magnetism from the irresistible lodestar of 'the overseas', the permanent projection of distance and re-settlement. At bottom this projection relates not to the 'overseas' imperium alone, but to its driving force: the identity I call 'Britannic' above, since an old-fashioned term now expresses its decline more appropriately.

The mechanism of self-colonization was made possible by 'Britain', projected as the grander entity that not only reconciled the bitter enemies of earlier times, but was universal in tendency. It bore with it originally the promise, at least, of civilizational status and permanence, manifested in an actual command of the oceans and other places. After their final gamble, the Scots had to fall again under its wheels, or try to get aboard. And once aboard, they had to make themselves useful and welcome. For the latter course, the best strategy is that style of over-compensation I described already. The minority ('junior partner', etc.) makes sure of its rights by overdoing allegiance: in this case, by being more 'British' than the English. Representing over eighty per cent of the British Isles population, the latter did not have to work so hard at this identification problem: they assumed (and still do) that England and Britain mean much the same thing. But for the Welsh, the Northern Irish and above all the Scots, a lot of ideology was called for to make the system viable.

It still is being called upon. Indeed, as the United Kingdom declines into its own version of self-colonization (with the USA), a distinctly more Scottish edge has shown through London government. Under Blair's New Labour régime this has escalated to the point of being unmissable, and frequently deplored. Commenting on the 2005 election, for example, Australian journalist Peter Wilson underlines the possibility of Westminster becoming still more Scoticized:

Even before Mr Blair leant on the popularity and credibility of his more trusted Chancellor to help him win a third term in government, there were unhappy mutterings in England about the political influence of what some call a Scottish mafia, or Scottish Raj, ruling Britain . . . The Scots make up only 5 million of Britain's 60 million citizens but they are already massively over-represented in cabinet thanks to heavy-hitters like Mr Brown, the former health secretary and new Defence Secretary John Reid, Secretary of Transport Alistair Darling, party chairman Ian McCartney, and Secretary of Constitutional Affairs Lord Falconer. [11]

But the real reason for the salience is that, in this situation, Scots are more convincingly 'British' than their English colleagues. The latter are still liable to take the English-British alloy for granted. Mr Blair's 'trusted Chancellor', the Scot Gordon Brown, would never make this mistake. The English may mutter unhappily, but now have no separate political identity to fall back, other than the Britannic shell. Brown understands that he and his post-imperial ruling class can't long endure without that shell — the vehicle they boarded after 1707. It badly needs more armour-plating — just the kind of thing 'Scotch philosophers' have laboured at since the 18th century, and (he thinks) may still perpetuate in the 21st. [12]

But of course *this* is another 'final gamble': the opposite of the one some of Brown's ancestors probably supported over Darien, in 1698. Today's Scottish mafia has to defend the core of Britishness to the last, because its own existence depends upon it. Nor is this merely a matter of job-preservation, blind servility or Party fidelity: it goes without saying they're 'sincere' — that their adopted or surrogate national identity shows all the features of over-compensation and passionate embattlement I mentioned above. Such features are normally conceded (and often wrongly dismissed) in cases like the Reverend Ian Paisley and his DUP battalions in Ulster. What are these are but the genuine visage of Britain in her last ditch, as distinct from the well-meaning 6th form ramblings about principles and values so dear to Westminster's *intéllos*?

Identity Re-building

On the way to work each day my tram rumbles past the Scots Kirk in Collins Street, downtown Melbourne, just before the long downhill slope disclosing the city's more characteristic vista, a southern road straight to infinity. In the emigration, as at home, religion has been somehow too important in the support of national identity. Although the first free immigrants from Scotland only arrived in 1814, by 1839 Melbourne was 'a Scotch colony. Two-thirds of of the inhabitants are Scotch'. [13] The prominence of Kirk missionary activity was (as historian Gordon Donaldson noted) 'an outward-looking characteristic in some ways in accordance with the earlier traditions of the country', and distinct from those of the English. [14]

The prominence of such traits has the same logic as that of the homeland: 'civil society' as *substitute* for a national state and political identity. The kernel of validity in civil society mystification lay with this peculiar necessity. A grander philosophical deployment of the idea by Hegel and Marx then produced the socio-economic notion of 'civil' as meaning merely distinct, or partly separate, from the state. But in its post-1707 origins, it had been forced compensation for an agreed absence of the latter. A de-politicized society was forced to make up for this, by bestowing abnormal rigidity and normative force upon institutions. In such unusual conditions, 'surrender' had to mean surrogacy, and the terms of replacement were spelled out in failure's reward, the Treaty of Union. Many of the stabilizing and continuity-bonding functions which had elsewhere fallen to the Absolutist and post-Absolute states — the 'nation-state world' — now devolved upon it. A unique chain of mishaps, from Cromwell to Darien, was compelled to 'pass over' into subordinate institutions like religion, and the legal, property and educational systems.

And then, inevitably, this was exported, in living emigrants as well as in the famed and secular *rayonnement* of Smith, Hume and the rest of their cultural machine. 'A movement so vast in scope, so prolonged in time and so complex in its nature will clearly not admit of a single or a simple explanation', warned Gordon Donaldson forty years ago. Yet he himself goes on to identify precisely such a common and persistent trait: frustration. This *Angst* has changed its forms in time, but never the essence of wanderlust:

> The energetic Scot who felt that there was no outlet for his vitality at home had become a soldier of fortune on the continent of Europe in earlier times and was to become an eager and restless colonist later . . . (and) . . . The sense of community among so many Scots, and the readiness of Highlanders at least, to accept, or submit to, leadership. contributed to the making of emigration the mass movement it became. The 'epidemic' character of emigration, the snowballing effect which is discernible from time to time, were fostered by the cohesion of the family, of the kinship group, of the local community (*ibid.* pp.201-2 and 204-5)

Thus the celebrated localism and extended-family *habitus* of Scottish society served to boost a nomadic emigration, rather than to restrain it. Following 1707 there was nothing in between, and a bequeathed identity had to make the best of it. This was a version of 'species-being' in which the outward-going or migratory trait reconfigured *Heimat* itself, through force of circumstances. [15] It found one its strongest expressions in the writings of Robert Louis Stevenson. 'In his letters', notes biographer Ian Bell, '. . . there is a sense of suppressed energy, a though the mainspring of his imagination was overwound'. [16]

The converse of the Scottish configuration was an unnatural density and compression in the institutions forced to bear the burden. 'Civil society' could only be an effective substitute for nationhood by stiffening all its own sinews — by becoming an environment at once localized, over-normative and suffocating; which of course then multiplied the 'frustration' fuelling so much exit, and made haemorrhage seem quite natural. The odd lack of self-confidence lamented by Carol Craig and others derived less from the Kirk, than from the ridiculous weights placed upon it, as well as upon education, local government and other institutions. In that dismal sense, 'Scottishness' represented a partial rigor mortis of the collective identity, not a soul-blight remediable by either Jungian therapy or the willed cheerfulness of self-help. It implied that to 'be oneself' was a choice between chronically looking over one's shoulder, and flight; is it surprising that so many chose the latter for so long, or still do so? Or that 'devolution' has been in some ways simply a clearer awareness of this intolerable dilemma?

Each Scot carries a bit of the ancient State within him — or herself: a fragment of the true cross, as it were. It may also be seen as a small piece of Immanuel Kant's 'crooked timber', blessed by God and the British Crown: erstwhile State plus transcending aureole, the fading British surrogate neither renounceable nor (until recently) easily denounceable. [17] The stiffening effects of that common predicament have been indeed remarkable: as Craig has shown, suffocating sameness and a depreciative (or levelling-down) conformity have been part of the deal. And getting out of it has been the answer for a very long time, albeit in successive and differing waves. Devolution was intended to entrench this and other traditions, ensuring that progress would remain safely in Britannic hands. It has not been entirely unsuccessful in its aim.

My own emigrant fate has been to study the wider process of 21st century migration and mingling, 'globalization', in a research unit at Australia's MIT, the Melbourne Institute of Technology. This is a wonderful opportunity, in a city as great as Seneca's Rome, inter-war Paris or today's Los Angeles: 'no place of exile' as the Roman put it, in a world where indeed nothing is alien to men.

Yet I must admit something else occasionally surfaces, in Collins Street —
or it may be at the sound of an accent, or a turning on a country road where
the Southern Ocean comes suddenly into view. The feeling that rises is like
that in Gabriel Aresti's famous Basque poem 'The House of My Father' (1963):

> I shall die,
> my soul will be lost,
> my descendants will be lost;
> but the house of my father
> will endure
> on its feet.

Only, it's not so confident. It's like what Stevenson voiced this way: 'Where
I was standing . . . there went through me or over me a wave of extraordinary
and apparently baseless emotion. I literally staggered . . . And then the
explanation comes, and I knew I had found a frame of mind and body that
belonged to Scotland . . . Very odd these identities of sensation, and the world
of connotations implied . . . and that indescribable bite of the whole thing at
a man's heart, which is — or rather lies at the bottom of — a story'.[18] The
feeling is inseparable from a shiver of loss and apprehension; for the fact is,
our father's house did not endure. It was reduced to permitted foundations
for so long, that reconstruction is difficult. So getting it 'on its feet' demands
a reorientation of the will, not just of policies and principles. and though it is
at last being rebuilt, too many fled it for far too long, and it's returning into a
time of huge changes and uncertainty.

Crooked Timber: a Future?

However inadvertently, Devolution has at least opened new doors, and with
its leaven of democracy made the return of real self-rule conceivable. A re-
building of national identity is under way, and on one way or another is
likely to restore statehood, and demand (at least) a rewriting of the Treaty of
Union, if not its abandonment. So how will this affect exiles and emigration?
And how could they affect it?

One answer is suggested by another of Donaldson's conclusions. 'With
all their successes', he wrote —

> . . . in so many walks of life, the impression the Scots have made on the new
> English-speaking nations overseas has been curiously limited . . . Here the Scots'
> capacity for assimilation comes in: when transplanted from his homeland he seems
> to find no difficulty in accustoming himself to unfamiliar terms and institutions.
>
> (*ibid.* p.207)

For communities assimilated to that extent, and with a diminishing 'Highlandism' as their main ethnic resort, it could be thought that the re-emergence of a homeland state might mean very little. All the less, perhaps, since it's happening under the new conditions of globalism, often held to imply less significance for all nation-states, new or old?

I doubt it. It is economists' mythology to believe the globalization has such consequences. The reality is already beginning to appear quite differently, and I suspect that something closer to the opposite may be true.[19] The closure of the world generates a greater thirst for identity, rather than the feared effacement of 'economic man' and woman. This fear is authentic, and it is surely no chance that all dystopias from Huxley's *Brave New World* down to the *Matrix* film trilogy have expressed the same thing. It goes to the heart, *le coeur du mystère* that anthropologist Emmanuel Todd evokes in his recent study of passing American power, *Après l'empire* (2002).

'Identity' is not an individual trait, but a unique individual-societal nexus: it depends upon diversity, the wider differentiation formed through communities — and above all, extra-familiar communities. Being 'oneself' relies on this formative nexus, and hence on a particular community of language and emotion. Seneca noted that one such community may give way to another, or others: once constituted, the nexus is movable, or displaceable, whether the switch be chosen or forced — emigration, or exile. And this may be gain, as well as loss. However, what is non-negotiable is *some* particular origination, as distinct from formation by general or universal rules (which would amount to 'cloning').

Diversity was interpreted by the 20th century idea of 'ethnicity' as something inherited, or given by a past out of mind — hence fixed, and to be transcended by the present. But the circumstances of globality force us to see more clearly there was nothing fixed about it: the fantastic cultural diversity of 'species-being' has always been 'under construction'. It simply happens that, at any given moment, most preceding phases of the process are hidden from its participants, and hence seem fixed, or 'essential' — not merely handed down but consecrated and permanent. But the process itself remains kaleidoscopic and continuing. And *this* is what globalization has to protect, or even to intensify. Because so much more will now be held in common, the sources of diversity will have at least to keep pace with it.

Literature finds it easier to voice this than social science — as for example in Alistair MacLeod's *No Great Mischief* (2000), a novel about the Scots of Cape Breton in Canada. In Chapter 23 one of them recounts (through someone else's voice) a return visit to Highland Scotland, where she got soaking wet in the 'rough bounds' of Moidart. People gather round to assist her, speaking Gaelic, and she suddenly feels she 'had been away from the language for such a long, long time', and replies in it:

> I don't even remember what I said, the actual words or the phrases. It was like it just poured out of me, like some subterranean river that had been running deep within me and suddenly burst forth. And then they all began speaking at once...as if they were trying to pick up a distant but familiar radio signal even as they spoke. We spoke without stopping . . . And then all of us began to cry. All of us sobbing, either standing or sitting on our chairs in Moidart. 'It is as if you had never left', said the old man. 'Yes', said the others all at once, 'as if you had never left'.

The point isn't that it was Gaelic (or, elsewhere in *No Great Mischief*, québecois French). Nor is it that the narrator is somehow disqualified or prevented from being also Canadian. Such rivers run deep within everyone, and are inseparable from shaping emotions which come out of kinship and inform everything else. The radio signals of familiarity become intermingled with others, yet go on influencing how the latter are received and interpreted. This is how deeper attitudes and mind-sets are passed on, and why they endure so long, and are transformed in so many different ways. 'Old clothes' indeed; yet without them the individual would be not so much naked as inexistent. In time, they become like underwear, beneath new uniforms like 'Canada' and 'Britain'. After three fairly lengthy experiences of emigration, to Italy, the Netherlands and Victoria, I've endured my share of the Moidart-effect — most strongly in the English-speaking environment of Melbourne.

And this is why I suspect that re-constituting a Scottish state would affect our vast emigration rather deeply. Because the fate of emigrant communities is less in the blood and more in political negotiation, most emigrants remain partly conditioned by homeland development (sometimes by fighting yesterday's battles rather than today's). Melbourne's Slavs go on re-fighting the post-Yugoslav wars, while its Greeks enjoy re-running the Cypriot debacle, usually with some more satisfactory conclusion. The Scots haven't been kept going by this kind of thing, but there are positive sides to that as well. Having no homeland in the requisite sense, they have of course been more affected by the Empire's misfortunes and long decline; this relates to Donaldson's point about their relative invisibility, or adaptability. They may have done little to assist nationalism at home, because it wasn't part of their culture of exile. On the other hand, this doesn't mean they would not respond to a recreated state-country without so many burdens of resentment, and less affected by the scars of conflict and irredentism. [20] I'm assuming here that a reasonably 'velvet' divorce or separation will be possible, most probably via farther advance in devolution *and* new political and constitutional reforms at the Westminster centre.

So far, the devolved parliamentary regime has had little success in healing the old haemorrhage by attracting natives back; but a more independent country might do much better. All the wrong way round, of course: but then, hasn't that been the underlying story, all the way from Darien down to Jack McConnell and Gordon Brown? As Bell puts it in that study of Stevenson quoted earlier: 'The task is to take the story forward — to give it sense, to follow it to the finish. So must we.' (p.21)

References

1   On *Wide World*, see the comprehensive account on the Australian website www.collectingbooksandmagazines.com It was a widely read illustrated publication famous for tall tales, edited by Victor Pitt-Kethley from the 1930s up until 1965. The most notorious series it published was by one 'Louis de Rougemont', who claimed to have spent years roaming the Australian outback with a tribe of cannibal aborigines.

2   See Don Watson's study of Victorian Gippsland, *Caledonia Australis: Scottish Highlanders on the Frontier of Australia* (1985).

3   *The Scottish Nation 1700-2000* (2000) pp. 244-5

4   In his contemporary ballad the 'Freedom-Come-All-Ye', often regarded as an anthem of democratic or left-wing Scotland.

5   'Memoirs Concerning the Affairs of Scotland from 1702 to 1715', from *The Lockhart Papers* vol. 1 (1817), pp.249-261. The text is also in *Scotland's ruine: Lockhart of Carnwath's memoirs of the Union* (Association for Scottish Literary Studies, 1995). Like all concerned with the subject, I owe a great deal to the invaluable pages on 'Emigration' in Michael Lynch's *Oxford Companion to Scottish History* (2001), pp.228-234, by David Herbert, Owen Dudley Edwards and Marjorie Harper.

6   I recently tried to analyze 'self-colonization' at greater length, in a consideration of Scottish historian Niall Ferguson's work on the British and American Empires: see the Open Democracy website at: www.opendemocracy.net – link under my name in search box.

7   As cited in Michael Lynch's *Scotland: a New History* (1991), 'Darien and the seven ill years', pp.307-310.

8   Penguin Books 'Great Ideas' edition (2004)

9   'One in three young Scots would leave the country if they got the chance, according to the most comprehensive survey ever undertaken of the nation's youth. Even more – one in two – could imagine moving away in the future. The study, Our Lives, Our Scotland, was conducted for YouthLink Scotland by Mori Scotland from May to July this year. More than 3000 people between the ages of 11 and 25 were interviewed and answered questionnaires.' *Sunday Herald*, by Stephen Naysmith, October 19 2003. *The Scotsman* of April 5 2005 revealed that: 'The SNP today released figures predicting that Scotland's population will suffer a drop of 1.4 million by 2073. The statistics stated the number of people in Scotland would decline from five million in 2004 to 3.6 million in 2073 - a drop of 27 per cent. And over the same period the UK's population will increase by 11 per cent, according to the forecast which the SNP said it had obtained from the Government Actuary Department.'

10   On the history of 'civil society', see the present writer's 'Civil Society: a Scottish Myth', in *Liber*   quarterly, June 1995 (pp.141-144), and also Krishan Kumar's much more extensive indictment in *The British Journal of Sociology*, vol 44, No.3, September 1993.

11   *The Australian* May 2005

12   See the April 2005 issue of *Prospect* magazine, where Brown held forth at length on the supposed values and ideals of Britannic civilization and identity, just before the election. This pitiable diatribe served mainly to emphasize the bankruptcy of his government and its policies. But behind it lay a party-spirit linked inexorably to maintaining British identity (and therefore his own), after a Middle-Eastern war devoted to the same purpose. A month later he and Blair were re-elected in the most depraved and unrepresentative contest of modern times — I'm quoting the Electoral Reform Society's verdict, as well as that of Iain Macwhirter,

Scotland's leading political journalist — see *Sunday Herald*, May 8th 2005, 'The Most Unfair Election in British History'.

13 Margaret Kiddle, *Men of Yesterday* (Melbourne University Press 1961). A similar interpretation can be found in the Presbyterian Malcolm D. Prentis's study *The Scottish in Australia* (Latrobe, 1987, Australian Ethnic Heritage Series).

14 *The Scots Overseas* (1966), p.21

15 A recent general history where the theme constantly surfaces is Michael Fry's *The Scottish Empire* (2002), an account based on distinguishing the English and Scottish motives for colonization and settlement.

16 *Dreams of Exile: a Biography* (1992), an interpretation of Stevenson stressing the role of exile in his later creative personality. For 'RLS', he shows, 'The three things that mattered were: illness, Scotland and travel . . . ' The result was 'an ambivalent exile' similar to that of many others; 'Scotland's exiles have always defined their country. The nation has a relationship of mutual ambivalence with its diaspora; less love and hate than love and valediction; a prolonged goodbye' (pp.13-14)

17 'Out of the crooked timber of humanity no straight thing was ever made' (*Gesammelte Schriften*, Berlin, 1900) vol.8, pp.201-206. The phrase was constantly quoted by Isaiah Berlin in his essays, e.g. The Proper Study of Mankind (New York, 1997-8) Foreword, p.xv, and 'In Pursuit of the Ideal'. p.16

18 As quoted in Frank McLynn's *Robert Louis Stevenson: a Biography* (1993), p.476, from the 'Baxter Letters'.

19 One very helpful study of this is *Economic Nationalism in a Globalizing World* (Cornell U.P. 2005), edited by Eric Helleiner and Andreas Pickel. From the angle indicated here, Patricia Goff's essay on 'Geography and identity' and Jacqui True's on New Zealand are probably the most interesting. But Helleiner's study of Quebec, 'Why would Nationalists Not Want a National Currency?' is also very relevant.

20   In *The Break-up of Britain* (1977, new edition 2003, from Common Ground
     Publishing, Melbourne) and *After Britain* (1998, Granta Books) I tried to
     explain the weakness and belatedness of political nationalism in Scotland
     in terms of internal social factors, like the role of the intelligentsia and of
     Scottish institutions. But both these efforts, and most of the criticism
     they attracted, were weakened by inadequate grasp of what national-
     ism was about. In retrospect, I think we all confused the ideologies of
     1870-1989 with more profound traits of nationality and culture — those
     factors that long preceded the imperial era, and have survived into the
     successor period of globalization. These are not 'primordial ' in any
     essentializing sense, but do belong in various *longues durées* that do go
     back as far as anyone can at present decipher.

Alasdair Gray

Born Glasgow, 28th December 1934

WRITER AND PICTURE MAKER

Saltire Book of the Year, Lanark, 1982

Self Portrait

10.30pm, Monday the 18th May, 1987

According to my birth certificate I am 52 years, 167 days, 40 minutes old. According to my passport I am 1.74 metres or 5 feet 9 ¼ inches tall. According to the scales in the lavatory I weigh 13 stones 7 pounds in my socks, semmit, underpants, bath robe, national health spectacles and false upper teeth: from all of which a doctor will deduce I am not in the best of health. I have the lean, muscular legs and small bum of the brisk pedestrian but the bulging paunch of the heavy drinker, the fleshy shoulders hunched too near the ears of the asthmatic with bronchial tendencies. The neck is thick; hands and feet and genitals small; the chin strong and double with the underside not yet grossly pendulous; the moustache pale sand colour; the straight nose survives from the years when I was thin all over; the eyes are small and sunken with blue-grey irises; the brow straight and not deeply lined; the hair of the scalp is fading from the nondescript brown to nondescript grey and thinning behind a slightly eroded scalpline. In repose the expression of the face is as glum as that of most adults. In conversation it is animated and friendly, perhaps too friendly. I usually have the over-eager manner of one who fears to be disliked. When talking freely I laugh often and loudly without being aware of it. My voice (I judge from tape-recordings) is naturally quick and light, but grows firm and penetrating when describing a clear idea or recollection: otherwise it stammers and hesitates a lot because I am usually reflecting on the words I use and seeking to improve and correct them. When

I notice I am saying something glib, naïve, pompous, too erudite, too optimistic, or too insanely grim I try to disarm criticism by switching my midland Scottish accent to a phony form of Cockney, Irish, Oxbridge, German, American or even Scottish.

At present I sit on a low comfortable chair in the room where most of my work and sleeping is done. I wear the aforementioned socks, semmit, etcetera, and am being painted by Michael Knowles B.A. (Hons), a quiet-spoken English artist living in Edinburgh who hopes to sell the portrait to the Royal Scottish Museum. I like and fear the idea of becoming a thing with a lifeless public shape, but obviously like it more than fear it for I am embalming myself in words for the Saltire Self-Portrait Series while Mr Knowles paints me doing so. I had planned to start less blatantly with a platitude everyone would accept, a platitude told in rhyme to make it seem original. I would then cunningly shift to an account of the people who made me, using old certificates and memories but mostly some pages I once asked my father to write about his early life. I was reading these pages an hour ago when Mr Knowles arrived. I laid them down, we arranged the furniture to let the window-light fall equally on me and on his canvas, then the pages could not be found, though we rummaged for them in all the places I could think of and a few where they could not possibly be. From childhood this habit of slyly, casually hiding valued objects from myself has deprived me, sometimes permanently, of money, travel, tickets, useful tools, keys, paintings, notebooks, manuscripts and appliances to assist breathing when the asthma is bad. A psychiatrist once suggested these losses were caused by a hidden wish to attract attention and get proofs of love from those close to me. I doubt it. I have often inflicted such accidents on myself when nobody is close and nobody notices. The cause is surely that sneaking appetite for disaster which Edgar Alan Poe calls *The Imp of the Perverse* and associates with alcoholism, irrational vertigo and procrastination. The older Freud calls it *The Death Wish*, perhaps too sweepingly. It has done me no lasting harm. Perhaps a defective grasp of solid externals is sometimes not caused by unconscious will, but by too much reflecting on mental innards. I'll find the lost pages eventually (for they are certainly within arm's reach) and use them to add dignity to an otherwise selfish narrative.

Meanwhile, what am I for? What does this ordinary-looking, eccentric-sounding, obviously past-his-best person exist to do apart from eat, drink, publicise himself, get fatter, older and die? Stars, herbs and cattle exist without reasons, they fit the universe wherever they occur without the need of language to maintain their forms, but a born human has no foreseeable shape.   It is turned into a Chinese housewife, a Neolithic hunter, an unemployed car mechanic or Ludwig von Beethoven by an always changing *when* and *where* pressing on a unique yet always ripening or rotting bundle of traits: traits joined by a painfully conscious need to both stay the same and grow different. This need generates ideas, arts, sciences, laws and a host of excuses, because one of our traits is garrulity.   Even in sleep we talk wordlessly to ourselves. So what are you for, Gray?

At present I do not know.   Until a few years ago I wanted to make stories and pictures. While writing or painting I forgot myself so completely that I did not want to be any different.   I felt I was death's equal.

We live and have lived, die and will die in this place
and millions have been and will be forgotten
with hearts and faces we struggle to keep
until folded in sleep or gone rotten
and most, before dying, give blood to son or daughter
and when the bones of these children crumble, remain
not even memories — names cut on stones, perhaps:
otherwise we are a procession as featureless as water

unless we get into a lasting image or repeatable pattern of words.   But the most necessary and typical people are seldom commemorated in art and history which whore after the rich, the disastrous, the eccentric and love, above all, monstrous folk with one ability, one appetite so magnified that they seem mere embodiments of it — that is how our heroes and gods get made. I tried to tell convincing stories by copying into them pieces of myself and people I knew, cutting, warping and joining the pieces in ways suggested by imagination and the example of other story-makers, for I wanted to amuse, so my stories contain monsters.   I do not decry them for that, but I have no new ideas for more.   Can I entertain with some of the undistorted facts which generated them?

Early last century a Scottish shepherd whose first name is now unknown fathered William Gray, a shoemaker who fathered Alexander Gray, a blacksmith in Bridgeton, east Glasgow, a district then brisk with foundries, potteries and weaving sheds.   And Alexander married Jeanie Stevenson, powerloom weaver and daughter of a coalminer, who became his housewife and bore another Alexander, who became a clerk on a weighbridge on a Glasgow dock, then a private in the Black Watch regiment in France, then a quartermaster sergeant there, then worked a machine which cut cardboard boxes in a Bridgeton factory until another world war began. While some of this was happening Hannah, wife of a Northampton hairdresser called William Fleming bore Henry Fleming who became a foreman in a boot-making factory, and married Emma Minnie Needham. Henry, nicknamed Harry, also became a trade-unionist, and his bosses put his name on a list of men not to be employed in English factories. He and Minnie came to Glasgow where she bore Amy Fleming who first became a shop assistant in a clothing warehouse, then married Alex Gray the folding box maker, thus becoming a housewife. She and Alex lived in Riddrie, a Glasgow corporation housing scheme where she bore Alasdair James Gray who became a maker of imagined objects, and Mora Jean Gray who became a physical exercise and dance teacher in Aberdeen, and married Bert Rolley from Portsmouth, a chemist who analysed polluted water. Alasdair Gray married Inge Sorenson, a nurse in an Edinburgh Hospital, thus making her a housewife in Glasgow, though only for 9 years; and she bore Andrew Gray who became a supplies clerk in a Royal Air Force base near Inverness. But long before Mora and Alasdair got married all the workers preceding them in this crowded little tale were dead, excepting their father Alexander. After cutting cardboard for 21 years he became manager of a hostel for munition workers, then a builder's labourer, a wages clerk, a persuader of hoteliers to subscribe to the Scottish Tourist Board, a remover of damaged chocolate biscuits from a conveyer belt, a wages clerk again, a warden and a lecturer for the Scottish Youth Hostels Association, a guide to walkers over mountainous parts of Scotland, England and Wales, and finally a house-husband in a polite little town called Alderly Edge in Cheshire, England, where he died a month before his 75th year on the fourth March 1973.

Here follow some of my dad's earliest memories, starting with memories of his own dad. I have cut out five conjunctions, replaced two pronouns by the nouns themselves and added three commas and a period. Nothing else is changed.

NOTES ON EARLY LIFE IN GLASGOW by Alexander Gray

My Father was the product of an age when children left school at 10 years and were sent to sea to learn the ways of the world. He served on two voyages, one when the crew were men released from Barlinnie Prison to man the sailing vessel, while on the second the ship had to leave Cuba because of the war with USA. On reaching home he was made drunk by the crew (he being a popular cabin boy) and taken home were his Mother found him at the door, sitting on his box, the crew members having knocked on the door and run off. That ended his sea-fairing education.

By the age of 25 years Father must have become a blacksmith. He had made two journeys to London from Glasgow, working his way from casual job to job, for walking was his passion and recreation. He had married, had two sons, William and James, after which his wife died. He married again and I was his third son by his second wife and I had a sister Agnes. He died in 1921 aged 70. His grandfather was a shepherd on the Earl of Home's estate at Douglas Water. His Father was a high class bootmaker whose shop was in (now) London Road near Glasgow Cross.

My Mother came from a mining family in Wishaw. I had several Uncles and Aunts from both sides of the family and it was our Sunday afternoon and evening visitations to them or being visited by them that provided the changes in the domestic routine, for all were within walking distance or tram distance from home in Bridgeton.

My early recollections were of our room and kitchen in a street off Main Street, Bridgeton, in a dirty grey tenement of three storeys. My step-brothers slept in the room while Father and Mother slept in the kitchen bed. Agnes and I slept in the hurley bed, kept below the kitchen bed during the day and rolled out at night. The lighting was by gas on a long piped bracket fixed to the mantelpiece, which could be angled to suit a reader. The light was poor not white as was later the case when gas mantles were introduced, first by vertical mantles and later by the small mantles now used on calor-gas lamps. The fire-place was blackleaded with the door handles and fire-irons in polished steel, the polishing of them being my weekly job, together with the oval dishcovers which hung on the kitchen wall below the shelves of the crockery and other dishes.   In front of the window in the kitchen was the jaw-box or sink with the brass water pipe, another of the weekly polishing jobs, which provided the cold water.

Father worked in a smiddy some 10 minutes walk from home, which lay between the Clyde and French Street.   These were the days when work started at 6am and breakfast was taken during a break about 8am. Midday dinner was around 1pm and work ended around 6pm. Father would have a cup of tea and buttered bread before work and return for a breakfast of porridge, an egg or other "kitchen" (cooked food like bacon or sausage). Dinner was of soup or broth, meat, potatoes, veg. followed by a milk pudding or fruit. Tea would be bread, tea bread, scones, cheese and tea, while supper would be porridge or peas brose.   During school holidays, Father would have his dinner at the smiddy and I carried his soup in a can and his main course in plates tied in a towel. There I would pump the bellows so fast that the fire would blaze. Sometimes I would look over the wooden fence to Auld Shawfield, the football ground of Clyde before they moved to the site of the present stadium and I can remember seeing players in red shirts running around, though whether training or playing a match I cannot remember.

When the season for running girds[1] came around, Father would make iron girds and cleeks* for my friends and me and we would make the iron ring as we ran round the streets in Bridgeton or made expeditions to the Sauny Waste, the open ground in the loop of the Clyde upstream from Dalmarnock Bridge. From the short street which gave access to works and a piggery on the Rutherglen bank, an earth path followed the river bank. It was uneven, with hills and dales which required skill with the gird to maintain an uninterrupted run. Hills and hollows of sand filled the river's loop in the middle of which was a flat hollow where we could play football. Often at the two ends of the loop a man would be on the lookout for the police for in some hollow there would be a pitch and toss school of some two dozen men. In the centre a man would swing a leather belt to keep the ring clear, while one man would be laying the bets with the surrounding crowd, another would be balancing two pennies on a sliver of wood or his fingers as a preliminary to tossing them high in the air to descend as head or tail, as two tails or two heads. A head and tail was a neutral toss and it had to be repeated till they both came down head or tails. With tails the crowd was happy at its win and with heads put up with a loss in the hopes that the tosser could not continue in a winning vein forever. We small boys were not welcomed to such a ring, but we would crawl through the grass to the rim of the hollow and peep down over the heads of the gamblers and run when we were spotted, to return to our street by the river bank or the joining street. Football was of course our favourite pastime. The streets were cobbled, the ball did not run true or stot in the expected angle, except when the wall of the houses was used when passing an opponent and the lamp posts were the goals. When each team was of two or three, the near posts on each side of the street would be used, but if more boys were available, two near posts on the same side would be used thus providing a longer pitch. Such football was not looked upon with pleasure by the folks who lived on the ground

---

* A gird was a thin hoop, originally a barrel hoop, at least waist-high to the child racing it but the bigger the better. A cleek was a short iron rod ending in a hook or ring enabling the racer to drive the hoop. The pleasure of this was the pleasure of running as fast as a big wheel running beside you, a wheel which depended on your skill for it to turn corners, avoid obstacles and leap over holes without either of you losing speed or falling down.

level and sometimes by those above, for windows could be and were broken. Sometimes a policeman would appear so the ball was snatched up and we all disappeared up the various closes to cross the intervening walls of the backcourts to adjoining streets and freedom. Leave-O or kick the can were alternatives to football, while the girls either had wooden hoops or peever and beds, or hop-scotch. Sometimes selected girls would play with the boys at hide and seek and the closes and dunnies provided scope for initiative in avoiding discovery.

Father and Mother were deeply religious. Father was involved in the creation of the Congregational Union, i.e. the union of Congregational Churches.* He sometimes took the pulpit when the Minister was ill, was superintendent of the Sunday School, an elder, and when a new church, Dalmarnock Road CC, was created, gave some seven years service as church officer as his donation to the new church. Mother, because the Minister's wife was an invalid, was President of the Mothers Meeting. Both were to my mind examples of Christian living for they not only observed the daily observancies but in their treatment of people of all religions or none, were helpful and kind and tolerant. We had grace at all meals, and each night before retiring to bed, Father would read the daily lesson from the Bible and Mother would say a prayer or the roles would be reversed and sometimes I or Agnes would be asked to take part in the service.

Father and Mother were both mild of temper. I never heard them raise their voices in discussion or argument between themselves or with others. These days in the first years of this century had no social security or health insurance and doctors bills had to be avoided. I remember Father coming home with his face and hands bandaged after he had been splattered with molten lead at work. He came from hospital where he had the pieces of lead picked from his skin, had his dinner and went back to work. On another occasion when our home had been burgled and drawers and dressers and cupboards ransacked and clothing etc taken, he returned home to learn of the theft. His first thought was for his working clothes and all he said was "Well, they have left me the best suit, the one I need for my work". After 40 years with the same firm he reached the age of 65 and was told he was getting too old for his work as a blacksmith. Without warning he was handed his

* The Congregational Church was the church of Cromwell and Milton. and for a short time during the Protectorate almost became the legally established church of England though it more clearly resembled the established church of Scotland in its lack of liturgy and ornament. But Church of Scotland clergy ordain each other and are partly paid from the revcnues of the state. Congregational clergy are ordained and supported by their congregations.

weekly wage, which I don't think ever exceeded 30 shillings, and thanked for his long and useful service and was given the advice to look for a lighter job. His hand was shaken by the owner, and he left, knowing that at his age he would not be able to get a tradesman's job. His last five years of labour was a hammerman to blacksmiths at Stewart & Lloyds at Rutherglen, much heavier work than the men he worked for. I never heard him complain. He was a teetotaller and did not smoke. His weekly spending was for butter scotch, the odd tram fare when on his Saturday afternoon walk. Often he would rise on Sunday morning and walk up to ten miles before going to church at 11 am. Before I played football on Saturday afternoons he would take me on walks along the paths round or over the hills which surround Glasgow, the paths which Alexander McDonald wrote about in *Rambles Round Glasgow*. When Mother, after an illness, spent a week at Strathaven, Father and I walked there and back each Saturday having taken the tram to Cambuslang.

One of my treats was to be taken to Celtic Park by Uncle John, who was Mother's brother and manager of the newside at Beardmores' furnaces. The oldside was hand-fed furnaces, where Uncle Tom was the leading hand. Both lived at Parkhead: I still can hear the hush of the thousands on the terraces as Jimmy Quinn barged his way toward goal with his opponents floored by his strong shoulders to be followed by the roar which exploded when he cannoned the ball into the net.

Mother was good with her hands. She knitted, crocheted, made jam and baked and had time for church work. Her contribution to the family purse always ensured that at Glasgow Fair the Grays had a week's holiday. Never once did we stay at home at that time. Occasionally we also had a day Doon the Watter* on other days of holiday.

In politics my Father was a radical liberal, though he never was active as a political worker. He knew Keir Hardie and was instrumental in getting K.H. to speak at Dalmarnock Congregational Church where the Minister at that time was the Rev. Forson. Incidentally Father had a bible class at the Sunday School and from his class came the two Graingers who later were medical doctors in Bridgeton and three Forsons, all of whom became ministers in Congregational churches, one of whom became minister to Father's own church.

---

* This was a trip by paddle-steamer on the river from the centre of Glasgo to one of the many resorts on the Firth of Clyde and its islands; the trippers usually returning the same day in the same ship.

I went to John Street Higher Grade School as an infant and later in the higher school, where I was a mediocre scholar, being better with my feet and hands than with my head. I remember the celebrations when George VII* became King. We each received a small box with the heads of the King and Queen embossed on the lid. We were marched from school to Glasgow Green for fun, games and sport, but what I did is now beyond me. Glasgow Green was not only where football was played, part was the bleaching field and the nearby folk after the weekly washing would spread out or hang their clothes and water them for the sun to make them white. It was nearby what was to become the Greenhead Baths. It was also here where we school children were taken for swimming lessons. We would line up outside, having raced for first place from school to the baths where we prepared by partially undressing so that no time would be lost in the boxes beside the pool.

Every New Year all the Stevenson family visited Granny who lived above a wide pen just beyond the present Tramway Garage at Parkhead. All the Uncles and Aunts and their children were present, four families in all. The youngsters sat down first and had steak pie followed by plum pudding in large helpings. They were sent out to play while the parents had their dinner. Through the pen there was a large gable end where we played hand ball. We picked sides and each side in turn had to hit the ball against the gable end, the ball being hit after it stotted once on the ground. The side which failed to do so, that is return the ball to the wall after one stot, lost a point and the side reaching perhaps 10 points lost the game. Once the elders finished washing up after the meal, we all returned to the house and games and song passed the afternoon, each person reciting or singing his or her party piece.

It was on Sunday that the morning coats were worn for church. Father, Bill who was church organist and choir master, and Jim, who sang in the choir (he also sang in the Orpheus Choir) wearing their tall hats. When Father died in 1921 I was an out-patient at Bellahouston Hospital, a military hospital, being given treatment following a war wound. In order to maintain the dignity of the family at the funeral I also had to get a morning coat and tall hat.

END OF ALEXANDER GRAYS NARRATIVE

---

* This is an error. My father muddled Edward VII who was crowned in 1902 with George V who was crowned in 1910.

You are reading this pamphlet because you are interested in Alasdair Gray, the maker of imagined objects, so I am sorry this essay is a preface to an autobiography instead of a sketch for one, as I intended. I am too fond of precise details to be capable of a broad quick sketch. Yet my father's self-negating account of his family — even the style of his language — tells much about those who made me, though the gentle radical blacksmith who taught Congregational clergymen died thirteen years before I was born and I don't know when his wife died. I first learned of them in my late teens, when I had bouts of asthma which sometimes made me feel all life and history was a bad disease, a disease which could only be cured by a god of love in whom I had no faith. My father was a radical atheist who believed, with Marx, that humanity would one day solve every problem it had the sense to recognise. As he could not persuade me of this he tried to help by introducing me to the god of his parents in words which respected both their faith and his own. I made a note of these words (which told some things his later account does not) and eventually paraphrased them in the 26th chapter of a very long novel:

> My father was elder in a Congregational church in Bridgeton: a poor place now but a worse one then. One time the well-off members subscribed to give the building a new communion table, an organ and coloured windows. But he was an industrial blacksmith with a big family. He couldnae afford to give money, so he gave ten years of unpaid work as church officer, sweeping and dusting, polishing the brasses and ringing the bell for services. At the foundry he was paid less the more he aged, but my mother helped the family by embroidering tablecloths and napkins. Her ambition was to save a hundred pounds. She was a good needlewoman, but she never saved her hundred pounds. A neighbour would fall sick and need a holiday or a friend's son would need a new suit to apply for a job, and she handed over the money with no fuss or remark, as if it were an ordinary thing to do. She got a lot of comfort from praying. Every night we all kneeled to pray in the living room before going to bed. There was nothing dramatic in these prayers. My father and mother clearly felt they were talking to a friend in the room with them. I never felt that, so I believed there was something wrong with me. Then the 1914 war started and I joined the army and heard a different kind of prayer. The clergy on all sides were praying for victory. They told us God wanted our government to win and was right there behind us, with the generals, shoving us forward. A lot of us in the trenches let God go at that time. But Duncan, all these airy-fairy pie-in-the-sky notions are nothing but aids to doing what we want anyway. My parents used Christianity to help them behave decently in a difficult life. Other folk used it to justify war and property. But Duncan, what men believe isn't important — it's our actions which make us right or wrong. So if a God can comfort you, adopt one. He won't hurt you.

This speech — or, to be accurate, the words it paraphrases did not help me at the time, for words cannot cure a physical pain unless they are a sort of hypnotism. But when my health mended it helped me believe what I still mainly believe: that original decency is as old as original sin and essentially stronger: that those who pray are consciously strengthening wishes which (whether selfish or not) are already very strong in them, and which decide the nature of the god they invoke.

I swear that the above quotation contains no inventions of mine, just two bits, of condensing and one exaggeration: I turned 7 years of voluntary service into 10. It also contains an image I used in another piece of writing: the image of a small boy at family prayers who suspects he is at fault because he feels God is not with him. This became part of *The Fall of Kelvin Walker*, a play I wrote in 1964 which was televised by the BBC in 1968 and published as a novel in 1985. This is a fable about a monstrously pushy young Scot getting rich quickly in London. He is buoyant with energies released by his escape from a nastily religious father who has used the god of Calvin like a rubber truncheon to batter his children into submission. Neither father nor son in that fable much resemble my father, or his father, or me, and none of the incidents in it befell any of us. When copying a thing from the experience of myself or acquaintances I often gave it a context like the one where it happened, and often did not. My most densely and deliberately autobiographical writing is in books 1 and 2 of *Lanark*. Apart from the encounter with the Highland minister, the encounter with the prostitute, the fit of insanity and the suicide, nearly every thought and incident is copied from something real in context where it happened, but so much of my life was not copied that *Lanark* tells the story of a youngster estranged by a creative imagination from family, friends, teachers and city. I hope this is a convincing tragedy, though it never befell me. My family and at least half my schoolteachers deliberately encouraged my imagination. They did it in a Scottish way, allowing me the materials and almost all the time I wanted to paint and write in, never praising me to my face but talking and boasting about the things I made when they thought I could not hear them. My family and schooling made art seem the only way to join mental adventure, physical safety and social approval. Indeed, they pressed upon my bundle of traits in a way which made other work dull or threatening.

The foregoing paragraph is written to emphasise the connections and divergences between life and art. To those who want more information on this fascinating topic I offer:

REPLIES BY ALASDAIR GRAY, TO QUESTIONS FROM
CHRISTOPHER SWAN AND FRANK DELANEY, AUGUST 1982

Q. *What is your background?*

A. If background means surroundings: first 25 years apart from five years
during the 2nd World War were lived in Riddrie, east Glasgow, a well-
maintained district of stone-fronted corporation tenements and semi-
detached villas. Our neighbours were a nurse, postman, printer and
tobacconist, so I was a bit of a snob. I took it for granted that Britain was
mainly owned and ruled by Riddrie people — people like my father.

If background means family: it was hardworking, well-educated and very
sober. My English grandad was a Northampton foreman shoemaker who
came north because the southern employers blacklisted him for trade-union
activities. My Scottish grandad was an industrial blacksmith and
congregational kirk-elder. In the 30's, when my father married, he worked a
box-making machine in a factory, hiked and climbed mountains for a hobby,
and did voluntary secretarial work for the Camping Club of Great Britain
and the Scottish Youth Hostel Association. My mother was a good housewife
who never grumbled, but I now know wanted more from life than it gave —
my father had several ways of enjoying himself. She had very few. They were,
from that point of view, a typical married couple. I had a younger sister I
bullied and fought with, until we started living in separate houses. Then she
became one of my best friends.   Sister Mora was a major influence on my
dramatic fictions because she listened eagerly to a long serial monologue, an
endless adventure story with a boy like me as hero, which I told her as we
walked to school or lay in bed with doors open between our adjacent rooms.

Q. *What was childhood like?*

A.   Apart from the attacks of asthma and eczema, mostly painless but
frequently boring. My parents' main wish for me was that I go to university.
They wanted me to get a professional job, you see, because professional people
are not so likely to lose their income during a depression. To enter university
I had to pass exams in Latin and mathematics which I hated. So half my
school experience was passed in activities which felt to my brain like a meal
of sawdust to the mouth. And of course there was homework. My father
wanted to relieve the drudgery of learning by taking me cycling and climbing,
but I hated enjoying myself in his shadow, and preferred the escapist worlds
of comics and films and books: books most of all. Riddrie had a good library.

I had a natural preference for all sorts of escapist crap, but when I had read all there was of that there was nothing left but good stuff: and myth and legend, and travel, biography and history. I regarded a well-stocked public library as the pinnacle of democratic socialism. That a good dull place like Riddrie had one was proof that the world was essentially well organized.

Q. *When did you realize you were an artist?*

A. I did not realize it. Like all infants who were allowed materials to draw with, I did, and nobody suggested I stop. At school I was even encouraged to do it. And my parents (like many parents in those days) expected their children to have a party piece — a song or poem they would perform at domestic gatherings. The poems I recited were very poor A. A. Milne stuff. I found it possible to write verses which struck me as equally good, if not BETTER, because they were mine. My father typed them for me, and the puerile little stories which I sent to children's magazines and children's radio competitions. When I was eleven I read a four-minute programme of my own compositions on Scottish BBC childrens hour. But I was eight or nine years old when it occurred to me that I would one day write a story which would get printed in a book. This gave me a feeling of deliriously joyful power.

Q. *What sort of things did you draw when you were a child?*

A.   Space ships, monsters, maps of imaginary planets and kingdoms, the settings for stories of romantic and violent adventure, which I told my sister when we walked to school together. She was the first audience I could really depend on in the crucial years between seven and eleven.

Q. *How did your parents react to your wish to become a professional artist?*

A. They were alarmed. They wanted art to enrich my life in the spare time left over from earning a wage, but they thought, quite correctly, that living to make it would bring me to dole-queues, and wearing second-hand clothes, and borrowing money, and having my electricity cut off — bring me to the state many respectable working folk are forced into during depressions, for reasons they cannot help. That I should choose to become a seedy parasite in order to make obscure luxury items hardly anybody wanted worried them, as it would worry me if my son took that course. So till a few years ago I was embarrassed when I had to tell people my profession. But that feeling of shame stopped last year when I earned enough to pay taxes, so it was not important.

Q. *Is it possible that your concentration on Scottish subject matter will make* Lanark *inaccessible to the non-Scottish?*

A. You would not be interviewing me if my book was only accessible to Scots. And all imaginative workers make art out of the people and places they know best. No good writer is afraid to use local place names — the bible is full of them. No good writer is afraid to use local politics — Dante peoples Hell, Purgatory and Heaven with local politicians. I don't think Scotland a better country, Glasgow a better city than any other, but all I know of Hell and Heaven was learned here, so this is the ground I use, though sometimes I disguise the fact — just as Dean Swift pretended to describe an island peopled by pygmies, when describing England.

Q. *What made you write* 1982 Janine?

A. I wished to show a sort of man everyone recognizes and most can respect: not an artist, not an egoist, not even a radical: a highly skilled workman and technician, dependable, honest and conservative, who should be one of the kings of his age but does not know it, because he has been trained to do what he is told. So he is a plague and pest to himself, and is going mad, quietly, inside.

Q. *What are the main themes of your painting?*

A. The garden of Eden and the triumph of death. All my pictures use one or other or both. This is nothing abnormal. Any good portrait shows someone at a point in the journey from the happy garden to the triumph of death. I don't regard these states as far-fetched fantasies. Any calm place where folk are enjoying each other's company is heavenly. Any place where crowds struggle with each other in a state of dread is a hell, or on the doorstep of hell.

Q. *How important to you is religion as a theme?*

A. Religion is not a theme. Religion — any religion — is a way of seeing the world, a way of linking the near, the ordinary, the temporary with the remote, the fantastic, the eternal. Religion is a perspective device so I use it, of course. I differ from church people in seeing heaven and hell as the material of life itself, not of an afterlife. Intellectually I prefer the Olympian Greek faith. Emotionally I am dominated by the Old Testament. Morally speaking I prefer Jesus, but he sets a standard I'm too selfish to aim for. I'm more comfortable with his daddy, Jehovah, who is nastier but more human. The world is full of wee Jehovahs.

POSTSCRIPT   6th July 2005

I am now 70 years 187 days and several hours old.   Height and weight are unchanged since I measured them in 1987.   To the single inhaler that then kept my asthma painless have been added two others (serevent and beclozone), a nitrolingual pump spray, also montelukast and pravastatin sodium pills taken on going to bed, aspirin and ramapril and vermapil hydrochloride pills taken on rising.   Most of that counteracts high blood pressure and incipient diabetes diagnosed in 2003 after a small ruptured artery in my brain and something like it in the chest briefly paralysed the right thumb and forefinger (needed to paint and write with) and caused a small heart attack.   The crumbling that will destroy this body in a few years is accelerating but I have never been so lucky and happy with wife, friends, work and wages.   I am in the midst of painting ceiling and walls of the Oran Mor leisure centre, a scheme of decorations that combine nearly all of the best of my earlier murals, including those in the Glasgow Church and synagogue that were demolished and the Scottish-Soviet Society that were papered over.

To my astonishment this work is already popular with Oran Mor workers, performers and audiences though I will need two or three years to finish it. Most of my weekdays and some weekends are spent on this job with two good assistants (Robert Salmon, Richard Todd) who, like me, get paid £15 an hour with material and scaffolding provided.   In a busy week I often earn £600, so income from writing accumulates in my bank account.   Some of that is advances for an autobiographical art work, *A Life in Pictures*, for delivery to Canongate in 2005:   advances from Bloomsbury for *Three Men in Love: A Triptych*, for delivery at the end of 2006.

I hope one day to edit, introduce and design *The British Book of Popular Political Songs*, despite the death of one literary agent who liked the idea and the unenthusiasm of my usual publishers.   Being born of hard-working people I want to die working.   While at work my time passes unconsciously, is painless, can amount to satisfaction.   Alzheimer's or some other form of senile decay is also a possible ending: in which case I hope to accept it as a holiday.

Stewart Conn

Born Glasgow, 5th November 1936

BBC PRODUCER, POET AND PLAYWRIGHT

FIRST EDINBURGH MAKAR

A Sense of Belonging

Mark Twain observed of being tarred and feathered that if it wasn't for the honour of it all, he'd as soon skip the whole business. My response on being offered Edinburgh's first official poet laureateship was astonishment mingled with trepidation. But not for a moment did it cross my mind to decline. The term *makar* evokes the great mediaeval flowering of Scottish literature. Yet in laying claim to no more than the *crafting* of poetry, it has to my ear a reassuringly down-to-earth and egalitarian ring, as against 'laureate' with its whiff of Parnassus.

Aside from photo-spreads in *The Times* and *Evening News*, a spacious *Herald* piece made play of my having been born in Glasgow and brought up in Ayrshire. Glasgow's Lord Provost was even quoted, wishing me well. For its inaugural makar, they were saying, Edinburgh had to resort to a migrant from the west.

One writer resident in the capital had already murmured that I wasn't native to his city: 'nothing personal, of course'. I decided that in the event of a recurrence I'd encourage those from my old stamping-ground to regard me as an infiltrator. For Edinburgh complainants the other barrel was primed: when Robert Fergusson died in penury in 1774, ungarlanded by the literati of the day, it was thirteen years before a memorial was raised over his unmarked grave in the Canongate kirkyard — by an Ayrshireman, Robert Burns.

What surprised and relieved me was that no-one brought up (at least within earshot) my poetry not being written in Scots. My musings on this were sharpened by an invitation to address the Association of Scottish Literary Studies on 'the health of Edinburgh poetry today'. Fears that it might prove a poisoned chalice were heightened by my proximity to the body up whose orifice it was assumed I'd plant my thermometer. Against this, and even after many happy years in the city, I still regard myself as residually an outsider.

My wife and I spent close on two decades in Glasgow, where both our sons were born. We lived near Kelvinbridge, handy for the BBC. In 1977, in the run-up to the launch of Radio Scotland, I was among those moved "to temporary accommodation in 5 Queen Street, prior to the provision of new broadcasting premises" adjacent to the impending Parliament building. The 1979 referendum put paid to that. In 1992, finding it hard to stomach an imminent and what would prove virtually total surrender of editorial autonomy to London, I resigned. Eventually the still makeshift studio premises were sold, some staff being moved to the Tun, others back to Glasgow.

I remember it coming as a bolt from the blue that the years we'd lived in Edinburgh weren't just a postscript to those in Glasgow, but exceeded them: twenty-seven now, and counting.   I recall too how on arrival the writer in me, geared to a sense of possession and dispossession, had felt a need to redefine if not re-establish an identity. This was achieved largely through a tie of the blood.

Though my father was a minister his side of the family had farmed on the slopes of Craigie Hill, outside Kilmarnock, since Burns's day. Much of my early poetry drew on rural images, animals and people. In due course I'd write of *"my shoes / holding a sprinkling of rich Ayrshire soil"*. Now for the first time my mother's background took on fuller meaning.

My antennae were already attuned to Edinburgh's history and architecture, its literary and cultural inheritance, and the interweaving of these. I thrilled to the New Town's elegant Georgian facades, and to picturing their former habitués; to passing where Scott wrote, Hume lodged, Stevenson dallied, or Lord Cockburn stood listening to the corncrakes in the dewy grass; or among the ghosts of the Old Town, envisaging a dramatically darker and more threatening world. But there was a more intimate link.

My mother's first home had been near the Meadows and she was married in Hope Park Church. Eldest of four sisters she went to 'Varsity' here before spending her wedded life in the west, and all her days spoke wistfully of her birth-place where, widowed, she would return and pick up the threads of friendships. My one regret on being made makar was that she wasn't around to take pleasure in it. What I took on board only latterly was that her father's licensed grocer's had been in the High Street — adjoining the old police-station and where the Fringe Office now is, in the shadow of the *air-cock o' Saunt Giles*. On chill winter nights, he left a dram on the window-ledge for the constable coming off his beat.

An 'Edinburgh poetry' first impinged on me in Kilmarnock's Dick Institute library, while I was still at school. In May 1955 I had a poem in an issue of *Lines Review* edited by Sydney Goodsir Smith. That month I bought and was bowled over by Norman MacCaig's *Riding Lights*. In due course an attachment to George Bruce's BBC arts department, during which I stayed with an aunt and uncle and cousins in Granton Road, gave me peripheral entrée to Norman, Sydney, Robert Garioch and others — bonnie fechters, a' wede awa — mainly in the howffs they habituated; and often with MacDiarmid, who signed my copy of his *Collected Poems* in Milne's Bar, in 1962.

Of those bohemian days, which have since entered folk-myth, I was struck both by the poets' stamina and by the diversity of their output. Of those in the *inner sanctum* Sydney, warm and rumbustious and an enthusiastic water-colourist, wrote of his adoptive *rortie city* in a rhetorical "willed" Scots. Garioch, self-effacing sipper of half-pints and now sadly under-estimated, impeccably melded traditional verse-forms and living speech-rhythms. Also to the fore in Scots were Tom Scott, JK Annand with his children's poems and across the tracks, the ebullient Hamish Henderson garnering folk-songs.

MacCaig wrote from the outset in the Scotticised English he spoke. Some called him a quisling until, deciding some of his work was rather good, they said he had a 'Scots accent of the mind': "whatever that is", he'd add, darkly. Given MacDiarmid's fierce advocacy of Scots, and their closeness, I once asked Norman if the issue had been a bone of contention between them. "We were good friends", he replied simply: "he never attacked me".

The 1950s and 60s remain the most recent period whose poets in stature, engagement with place and commitment to Scots I think of as truly representative of — whose voices cumulatively *embodied* — Edinburgh. I enjoyed my glimpses of them. Geerie (as he tended to be known) used to like walking through Queen Street Gardens, until dog (as against child) owners took over. He took to "sticking a wee bit of wood in the grass, beside each poo . . . until it started looking like Flanders Field". Once as I drove him to an event in St Andrews he peered up at the thousands of pinkfoot massing over Loch Leven; eventually murmuring, "some kinna bird". At the Byre after I had elaborated on my poems' country origin and imagery, he impishly began, "This is my only nature poem: it's criet 'Worm'."

MacCaig didn't beat about the bush. The first time I shared a platform with him I over-earnestly predicated the themes patterning what I planned to read. He began sardonically, "Here are a few random snowflakes from a pile of slush". Another time when Liz Lochhead and I were sharing the bill with Norman and George Bruce, the first half spectacularly overran. George announced that when he'd timed his poems on his office stopwatch, they'd come to exactly 15 minutes. This got the full MacCaig glower: "Aye George, but did you time what you were going to say in between?".

In those days the city was still a prim spinster; or a dowdy dowager, proud of a privileged past but blinkered . . . and irremediably 'east windy, west endy'. The tenement entries had their old brass bell-pulls. Queues of seamen formed outside Dora's, in Danube Street. George Street's pillars fronted banks, not teeming clubs and wine bars. George Square was yet to be desecrated by the University. The Caledonian Station, now defunct, could still be a cauldron of steam. The Traverse Theatre Club had ruffled the feathers of the city's self-appointed moral guardians; Richard Demarco's Open 100 Exhibition taken the douce arts world by the short and curlies.

Today's capital is very different. Still the filmic backdrop of the Castle and Arthur's Seat. But while steadfastly retaining its gulf between rich and poor, and pockets of parochialism, it has felt a gust of fresh air attributable not least to the Festival and even more the Fringe. With its year-round tourist-influx, ubiquitous student population and affluent financial whiz-kids it is revitalised, sophisticated, cosmopolitan, hedonistic and international. To Alastair Reid, after long away, it is "a young city" again.

There has also been a sea-change linguistically. I recall flutterings in the doocots, over style-sheets and attempts to impose a uniform Scots spelling. Many of its devotees saw Lallans as inseparable from a sense of national identity, in the fight for Devolution and Independence. With our Parliament re-convened one barrier has been breached – but a plateau reached. Scotland now seems stuck at a half-way house, hopes of Independence very much on hold. This has undermined one advocacy of literary Scots. Concurrently TV, the education system and other forces have irreparably devalued the spoken word which was to Garioch both source and tuning-fork.

Glasgow where I cut my teeth when G12 was still W2 was very different. BBC staff tended to regard colleagues in Edinburgh and the other 'out-stations' as peripheral if not quite country cousins. More widespread was Weegie glee at any chance to ca' the feet from those snotty Edinburghers. This lingered close to the surface. In 1999 after a writers' workshop in Pollok I sat on the bus beside a little lady who enthused warmly about it. Rising to get off at Bridge Street she asked how far I was going. I said back to Edinburgh. "Aw" she cackled, as the doors swished shut, "we fair pipped youse fur the architecture."

One marked divide was in the cities' respective poetic usages. To Tom Leonard his urban demotic was not a *patois* but the language of his art. It was also fiercely political: but socialist, not nationalist; not merely to avoid being tarred with the Lallans brush but, as with the fervour and integrity of James Kelman's prose, to expose a whole system of language dominance and reaffirm the dignity of what was seen as a deprived underclass.

If inter-city antagonisms have eased, a catalyst may well have been the perception of Edwin Morgan as staunchly Glaswegian, yet in the best sense 'common property'. Straddling geography and genre, his work over decades has influenced a far-flung body of younger writers. Already Glasgow's laureate, his appointment as Scotland's national poet (though handled with blatant opportunism by the First Minister) met with wide approval.

With its plethora of prizes and pamphlets, and proliferation of web-sites, poetry is now not just respectable but fashionable. The Scottish Poetry Library flourishes, off the Royal Mile. Outwith the cornucopia of the Book Festival, Edinburgh has constant poetry events — and a Mushaira of Asian Poetry hosted annually by the City Council. There are memorial plaques to Scottish writers, in Makars' Court. The Writers' Museum holds the fort, pending adequate housing and display of our literature past and present — ideally with a centre for Scottish PEN. Sculpted herms (poets' heads on plinths, a notion some might applaud) embellish Edinburgh Park.

Being mercifully under no onus to produce 'civic' poems my activities veered from judging competitions, and having poster-poems displayed on local buses, to editing an anthology for young children and another celebrating the quincentenary of the Royal College of Surgeons of Edinburgh. Couplets lasered in the pavement to mark the regeneration of Holyrood's Clocktower site survive (so far) the passage of pedestrians and skate-boarders.

My good fortune was to have two very different events fall within my tenure of office. First, thrillingly, came the presentation in the Unesco building in Paris — among a throng of nationalities, the Eiffel Tower silhouetted in sparklers — of the dossier advocating Edinburgh as the first world City of Literature. Having been invited to provide a poem for the occasion, I was able later the same evening to share in the incredulity and exhilaration when — months ahead of expectation — the acceptance of the bid was announced. For our small group sauntering along the *quais* next morning, it was like walking on air.

The following Sunday, with propitious timing, a dedication service was held in the Canongate Church prior to the unveiling of David Annand's statue of Robert Fergusson. Again approached for a short poem, I'd asked what was meant by 'short'. The reply was to the point: "It's to be in the open air — it might rain". Luckily it didn't. It has been suggested the spritely figure of the poet could be striding towards the new Parliament: from his smirk I suspect he may have less salubrious quarters in his sights, en route.

For all the favours poetry receives, it does not seem to have benefited from the high tide for prose which has boosted many a publisher's coffers. And the mega-bookchains can treat it grudgingly. Yet I'm not sure that it is so hard done by. After all it has to compete in the market-place with best-sellers and Film. And too many aficionados won't put their money where their mouths are — a nail Kenneth Patchen hit on the head: "People who say they love poetry and never buy any are a bunch of cheap sons-of-bitches".

Indeed the whole poetry industry can seem counter-productive; burgeoning residential and other courses, and the popularity of writers' groups and workshops, arousing a suspicion that fewer folk are actually *reading* the stuff than trying to *write* it. The idea that this produces more cream doesn't allow for the ratio of poetry to verse, by which I sometimes feel so beleaguered as to contemplate a moratorium, even a selective cull (just joking).

With this hive of activity, what of the honey? There has been one seismic shift. St. Andrews University's English Department houses a phalanx of high-profile poet-critics: Douglas Dunn, Robert Crawford, Kathleen Jamie, John Burnside and Dundee-born Don Paterson. WN Herbert's register-hopping Scots is spiced by phonetic Dundee-speak. StAnza Poetry Festival further widens horizons. And the over-all climate reflects a hard-won freedom in the mind and in the fluid interplay of whatever tongue or tongues come naturally. The fallacy of preserving one language's 'purity' has been blown to smithereens.

Contributing to Edinburgh's new harmonies is an influx of poets from Shetland, Brora, London, Ireland, India and elsewhere. Despite long-term residency many, among them Valerie Gillies, would refute any restrictive 'Edinburgh' tag. So might Brian McCabe and Ron Butlin, both born here; and those who like Elizabeth Burns, or Tom Pow with his moving familial poems set in the city, have moved away but without severing links. This does not preclude an intense loyalty to the city, displayed also by writers as varied as Angus Calder, Colin Donati and Donald Smith; each conscious of a dual belonging.

I thought I'd resolved this by telling myself my head was in the east, but my heart in the west. Now I'm less sure. On a recent visit to Kilmarnock I was driven up the hill and past the road-ends of the farms which were my boyhood terrain. I felt completely detached. Maybe I've been away too long. Or previous poems have exorcised a psychological need, severed an umbilical cord. There can be so many intricate and equivocal belongings: to where one was born or grew up, to one's ancestry, where one moves to or settles; with perhaps crucial, whether and where relatives remain, or no longer hold sway.

Ideally such disparate sources will prove cumulative and complementary, not reductive or destructive. Regions and dictions can form a complex mosaic, as researchers have found in trying to pin down the 'locations' of Scottish writers. In the long term the most any of us can count on, wherever we end up, is being if not totally at home, at least as minimally alien there as anywhere. One hopes the poetry will not turn locations to dislocations, but detect some organic unity of theme. Simply stitching on name-tags, though a guide to topography, is no guarantee of a poetry having put down a tap-root.

While working on a sequence set in the Royal Mile there came a point where I realised I was being driven by a self-imposed sense of obligation: as damaging for poetry, as in any love affair. This was a timely reminder of the potential danger and discomfiture of seeing myself, or being seen by others, as a spokesperson for the city. Whereas what I needed was the confidence to give instinct free rein and let the city and its rhythms work on me, if they so decided, rather than try to take them by the scruff of the neck or change my spots: as William Soutar put it "to curb the fretful brain, and trust the blood".

As for 'Edinburghness'. . . what harm if its poetry should have a less particularised thumb-print? Remarkably few of Norman MacCaig's poems are, let's face it, set there. He was all too aware of being split between the city and Assynt, where each summer he'd escape with his trout-rod. How totally in any case can identity be attributed to location, without regard to perception and sensibility? But what ultimately matters, surely, is that the poetry should be informed by a high seriousness and cultural breadth, underpinned by a concern for craft.

In his last radio interview I asked Norman what being Scottish meant to him: was it *pride*? "No, it certainly isn't pride. I can never understand why people say I'm proud to be a Scot'. He's only Scottish by a bunch of accidents. What's there to be proud about? Pleased if you like. I'm very *pleased* to be Scots. But I see things wrong in Scotland that I'm not proud of at all. That's common sense, isn't it?" This is another reminder that as a city of literature Edinburgh, responding with both confidence and humility to its wider validation, must constantly re-earn its spurs — not take them for granted.

This is for the future to evaluate. The onus on today's poets, with a finger on the pulse of social and cultural as well as literary change, is to make as open-minded and spiritually sustaining a provision as possible, for that future. Differences must be celebrated; the resultant poetry be *in*clusive, not *ex*clusive. Not as marketing fodder or to satisfy some passing academic penchant, but for poetry's own sake and for the vibrancy and joy of creating it. In the hope that the heart's song interwoven with that of the city will continue to communicate, enrichingly and humanely, their unique rhythms and cadences.

(Thomas) Hugh Pennington

Born Edgware, Middlesex 19th April 1938

MEDICAL MICROBIOLOGIST

E.coli, smallpox and other things

I am only a Scot by domicile, being born in London in 1938. My family returned to Lancaster, my parents' home town, not long after because of the Second World War. I spent my childhood and went to school there. The town had been burned in 1322 by two Scots armies, one coming over Shap and the other through Furness in Cumbria and over the sands of Morecambe Bay. With the passage of Jacobite armies from the north through the town in 1715 (with some local support and little plunder) and in 1745 (with no local support and much more plunder), this serves notice of its closeness to the border. Scotch influence is therefore to be expected; arson and plunder have been forgotten; and in my childhood doctors and nonconformist ministers all seemed to come from Glasgow, so a good deal of the intellectual life there in the 1940's and 1950's had a strong Gilmorehill flavour.

My general practitioner was a Scot and so was the Congregational minister of the church to which I was taken by my parents, so I suppose they must have had some influence, although what it was is hard to identify now. It was not so with my parents and other close relatives. My mother had high expectations and approved of intellectual things, although her attempts to make me learn the violin and to like Latin failed. The latter defect saved me from the ministry, my father's ambition for me, for which I am grateful because of a lifelong suspicion of all things metaphysical. There was a long tradition on my mother's side of the family of hospital work; as constructors of them or nurses. Most of this activity centred on the huge local psychiatric hospital known seriatim as the County Asylum, the County Mental and Lancaster Moor. Relatives had been involved as builders from 1812 and on through the nineteenth century, and as nurses of all grades, with a great aunt its matron, and my grandfather the chief attendant in the 1930's. All this health work made medicine a natural choice for others to make for me. It was facilitated enormously by first class science teaching at Lancaster Royal Grammar School. Rigorous and deep, it also encouraged breadth; as joint curator of the school museum (it had an extensive collection of stuffed birds and the job excused me from some of the field sports at which I was no good) I had my first media experience being "interviewed" on a Manchester produced bit of Childrens Hour on the BBC. "Interviewed" because everything was read off a typewritten script.

With hindsight my grandfather's success in moving from being a railway engine cleaner to the top job in his field should have inspired, but as a youth one takes so many things for granted. My Uncle Jim's doings impressed much more directly. He was an undertaker. He bought the white-tiled ice cream shop next door to his office as a chapel of rest — it needed minimal modification. I saw him operating his network of necrological contacts in the town to find out who "had got it" whenever a citizen died. He was a straightforward person who had fought in Iraq — Messpot he called it — during the First World War. He caught rabbits with ferrets, was called in as a carpenter when a Saturday afternoon fight in the main shopping street between Lancaster's Poles and Irishmen collapsed through Woolworth's windows, and was philosophical when told he had terminal lung cancer — it was time to go and he had had a good life. His example taught me to aim to be realistic and unsentimental and practical about things, like his speciality.

Asylum connexions strengthened this way of looking at life. While still at school I got a job in its laboratory. It had changed little since its establishment in the 1890s. I was given the task of testing urines passed overnight for sugar by boiling them with reagents over a Bunsen burner. They had a tendency to erupt suddenly out of the test tube. The smell dominated the morning. The rest of the day went on with the search for tuberculosis bacilli in sputum samples and the testing of stomach contents. Downstairs there was the occasional post-mortem (the attendant was a patient) and a steady trickle of new arrivals to be photographed. Most were transferees from Broadmoor and other forensic establishments.

The first two years at medical school in London were less interesting. St. Thomas's being traditional, they were dominated by anatomy; notably the dissection of the shrivelled-up corpse of an old hunchback. Biochemistry was pre-DNA and physiology focused a lot on the heart of the frog. Relevance seemed remote and the main task was to pass the examinations. Lancaster was still teaching me more. Its coroner was a family friend and he introduced me to the pathologist at the Royal Infirmary. He was happy to have me at his post-mortems, and I went regularly during vacations. The PM is not only a brilliant teaching tool, but has about it the excitement of discovery; one never knows what will be revealed when the skull cap is removed or the abdomen opened. The commonest conundrum requiring resolution happened in the summer when visitors came to Morecambe to enjoy the sea air (a goodly number from Glasgow). Every year some would be found mortally ill in a coma at the foot of the stairs in their hotel or boarding house. At PM it was clear that they had bled into their brains. Was this due to a stroke which had caused them to fall, or was it caused by a head injury sustained on the way down? Giving the coroner an unequivocal answer was not always easy. The general lesson was that applying science to medicine is often difficult, and the particular one was that diagnosing a definitive cause of death is commonly hard, and sometimes impossible.

Useful as attending PM's was, its influence was far less than that of the third big hospital in Lancaster, constructed in the nineteenth century for the "Idiots and Imbeciles of the Seven Northern Counties." Another relative worked there as an administrator, and he smoothed the way for me to get a nursing job there one holiday. It had also changed little since the 1890's. It was grim. I was assigned to the infirmary block in which patients not only had severe learning difficulties but physical ailments as well. The bedridden schizophrenic (who thought he was Tom Finney, the Preston North End football star) with Down's syndrome and a hole in the heart was better off than many there because he could speak and was only occasionally incontinent. What I saw, smelled and heard eliminated the last vestiges of my religious faith. The blows of fate that had caused the patients to be there were compounded by the harshness of the regime. Not all the nurses were unkind; but some were.

Life at medical school was now getting interesting as we had gone on to the wards. I had always had a doubter's approach to revealed truths — perhaps of genetic origin — as I had been baptised Thomas, a family forename. Scepticism was reinforced by the teaching at St Thomas's. The most powerful influence came from Professor Edward Sharpey-Schafer. I was a student on his medical firm and worked for him as his last houseman before his premature death from smoking. His father, a naval commander, had been killed at the Battle of Jutland, and he was brought up by namesake, his grandfather, a formidable personality and Professor of Physiology at Edinburgh. Schafer was a brilliant experimentalist on the human circulation. His obituarist said that "he published a great many papers without repeating himself." I can vouch for the comment that at times he "exploited a nihilistic image to avoid uncomfortable personal involvements". Research excellence and the rational treatment of disease (which meant avoiding drugs for which there was no evidence of efficacy, ie most of them) were his hallmarks. It was commonly held that the surest mark of his approval was to be sworn at; my predecessor knew that he had made it when he was called a f . . . . . g sheep; I must have failed because I was never thus blessed. Nevertheless his succinct and direct speaking and writing styles have been my models ever since.

Focusing on pathology and the whetting of the appetite by mortuary work paid off. I was offered a job in bacteriology by the Professor at St Thomas's, Ronald Hare. Close to retirement, he had been mentored by Alexander Fleming. The department was in an asbestos shed on the roof of the medical school. The view of the Palace of Westminster was magnificent and we used to time experiments by Big Ben. It was just as well that we could see and hear it, because Hare had been brought up in the string and sealing-wax era and had a deep aversion to buying equipment that used electricity. In any case, there was no money. A new professor came on his retirement, Tony Waterson, a virologist from Cambridge. His honeymoon funding electrified the department and we soon had an electron microscope and an ultracentrifuge for analysing viruses at 40,000 r.p.m. The era of molecular biology had arrived. Tony got big research grants and I was put to work analysing virulence in Newcastle Disease virus, which caused disease in chickens. The main reason for working on a veterinary problem was that it was a good model for viruses in general and that it had certain technical advantages. But for me it was a lucky break because it introduced me to the world of animal diseases, which was to stand me in good stead thirty years later with *E.coli* 0157. Mentoring by people like June Almeida, a world-class electron microscopist from Canada who had started as a laboratory technician in Glasgow, and meeting people like Fred Brown, the brilliant foot and mouth disease biochemist, was making me into a scientist.

The traditional way to finally achieve independence as an investigator is to work for a while in another laboratory, preferably in the US. Tony Waterson had contacts in Madison, Wisconsin, and in late 1967 my wife and I moved there. Its science was very good — one of its biochemists, H.G. Khorana (trained in India and Liverpool) won the Nobel Prize while we were there — but so was the broad experience. Going there on a 4,500 ton cargo boat was challenging, particularly when the Jaguar cars and cocoa butter in its hold shifted during a mid-Atlantic storm. Vietnam was at its height and it was a Presidential election year. We gave out leaflets for the Democrats, but Nixon still won. Meeting Flathead Indians while camping in the Montana Rockies and brushing against Richard Burton and Elizabeth Taylor leaving Trader Vics at the Plaza Hotel in New York as we were going in compensated for the inane TV "specials" and second-rate newspapers. And the university was excellent. Although really a collection of departmental fiefdoms held together by hostility to the institutional car-parking policy (even Khorana had to use Lot 60 which was a long bus ride from the campus), its lavish local and federal funding (from bodies like the National Institutes of Health) had made it a world leader in many fields without being elitist – it had a Professor of Marching Band who trained football cheer-leaders and one of its main auditoriums had the notice "Beef Cattle" over its door.

In Madison I had continued a fly-collecting hobby. Blood-suckers were a particular interest. A decision had to be made about where to go next and I wrote to the Medical Research Council in London enquiring about jobs in their tropical establishments, where entomology and virology came together in the study of mosquito-transmitted infections. The reply said that there were no vacancies but there was one in Glasgow, in the Institute of Virology. We flew there via Shannon, meeting an old Irish friend whose husband was warden of Wolfson Hall, so had accommodation to tide us over while we confirmed arrangements to stay in an "Executive" flat in Cumbernauld. It was in a 12-story tower block. The only executive thing about it was the rent. The uriniferous lifts reminded me of the morning smell of the asylum laboratory, and the "Ronan Point strengthening", steel bars reinforcing the corner of the living room, coupled with a sway in strong winds, were unsettling. But the 10 floor views were magnificent. So was John Subak-Sharpe's ability to get funds for the Institute. He was its Director. I had a personal technician, my own laboratory, fantastic support facilities, virtually unlimited funds for supplies, and clever colleagues. The research start was straight into the deep end. John had just discovered that rifampicin, an antibiotic, blocked the growth of vaccinia virus, the smallpox vaccine. I was instructed to find whether it had the same effect on smallpox virus itself. It was deemed to be too dangerous to do the work at the Institute, which didn't have the necessary isolation facilities, and so I was sent to Birmingham. Henry Bedson had a laboratory in the medical school there which worked on smallpox. It was before the era of safety cabinets. Making sure that everyone was vaccinated was the main way of stopping the escape of the virus, which we handled on the open bench. My experiments worked, and after a month I returned to Glasgow, where I continued to do research for the next decade, with forays into various virus families but mostly on viruses related to smallpox. One of the last things to happen before leaving was to be asked back to Birmingham to examine a PhD on smallpox. By this time the virus had been eradicated and Bedson's laboratory, although much safer than when I was there ten years before, was scheduled for closure because it didn't come up to the high standards now deemed to be necessary. So a batch of final experiments was being rushed for completion. I was unhappy enough about conditions there to revaccinate myself vigorously on return to Glasgow; tragedy struck a few months later when the virus escaped, killing a secretary in the department on the floor above Bedson's laboratory. He cut his throat.

Working in Glasgow was good. Unlike St. Thomas's, it was a proper university. To remember that Lord Kelvin and Lord Lister had done their important work there put a spring in the step. To see Ian Donald, the originator of medical ultrasound, in the bank on Byres Road confirmed that things were still going well. Despite sectarian graffiti, the need to step over drunks in the gutter at Partick Cross at 10 in the morning, and another asylum laboratory olfactory reminder, the smell of the subway, the quality of life was good. Scotland had become home. So to go for the Chair of Bacteriology at Aberdeen was the right move.

My application was successful, and we moved north in 1979. It was the calm before the storm. For many years, Aberdeen had been very successful in getting funding from the University Grants Committee. Its science department were lavishly staffed and were in big buildings. Its medical school had budgets that allowed its staff to provide a good deal of the hospital care, particularly at Foresterhill. All this changed with Thatcher's "Value for money". Per student Aberdeen's funding was nearly on a par with Oxford's — but not even the most loyal alumnus could say that all our outputs were of the same quality. And recruiting science students was difficult. So in 1981 Aberdeen was deemed to be overstaffed to such a degree that its funding was reduced by more than a fifth. Many had to go. This fell particularly heavily on the medical school. A quarter of hospital consultants were university employees. Even counting them in, Aberdeen's medical staffing levels were still lower than those in the rest of Scotland. So there was no slack. Another penalty was that for the first time, research activity determined funding. Many academic doctors in Aberdeen did little, because of their big NHS commitments and their teaching. So it was part 2 of the Matthew principle: "from him that hath not shall be taken away even that which he hath". Sorting out these problems was a dominant activity for the next decade. One solution was for university staff to become NHS employees. Tricky pension problems lurked. One of my colleagues described some of the negotiating sessions as "mangling meetings." But at the end of the day a leaner medical school and one, I think, really fit for purpose, emerged. Teaching is thoroughly professional, and research quality unrecognisably better.

Moving to Aberdeen changed my personal research programme. Applying the molecular biology methods used to study viruses to bacteriological problems made sense because bacteria are much easier and cheaper to grow in the laboratory — thus getting over the problem of limited resources — and because for a long time I had been interested in developing fingerprinting methods to track the spread of infectious agents. Attention turned to organisms like *Staphylococcus aureus* — the cause of boils and parent of MRSA, the bacteria that cause meningitis, food poisoning bacteria like *E.coli* 0157 and *Campylobacter*, and *Streptococcus pyogenes*, the cause of scarlet fever.

Then came the flesh-eating bug. It was, in fact, *Streptococcus pyogenes*. Because my name was on a list held by the British Medical Association I became a port of call for print, radio and TV journalists for the ten days in 1994 that the story was headline news. Necrotizing fasciitis was not new. The number of cases almost certainly had not increased in the 1990's. There was no epidemic. It was a media outbreak caused by the propensity of journalists to feed on themselves for news, helped by the fascination of the public for accounts of horrible things happening to ordinary folk and the skill of reporters in finding victims to tell their stories. The whole thing had been set off by a *Daily Sport* reporter casting round for a lurid story at a quiet time and finding a Press Association item about a small cluster of cases in Gloucestershire. His headline ran "BUG THAT EATS YOU ALIVE. Killer virus scoffs three." Before the story died it was running on Canadian television and Australian radio. An announcement by the Prime Minister, John Major, that he was going to do something about beggars killed it.

A short period of intense media experience is a good way to learn technique and work out the ground rules. Experts who cannot summarize complicated science in three snappy jargon-free sound-bites will not be asked back. Being unfazed by responding to a disembodied voice in an ear-piece (that feels as though it is about to fall out) and speaking confidently to a camera controlled by an engineer hundreds of miles away is essential. Finding out about these things was invaluable for what was to follow.

The *E.coli* 0157 food poisoning outbreak in Central Scotland first showed itself on Friday 22 November 1996 when public health officials became aware of illness affecting a number of residents of Wishaw in Lanarkshire. It soon became evident that the outbreak was going to be big. By the Wednesday afternoon five victims had died. My laboratory was the Scottish reference centre for *E.coli* 0157 microbiology, and on the Thursday I received a call from a senior Scottish Office Medical Officer to ask whether I would chair an expert group to enquire into the outbreak and make recommendations about the lessons to be learned and the implications for food safety. The feeling that the outbreak was very serious was right. Eventually, more than five hundred were affected and the bacterium killed seventeen. My group was under pressure to report speedily. Not only was this another big food scare to add to the linking of BSE and vCJD earlier in the year, but a general election was coming soon, with bad omens for the Tories in Scotland. Michael Forsyth, the Secretary of State, had become tartan and pragmatic. There was never a better time to drive forward food safety policies that normally would have been too radical to contemplate. Our proposals went forward with Forsyth's enthusiastic support. The only real opposition came from Westminster departments, probably because of their firm view that only they should make policies affecting the whole of the UK. It was out of order for "Territorial" departments to meddle seriously in their affairs. The way that Scottish civil servants used the machinery of government to ding down their colleagues south of the border was pure "Sir Humphrey". The "Pennington Report" was published in April. It received parliamentary approval in a debate – the issues transcended party politics.

I retired in 2003. The changes in medicine since my asylum jobs in the mid 1950s have been immense. Then a diagnosis of leukaemia, or renal failure, or testicular cancer was a death sentence. Organ transplants, coronary artery bypass grafts, and artificial joints were the stuff of science fiction. The benefits brought by science have been very great. I was advised early in my career against microbiology, because vaccines and antibiotics were making infectious diseases a thing of the past. But even then HIV was evolving into a human pathogen, and the first MRSA strains were being isolated at St Thomas's. So sticking with microbes was right. Nevertheless, I feel a failure. Some of our current problems, like MRSA, are due to not doing things that have been known for generations – simple scientific messages have not been got across. Even worse has been the persistence, and even growth, of irrational and anti-scientific attitudes in medicine. Homeopathy has never been stronger. And medical students probably receive less science education now than in the eighteenth century. Thank goodness for paramedics who know how to use defibrillators!

I have been very lucky, starting as a child with a nutritional head start from the 2nd world war Drummond diet, through strong parental support and then the same from my wife and academic colleagues and my secretary.

Having a public profile has brought part 1 of the Matthew effect into operation: "Unto every one that hath shall be given, and he shall have abundance." Being put on committees at the Food Standards Agency and the BBC has been a privilege. Being interviewed on TV has been a challenge, but not as great as giving the keynote address at the Christmas Carcase Competition at Inverurie slaughterhouse. Being asked to write essays like this one is enjoyable. Rewards have been enormous: receiving a facsimile plaque of "The Mask Play of Hahoe Byeolsin Exorcism" (Important Intangible Cultural Asset No. 69) from the South Korean Broadcasting Service was a pleasure even greater than sitting on the GMTV sofa. But two stand out. The best is to see the successful careers of young people who have worked in my department. But I fear the one that will be remembered longest is the notoriety from responding to the assertion that we have become "too clean" made in an early morning unscripted interview on the "Today" programme. I said "bollocks".

Allan Massie

Born Singapore, 16th October 1938

NOVELIST AND COLUMNIST

Saltire Book of the Year, A Question of Loyalties, *1989*

In Converse with Imaginary Characters

In 1926 my father went to Malaya to take up a post as assistant manager of a rubber estate. He was eighteen or nineteen, and had never been out of Scotland before. Indeed I doubt if he had been south of Perth. He would have preferred to farm in his native Aberdeenshire, but, as he said, he had no capital; so this was impossible. A few months in an uncle's law firm convinced him that office life was not to his taste; and so, Malaya, which is why I came to be born in Singapore. This makes me a child of Empire like so many Scots.

My roots however are in the north-east, in lowland Aberdeenshire. Most of my ancestors were farmers, as far back as we know. Some, collaterals perhaps, were ministers of religion or schoolmasters. The names in the family tree — Massie, Johnstone, Forbes, Allan, Martin, Hill, Fordyce, Greig, Troup — are all Lowland rather than Highland. Late in life my father was asked if he would be wearing the kilt to a grandson's wedding , He replied, "I'm a Lowlander, I've never worn a kilt in my life." In the nineteenth century those I know of adhered to the Free Kirk in religion, and to the Liberal Party in politics. They believed in hard work and self-respect. I have a notebook belonging to a great-aunt in which she praises "thrift, allied to all the virtues" and declares that "a wasteful man or woman is regarded as a dangerous member of society".

I have no memories of Malaya. We came home when I was only a few months old. Then, when my father returned at the end of his leave — six months at home every four years— my mother stayed behind with my brother and me. She was expecting another child, and war with Germany had broken out. My father was taken prisoner at Singapore and nearly died in the Jap POW camp.

He had at first no wish to go back to Malaya after the war. My mother had inherited a farm from her father. He was keen to run it and went so far as to buy a herd of Ayrshires. Then his company, Sime Darby, approached him with a handsome offer, promises of promotion, glittering prospects. He accepted.

My life might have been very different if the decision had gone otherwise. We would probably have gone to school in Aberdeen — the Grammar or Robert Gordon's — whence I would have proceeded to Aberdeen University, perhaps to study law and go into a firm whose senior partner was married to one of Father's cousins. I would then have been at the right age to do well out of the oil boom, and might, like so many Aberdeen lawyers, have become rather rich.

Instead we were sent to boarding school, first to Drumtochty Castle, a prep school in Kincardineshire, and then to Trinity College, Glenalmond (which now calls itself Glenalmond College). I was notably well taught at both schools, especially in English and History, and have no cause to complain of either.

Glenalmond was a nineteenth century foundation, unusual in being Episcopalian. Its founders included the future Prime Minister Gladstone, the Duke of Buccleuch, the Earl of Home and Sir James Hope-Scott of Abbotsford, whose wife was Sir Walter Scott's grand-daughter. Their intention was to make it unnecessary for Scottish Episcopalians to send their sons to England for their education. It was still Episcopalian, in my time though probably more than half of us would have been brought up in the Church of Scotland. Nevertheless the seven bishops of the Episcopal Church were ex officio members of the Council. Many Scots, ignorant of history and of the Episcopalians' devoted adherence to the Jacobite cause, call the Episcopal Church "the English church".

Many also regard independent boarding schools like Glenalmond as English imports, alien to the Scottish tradition. This is not unreasonable, though it never occurred to us that the school was anything but Scottish, and the few English boys there were often given a hard time. Nevertheless most of the senior masters were themselves English, and it was understood that clever boys were being prepared for Oxford or Cambridge rather than for a Scottish university. The truh is, perhaps, that while Glenalmond was not English, it was unquestionably, — and unquestioningly — British.

Cambridge which I went on to was British also. The town itself was of course English, to me curiously and agreeably English, especially in the seedy pubs around the Lion Yard where you might meet decayed stable-hands and struck-off solicitors. The college servants were English, but the university itself never seemed to be that. This was partly because so few of my friends and acquaintances had two English parents Indeed even some I took to be English turned out to at least half-Scots — or Russian, American, Jewish or Greek. The truth was that Cambridge belonged to the British Establishment, which was the creation of Scots as much as of the English.

I assumed I would make my career in London. We almost all assumed that's what we would do. This was natural, and I suppose that if some foreigner had asked me what was the capital of my country, I might have answered London, not Edinburgh. And why not? London, like Cambridge, seemed to me British rather than English. Though vastly changed in the last forty years and more, that holds good, and it is noticeable that the children of immigrants tend to call themselves not English but British.

Perhaps if I had worked harder and made plans for the future instead of giving myself to pleasure, I would indeed have found a job in London and made a career there. As it was I found myself with a degree, numerous debts, and no employment. So I became a schoolmaster at my old Prep School.

I taught there for ten   years making only a couple of half-hearted attempts to break away. I remained because the life was agreeable, I enjoyed teaching, liked my pupils, was accepted as one of the family and fell in love with one of the headmaster's daughters, whom indeed I married eventually. I remained also partly because my will to leave was weak, and partly from a sense of loyalty, for it was evident that the school, though educationally successful, was heading, financially, for the rocks.

When at last it was wrecked on them, I had a bad year. I was without direction and drinking too much. So, like Johnson's friend Savage, "having no profession, I became of necessity an author". I had always intended to write; now I had nothing else to do, and managed to sell my first short stories, to Alan Ross, editor of *The London Magazine* He gave me good advice and much-needed encouragement, for which I am grateful. Writing was also a means of regaining my self-respect.

Then I took off for Rome. It seemed the sort of thing for a novice writer to do. I lived there for three or four years supporting myself by teaching English, incompetently since I did it without interest, and by selling the occasional story and newspaper articles. We got married in Rome, on the Capitol, and our first child was born a year later. My novel made no progress, then died.

We returned to Scotland, to Edinburgh and found a flat in Drummond Place. It was a difficult time for my wife especially. We were very poor and had few prospects. I was approaching forty and had achieved little. I taught at a couple of tutorial colleges and wrote at night. Then, thanks to the friendship of the poet and novelist Robert Nye, and the influence he exerted on my behalf, I began to review books regularly for *The Scotsman* and to write other pieces for the paper. I discovered that years of writing History essays at school and university had given me a certain journalistic facility.

Book reviewing was a stroke of luck. One piece attracted the attention of Euan Cameron, an editor at *The Bodley Head*. He asked *The Scotsman*'s literary editor Willis Pickard who I was, and Willis said he believed I was writing a novel. Euan Cameron wrote to say he would like to read it. This spurred me on to finish the book. It was accepted and published when I was a few months short of my fortieth birthday. In retrospect it seems a good thing to have embarked on a new career in early middle-age. Novelists who publish when they are young use up material at a time when they should still be acquiring it.

Since 1978 I have published some thirty books, most of them novels, and written more newspaper articles than I care to try to count, on literature, theatre, politics, public affairs, ethics, and rugby, other subjects too doubtless. I suppose I have averaged about two hundred a year. Yet, though I would like to call myself a newspaperman, I doubt if I merit the description. I have never been employed on the staff of a paper, never known the urgency of late editions or the mingled camaraderie and rivalry of the newsroom. I am happy enough however to style myself a hack.

At the age of sixty-six I find myself compelled to accept that I have probably done the best work, written the best novels, of which I am capable. I think well of most of these books, and am happy to believe that they have given pleasure to some. It's a minor irritation that, because few of my novels are set in Scotland, I am sometimes not regarded as a Scottish novelist. Not that it matters greatly.   I am certain myself that even those novels set in Ancient Rome, and more assuredly those which deal with the political and moral crisis of mid-twentieth century Europe, betray what Stevenson called "a Scotch accent of the mind". Nevertheless it's been clear to me for some time that I am out of the mainstream of contemporary Scottish writing, well out of it indeed.

Eric Linklater, the twentieth century Scottish novelist I most enjoy and admire, was asked, near the end of his life, when he had been happiest. He replied "when I was at work on a novel and it was going well". I might say the same thing. He added, "and I don't think I shall have that experience again". I trust I will, even though I can no longer persuade myself that what I write is of great significance, and though I have come to accept that the novel no longer occupies the central place in western culture that it held for perhaps a century and a half, from, say, the publication of Waverley in 1814 to the nineteen - sixties I think my novels mostly well-made, better-made certainly than many hailed as works of genius, and I shall go on writing them, even though it's unlikely I shall hit on a new theme or find anything new to say, but must instead rely on what Evelyn Waugh called "professional trickery" to make them agreeable to readers.

The life of a writer is necessarily uneventful, unless he is one of those who ranges the world, with ever greater anxiety, in search of new material. He spends his time alone, at his desk, in converse with imaginary characters. The hardest thing is to retain his sense of curiosity about other people.

That very good novelist Alan Sillitoe once said that "to write a novel you need observation, memory and imagination". All grow duller with the passing years. Yet one keeps going. What else is one to do?

In 1982 we removed from Edinburgh to the Borders, renting a house in the Yarrow Valley, and have never for a moment regretted it. The country is beautiful, not yet despoiled, despite the threat posed by plans for wind-farms. There is still individuality here and a robust common-sense attitude to life; not different from what I knew in Aberdeenshire in my youth. My marriage has lasted; without my wife I would have gone to pieces and, probably, died of drink. As it is I gave up alcohol ten years ago, and am the better for having done so. Our children have grown-up, are doing well, and seem to me admirable well-balanced people. We live surrounded by animals — Clumber spaniels, cats, horses and hens. The French novelist Colette once wrote: " our perfect companions seldom have fewer than four feet". I often find myself in agreement, my wife always. I take pleasure in walking the dogs and watching rugby. I intend to die here, if not quite yet, and to be buried in Yarrow kirkyard. When I travel now, I prefer to return to places where I have been happy, notably Paris and Rome. I am a European rather than an Atlanticist.

Reading remains a delight and a consolation. The novelists I most admire are Scott, Stendhal, Dickens, Proust, Hemingway, Lampedusa and Andrei Makine. About Makine, a Russian who writes in French, I feel as Chekhov did about Tolstoy: as long as he is writing it matters less that I have failed to achieve what I set out to do.

There are regrets. Of course there are. One would have to be very self-satisfied for there not to be. I regret weakness of will, indolence, failures of sympathy and generosity too frequent irresponsibility, and ingratitude. More trivially, I should like to have written a successful play and to have played rugby for Scotland. The first might have been possible, the second never. I admire physical and moral courage and generosity of spirit, in all of which I have been deficient.

I retain an interest in politics and the behaviour of politicians, while no longer believing in solutions, and agreeing with Johnson that most schemes of political improvement are "very laughable things". I still think of myself as British, while recognizing that the feeling of Britishness has weakened in my lifetime especially here in Scotland and will probably wither away.

I don't think an independent Scotland would be a disaster, but neither would it be paradise regained. Independence would, I suspect, make less difference than either its promoters or its opponents suppose. Nationalism seems to me rather dotty, but so are a great many other things in the modern world. Nevertheless in some respects that world is better than the one I knew in my youth. It is more tolerant, there is less social bitterness than there was then and relations between the sexes and between the generations are easier than they used to be.

Duncan Macmillan

Born Beaconsfield, 7th March 1939

ART HISTORIAN AND CRITIC

Saltire Book of the Year, Scottish Art, 1460-1990, *1991*
Andrew Fletcher of Saltoun Award, 2004

Scottish Art reinstated

On 30th September 2004 I retired from Edinburgh University. I had served a full forty years to the day in the same institution, for I was appointed on 1st October 1964. For much of that time, I have lived at the same address in Edinburgh's New Town. It does not sound like an adventurous life, nor the stuff of an autobiography, and if that were all, this memoir should be very short indeed. I hope, though, that in that time, even if I have stayed at home, I have had some intellectual adventures that may be of interest and they are my subject.

My story began near London on 7th March 1939. My father was working as a freelance academic and author at the time, or he may already have been working for the BBC as he did for the first two or three years of the war, I am not sure. I am glad to say, however, that my presence in Scotland as a very small baby is recorded in a photograph taken in Glen Urquhart that year during the last summer of peace. War was clearly imminent and it was then, as a retreat from it for his new family, that my father bought the house in Glen Urquhart, his ancestral home, where I spent much of the first five years of my life.

My grandfather was born in the Glen. The family was cleared from good land to bad around 1839, but at least they were not exiled. My great-grandfather, Ian Ban Macmillan, was a tacksman and so had some small security of tenure. Brought up at Drumclune, a marginal farm high up above the Glen on a north facing-ridge, my grandfather was the youngest of seven children. He left the farm to go to King's College, Aberdeen, as it still was. After graduating in divinity in 1858 and marrying my grandmother, Elizabeth Lindsay, daughter of a Glasgow builder, he went to teach in Madras in India. After fifteen years or so he returned to Scotland to teach in his own school in Aberdeen. It was there that my father was born in 1885, but, peripatetic Scots, my grandfather and grandmother, now with seven children, then moved to Stellenbosch in South Africa. My father spent his school days there to return to Britain in 1903 as one of the first Rhodes Scholars. As a young man he retained his links with Scotland, however, and especially with Glen Urquhart and so, years later, when war seemed imminent, he returned there with me as an infant in 1939. The house there was sold to him by his first cousin, Tavish Macmillan. Tavish whom I knew well, though he was born in 1864, is a story in himself. He had left the Glen to go to the gold rush in Montana in the early 1880s. He made a handsome living running a store there for twenty years and returned to marry another cousin, Tina Macmillan, also a remarkable lady and a particularly fine speaker of Gaelic, I was assured by colleagues at the School of Scottish Studies who recorded her.

My father had spent most of the intervening years in South Africa as professor of history at the new University of Witwatersrand. He was a Fabian and I think I owe my existence to that fact. He always said it was Bernard Shaw and Beatrice and Sidney Webb, the leading Fabians, who had insisted that he should not enlist in 1915 — he had returned from South Africa to do so — but should go back and carry on what he was doing there, writing pointedly relevant history and campaigning against the injustices it revealed. It was perhaps in recognition of the place of the Fabians in my life, even before I was born, that my godmother was Ellen Wilkinson MP, leader of the Jarrow marchers.

As a Rhodes scholar my father had gone to Oxford where he was clear he learned nothing at all. But he used the balance of his scholarship to go to Berlin and there he learned a new, engaged view of history which shaped his life. What he learned there and I hope passed on to me is that the justification of the academic life is its potential impact on the wider world.

In South Africa he had had a twenty-year, childless marriage to Jean Sutherland. But the marriage broke up under the stress of his isolated opposition to what was later to become apartheid; isolated in the white community that is. He became the lonely champion of the black. It was at this time that he met my mother. Traditionally this happened when he was chairing a lecture by Shaw which she had been forbidden to attend, but had done so all the same. Their affair scandalised South Africa. He was married, a socialist and a Presbyterian. She was a catholic and the eldest daughter of Sir Hugh Tweedie, Admiral of the South Atlantic Fleet. (My maternal grandfather was the second generation of a Borders family to serve in the armed forces.) There was also a twenty three year age difference between my father and mother. To add to the scandal, they were not married till shortly before I was born several years later, and I was the second child. Wedding anniversaries were not a feature of the family calendar.

We spent the war between Penn in Buckinghamshire and the house in Glen Urquhart. The Glen then was another world. The older generation were all Gaelic speaking, but Gaelic was spoken very little. The old folk also still led their cows to pasture in the mornings. There was no electricity. John Mackenzie, better known as John the Baker, another cousin, not only ran the shop and the bakery in Milton, he was also the butcher. I think we lived comparatively well on offal, which was not rationed, and eggs and rabbits and such like unofficial food. He teased us children by talking Gaelic to us, but that was as close as I came to learning the language of my forefathers.

My education was anyway always more a matter of chance than of design. It began at my mother's knee in Glen Urquhart, where I learned to read by candlelight. But this brief idyll was rudely interrupted and at the age of five, I was sent away to board in Crieff in an institution known euphemistically as a Children's Hotel. It was not Dotheboys Hall, but it was distinctly Victorian all the same. I remember being beaten for telling a lie when I knew full well it was one of the adult carers who had told the lie, not me. Later the following year, however, my mother also moved to Crieff with my younger brother, who had been born in January, and VE Day was celebrated there while we were waiting to move into a house at the top of the town my father had chosen for the view over the valley of the Earn.

The primary school of Morrison's Academy was not memorable. Two spinster ladies taught us. One was tall and thin and grey, the other short and fat and florid. I am not sure that they liked children very much. I must have been deemed to have learned something, however, as I remember competing to be top of the class and in the end sharing the prize.

I moved to the junior school of Morrison's Academy, where the tawse was still an instrument of instruction, and where what I remember most from my lessons is being introduced to Scottish history by a charmingly eccentric teacher known as Bobo Fletcher. It was a subject not broached again till I was at St Andrews University. Then the family moved once more. Surprised perhaps by the arrival of a fourth child, my sister Catriona, my father was faced with the need to make more of a living than freelance writing and broadcasting could provide and so he took up an invitation to teach at St Andrews University. His subject was called Colonial Studies and was, more broadly, contemporary imperial affairs and the history of empire. I was eight when the family was transported in a Rolls Royce taxi (the Rolls was the standard taxi in small Scottish towns in those days) from Crieff to St Andrews to another house chosen for the view, a Victorian Gothic pile on the Scores with a cliff and the North Sea at the bottom of the garden. The wind whistled through it; my father could not bear to be in a room where the windows were closed — ever. The ceilings were immensely high, but the only heating was provided (at best) by three coal fires, one on each of the main floors. (There was also an enormous, spooky basement.) The bedrooms were entirely unheated and the house was supposed to have a ghost. It was Hogmanay, 1947, when we arrived in this Hitchcock edifice. We were entertained to dinner that night by our new neighbours, Principal Sir James and Lady Irvine. It was a scene more from Orchardson than Hitchcock, though pretty strange all the same. Our hosts sat at either end of an immensely long mahogany table in a gloomy room with a butler, or some other servant, hovering obsequiously in the shadows.

I started a new school, New Park, an undistinguished prep school where I did not do very well at first. I did not know what French and Latin were, nor indeed geometry or algebra, but I suppose I eventually got the hang of them. I certainly learned to love geometry for its visual elegance. I must have evinced an interest in other kinds of drawing too for I remember Joseph Sikalska, a Polish artist who was briefly art teacher there, taking an interest in me. A better education than school was to be had in St Andrews running on the rocks with school friends, playing chicken on the pier with the great waves that rolled in on the January gales, or risking our boyish necks climbing cliffs with washing lines and bicycling, careless of traffic for there was none, round the empty roads of East Fife. My particular friend, Alexander Macdonald, was passionate about boats from an early age and with him I also risked drowning, sailing on rafts we had built, or paddling around in canoes. Later we learned to sail.

I also learned to love birds. Placed between the cliffs with all their seabirds and the tree lined gardens of the Scores, the bird life was wonderfully rich. As boys do, I also collected stamps. It was definitely an aesthetic pastime. Stamps are miniature pictures and I remember the pleasure they gave. Perhaps arranging and cataloguing them prefigured my interest in art history, although cataloguing was never an aspect of the subject that really excited me in later life.

Among my other boyish pleasures was the cinema. There were two in St Andrews. Both in North Street, they were only a short walk from home and they each changed their films twice a week. There was always something to see. Westerns, musicals, Ealing comedies, war films, I took them all in. A little later there was also the Film Society. I began going to the films shown there while still in my early teens and continued to see everything that was shown when I became an undergraduate. That really was an education. Jean Renoir, Marcel Carne, Kurosawa, Bergman, Fellini, Ozu, all their films came to the Film Society. When they did, they were not yet seen as classics and so it was possible to watch them without any conditioned response. They provided my real introduction to contemporary culture.

My rather ragamuffin existence was interrupted on Sundays by the ghastly ritual of church. (My mother did not practise as a Catholic during my childhood. Later she was coaxed back into the church by a wily priest in St Andrews.) I remember the peculiar joylessness of the church bells clanging out in the stillness and silence of St Andrews on a Sunday morning. The Town Kirk had a carillon on which the hymns to be sung in the service were clanked out at a funereal speed. Years later I realised that this was a fascinating historic link with the Netherlands, but when I was a boy it just meant putting on my Sunday best which I hated. I argued that if God's interest was in my soul, why would he care how I was dressed? But I was overruled. Then the service was followed by stiff family walks along the golf course or the Kinkell Braes with all the other douce people of the Kirk. A scene from Dutch painting if I had but known it, nevertheless not diverting for a small boy. It was even worse when church was in St Salvator's College Chapel. I had to don a kilt and walk down the aisle between the ranks of students, men facing women on either side, to take a seat beneath John Knox's pulpit among the staff wives with their moustaches and their hats. (The gowned staff sat opposite in Gothic stalls.) It was an icy plunge into the coldest depths of Presbyterian respectability.

New Park was a prep school geared to Common Entrance and scholarships. I would certainly have been much better going to Madras College, the distinguished grammar school in St Andrews, and staying there, but the town, though so small, was socially stratified. Madras, in consequence, was unthinkable to my mother who never quite forgot the social pretensions of her upbringing, though I believe my father favoured it, and so the next stage was a choice between Fettes and Gordonstoun. I had to try for scholarships at both as it was made clear that the family finances would not support a fitting education otherwise. Apparently I got a larger scholarship to Gordonstoun and so that was where I went. My education, if it had been pretty haphazard so far, was seriously haphazard now.

The choice of Gordonstoun was suggested by an old friend of my father's, John Murray, a contemporary at Oxford who had been at Christchurch with Kurt Hahn. He had in fact had the rooms beneath him and Hahn, who could not spend time outside because he had suffered severe sunstroke, was practising the standing high jump in his rooms to the acute discomfort of his neighbour below. Surprisingly they had become friends and now my fate hinged on it. Hahn was still in charge when I went there, but he was shortly afterwards pushed out to be replaced as headmaster by an appalling individual called Geoffrey Brereton.

My housemaster, Eric Meissner, was a very strange character. He had thick, square glasses, white hair swept back and a face like a cliff in bad weather. If his scowl was ever relieved by a smile, it looked uncomfortable. He wore a duffel coat and in winter his pyjamas were clearly visible poking out from under the legs of his trousers. He spoke in a caricature German accent, the spoken equivalent of Gothic script, 18 point in bold, and was always accompanied by a huge, smelly, unwashed and untrimmed poodle called Ponto. It was easy to mock him and we did. Unfairly perhaps. He had made a courageous stand against Hitler at Gordonstoun's parent school in Germany. I drew caricatures of him and of the other masters. Nevertheless we respected Meissner and in his own odd way he was charismatic, the first teacher with any charisma I had encountered (except, briefly, for Bobo Fletcher.) He taught history very erratically, but inspiringly, and some Shakespeare. He also read to us, Homer, Tolstoy and other classics.

Most importantly Meissner was a real painter and the school was decorated with his moody, romantic pictures. Many of them were rather visionary, or perhaps symbolist pictures of the place itself which vividly conveyed his sense of its magic. For those of us who admired them, they imbued it with a sense of romance. For Gordonstoun — not the school, but the place — is romantic, tucked in behind great sea cliffs, with its eighteenth-century house and wonderful seventeenth-century stable block, the Round Square, the circular steading built by Robert Gordon, the Wizard of Gordonstoun, according to legend as a refuge from the Devil. It has crow-stepped gables and a roof-line that varies every thirty yards or so. I lived in it for most of my time there and painted pictures of it in an imitation of Meissner's symbolist style. This building was my introduction to the inimitable charm of Scottish vernacular architecture.

Meissner taught nothing systematically, but he encouraged a small group of us to take an active interest in art. We spent Saturday mornings painting in his room and I therefore owe him a debt which I am glad to acknowledge. It was certainly with him that the interest which was to take over my life began to take real shape. Art, and the excitement of language shared with friends, one of whom, Nicholas Otty (now, after a second marriage, Delavergne-Otty) is still a close friend, became my principal interests at Gordonstoun. There were no girls.

The staff consisted of eccentric refugees, strong on inspiration, short on system, and a crowd of perfect dullards, among them the official art teacher, Roy McComish. (Meissner's art teaching was unofficial.) It was from McComish, in preparation for A-level art, that I had my first ever lesson in art history. It was not very illuminating. It was a subject about which he plainly knew little and cared less. The one or two good teachers were in maths and physics and for a while I thought that my interests would go that way. I loved aeroplanes and it would have been a logical direction to take. In the end I turned away from science, however. I suspect that disastrous maths teaching at A level and the pull of art probably conspired to decide for me. I certainly don't remember any discussion or advice from anybody.

Nor do I remember any real discussion about my next choices. The assumption was that I would go to University, but it was also assumed that art school was out of the question. It simply was not an option and it was only years later that I realised it might have been. As a subject, art history barely existed in universities at the time. Exam passing was not Gordonstoun's forte, the teaching was so erratic, but I did eventually get four A levels, as far as I remember. I was supposed to go to Oxford, but that was out of the question. Even St Andrews was a struggle as I had to pass A level Latin to qualify. This I eventually managed, or it might have been Higher Latin that I passed, for I took that too, and so I started to read history there in October 1957.

The agony of Latin continued, however. It was still a compulsory part of an arts degree at St. Andrews. General Humanity it was called. At the very end, as I worked for a resit, I began to get a glimmering of why Latin was worthwhile and for the first time to enjoy it, especially Tacitus, Horace, Catullus and Virgil. I am glad I did. History proved a mixed blessing, however. Norman Gash, Professor of Modern History, was the dullest teacher you could imagine. His supporting staff were not much better. But Lionel Butler, Professor of Mediaeval History, was the opposite. A vivid teacher and a man of infectious enthusiasm, he made the vital link for me between history and culture and especially with my interest in art. Indeed he later went on to establish art history as a discipline in St Andrews. He is the second teacher to whom I know I owe a debt, but I also do to Ronald Cant. He taught Scottish history in lively, informal lectures. I remember him telling us that the Celts had no problem with class because they were all aristocrats, an elegant idea even if it was not true.

Philosophy was also compulsory and that turned out to be an unexpected joy. Playing with words and ideas was fun. Drinking was fun too, however. Worrying about sex was not fun. In the late fifties, it was still the chilly age of chastity. Nice girls didn't do it. And so if they were to be approached at all, it was under the impression that they would be doing you a large favour, not because of any mutual desire. It was not a position to inspire confidence. It took some time to understand that such things could indeed be a shared delight. This is an intellectual memoir however, not an emotional one, and so it is not the place to pursue that narrative, though I do think that the separation of these things is often artificial. Eros can be part of our motivation when we least suspect it and it is also a much larger part of art than is generally recognised in the dry narrative of art history.

But after moving into a university residence, St Regulus Hall, in my second year when my parents spent a year in Africa, I cemented a lifelong friendship with John McLean with whom with other friends I shared both the pleasures of drink and the anxieties of sex. With John, however, I also shared a love of painting and that was a tremendous encouragement both then and afterwards. I owe him a debt for it. John also had a picture in his room unlike anything I had seen before. The Cézanne, Monet and Gauguin exhibitions at successive Edinburgh Festivals had introduced me to painting as it figured in the wider world. They made a huge impression on me. Indeed I see the Cézanne exhibition in 1954 as a turning point in my life. But the picture John had was abstract and contemporary. It was something quite new. It was by his father, Talbert McLean. At some point in my second year, I travelled with John to Arbroath and met Talbert and saw his paintings. He was a wonderful man, modest and quiet, but with an integrity and inner strength which shone through both the man and his art. It was a vital connection that he made for me: that good and bad in art were a reflection of good and bad in life itself. It was the same year, I think, 1958, that the exhibition in Edinburgh of School of Paris painting from the Moltzau Collection introduced me for the first time to abstract painting more generally. I think I painted several pictures afterwards in the style of Manessier.

Meanwhile, however, I had not given up my love of aeroplanes. I joined the University Air Squadron and learned to fly. I went solo from the tiny wartime airfield above the cliffs at Crail. Then the squadron moved to Leuchars where the runway was so huge that on one occasion the instructor I was with took off across it. He was incensed by the mockery of the crews on stand-by with their jet fighters at the beginning of the runway, so he sent them running for cover by taking off over their heads.

I realised fairly quickly that the conformity required by the RAF was not for me, but not before I had got a lot of pleasure from flying and had also usefully supplemented my income, for the Air Squadron paid quite generously. My student grant was minute and I do not remember any other subvention. After a summer camp at Tangmere in Sussex, flush with £25 pay in my pocket, I set off for the first time to France. I had travelled to South Africa when I was eleven and to Jamaica one memorable Christmas as a teenager when my father was spending a year at the University College of the West Indies, but I had never been on the Continent. I had also studied French for a good many years, but I had never heard it spoken. The way I had been taught, it was as dead as Latin. I arrived in France and could not speak a word. I learned the hard way, working as a night porter in a dim hotel in Montparnasse, dealing with drunks and throwing out whores if they sneaked in.

The *patron's* wife was a Scot and I had arrived there after calling on the Scots minister in Paris who, it was rumoured, was willing to help indigent young Scots like myself. He was Donald Caskie, a war time hero and a remarkable man, if a little strange. He put me up for a little while and I helped him by doing odd jobs. Then he found me this position in the Hotel des Colonies. I had a room, but virtually nothing to live on, roughly a hundred old francs a day, about ten pence I suppose. My breakfast of half a baguette came with the room. Otherwise I think I lived on beans. I was mostly kept alive by a charming Franco-Scottish lady, Netta Mackintosh, a friend of Donald Caskie's, and a lifelong resident of Paris, but also a sister of one the proprietors of the Children's Hotel in Crieff. She had stayed in Paris throughout the war and had played her part in the Resistance hiding escaping prisoners of war as they moved through the city. She wore the Legion d'Honneur that her courage had earned her, a tiny ribbon on her ample bosom, and lived with her brother, who had served in the British army in the war, in a little flat near the Avenue Felix Faure. She invited me regularly to eat, always tactfully, and her warmth and kindness then perhaps made up for my experiences as a five year old in her sister's dreadful establishment.

Paris was romantic. There were glamorous strays playing music under the bridges. I went to the Academy of La Grande Chaumière and drew from life. The Louvre was open free on certain evenings and I wandered there, and in the Jeu de Paume where the Impressionists were displayed, wondering at what I saw. My loves in painting had started with El Greco, but I had quickly abandoned such extravagance for the miraculous serenity of Piero della Francesca and the artists of the Quattrocento. But I was also still fascinated by the Post-Impressionists, by Cézanne and Gauguin, whose work I had first encountered in Edinburgh, and by Van Gogh whose paintings I saw here for the first time.

I was also enthralled by the Romanesque. I don't know where my love of its austere and tragic dignity came from, but it has endured, and it was with the vague intention of visiting the great Romanesque churches on the pilgrimage route to Santiago de Compostella that I set off hitch-hiking southwards some time towards the end of August. I slept in the fields and reached Le Puy and the Auvergne before the chance of a lift diverted me down the Ardèche to the National Sept and thence to St Tropez. Just then Brigitte Bardot had burst on to the cinema screen as the fascinating image of female sexuality as an active, not a passive thing, and I am sure her residence in St Tropez had something to do with my chosen route. I did not find her there, nor any substitute, but from there I travelled west in search of the grape harvest to earn the money needed to take me home.

I picked grapes for a month or more in the little town of Nissan-les-Ensèrune. My pay was largely in wine, three litres a day; and I still have the ancient black bottle that was found in the corner of a barn to give me my first litre and so seal my contract. It was 'truck' in fact — as in to 'have no truck with' someone — payment in drink. The rest of my wages amounted to no more than £1 a day. The old people spoke Languedoc. Everybody cursed the priests as 'les corbeaux'. The Albigensian crusades were not forgotten, nor were the Germans. One day I had a scary encounter with two very large, motor-cycle gendarmes dressed in long boots, leather jackets and helmets. They demanded my papers. I had nothing on but a pair of shorts. I could hardly have been carrying my passport as they well knew. They became very threatening and started to cross-examine me. I am fair in colouring and they had taken me for German. But when I told them I came from Scotland and was studying philosophy, as that summer I had decided to do, their attitude changed dramatically: "Alors! Vous êtes Ecossais? Vous n'êtes pas Allemand? Et vous faites vos études en philosophie? Eh bien! Allez! Les philosophes n'ont pas besoin des papiers!" Also reflected in that exchange was the always touching folk memory of the ancient friendship between France and Scotland.

The other workers were Spanish migrants. The first litre of wine was handed out at seven o'clock, the second at ten and the third in the lunch break. We knocked off at four. The patron's wife supplemented this ration of alcohol with absinthe, or something very like it, mid-morning. The work was hard, but the day passed in a pleasant enough alcoholic haze. I lived on bread, wine, grapes and boudin and was innocently courted by the village girls below marriageable age. The older girls could not be seen speaking to me, nor would my life have been safe if they had done so.

I found my way back to Britain in late September to find my parents had moved house from Scotland to Long Wittenham near Oxford. Returning from there to St Andrews, in spite of what I had told the gendarmes, and I had indeed intended to change to pure philosophy, I decided to compromise, drop modern history, but stick with mediaeval and combine it with moral philosophy. It was an odd combination, but it worked. The teaching of philosophy, or rather metaphysics, in second year by Professor Johnny Wright was inspiring. The later years proved less so, but the books were marvellous, Plato, Aristotle, Rousseau and especially Hume. There was something about his language and the luminous humanity of the thought for which it was the vehicle that I found utterly compelling. It made the superficial nonsense of the Oxford logical positivists, whose work we were also obliged to read, seem just that. I could not comprehend why we were supposed to see them as equally relevant, or as even engaged in the same pursuit.

The teacher in my final year at St Andrews from whom I learned most, however, was Robin Adam. With him, I studied the Norman Conquest and the Domesday Book for Herefordshire in detail as a special subject in mediaeval history. It was my first real introduction to historical method and to how the wider picture in history is a function of accurate detail.

I took my degree in June of 1961. I was not sure what I was going to do next, but at some point I found out about the possibility of being an Assistant in France and so in the autumn of 1961, I found myself in Marseille where I spent a year. It was at the height of the Algerian crisis. Bombs went off every night and the city was full of the *pieds noirs*, the French refugees from Algeria. There were other kinds of violence too and guns were much in evidence. The whole centre of the city was in hock to protection racketeers, but the only fiery drama I experienced directly came when a gas heater in my room leaked, a bed caught fire and I had to throw it into the street below. It sat burning in the middle of the street, the Canebière, the main street of Marseille, till the pompiers arrived on their fire engine wearing great brass helmets. Otherwise in Marseille I mostly managed to live peacefully enough in a polyglot group of the other British assistants, faded French aristocrats, Corsicans and various Mediterranean strays.

I read a lot that year, especially Camus, Sartre and the Existentialists. The Existentialist idea of the absurd seemed profoundly logical in a world which it was generally assumed would sooner or later be blown away by nuclear war. The merriment of the sixties was surely a huge reaction of relief after the Cuban missile crisis made that fiery holocaust seem no longer inevitable. I painted too. I also travelled to Italy for the first time and spent the Christmas of 1961 in Rome.

But I had to decide what to do next. The only thing I was sure of was that I wanted to work with words, ideas and art. I went for an interview in Paris for a job with a French art magazine. They did offer me something after a delay of a month or more, but by then I had already decided to return to University. I had earlier toyed with the idea of going to Dundee to study architecture, but in the end I applied to the Courtauld Institute in London to do a post-graduate course. I spent two academic years there from October 1962 to June 1964.

Most of the art history that was taught at the Courtauld seemed to be like the writings of the logical positivists, an effete academic ballet. People like John Sherman struck elegant attitudes and said very little. It was notable that the only time I was ever taken to see an actual picture was in a class on conservation and the purpose of the visit was to look at the back of an altar piece, not the painting on the front. But Alan Bowness was friendly and encouraging and took a real interest in his students. John Golding was intense and at least approached the subject from the point of view of a painter, though I suspect he had never heard of Bergson when I gave a tutorial on Futurism and deployed some of my rather eclectic reading in philosophy to suggest that he was an influence on Boccioni. Rayner Banham was also interesting. The person who made most impression on me, however, was Anthony Blunt.

Blunt had passion and did not conceal it, nor did he hide his real sympathies. In fact we were all aware of his career as a spy. I studied Picasso and the Spanish Civil War with him, pretty much one to one. It was a subject close to his heart and an exciting experience. There was no ballet here, no posturing. I had always known it was important, but now for the first time it became clear to me that the reason why art mattered was because there the deepest concerns could be expressed and argued over. It might even change the world and art history could illuminate all this.

Blunt was also kind to me and encouraged me. I proposed a thesis on Picasso and Surrealism and he was enthusiastic. He was correspondingly disappointed, I think, when I asked him for a reference to apply for a job at Edinburgh. Why did I want to go there? he asked. Scotland was where I came from and I felt perhaps I could do something there, I replied. I don't know exactly what it was I thought I could do, but I do clearly remember saying that to him. I also had no money. Indeed I was in debt. I had to have a job. I don't think Blunt understood that. I had kept myself in London as best I could by writing for various dictionaries. One of them was published by Phaidon, I think, but I am not at all sure what I wrote in it. Nevertheless these articles were my first professional publications. I did the research in the V&A library and hammered the articles out on an old portable typewriter, learning to type as I did so, if to this day rather inefficiently.

In July I went for interview in Edinburgh with David Talbot Rice in the newly built David Hume Tower. I was given the job, presumably on Blunt's recommendation, though I was ill enough prepared for it. The subject I was to teach was the art and architecture of the seventeenth and eighteenth centuries in Britain and Europe. I knew nothing about it at all. At the Courtauld I had studied the art of the Renaissance and that of the twentieth century. The bit in between was a blank.

I moved to Edinburgh in August with no money and I did not get paid till the end of October, so I continued to write dictionary articles to keep myself. I took a room in Northumberland Street and embarked on a private crash course in my new subject. Among the books I read while I did this was Frederick Antal's *Hogarth and his Place in European Art*. It left an indelible impression on me. Here was art seen as an integral part of the history of human ideas and radical ideas at that. It was only years later when I read Miranda Carter's admirable biography of Blunt that I connected him directly with Antal and realised how much personal continuity there was between them and how what I had learnt from Blunt tied up with what he had learnt from Antal. But the first lecture I gave was on Claude. I have had a very special affection for Claude ever since. He is the most magical of painters. I also had to teach the first year, already an enormous class and quite a challenge though one that I learned to enjoy. I also began to teach extra-mural classes and continued to do so for many years.

As well as Hogarth and Claude in these first years in Edinburgh, I discovered Blake, Turner, Constable and the Dutch. From the beginning I took great stimulus from teaching and the habit of linking teaching and research stayed with me. Often, indeed, my teaching led my research.

I found that the literature on Dutch art was very sparse and even less illuminating. Somehow the Dutch painters had never been accepted into the canon. What was written about them presented them as apart from the mainstream. It was often even apologetic. Much later, Kenneth Clarke's *Rembrandt and the Italian Renaissance* was a brilliant exception to this and gave me great inspiration. At the time however, the literature was condescending and this did not make sense. It seemed to me that the landscape painters of the 1620s and '30s, Jan Van Goyen, Salomon van Ruysdael and the rest, carried out a revolution in painting every bit as radical and profound in its consequences as Cubism and that the great artists who followed them were in a real sense already modern.

I studied the great collections of Dutch painting in London, but then, to find out more, in the spring of 1966 I set out on a pilgrimage to Holland and spent three weeks driving around in the ancient Morris Minor convertible that I had bought the previous summer. It was my first car and the first of a series of these wonderful little cars that I drove, travelling in them as far afield as Munich, Rome and Barcelona. On this trip, I visited all the major centres in Holland and some of the minor ones too. I also went south into Belgium to Antwerp and Ghent. I learnt a lot and began to see that the Dutch painters really were the main line and that it is the canon that is wrong. Later it proved to be the same with Scottish painting. The two were also certainly connected and indeed, as it transpired, the next chapter, the eighteenth century part of the alternative canon that I began to formulate for myself, proved to be in significant part a Scottish story.

In various revisions of the degree courses in Fine Art and with the introduction of an art history degree, which I think I initiated, there was more scope for specialist teaching and I focussed more closely on British art. First on the Pre-Raphaelites and then more and more on Scottish art. I remember an incident that made me realise early on how much there was to be done. I came across a passing reference to the paintings by Alexander Runciman in the Cowgate Chapel, now St Patrick's Church. I was intrigued by the fact that a major painting might have been lying unseen for a century and a half beneath a coat of paint. I went to the church and worked out that Runciman's huge painting of the Ascension must indeed still be there. In 1966 I managed to establish by a technical examination that it was. Maybe this was symbolic of a wider search for the hidden story of Scottish art, I do not know. But I began to think that I should pursue this as my main research. I wrote to Anthony Blunt saying I wanted to write my PhD on Alexander Runciman, not Picasso. He replied he had never heard of him and I think gave me up for lost.

My access to Scottish painting before this had been slender. In St Andrews my mother used to buy up old paintings of Highland cows in the salerooms and occasionally I reused the canvasses, not a very dignified first approach to the subject to which I have since devoted so much time. But where could I have learnt about it? In spite of Caw and Cursiter and the honourable exception of Ellis Waterhouse in his Pelican History of Art volume on Britain in the eighteenth century, generally, if Scottish artists were written about at all, it was simply by selectively incorporating them into the history of English art. I remember years later finding a catalogue in Amsterdam, a British Council publication from the sixties, that summed it up. It was an exhibition that professed to be of English art, but it included Raeburn, Ramsay and other Scots. There was also a helpful map at the beginning which showed the British Isles, but cut off at Berwick and without any indication of Scotland at all.

But the contemporary scene was not encouraging either. From Talbert McLean I had learned about James Cowie, but Cowie was a bit of an outsider and Talbert did not have a very high opinion of the Scottish art establishment otherwise. It had not been kind to him and when I came to Edinburgh and met some of the leading Scottish painters, I was inclined to think he was right. When David Talbot Rice introduced me to Robin Philipson, for instance, he greeted me by saying: "Ah, you are another of those art historians hired to mislead our young painters," or words to that effect. There were Board of Studies meetings too when the staff of the Fine Art Dept. would sit down with the staff of the College of Art. TR presided, patient as a Buddha. Gillies would sit like the Dormouse at the Mad Hatter's Tea Party, smoking his Woodbines. Robin, who was then Head of Painting, would go on flamboyantly about the 'craft of painting' — crafty painting might have been more accurate. Eric Shilsky, Head of Sculpture, would ramble on endlessly about how six years was not nearly long enough for a student to study sculpture and so the Fine Art Course should last at least a lifetime. It all confirmed the feeling I had got from Robin's welcome that contemporary art in Scotland was distinctly anti-intellectual.

But there was also another side to contemporary art. The Traverse had just opened and Richard Demarco was presenting his first exhibitions. There was the Paperback Bookshop on the corner of George Square and there were Happenings like the famous 'nude in a wheelbarrow' during the Festivals of those years. Soon my friend and colleague Ivor Davies was entertaining us by blowing things up in the name of Destruction in Art. During my first summer in Edinburgh, too, John Bellany and Sandy Moffat held the second of their open air exhibitions and in my very first tutorial, the first class of my whole academic career, I had to cope with a bellicose Alan Bold spouting MacDiarmid and Marxism.

It was the sixties and life was fun. But I did begin to write my PhD and in 1970 published my first academic article. It was on Alexander Runciman in Rome in the *Burlington Magazine*. It is a pretty stiff and boring read. Publication was also delayed because somebody at the Courtauld had decided to write on Runciman too and my article was held back so it could appear at the same time as she published hers in the *Warburg Journal*, very fair-minded I am sure, but not encouraging. I also published an article in the *Art Bulletin* later the same year on Holman Hunt's *Hireling Shepherd*.

I went to Rome several times in pursuit of my research. There I followed the eighteenth-century Scottish artists round the monuments and up into the Alban Hills. I traced their lodgings in the *Stato degli Animi*, the annual Easter censuses prepared by the parish priests, and I found them all living on top of each other around the Spanish Steps. Back in Edinburgh I found that theirs was the world of the Cape Club, a whole subculture of hard-drinking artists, actors and poets, a rumbustuous world beneath the more socially decorous layer of the recognised Enlightenment. These were the beer drinkers. Polite people drank claret. The records of the Cape are one of the more unusual treasures of the National Library, beer stained lists of the nightly sederunts with occasionally the bill for green stoups of porter totted up on the back. It was an exciting and excitable group of people and they were also self-consciously Scottish. I treasure the remark by the younger Thomas Ruddiman in the first editorial of the *Caledonian Mercury*: his new paper should be 'not a flimsy retail shop of imported foreign articles, but a genuine Caledonian magazine.' It was a point of view that it seemed to me was vividly reflected in the Runciman drawings that I was studying in the National Gallery Department of Prints and Drawings at Ainslie Place and in photographs of the lost ceiling of *Ossian's Hall* in Penicuik House. I got to know and admire Keith Andrews, Keeper of Drawings, but as the conservation department was in the same building, I also got to know Harry Woolford and John Dick. John especially shared my developing interest in Scottish art.

My thesis took years and never had a single minute's supervision. The time it took was partly because I was teaching full-time and sabbaticals were not so fashionable then, but it was also because I discovered very quickly that I could not write a meaningful biography of an eighteenth-century Scottish artist whose career was divided between Edinburgh and Rome without writing the history of the artistic context in which he lived and worked. Basil Skinner had opened up the discussion about the Scots in Italy, but there was a mass of primary research to do. There still is. I eventually wrote most of my thesis in a sabbatical term at the British School in Rome early in 1971, my first sabbatical. It was in June that year too that I got married. I met my wife Vivien when she was still a student on the Fine Art course. I think the last time I saw David Talbot Rice was at our wedding. Vivien was one of a very lively year, many of whom are still friends, that I took on a memorable art historical tour of Italy, the second one that I organised. My best man was Bedros Vartanyan. We lived first in Royal Park Terrace, in a flat I had bought a few years earlier, in the family tradition for the marvellous view. Arthur's Seat filled the windows. The following year, however, we moved to Nelson Street to the flat in which David and Tamara Talbot Rice had lived. It did not have a view, but we have lived there ever since. The following year, in 1973, our first daughter, Christina, was born. Our second daughter, Annabel, followed in 1976.

I finished my PhD in 1973 and graduated the following year. My father was awarded an honorary degree at the same time, but he died later that year. I was pleased that in the last years of his life I was able to take him back to Glen Urquhart several times. It was a place he had always loved as I have done also. I bought a house there myself in the late 1980s, a smallholding that had belonged to three unmarried cousins, the two brothers and sister of Tavish Macmillan's wife Tina and the last Gaelic speaking members of the family.

It was soon after I had finished my PhD that I first began to think of writing a full history of Scottish art. Why should we not have access to our own artistic heritage, I felt? A nation without access to its history is an amnesiac. It took a while to realise my ambition however. I was teaching a great deal and so once again, my research had to follow my teaching. My project was also set back by the publication of David and Francina Irwin's book, *Scottish Painters at Home and Abroad*, in 1975. But while it inevitably made publication of another book on Scottish art more difficult, I reviewed it in the TLS and that cleared my mind and so helped focus my own project.

The Irwins took great exception to what I wrote in my review and a rather heated correspondence ensued, but I don't think I was being unkind. The book reflected the universal problem for academics at the time: to claim something was Scottish and was of value was fine so long as it was also clearly subordinate to the English view of history. Even in their title, the Irwins, it seemed to me, had bent over backwards to conform to this rule and not make the mistake of claiming a Scottish identity for their subject. The book itself was, as I said in my review, a fine piece of research, but it was a mine or a quarry rather than a construction. It had no central proposal to make about what, if anything, made Scottish art distinct, nor how it was part of any wider Scottish intellectual or cultural history. Indeed, though they followed Caw in this, the Irwins did not even discuss a 'Scottish school' till they got to the mid-nineteenth century when such a thing was noticed for the first time in England. It seems characteristic of this story that the Scottish school had been a matter of discussion, admiration and even imitation in France a good deal earlier than that.

The challenge I had set myself was therefore to take the tumbled stones of the history of Scottish art and build with them a meaningful structure that we could recognise, not only as the history of our art, but also, past and present, as an integral part of the greater edifice of our cultural history, indeed of our identity and its place in the wider world. The story of Scottish art properly told must also change the wider story of European art. The key to this was what I had realised writing my PhD: that painters, poets and philosophers naturally shared the same ideas and the same concerns.

About this time I also set out to make my thesis publishable. I had a sabbatical in the autumn of 1976 and we went to Italy. Our youngest daughter, Annabel, was a baby and we rented a freezing cold house in remote countryside outside Florence. My plan was to write from six in the morning till twelve and then spend the rest of the day with the family. I stuck to it pretty well and wrote a significant part of a manuscript, but for some reason I never completed it after returning to Scotland. I think my ideas had moved on and I was already thinking about the wider picture of Scottish art. A single biography, and one that I had already written in effect in my thesis, was not the answer.

Writing about Runciman, I had soon realised how important Gavin Hamilton was, for instance, not just in British art, but in European art as a whole. Thus it became clear that this was a story that had implications for the wider history of the art of the time. But I also learned how difficult it was going to be to change received opinion when I had an article on Hamilton accepted by the Art Bulletin, but had to withdraw it at the last minute because some anonymous academic reader did not approve of what I had written and asked me to change my conclusions. Of course I could not do so. They were the point of the article.

In the late '60s and '70s, it was still normal in academic circles to ignore the Scottish dimension in the Scottish Enlightenment, if not to deny it actively. It was as though the fact that the Enlightenment happened in Scotland was a fluke, best explained by the blessings that came with the

Union, which had at last made Scotland respectable. There is an amusing updating of that in Melvyn Bragg's recent invention of the English Enlightenment. But I was excited to encounter a brilliantly stated alternative view in George Davie's *The Democratic Intellect*, a book that profoundly influenced me. I also treasure the memory of seeing George in action for the first time. It was at a lecture given by Trevor Roper on the Enlightenment. He gave the standard view that it was all thanks to the Union, finished and sat down, but after the usual polite applause there was a kind of volcanic rumble from the back of the room. It was George Davie exploding to blow away the flimsy edifice of Trevor Roper's argument as though it were no more than a pile of autumn leaves.

It must have been just before this that Suzanne Sinclair had first introduced me to George. Suzanne and I had met on a committee that dealt with the University's development of Milne's Court as a student residence. There, in our innocence, we had exposed some criminal skullduggery by Maxwell Young, Factorial Secretary of the University, and the architect John Reid. The Georgian buildings immediately to the west of New College were unsafe, we were told. They must come down immediately. Naïve junior that I was, I asked for the engineer's report that said this was so. Suzanne backed me and of course it transpired after several meetings and even more evasions that there was no such report, though a brochure had already been printed showing John Reid's proposed building on the site where the Georgian buildings stood. Nobody was prosecuted for conspiracy though they should have been. The Georgian block is still there however, I am proud to say, safe and solid as it ever was.

I was very much involved in conservation generally in the late sixties and early seventies. My first public foray was over the proposed demolition of the Cafe Royal. With a group of like-minded people, I helped organise a petition. We collected ten thousand signatures and I think I addressed the Planning Committee when we presented it. We won our case. I then became the first chairman of the South Side Association which grew out of the same pressure group formed with Peter Pharoah, Oliver Barratt and others. In the question of the South Side it seemed that the attitude displayed by Trevor Roper also shaped planning. I published an article about the plans for the area which I called 'Where the Luftwaffe Failed'. It was an attack on Percy Johnston Marshall whose plans threatened to demolish most of the South Side as effectively as ever the Blitz could have done had the Luftwaffe been so minded. Percy's response was interesting: "Good to see you young chaps interested in conservation, but what you should really be worrying about is the New Town." It was the same problem as with Scottish art. The New Town, however much it actually enshrines the thinking of the Scottish Enlightenment, is nevertheless recognisably international in style, not obviously Scottish. It was deemed worthy of attention because it was capable of adoption into an anglo-centric view of history, but the South Side is vernacular, merely Scottish therefore, manifestly not part of that wider history and, in Percy's view, expendable.

We lost the two triangles of eighteenth century flats with all their pubs and shops around Bristo Street and Crichton Street, thanks to a cynical move by the egregious Maxwell Young. He realised that the conservation lobby was growing in strength and if the buildings were not destroyed quickly, it would be difficult to get rid of them. They were knocked down over the summer while I was away on holiday. That autumn there was an accommodation crisis for students. Thirty five years later the site is still empty. I have never set foot on it, nor will I till something worthy has been built there. We did win the struggle over Buccleuch Place and the adjacent streets, however. They are still standing.

While I developed my study of Scottish art, my interest in contemporary art did not fade. Indeed I always saw them as complimentary. This was confirmed by a new departure, art criticism. I had begun to write book reviews and the like for some of the ephemeral magazines of the time, *Q Question*, *The New Edinburgh Review* and later *Cencrastus*. Indeed I served on the advisory board of *Cencrastus* for a little while. But for an art historian, art criticism was a doubtful enterprise at that time. The art critic and the art historian were seen as almost in opposition. Art history presented itself as a rigorous academic discipline. It could have nothing in common with the sloppy, subjective habits of the art critic. I already believed the contrary, however, that art history is a necessary part of the equipment of the art critic and that to an extent the opposite is also true. Surely the purpose of both is to give access to art of whatever period so that it can give pleasure and illumination to our present world?

My first contemporary art review was in *Studio International* on a painter called John Copnall showing at Demarco's Melville Crescent Gallery some time in the early '70s. When the editor of *Studio*, Peter Townsend, after being unceremoniously sacked from his post, started *Art Monthly* with Jack Wendler in 1976, I had an article called *Art and Devolution* in the first number and thereafter wrote regularly for a number of years. I also began to write catalogues for the SAC around this time. I think the first was for Gavin Scobie in 1974. Gavin had seen my John Copnall review in *Studio*. He liked what I had written and asked me to write the text for the catalogue for an exhibition organised by the SAC. Later I wrote a short book on Gavin's work.

It was through *Art Monthly* that I went to interview Miró in Majorca in 1978. I had taken the family to Catalonia regularly. The analogy with Scotland that I saw there was intriguing and it was that which first led me to take an interest in Miró who seemed such a potent focus for Catalan identity. Meeting him was a memorable experience. What he told me in an hour's conversation, as I digested it later, was, I realised, quite startling. He offered a whole alternative to the conventional view of Modernism. He told me that the thing that mattered most to him was what he called 'les grands projets', his public art. I realised that he was quoting William Morris, Walter Crane and Owen Jones, almost verbatim. He offered me what seemed an invaluable insight, not only into his own motivation as an artist, but into what was essentially an extension of the Arts and Crafts tradition going back to Gaudi's indebtedness to Jones and, in radical opposition to the ego cult of modernism, embracing the idea of the artist as the anonymous servant of the community. Later I found this same vision championed by Patrick Geddes and embodied in the Scottish National War Memorial. I published my interview with Miró in *Art Monthly* and *Arts Canada*, but a couple of years later, thanks to Jacques Dupin, Miró's friend and agent at the Galerie Maeght, I also became involved with a major Miró exhibition in Houston, Texas, for which I did extensive research into his public art and indeed visited a great many of the sites. The work I did was published in 1982 in a truncated form in the catalogue of the exhibition, *Miró in America*.

In 1977, I organised an exhibition at the Fruitmarket of the work of John McLean, Fred Pollock, Douglas Abercrombie and Alan Gouk, four Scottish artists working in London. Through John, I invited Clement Greenberg over to give a talk. That was quite an experience. Most vividly I remember a lunch at Edinburgh College of Art when John Brown, College Treasurer, who had been warned that Clem liked his whisky and had recognised a kindred spirit, stood behind his visitor's chair, whisky bottle in hand, throughout the meal. But getting to know Clem was a privilege. I took him up to meet Talbert McLean in Arbroath because in my mind they stood for the same sense of values in art.

In 1978 I got into trouble however. I was invited to write an introduction to the catalogue of an exhibition of contemporary Scottish art in Finland organised by the Scottish Arts Council. It was a political initiative to placate nationalist feeling in advance of the forthcoming referendum on Scottish autonomy. Part of the deal was to be a trip to Finland for everybody involved as guests of the Finns. But when the time came I got no invitation. Richard Demarco was sent in my place. It was only when the group came back that I learnt why I had been excluded. The British Ambassador had been shown my introduction by the British Council before it was printed and was so incensed by my explicitly Scottish point of view that he wanted it suppressed. It was pointed out to him that published in Finnish it was unlikely to cause much stir back home, though suppressing it certainly would. He contented himself by making sure that I was not invited and in my absence by attacking me publicly in his speech at the opening of the exhibition, much to the surprise of the Finns. When they found out what had happened, however, they asked me anyway and I spent ten days in Finland the following spring.

When I told this story to George Davie he responded by writing a moving letter telling me how much pressure had been put on him by Sir Edward Appleton when he published *The Democratic Intellect* because of its independently Scottish point of view and how much this had inhibited him from publishing more. That he eventually did start to publish again was I think in large part due to the encouragement of Murdo MacDonald.

In 1973 the first phase of the Talbot Rice Gallery was opened. I took the opportunity it offered to repay a debt of honour and present an exhibition of the work of Talbert McLean. Then with Ivor Davies and Giles Robertson, I helped supervise the conversion of the White Gallery from a bare space that had formerly been the Library Periodical stacks. The architect was once again John Reid. Much to his disgust, we rejected his plan to fill the gallery with a monumental staircase and insisted instead on the simple space we now have.

It was only with reluctance that I took over the Gallery after Ivor Davies left in 1977 or '78. It is not that I was not interested, but at the time the gallery was a lame duck. A victim of a stand-off between the SAC and the University, the annual budget was £1000, £500 from each of them. Nor, when I took it over, was any allowance made for the additional demand on my time. It was only several years later that I moved onto a split contract whereby a teaching half-post was paid from the Faculty of Arts budget and the other half, my Curator's salary, from the Central Administration budget. I reported directly to the Secretary of the University.

The only staff in the Gallery was an attendant, Frank Moran, a charming man. An ex-plumber, he and a mate had together been responsible for the British Army's successful crossing of the Rhine. They had spent a night splicing the cables that hauled the temporary bridges into place. But as an old soldier Frank was also a student of the British principle of economy of effort. I remember being introduced to this at school where I was punished for some misdemeanour by being sent to work on the estate. One task was moving tree trunks. My partner in this seemed to me to be old and frail, so naturally, being young and fit, I strove to carry more than my strict half of the load. The foreman took me to one side to explain that if you carry a tree trunk, or any such load, you must always lift it by the extreme end, that way you will not carry more than your share. I then shocked the authorities by shifting a ton of sand in half an hour when nobody was looking. This was so unprecedented that I was accused of getting my friends to help. Anyway, it meant that in the Gallery, Frank, though he was a kind man, was strict in only lifting his share of the metaphorical tree trunk.

The gallery gave me an opening in a quite new direction, outwards towards the public and towards contemporary art and its meaning in the modern world. For this I am immensely grateful. If I had not had this chance to diversify what I was doing and to work independently, for no-one interfered with me, I would never have survived another twenty five years and more in the University. When I took over the Gallery, too, the stand-off between the University and the SAC came to an end. Early in 1979 Lothian Region intervened to provide a grant of £5000. This shamed the other two parties into matching it, or at least coming close to doing so, with grants of £3000 each. From there forward it was possible to plan a proper exhibition programme.

My first major project and my first modest catalogue was an exhibition with Eduardo Paolozzi during the Festival of 1979. The following Festival I held an exhibition of the work of the Canadian painter Jack Bush. Since then I have lost count of the number of artists I have exhibited, or for whom I have written catalogues. They have mostly been Scottish, but I have also formed several friendships outside Scotland with artists I have shown and I have gone on to write for several of them in their home countries including Peter Brandes from Denmark, Eugenio Carmi from Italy and Toshihiro Hamano from Japan.

Running the gallery was often a struggle and I was never sure from one year to the next if it would survive. I tried to ensure that it did by distancing it from the Fine Art Department and the Faculty of Arts. I reckoned it would be too easy to close it down to save money if it was part of the struggling Humanities where horizons were always limited. It had to be seen as a University asset. If I was successful in this, it was largely because I was supported by successive Principals, John Burnett, David Smith, Stewart Sutherland and Tim O'Shea. I am grateful for their vision. Politics apart, the Gallery was an exciting opportunity and a real chance to connect writing about art in the past with writing about it and promoting it in the present — presenting the historical and contemporary as continuous, in fact, not as quite separate things. Thus it was that in 1981 I undertook my first historical exhibition. I had realised that portraiture, far from being downtrodden and peripheral, closely reflected the main business of European art. It was concerned with the individual and it was social. Above all it focussed the question of otherness, the conundrum at the centre of empiricism. The exhibition was called rather grandly *Masterpieces of Scottish Portrait Painting*, but it did include such pictures as Ramsay's *Margaret Lindsay* and his *Elizabeth Montague*, two of the greatest ever female portraits, Raeburn's double portrait of *General Francis Dundas and his wife, Eliza Cumming*, and Orchardson's lovely portrait of *Mrs. John Pettie*, but perhaps the star of the show was Wilkie's astonishing *Chalmers-Bethune* portrait. It was completely unknown before then.

In the same year, too, I showed a major William Johnstone retrospective. Getting to know William Johnstone was a privilege. It was characteristic of him that this friendship began some years earlier with my receiving a letter in beautiful handwriting. He had seen something that I had written in *Art Monthly*. He had liked it and had written to say so. Not only was he still keeping up to date with the art press in his late seventies. It was typical of him that he also took the time and trouble to write a letter of encouragement to someone that, rightly or wrongly, he saw as promising. I was very much encouraged by his interest and support.

Meanwhile the Scottish content of my British art teaching gradually took over till, some time in the mid-seventies, I began to teach a purely Scottish course. It was the first of its kind, although now, I believe, Scottish art is taught in all the Scottish universities where there is an art history course. In my teaching I always used the marvellous resources in and around Edinburgh. The collection of Prints and Drawings at the Mound was the centre for much of my tutorial teaching, for instance, and what a privilege that was. Foreign students, especially, were amazed at the opportunity to study the work of Ramsay, Wilkie and others in such detail and at first hand. I was very touched when a Swiss student, Marguerite Droz-Emmert, went on to write a thesis and then publish it as what was, I believe, the first book in German on Allan Ramsay.

I also used to take my class to visit houses and collections as often as I could and the encounter from which the portrait exhibition was born was with the Raeburn double portrait of *General Francis Dundas and his wife* which I saw at Arniston on one of these visits. The picture's boldness astonished me, but it seemed it could not be just a display of virtuosity. It was reflecting on it that I came to realise how central portraiture is to the whole of this subject and, too, how in such a picture ideas about perception, identity, social awareness, all themes of Enlightenment thought, find as articulate expression as they do anywhere in the prose of the philosophers.

If this picture was the germ of that exhibition, it was perhaps also the germ of the project which followed in 1986, the book and exhibition, *Painting in Scotland the Golden Age*, or rather it was half the germ. The other half was the recognition through my PhD of the precociousness of Runciman and his friends in some of the key concerns of modern art. Though I think I was also so incensed by an article in *Art History* on Wilkie's *Knox Preaching at St. Andrews* which presented this great liberal picture as some kind of hysterical anti-Catholic tract, and along with this both Wilkie and Thomas Chalmers as blinkered and prejudiced Protestants, that I felt the record had to be put straight. The article was profoundly unscholarly and itself just recycled prejudice, but the editor of *Art History*, John Onians, would not publish a rebuttal. I had to find a way to present the truth and the counter-argument myself. In 1978 I had in fact published an article in the first number of *Art History*, not an experience I was ever to repeat.

Raeburn seemed to give the balancing, intellectual dimension to the precocious Romanticism of Runciman, though it was not until later that I discovered exactly how true that was. But my first task was to find out what really was the wider intellectual framework that linked Raeburn and Runciman and indeed reconciled as well the aims of painters as apparently diverse as these two with those of Allan Ramsay, Gavin Hamilton, David Allan, Alexander Nasmyth and David Wilkie.

The idea of writing this book had been in my mind for a while by then and in 1984 I wrote a series of essays in *Cencrastus* that were really the outline for it. I also suggested it to John Nichol at Yale University Press, only for it to be rejected as lacking a market. The breakthrough also came in 1984, however. Uncharacteristically I had let myself into organising the Art Historians Conference in Edinburgh that year. The job perhaps fell to me as I was Acting Head of the Fine Art Department for several years after Giles Robertson retired. At the conference I met Simon Havilland of Phaidon. I had formulated the idea of writing this book in conjunction with an exhibition on painting in the Enlightenment. My former tutor, Alan Bowness, now Director of the Tate, encouraged it. Simon Havilland took up the idea. So did the Tate and so we had the exhibition in Edinburgh during the Festival of 1986 and at the Tate in the autumn of that year. There were more than 200 works in the show including some of the most precious in Scottish art. Even the Queen's great Wilkie, the *Penny Wedding*, was included. It is a key Scottish picture but Oliver Millar, then in charge of the Royal Collection, at first refused to lend it. The occasion, he said, was not of sufficient importance, but I found myself showing the Duke of Edinburgh around the University and seized my chance to clype on Millar with the desired effect. I got a crawling letter from him a few days later agreeing to lend the picture.

Writing the book gave me a lot of pleasure. As the story unfolded, a real intellectual framework emerged and painting, poetry, philosophy and even medicine seemed to share an agenda. In fact the whole thing was so unified that I could even see where there was a gap. This happened with Raeburn. Although he had been so much part of my early thinking, when I came to write about him it became clear that there was something missing. There was an intellectual shape to what he did. The question was what formed it? Something led me to Thomas Reid and there I found a theory of perception which is clearly reflected in Raeburn's work and which also had the most radical implications for painting more generally. There are places where Reid seems to anticipate directly the aims of the Impressionists, just as Raeburn does. The fact that through Victor Cousin, his works became a set text for the Baccalauréat in France in 1842 surely has something to do with this apparent connection.

One major omission from the *Golden Age* book, however, is Adam Smith, though I have endeavoured to make that good since. Smith's idea that sympathy is the cement that binds society together, and that sympathy itself is a function of imagination, is the key to much that we see in Scottish painting from Ramsay's portraits to Wilkie's *Distraining for Rent*. Gavin Hamilton and Adam Smith were classmates and the idea of moral sense is also reflected in much that Hamilton did.

Trying to publish some of these ideas, I found the same old prejudices in place, however. A publisher's reader for Cambridge, I think it was, dismissed the whole argument out of hand. At one point where I had suggested that Courbet's *L'Après Midi à Ornans* was influenced by Wilkie's *Cotter's Saturday Night*, which it manifestly was, he/she wrote 'to suggest that Wilkie influenced Courbet is absurd.' It was not a matter of argument then, but of implicit, unquestioning belief in the hierarchy of art, in the canon, in fact. According to this, Wilkie, a Scot, is necessarily of inferior rank to Courbet, a Frenchman. I came across exactly the same thing with Lawrence Eitner, the Géricault expert. Géricault wrote a letter expressing his deep admiration for Wilkie's *Chelsea Pensioners*. Writing about Géricault, Eitner both quotes it and dismisses it. I met him at a conference on Géricault at the Louvre where I gave a paper and I took the opportunity to ask why he had dismissed it. He replied there was no way Géricault could really have meant what he had written about an artist as insignificant as Wilkie — so far outside the canon, he might have said. Géricault was evidently momentarily deluded when he expressed such an incorrect view.

After the publication of the *Golden Age* book I was more than ever conscious of the need for the book that I had first dreamed of writing that covered the whole topic of Scottish art. Again it was a chance conversation that turned this into a real project. Somewhere I was chatting to Bill Campbell of Mainstream and mentioned the idea of a book on Scottish art without supposing it would interest him. At the time Mainstream had not undertaken any art books, but he took up the idea immediately and the project was born. That was late in 1988. I spent a little while preparing my thoughts and I began to write in long-hand early in 1989, but the thing really did not take off till I bought my first computer in March. It was an Amstrad and was slow and clumsy, but it was magic compared to a portable typewriter. I began in the middle, got to the end and then went back to the beginning. I did not have any sabbatical leave, but continued to teach and to run the gallery. Nevertheless I managed to write just about a chapter, up to 15,000 words, a fortnight for more than six months. The text was finished by the autumn of 1989. I had RSI in one wrist at the end of it and I was ill that Christmas.

The original idea was that it would be quite a short book, but I am afraid it grew to more than 250,000 words, a massive bibliography and nearly 350 illustrations. It was a huge project, but Bill Campbell and his colleague at Mainstream Peter McKenzie stuck with it. I owe them a great debt, though fortunately not a financial one. The book was profitable.

Gathering the illustrations — many of them involved driving round the country with photographer Joe Rock to make them (which he always did beautifully) on the spot — preparing the end-matter and the design took most of the next year, but the book was ready to print in October 1990. Then I had an awful moment. It was to be printed at Butler and Tanner in Frome, Somerset. We had managed a deal with the Russell Trust that involved sponsorship in kind from the Russell paper works. I went down to supervise printing, but after the first sheet of 24 pages came off the press it became clear that the colour register was out at the edges. The whole stock of thirty tons of paper was warped and I had to decide to abandon printing and scrap the paper. By a heroic effort Mainstream got a fresh supply of paper and printing resumed again in November. I spent a week on the presses, but I think the result was worth it. The book looked good and it was a success. I was very flattered that it was short-listed for the Whitbread Prize and then won the Saltire Prize for Scottish book of the year.

The idea of *Scottish Art* was simple enough; to tell the story of art in Scotland as I had tried to do in the *Golden Age* book in a way that took account of the wider intellectual and cultural history of the country; in a way that was accessible to everybody; and too in a way that made its continuing relevance in the present quite clear. That is why the closing date of the book's time-frame was the original year of publication, 1990. The art of the past should not be a separate thing, inhabiting some remote and scholarly sphere. It should be part of our present self-awareness. Indeed it is a necessary part of our self-esteem. That I suppose was the essential motivation of all this. We are a nation with a remarkable visual heritage, but we had always been taught to think the opposite. It was part of the proverbial Scottish cringe that we had believed the black propaganda against the Reformation and the Iconoclasts and were inclined to suppose that, as their heirs, we were irredeemably philistine as a nation. It was an enduring misrepresentation which I hope my book has helped correct. I think that the failure of the 1979 Referendum may also have focussed this for me too. It raised questions of national self-esteem which it was clear would be resolved in the cultural field, long before they could be in the political one.

Even as I wrote the introduction, I was able to quote a current *Sunday Times* headline "Scots visual art and Calvinist neglect." It was because of the kind of prejudice reflected in that remark that I had started the narrative of the book in the fifteenth century. It seemed to me essential that the Reformation should be located as simply an episode in Scottish history, one that had extraordinary consequences certainly, but which nevertheless did not represent a break in historical continuity.

James III was plainly a Renaissance prince and the first great works that survive that belong in the modern world date from his reign. So 1460, the year of his accession, was the starting point. The record we have of the Renaissance in Scotland is only fragmentary. Nevertheless it became clear to me that even in that shadowy picture there are signs of a vivid and self-confident self-awareness that makes a great building like Stirling Castle the result, not of some provincial inability to understand the new art of the sixteenth century, but rather of a self-conscious determination to adapt it to the expression of a distinct Scottish identity. The Reformation was a product of this Scottish Renaissance, not its antithesis; nor indeed were its leaders fundamentally hostile to art. It was after all precisely the years of the

Reformation that saw brilliantly coloured painted ceilings become so much part of Scottish life.

The rest of the story followed remarkably smoothly. The Enlightenment inevitably stands at the centre, but there is much else besides. Wilkie's *Cotter's Saturday Night* was painted in 1837, the end of the Enlightenment by most reckoning. His ideal of a harmonious society unites, seamlessly, the philosophy of moral sense with the traditional Calvinist vision of the metaphysical society, but this it is not simply retrospective or nostalgic. It is forward looking. Here and elsewhere he anticipates Ruskin and also Geddes in his prescient understanding that the crisis of modern society will be moral and not simply economic. The picture also tells us about the compound of religious and social ideals that led to the Disruption six years later. William Dyce likewise reflects on the collision between traditional religious belief and the new scientific understanding. William McTaggart is also profoundly modern. In the *Sailing of the Emigrant Ship* we see not only his continuing social concern as he reflects on the dissolution of Gaelic society, but also how his chosen means of expression conveys his sense of the dissolution of the old order through the actual dissolution of the surface of the picture itself. Geddes himself, who impinges so directly on the visual arts, is not only the heir to much Enlightenment thought, he was also prophetic in the way he saw where it would lead if Enlightenment empiricism was separated from the ideal of humanity that shaped it.

Geddes already looks forward directly to twentieth century concerns. But Arthur Melville is also surely a major figure in late nineteenth century painting. Melville, an East Coast painter and never a Glasgow Boy though he is consistently lumped in with them, was a key figure for the Colourists and among them, J.D.Fergusson stands out. He was the only major British artist directly associated with all the excitement in Paris in the years before the first war. Strikingly however, he does not simply pick up new painterly tricks when he sets out to make a major statement as he did in *Les Eus*, for instance. That picture looks back to Wilkie and David Allan as much as it does to Matisse and to Gauguin's vision of Eden, though the society of sexual liberation that Fergusson proposes is one that was so far ahead of its time that that side of it has been carefully suppressed till now. Sexual mores aside, Fergusson, Mackintosh and Geddes represent between them a fascinating circle of Scottish modernists. Part of this modernity was the promotion of women artists. Geddes did not create Phoebe Traquair, but he did promote her very effectively.

One of the most satisfying things about writing this book was that this story, when told as a continuous narrative, proved that there was a vigorous, distinct and unbroken tradition of art in Scotland. The artists also served their own community well. They were never insular, but nor was their art ever simply a dim reflection of brilliant events on other shores. And this has continued down to the present. Eduardo Paolozzi, Ian Hamilton Finlay, Will Maclean and others clearly belong in a tradition that stretches back to the Enlightenment, but loses nothing in modernity by doing so.

In 1991 I visited Japan for the first time. The occasion was a proposed exhibition of work by Toshihiro Hamano. Several visits followed and in 1995 I had a fellowship that gave me three months in the country. I was pursuing a topic that had emerged in part from conversations I had with Hamano and, in parallel, a sense of the way in which western artists had almost intuitively found something in Japanese art, and especially in the Zen tradition, that answered one of the central puzzles that faced them, the inevitable confusion of subject and object that undermines a system based on empiricism; and that was what, it seemed to me, western art was essentially concerned with. Hume had identified this problem, but before him, so had Rembrandt. Then Whistler sought an answer in a kind of painting that dissolved the distinction in a way that was overtly indebted to Japanese art.

I spent some time in two Zen monasteries in pursuit of some understanding of the Zen approach. It was fascinating, though hard on the knees. The Japanese influence on Western art has often been discussed, but my own understanding of it is that Japanese art helped artists identify decisively a problem in Western thought, rather than that it provided a simple solution to it. The essential part of the argument that I was evolving is that the whole history of art in the West is part of the same empirical project as science. We are more familiar with it in science partly because scientists have had to maintain the fiction of objectivity, even though artists and philosophers had recognised early on that it was impossible. Both the latter groups have struggled since then to find a solution, but the artists did so, until recently at least, without abandoning the original objective: to describe experience. The difficulty of the search explains much in modern art. The Zen dissolution of subject in object offered a way of seeing this problem for what it was and Monet's great *Water-Lilies* do just that.

This argument also links many of the things that were apparently definitive of modernism in the early twentieth century with things that the Scots were doing in the eighteenth: the cultivation of the imagination, and to that end the emulation of the primitive as an imaginatively and morally superior model; the belief in the value of spontaneity and expression, and the consequent disregard of rules. These were all things that link the generation of Hamilton and Runciman and the philosophy of moral sense to that of Matisse and Picasso and the philosophy of Bergson. This of course is also where my early study of the Dutch painters joined up decisively with my study of the Scots.

After Scottish Art I published first a book on Will Maclean in 1992 and then a similar book on Steven Campbell the following year. Both accompanied exhibitions in the Talbot Rice Gallery. Their subjects were artists who, though very different from each other, were of real stature and whose work is rich and complex. I also collaborated around this time on exhibitions with both Eduardo Paolozzi and Ian Hamilton Finlay. These artists were all key figures in my next project, *Scottish Art in the Twentieth Century*. It might seem a paradox to treat the 20th century separately, given what I have said about the importance of continuity. I do believe that there is a degree of misleading hubris in the way that the 20th century saw itself as different from all preceding centuries and in consequence saw its art as somehow apart, different from anything that had gone before. Nevertheless, there can be no doubt that what is closest to us is of most interest, especially to the young.

In *Scottish Art*, though it did come up to the present, I had had to balance my treatment of the 20th century against all the preceding centuries and so, although in fact it was not really squeezed in proportion to the rest of the book, it was bound to seem so. Certainly there was less opportunity for illustration or indeed even to make mention of a good many artists whose work is nevertheless significant in the context of a single century. It had also been necessary largely to exclude sculpture from the larger book for reasons of space, something for which I was criticised at the time, unfairly I think as I made it quite clear in the introduction that sculpture was not to be part of the story that I was setting out to tell. *Scottish Art* was also a big, expensive book. For all these reasons, the case for writing a separate book on the art of the 20th century which could illustrate a wide variety of contemporary and near contemporary work was a strong one. It was also part of the project from the start that it should be priced at no more than £20 so it could reach the widest possible public. We could find no subsidy so this constraint of price meant that it had to be relatively short. It was only 192 pages.

In 2000 I published a book on Elizabeth Blackadder. This was at Elizabeth's invitation following a couple of catalogues that I had written for her for shows with the Scottish Gallery. Work on the book was mostly done in 1998 I think. I also continued to publish exhibition catalogues and in 1996, following a catalogue I published a couple of years earlier, I was invited to write a book jointly, or perhaps more accurately to share a book, with Umberto Eco on the Italian painter Eugenio Carmi.

In 1994 I had taken up writing regularly for *The Scotsman* on the invitation of Alan Taylor. Appropriately, my first review was of an exhibition of Dutch landscape painting in Madrid. The first there had ever been. I reckon I had published half a million words in the paper when I moved to a new paper *Business a.m* in 2000. It folded after two years, however, and I returned to *The Scotsman* in June 2002. In the mid-nineties, my position on the paper allowed me to engage directly in the battle over the proposed gallery of Scottish art. This was a shocking episode in the recent history of Scotland. The National Gallery, ably assisted by a ruthless and quite unprincipled Glasgow lobby, proposed to hive off the national collection of Scottish art into a separate gallery in Glasgow, dividing it from the international collections into a ghetto in fact. It militated against everything I had tried to do in presenting Scottish art as a significant part of the European tradition and, worse, it reflected the survival in modern Scotland of the old, anglo-centric prejudices, quite undimmed and unashamed, that I had encountered from the start. In the view of its director, the Scottish collection in the National Gallery was clearly expendable, if it was not actually an embarrassment, the provincial clay feet that would limit the Gallery's (and his) international ambitions. I said at the time that if this proposal went through, the National Gallery of Scotland would become the National Gallery of Nowhere in Particular, a bland, international collection that could be anywhere.

Even now the Scottish collection is still ghettoised within the National Galleries, though not in the Portrait Gallery which, because of its overt and inescapable Scottishness, was to be the sacrificial lamb in all this. It represented too visibly the offending inconvenience that the National Gallery of Scotland is located in Scotland. It was to be closed, a proposal that aroused dramatic public opposition. Paul Scott and the Saltire Society organised a public meeting in Edinburgh College of Art where the strength of feeling was registered not only by the speakers of whom I was one, but even more by the sheer numbers who attended, or tried to attend for the crowd spilt out into the open and relay speakers had to be provided.

But even when that round was won, the fight continued for several years over the idea of a gallery of Scottish art in Glasgow. I continued to be engaged heavily in it. So did the Saltire Society where an action committee was organised. The Glasgow lobby sought to polarise the argument as an Edinburgh-Glasgow issue, but it was a national one. The whole future of the national collection and the place of Scottish art within it were at stake. It was a fierce battle and it is extraordinary that the whole project went so far and indeed that so much money was spent on it. Old prejudices die hard. I am very glad we won the argument. I am not sure that Timothy Clifford has ever forgiven me for our eventual victory however. There is a certain irony in reflecting that it was only because of the efforts of myself and others in promoting Scottish art that it had become sufficiently important to be fought over in this way.

In 2000, I also published a new edition of *Scottish Art*. The additional work was limited by cost to two new chapters, rather than a complete revision. So I added a chapter to bring it up to date chronologically and a chapter to take account of the work I had done in the intervening years. In this, I outlined, for example, how I had come to realise how much, especially in the eighteenth and early nineteenth centuries, Scotland was a generator of ideas which mattered in the European context. Indeed I suppose the challenge was already implicit in writing *Scottish Art* in the first place to show how, when you take into account the story told there, you have to rewrite the history of European art to accommodate it. I explored this in outline in an essay on the 'Canon in Scottish Art' in 1994 in the first number of a new journal called *Scotlands*.

I embarked on this new research in 1991 when I had a short fellowship at Yale. It was only a month, I think, but as there was nothing else whatever to do in New Haven and the wonderful Yale Library was open till midnight, I got a great deal done. I have published a whole series of articles that started with work done there exploring the indebtedness of European artists to ideas first formulated in Scotland: the dependency of David and Canova on Gavin Hamilton, of Géricault on Charles Bell and Wilkie, of Bonington and Delacroix on Wilkie and Scott, and there is still more to tell. This discussion ties up with the broader discussion about empiricism and the origins of modern art and I suppose the problem that faces me now is how best to organise that argument: in broad terms working outwards from the Scottish experience, or as two separate books, one focussing closely on Scotland in Europe and the other on the wider theme of empiricism as the motor of modern art.

One of the last major exhibitions that I organised in the Talbot Rice Gallery before I retired, *Object Lessons*, in June 2003, explored a key aspect of this theme. It brought together all kinds of objects from across the University's diverse collections — its scientific more than its artistic collections in fact — to demonstrate their richness; but also more importantly to demonstrate how much the empirical tradition had always depended on the visual disciplines of observation, record and analysis whose instrument, from the very beginning, was drawing. It was a way of locating Edinburgh University and thus Scotland at the heart of the empirical tradition, but also of demonstrating more generally the close inter-involvement of the sciences and the visual arts throughout the modern period. It was therefore also a way of demonstrating the validity of the argument that in the modern world — that is since the beginnings of empiricism four hundred years ago — art and science have been two aspects of the same project. There have been digressions certainly. Nevertheless, I believe, the drive that produced modern art was the same as that which drove science. To recognise that more clearly might help us to understand both better. It would certainly make the way in which modern art developed much easier to understand and would show it as an integral part of the whole history of Western thought over that time. If the study of Scottish art can throw light on something so much bigger than itself, then perhaps that is justification enough for undertaking it.

Nevertheless the greatest source of satisfaction for me is here at home. It is to see how Scottish art, from being a forgotten and neglected part of our history, has become in recent years a central part of the national consciousness and above all of national pride and self-esteem. If I have contributed to that transformation in any way, then it has been well worthwhile.

John Byrne

Born Paisley, 6th January 1940

PAINTER AND PLAYWRIGHT

Life is the Clay

It was 1958 and I was in London, living in Harlesden and working undercover as a Counter Clerk (Temporary Grade) at the Labour Exchange in Medina Road, Holloway. It was the dullest job in Christendom but it did allow me the opportunity to trawl the galleries of Cork Street and its environs in search of that ladder of legend upon which I could set a toe. Prior to my unlucky break in securing that position with the Civil Service I had borrowed enough money from my pal Peter O'Neil to purchase a tin box of 'watercolours' from the toy shop underneath his mother's flat in Harlesden High Street and with the help of a tin of boot polish, a small rectangle of plywood prised from the skirting board of their bathroom, and some Brasso, managed to paint a circus scene of such glowing intensity that I had no qualms about hawking it round the fashionable galleries of Mayfair on my Saturdays off from work in the certain knowledge that not only would I get a foothold on that first rung but I would be scaling the ladder at such a rate that there was a definite danger that I might disappear into the clouds and be celebrated only after my death. I was 18.

Ten years later the penny dropped. I was working as a Carpet Designer with my old sparring partner A F Stoddard & Co in Elderslie, having gone through Glasgow School of Art, been to Italy on a scholarship, got married and had two small children, been accepted for the Painting School at the Royal College of Art (I was to share accommodation with a chap called Henk Onrust at their Halls of Residence) but hadn't gone — I discovered years later that the then Director of Glasgow School of Art, H. Jefferson Barnes, had paid me the huge, albeit back-handed, compliment of informing the

Bursar at the RCA, when asked to provide me with a letter of recommendation for a College grant that would see my family and me through the Painting School, that "... there is nothing more that you can teach him", thus putting the kybosh on that particular source of revenue (for which I say a prayer of thanksgiving each night) — and was not enjoying it one bit. What to do? I had by this time realised that those London galleries I'd visited my little circus picture upon were but shops, each with a particular clientele to be catered for with a particular kind of painting. I'd been back and forth to the metropolis in the intervening years and the glowing reviews I read in the art columns of the *Sunday Times* and the *Observer* never squared for me with the stuff on the walls. The smell of stinking fish? I thought I'd give it another go and set about making another little picture. Under the desk in the Design Studio at the Carpet Works. Of course, nowadays, it probably would be stinking fish but then it was a little painting of a man in a panama hat holding a bunch of flowers in the 'naif' style. I'd come across a feature in one of the colour supplements about 'the Innocent Eye' — self-taught painters and primitives — and recognised that what one needed was a 'hook'. If you could say that you were an ex-prisoner or a one-legged Trappist monk this was a hook the gallery could hang the show on. We had all of us while at Art School subscribed to the ridiculous notion that if one hadn't made it by the time one was 25 that was it – oblivion and Hell mend one. I was already 27 by this time. My days were numbered and them some. Six months on and I was dead meat. Never mind how it was accomplished. Never mind to what lengths one had to go. Better a One Hit Wonder than a Nobody, right? I picked the Portal Gallery in Mayfair. Wrote them a covering letter with The Man in the Panama Hat (in the 'naif' style), said it was painted by my 72 year-old father, an ex-busker, signed it with his name 'Patrick'. Got a letter by return. Rather a dry letter but they were 'interested' to know how to get in touch with my father and whether he had produced any other paintings. I wrote back saying that he was at his beach hut in Dunoon and that I was acting on his behalf and yes, he did have more paintings. Quite a lot of them. Enough for a show, certainly. My father was summoned to Mayfair. I went in his stead. Confessed to the ruse. The gallery said they'd already twigged but I could tell from the wheelchair that had met me off the bus and the uncorked bottle of Sanatogen Tonic Wine on the reception desk that they were fibbing. In the interests of fame and commerce we arrived at an understanding — if I didn't say too much to the press then they wouldn't either. 'Patrick's' debut show was a sell-out — bought by the rich and famous, reviewed in the pages of *Apollo* (in exchange for two tickets for 'Oh, Calcutta', the hit-show of the moment), celebrated in *Vogue* magazine with a photograph by David Bailey, and eventually undone in the Letters page of the *Observer* where the Registrar of Glasgow School of Art, on the instructions of my nemesis, the aforementioned H. Jefferson Barnes, revealed the true identity of the guilty 'innocent'.   Again, the trademark backhanded compliment — ". . . the most sophisticated student to pass through the Mackintosh building since Joan Eardley . . . winner of the coveted Bellahousten Award . ." but the damage was done, my cover blown.   I had fallen among thieves. Sold my birthright for a mess of potage.   What to do now??

In 1977 I sent off a theatre script to the doyenne of play agents, Peggy Ramsay.   It was called 'Writer's Cramp' and featured one Francis Seneca McDade, a self-styled author with a big hit for himself whose lack of success, despite his obvious genius, in the literary world resulted in penury, forcing him to turn his hand to painting (at which he was that 'rara avis', a genuine primitive) under the 'nom de pinceau' Sconey Semple, a one-eyed illiterate whose seminal work 'George the Baptist' – painted on the inside of a kettle using specially-designed brushes — was bought for the nation and is now on display at the McDade Memorial Archive, Shoogly Walk, Barrhead.

I was once told by Robin Philpson the then Head of Painting at Edinburgh College of Art where I'd transferred for my Third Year from Glasgow, that once I'd rid my work of its vulgarity I might have the opportunity of becoming a "proper painter".   I hadn't the gumption then to tell him that 'vulgarity' and 'life' were to me synonymous.   I have acquired that gumption now, though.   I would never have become a playwright nor, in my own estimation at least, a better painter (i.e. a painter from the 'life'), had I not been something of a vulgarian.   My work is suffused with the vulgar.   I have no time for 'ivory tower-ism'.   The worthy — the dead hand.   What is Art if not the embodiment, distillation, and celebration of Life itself?   We are born with gifts and weaknesses — the great triumph as I see it is to turn our weaknesses, our foibles, our failings, through our work as artists into something other.

Life is the clay — Art is the vessel.

Aonghas Macneacail

Born Uig, Isle of Skye, 7th June 1942

WRITER

Leaves from a Life: *some autobiographical notes*

Tapping these words into my laptop, I recall my father, who died when I was eight, turning a patch of fallow ground behind our house with an implement we knew as the *caschrom*, a foot plough. For Edward Dwelly, lexicographer extraordinaire, this "crooked spade" was "of great antiquity" and used to till stony ground unworkable by a plough.

The expression *b' eòlach do sheanair* (as your grandfather knew) meaning the exact opposite, would frequently be used in reaction to any new facility or contraption, from mains electricity and a plumbed water supply to synchromesh gears and transistor radios. The immediate post-war world we lived in seemed, nevertheless to be a stable one. But then, maybe every childhood except the most disrupted is lived in a cocoon of apparent stability

Our Gaelic grandfathers, whose links with antiquity were deep and diverse, cultural as well as economic, even if attenuated by oppressive theologies and dislocative politics, would be rendered speechless, utterly, by today's instantly global electronic world. I was born to their world where things like tractors and outboard motors existed, but elsewhere. Children hung up their stockings, but Christmas was otherwise an ordinary working day. We still had rationing, but I seem to recall being able to buy sticks of liquorice which we pretended were chews of black twist, the pungent tobacco favoured by the old men of the village.

My father, an able seaman on coastal freighters which plied between the main British and Irish seaports, who died when I was eight, I remember as a bringer of *Dinky Toys* and DC Thompson comics, first the *Dandy* and *Beano* and latter the *Hotspur, Adventure* and *Rover*. He did leave the sea, in order to see more of his family, but apart from a couple of months labouring on the site of the new village police station, he remained, essentially, an economic absentee, until cancer made his absence permanent. He was, I'd later learn from his contemporaries, a passionate reader of history books.

Our village was Uig, on the West coast of Trotternish, the most Northerly peninsula of the Isle of Skye. Now an important Hebridean ferry port, in 1942, my year of birth, as for many years after, it offered shelter, and little else, to a smattering of fishing boats, and every couple of weeks, the MacBraynes coaster, that carried small cargoes to similar ports throughout the islands. What I recall from those early years is that the dilapidated, and potentially dangerous, state of the pier, reckoned to be among the longest in the country, was a source of concern to the community, and occasionally to politicians, which made it an interesting place for village boys to go fishing.

Uig was, essentially, a string of crofting townships wrapped round a sheltered bay: the name derives from Vik, the Norse word for a bay. On the Northern wing, our township, Idrigil, which overlapped with Rha, overlooked the pier, and faced South Cuil, a scattered string of buildings where the school sat in a small cluster which formed the tip of the Southern tail of the village. Across a steep-sided stream from the school stood the John Martin Memorial Maternity Hospital, where I, and the great majority of Skye's population, for several generations, first drew breath.

One of my earliest recollections is of visiting my mother there, and being introduced to my new-born sister. When, a few days later, mother and daughter were brought home by the hospital matron, a cousin of mum's, I was, I'm told, anxious that the baby's "real" mother took her back to the hospital. That year a war ended, and I also have a memory of fire, on the hillside across the bay. For years, I associated it with stories of an American transport plane that had crashed into Beinn Eadarra, the three-peaked hill that dominated Uig: on reflection, I now think it more probable that the flames rose from a victory bonfire. It was, I'd guess, the following summer that a couple of English youth hostellers knocked on our door, hoping to buy milk or eggs. Hearing their language for the first time, I could only describe it as *bruidhinn bhuidhe*, the "yellow speaking".

A year later, I was introduced to an altogether English-speaking environment. Even though it was with a modified Gaelic accent, my first teacher's first job, that year as every previous year, was to teach her tearful new charges a foreign language, which most of us would soon learn to speak better than our own. I think I enjoyed the first four years of school: we were well shepherded into literacy and numeracy by Miss Ross (who was actually Mrs — being married to John Ross, the gamekeeper, who knew how to keep the gentry content while having ways of alerting less "licit" local users of the river that authority might be approaching).

The upper three years of primary were under the charge of a headmaster who, being the most formally educated elder in the Free Church, to which my family adhered, also ran the Sunday School — which condemned me to experience the lash of his authority six days a week. While he couldn't access his fearsome Lochgelly tawse, which we called the "strap", on The Sabbath, a rigid Highland Calvinist interpretation of the Bible instilled enough fear in us to ensure conformity. Texts and catechismic answers were learned by rote with due diligence. The descent of leather on extended hands was a regular weekday occurrence. The only belting I can remember receiving followed a foray down the out-of-bounds steep bank above that stream below the school, to gather ripe nuts from the hazel trees that grew in profusion there.

Although we weren't aware at the time, our headmaster suffered bouts of depression, which may have explained his frequent retreats to the schoolhouse, having set us work which was often completed long before his return. In Primary 7, our final year, that habit provided a particularly anguishing twist, as he would return in time to ring the bell for "school's out" but keep behind for revision those he thought likely to do well in the Qualifying exam. There was nothing sordid in this practice, just the tedium of arithmetic, and the knowledge that our peers were out playing their way home.

Apart from the coloured paper chains and bells, and sweetly pungent pine branches draped along the infant classroom wall at Christmastime, the only really good memories reclaimable from those years are the few occasions when a writing topic allowed the imagination full flow. In the playground, being an imaginary member of goody Stalin's army, before the Iron Curtain came crashing down on such simplicities, was fun too. But mostly, the good things happened outside school.

While I don't recall a single Gaelic lesson in his school, I do owe that old theocrat one favour: his advice to my mother that if she wanted me to be able to read Gaelic, I should be encouraged to read the parallel text New Testament, starting at John's Gospel, Chapter 1 — *Anns an toiseach bha am Focal* (In the beginning was the Word). Thus was gaining a degree of literacy in my own language brought forward, probably by a number of years.

Being able to include Gaelic as a Secondary subject became an even more attractive option, though I regretted not being able to pursue the alternative as well — French having the appeal of being a modern European language.

Being in a (small) class of Native Gaelic speakers, who were taught by a Native Gaelic speaker, through the medium of English, didn't strike me as odd, at the time. Nor did it occur to us to observe that, with apparently no literature beyond the early 19th Century, we were being taught that the language we spoke at home was as dead as the Latin we were *Amo-amas-amatting* our way through.

Secondary school was a fifteen mile bus journey away, in the great metropolis of Portree (population, then, around 1000). What do I remember about it? Being picked on, as I'd been at Primary school, for being fat and bespectacled (as I'd been at Primary school). Chemistry consisted of experiments that flared up or went *BANG!* Maths was a mystery which I was happy to leave in that condition. History was kings and dates. Music was a vaguely flamboyant teacher at a plink-plonk piano, encouraging us to sing *Shenandoah* and *Ilkla Moor Baht 'At*, with feeling. Art might have been OK if the teacher hadn't tended to splash her corrections all over your carefully brushed in works of art. Gym (as I think it was called — it had been "drill" at Primary) was athletes and others: I was an other. English depended on the teacher. The one with the French name threatened to make us act out *A Midsummer Night's Dream:* I think he perceived it as a promise. Long Will, with his sharp wit and relish for language, and how it worked, was great fun, except when his war wound bother him.

Not being allowed to learn German, by dropping Latin in Third Year — the usual procedure (I thought I'd found a way of accessing a modern European language) — because "French and German go together, Gaelic and German don't", according to the headmaster, killed any enthusiasm I might have had for school. Modern Languages were modern languages, and Gaelic was definitely among the dead ones. The thought was not necessarily articulated thus at the time, but on reflection seems apposite. What's surprising is that I didn't turn against Gaelic — in any way, as I recall. I just stopped working, in any subject, and a year later was out of school.

The pretext was a wish to go to sea, as father, uncles and grandfathers had done: and I'd grown up with stories of ships crewed entirely, from skipper to galley-boy, with mariners from the one Gaelic-speaking island. Bad eyesight meant I couldn't hope to follow the navigation route to the objective nearly every island schoolboy dreamed of, command of a ship. I didn't see myself in the engine room, which left two options, the galley or the radio operator's eyrie. While I've since learned to cook, the kitchen then remained essentially a woman's province: though I knew a ship's crew, including the catering personnel, was all male, I didn't see myself in an apron, so I applied to join a course in radio operating at the James Watt College, Greenock.

Learning to tap out Morse Code was the easy part. Absorbing the mystery of valves, resistors, capacitors was a bit more stressful. The basics of electricity were straightforward, but then a terrain was entered which I thought safely behind me in the school science room, where the lecturer spoke the impenetrable (to me) language of physics. Literally a non-swimmer, I was now figuratively also out of my depth.

At sixteen, stepping out of school for the last time had seemed like a huge adventure, like stepping of the edge of the world . . . It was a curiously lonely experience: where previously there had been a trooping from one classroom to another in a group, this was just me, acting entirely on my own. Perhaps the fact that I was naïve, gauche, inexperienced in the self-sufficiencies of tertiary education, protected me from being stricken by a sense of failure, as the big ships moored in the various docks became more and more removed from my expectations. Besides, at seventeen, I discovered sex, which, of course, changes everything

Having given up on the sea, I found employment as a clerk, in various offices, mostly in Glasgow, the first of which, in the city centre, was next door to a bookshop.

Enid Blyton's posh kid Fives and Sevens as well as the great fictional mariner Horatio Hornblower had informed my pre-teen reading. In my teens, Stevenson's *Kidnapped*, while it may have been a school text, provided enough excitement to be enjoyed for its own sake but Alan Campbell MacLean's novels with their familiar North Skye settings were sheer joy.

I had also subscribed to a Book Club while still at school, having developed a taste for "grown-up" fiction while in my early teens but, on leaving developed an inexplicable resistance to books — certainly to works of fiction. Modern art became my spare-time passion, both in what I read and what I attempted to reproduce. Round about the age of nineteen, I decided that art was either a dead-end or a hill too steep to climb, and began to write instead.

Three books bought in that bookshop near my first workplace provided an unlikely trigger for my writing career. The first was Virginia Woolf's *The Waves*: I think the blurb may have described it as "poetic"; I was certainly intrigued by its deliberately patterned rhythms. Samuel Beckett's *Malone Dies* was my next purchase; a most unusual, but utterly compelling day in the life of a bedridden solitary: what ought to be depressing in the extreme becomes, as filtered through the author's vision, a remarkable exploration of the survival instinct is how I recall it, nearly five decades later. I then turned to poetry, in the form of a *Selected Poems* of Dylan Thomas. His linguistic exuberance may offer a bad model, but as words to be spoken out loud, poems like "Do not go gentle" and "The hand that signed the paper", among others, are supreme. These were words to relish, but I'm glad to say that curiosity eventually drew me to seek out other poets, and seriously begin my apprenticeship.

Alongside this discovery of literature, as something that I could engage with directly, came a sense that there was something to be got from formal education. Evening classes in various subjects, at various establishments, led to a full-time year at further education college, followed by university. Langside College introduced me to both 20th Century Gaelic poetry and English literature as a contemporary phenomenon: our lecturer brought his pal Willie Macilvanney in to read his own poetry to us.

By the time I got to Glasgow University, I'd been obsessively attempting to write for about five years. I had also, some time before matriculating, met Philip Hobsbaum, whom I'd previously heard on radio, reading his own poem "KI" a dramatic monologue in the voice of Karl Marx speaking from his desk at the British Museum. It was Hobsbaum who identified, from a sheaf of hand-written scraps, my first workable poem, and offered the advice I've considered bedrock ever since; "Write about what you know". I've also learned through practice that "what you know" isn't always what's on the surface: poems have the ability to surprise their creator, though they'll only survive if they can be believed in.

Through Hobsbaum, I'd also learn of the presence among my fellow undergraduates of a poet I should know about. Philip may actually have shown me a copy of Tom Leonard's *Six Glasgow Poems*, a new way of seeing things, a new way of being heard. Through Leonard, I'd meet another Tom, McGrath, whose infectious enthusiasm for current trends in American poetry introduced a bunch of us to the Black Mountain School of Poetry, and its original mentor, William Carlos Williams, who encouraged us to listen to the way we speak, and to use that in our poetry . . .

Flashback; what was given at school, whether learned or not, is easy to catalogue: in the year I left school, my great-aunt died, at the age of 90. Her contribution to my education cannot be ignored. Increasingly debilitated by rheumatics during my growing up, she sat by the fire and reminisced — her memories reaching back to the days of rack-renting landlords, and incorporated floods, grinding poverty, hard labour, breaking down fences in breach of the law to reclaim land that had been promised her community then denied, and solo fishing trips in an open dinghy at a time when women weren't supposed to go fishing. I would, much later, realise she was feeding me history.

Flashback; sitting on the low benches in the school infant class, watching a whirring-in-the-background projection of John Wayne being *The Quiet Man*, Jack Hawkins sinking the German navy, and Alan Ladd walking tall, all courtesy of the Highlands and Islands Film Guild van, making its monthly appearance.

Flashback; rock 'n roll and transistor radios happened during my early teens. I preferred the Carl Perkins version (of Blue Suede Shoes) to Presley's. Perkins wrote the song. Through rock 'n roll, I learned about the Blues. Skiffle drew on the Blues and led to British rock 'n roll: it also led to the "Folk Song Revival" which allowed our own traditional songs to be respectable again, and freely sung, including the great Gaelic songs of previous centuries as well as those of several fine 20th Century poets still composing in the song tradition.

I started writing in English. Discovering Sorley MacLean and the other great modern Gaelic poets while at Langside College encouraged me to write in my own language. Writing in both languages, I considered English the medium for my "serious" poetry. Being invited to take a Writing Fellowship at Sabhal Mor Ostaig, the Gaelic College, in 1977, turned me into a Gaelic poet. A Fellowship at Glasgow University, in 1993, twenty-five years after I'd first matriculated there, turned me into a bilingual poet again.

Flash-forward; Scotland has a curious relationship with its Gaelic poets. It likes the fact that we're there, so long as it doesn't have to read us. It doesn't understand Gaelic, you see; even though we do translate our work into English. Being bilingual leaves us swinging transparently between two stools. The rest of the world is more open to what we have to offer. Being a Gaelic poet has taken me across the Atlantic, on more than one occasion, it has taken me to various corners of Europe, East and West, from the Capitol in Rome to the Arctic Circle, to St Petersburg, Vienna and Berlin, to Belgium, Poland and Croatia, to Japan and Jerusalem, and to Ireland on numerous occasions.

But does it, ultimately, matter? Plenty poets were never published in their own lifetime. We write in order to find out what we have to say. Audiences are a bonus. The act of writing is the act of trying to get it right. I'm often asked, when workshopping poetry with schoolchildren, "What's the best poem you've written?" and I answer, "The next one."

John Bellany

Born Port Seaton, East Lothian, 18th June 1942

ARTIST

My voyage through life

I was born on the eighteenth of June 1942 in Port Seton, East Lothian,
Scotland. A beautiful fishing village on the Firth of Forth. It was an idyllic
place to spend your childhood with all the beauty you could want. The
place itself had a deeply religious background with eight churches and
meeting places, e.g. The Harbour Meeting, and the whole tone was that of
respect and fear of death, very much under the wing of John Knox. The
corollary to this was the other side of village life where profanity ruled and
fun and games were the chief merits of their society.

So I was brought up with the SACRED and the PROFANE.

My father was a fisherman, as were both grandparents. My maternal
grandfather came from Eyemouth where a very similar way of life existed.
There I spent all my long summer holidays – wonderful.

I studied at Preston Lodge school in Prestonpans and went to the mighty
Edinburgh College of Art in 1960.

This really opened up the whole world of Art to me and also another huge,
exciting world full of joy and adventure and learning. There my best friends
were Sandy Moffat and Alan Bold who was a student at Edinburgh University,
and together we explored life's rich textures of the drink, the poetry, the art,
the music, the literature and the sex.

There was a great camaraderie of spirit among all the students at this
time and the sixties were an age of revolution led by artists of all beliefs,
shapes and sizes, from the Beatles to Alan Bold.

At Edinburgh College of Art I was taught by Sir Robin Philipson and Sir
William Gilles and their inspiration and generosity of spirit have never left
me. There were many other good teachers there and I had five years of intense

learning and understanding the meaning and the wonder of great art.   I cannot thank those individuals and friends enough for providing me with a rock on which to base my future.

In 1964 I married my wife Helen and she has been my muse, my love, and the mother of our three children Jonathan, Paul and Anya and seven grandchildren.

Then in 1965 I went to London to the Royal College of Art to study under Professor Carel Weight, and had the real introduction to living in the world's greatest metropolis which in the late sixties was the cultural centre of the Universe.   The great explosion that happened opened up so many different routes and my life was changed in the three years I studied there.   The paintings poured from my brushes and my vision was maturing and life was rosy.

In 1968 I received the Burton Award along with my 1st Class Honours Degree and went to Spain. The Goyas were an inspiration and off I went on my voyage through life.   In the seventies I taught at many Art Colleges throughout England from Winchester to Exeter, from Birmingham to Chelsea, from Falmouth to Canterbury, from Croydon to Goldsmiths where I ended up teaching along with the Royal College of Art where I started in 1965.   I stopped teaching all together in 1983 and gave all my time to being a full time painter.

During the seventies and early eighties I was painting flat out and teaching and living life as if every day was my last.   I had many exhibitions, all over the world from Australia to New York, from London to Los Angeles, Chicago and Hamburg. This took its toll and I found myself in St Thomas's Hospital in 1984 with liver failure.   In 1988 I was taken Addenbrokes hospital Cambridge, when under the supervision of Sir Roy Calne, I was given a liver transplant and painted my way in and out of hospital and the paintings were shown in the Scottish National Gallery of Modern Art and Aberdeen Art Gallery.

This Resurrection and Chapter 2 of my life had a huge effect on my paintings and drawings and the next year was very different.   I started painting in a much more lyrical way with huge flower paintings and the quality of the work was much more optimistic. My palette changed and the work was full of joy and wonderful bright colour.   I was now on a new journey.

The Nineties continued in a happier vein and then I bought 'Sipulicchia' a 15th century manor house in Tuscany, Italy. I fell in love with the place and painted my heart out. I then fell in love with the people of Fosciandora and Barga. I had three huge exhibitions in Barga in 2002 and the whole of valley of the Serchio came to the exhibition. I was treated so well by the Italians and the mayor gave me the Freedom of the City. Florence awarded me the Cavaliere medal, Barga gave me the San Christoforo medal and since then I have been treated like Picasso!!

George Bruce and I did a portfolio together — *Woman of the North Sea* — six poems and six of my etchings. I also illustrated the cover of his *Pursuit: Poems 1986-1998* which won the Saltire Society Award for the Scottish Book of the Year in 1999. He was an inspiration for me for the last decade of his life and it was mutual, as we were both from Scottish fishing stock and our shared memories of the town and village was immense. I miss his presence so much.

In 2003 I went to China and Helen and I were deeply impressed. I am having an exhibition at the National Gallery of China in Beijing in April 2005 and the Central Academy of Art in 2006. I have a painting in the new Scottish Parliament on permanent display and have had a solo show in London every year since 1971 and a retrospective at the Scottish National Gallery, and the Serpentine London, Kelvingrove Art Gallery and this year 'The Odyssey' of John Bellany at the Mitchell Library, Glasgow.

Sheena Blackhall (Middleton)

Born Aberdeen, 18th August 1947

WRITER

Leerie-Lichts and Gorblies

The circumstances of my birth were somewhat peculiar. Although I was a post war 'baby-boomer' born in Aberdeen's Cuperstone Nursing Home in 1947 I was actually raised in the nineteenth century. No, the reckoning isn't mistaken. The house where I lived for my first 25 years, and returned to when my marriage ended, was 15, Albert Terrace Aberdeen. The first map reference to the street was in 1849. Twenty years later the name was changed from Saint Mary's Road to Albert Terrace in honour of Queen Victoria's Prince Consort. As it was protected by rigidly enforced conservation laws, the street retains its cobbles, its gas lamps, its iron railings, slate and granite to this day.

The house was Dickensian, cold and rheumaticky. It stood on three levels, with three upstairs bedrooms and a large attic. My parents were middle-aged when I was born, arriving when the pram had been sold and my mother was 40. 'I could hae bin yer granny', she always said. This made for dreich Hogmanays. Usually, somebody had just died, and my father, who was tea-total would querulously raise his glass of lemonade to the chimes an say dolefully 'I winner if we'll aa be here neist year'. This, to a small child, was tremendously alarming, the thought that death was permanently camped out on the doorstep, waiting to pick us off.

Every year, my mother marched me down to a local book shop to buy my birthday presents. They never varied . . . I was allowed to choose anything by Dickens or Sir Walter Scott. Every night no matter how glorious the summer nights, I was sent to bed at 7pm to say my prayers and read. Around the age of 8, I discovered that masturbation whiled away the occasional moment, though I had no idea this was what it was called until I was much older. My mother told me never to sit too close to boys at school or I might get a baby (I assumed that babies brushed off on you, like dandruff). She zealously marched me to church every Sunday, Melville Kirk, presided over by the Rev. John Bell Deans, a hell fire preacher who once delivered a sermon on eternity so terrifying to a small child that I had nightmares for months afterwards, a recurrent nightmare of sitting astride a wooden painted carnival horse in a midnight carousel, whirling round the Milky Way forever. 'God is always near you, watching what you do,' was her favourite hymn. My own, invisible policeman. No escape then, from morality, as a child.

Her gift to me of Dickens was the best thing I ever had from her. I grew to love Dickens, to inhabit his world. One Spring morning, having been sent to bed early and wakened with the dawn chorus, I set off in my night dress up the cobbled street pretending to be Oliver Twist alone and lost in London. I got to the top of the road and was stopped by a mystified policeman. 'And where might ye be fae?' he asked, taking out his notebook. I could outrun any policeman at that time, and quickly shimmied over the dyke to safety. This was my first indication that mixing fact with fantasy might not be a good idea.

Until I was 16 years old I slept with my grandmother, Lizzie Booth, in her downstairs room at the front of the house. At ground level there was also a music room, parlour and kitchen. Behind the house was a small garden enclosed by high walls studded with broken glass to deter intruders. If mother was middle aged, granny was ancient. She sat by the fire cleaning the family brass and silver, or stitching tapestry. Once, when was stitching a huge floral tablecloth, I observed her keenly.

'Foo are ye makkin that tablecloot granny?' I asked. 'Ye'll be deid afore it's aa dane.'

Granny looked at me over the top of her spectacles. 'I've a gey lot o flooers left in me yet, quinie.' she retorted. She recited mysterious rhymes, which hinted at fey creatures — 'Pit yer finger in the gorblie's hole the gorblie's nae at hame — he's roon the back o the hen hoose, pickin an auld deid hen.' I conjured up terrifying images of the gorblie, a half-hedgehog half-human beast with the teeth of an alligator, savaging poultry and little girls by turns.

Neighbours were genteel but distant, apart from two elderly ladies, both from the Tarland region originally, who stayed at the end of the street. One old lady was a relative of my fathers. Her cook cum housekeeper was a third cousin who had worked for this old widow woman, at a hotel she had owned in the city. Their story was far more exciting than any I could have invented. The cook had witnessed her employer's daughter give birth to illegitimate twins, there being little or no birth control available then. Infanticide was commoner than believed. Subsequently, the babies were incinerated in the hotel kitchen fire. The cook had been raped as a child by her stepfather and ever afterwards was seen as 'a bittie touched.' The babies' mother, therefore, could not have anticipated that this 'natural' would have the foresight to scrape the burnt remains from the fire and keep them in her kist for the purpose of blackmail, though the cook did not describe it as this to my mother. 'It's ma wee bittie insurance' she told her. 'I'll aye hae a hame an a job as lang's I hae the evidence.' For many years the kist with its 'wee bittie insurance' sat in the old ladies' garden in Albert Terrace, and I always shuddered when I was sent there as a little girl with baking for the two old ladies from my mother. The cook used to take a bottle of stout from the pantry and doctor a drink of lemonade with it, sending me home very merry indeed.

Our immediate neighbours, of whom I saw little, were English. The head of the house was Sir Cyril Lucas, a distinguished scientist in the field of fishery research. I once received a smacked bottom for climbing up onto the partitioning wall between our houses and singing 'Scots wha hae wi Wallace Bled' whilst waving a wooden claymore at the astonished Lucases during a particularly virulent patriotic phase. My father had spent many hours lovingly creating a doll's house for me – my mother had bought a large china doll, with eyelashes like dead spiders. When I ignored both, father relented and made me boy toys. For some time I careered up and down our back lane snecking the heads off dandelions convinced I was Rob Roy reincarnated.

My parents were second cousins. My father's grandmother Sally Craib (1845-1914) was born on the farm of Strathmore, in the parish of Coull, which lies between Aboyne and Tarland, and my mother's grandmother Helen Craib (1862-1939) was her sister. Of those in that family of ten Craibs, three spent most of their adult lives in Ceylon, the others farmed in the North East. Isabella Craib married James Anderson, who managed the estate of Deeside, Maskeliya (Tamil name Taivakanda) in Ceylon . . . their daughter Catherine was born there in 1881. Her parents sent her home to study medicine at Aberdeen University, and my grandmother Lizzie, her cousin (1882-1964) was her housekeeper/companion at Whitehall Road during those student years. Dr James Craib MB CM MD (1855-1899) died in Ceylon. He was the district surgeon for Ambagamuwa and Kotmale, in the regions around Kandy. Alexander Craib (1850-1925) was a tea planter in Invery, Dikoya, (Tamil name Sinne Berrogolly) in Ceylon and is buried in Coull kirkyard. My first pay from the BBC was spent on purchasing my lair in Coull, ever mindful of my granny's saying, 'Yer a lang time deid.' The views of Lochnagar, Tomnaverie,

Morven and the ruined Castle of Coull from this airt are truly magnificent. Unfortunately, the area is plagued by moles, and when my father's ashes were due to be interred there it was difficult to know what was grave and what was mole-hill. The gravedigger was a third cousin. 'Yer da winna be lang here his leen — his cousin ower the hill is due tae dee neist year — ay, she's in a bad wye, puir wummin, an she'll be beeriet twa lairs ben. I believe yer comin here yersel, in time?'

In granny's room were books by Saki and Kipling amongst the Victorian nick-nacks. Much of my childhood was spent ill in this bedroom suffering from recurrent bouts of croup, the smell of Friar's Balsam filling the air, with an old smelly sock stuffed with salt draped over my neck, granny's folk-cure for 'hoasts an whizzles.' Usually, I enjoyed being ill, apart from the dreadful business of battling for breath. My father would come through in the evenings and sing to me — he had a splendid singing voice . . . Burns or some old favourite like Dream Angus — and I was allowed to take all granny's ornaments into bed with me, her brass monkeys and trumpeting ivory elephants, where I could pretend to be Mowgli and chat to them all. One horrid day, however, when my breathing was particularly bad, Dr Grieve the family physician was called. I could hear him discuss my condition out in the hall. 'Ye mean ye'll hae tae cut the lassie's throat?' gasped my mother. 'Not exactly, Mrs Middleton' came the reply. 'I MAY hae tae perform a tracheotomy, tae let air inno the windpipe if she disnae improve.' I gripped onto granny's three wise monkeys very tightly and stayed so still I could have been the old grandfather clock on the stairs that kept a constant whirring and chiming all day. By evening, I had recovered, so no throat cutting was needed.

Inbreeding was common in rural North East of Scotland. My great-grandmother Helen Craib was also the great grandmother of the Doric novelist David Ogston. According to my mother, this made him my second cousin. My mother, who had always wanted to be a writer, was extremely religious, and David's other occupation was that of the ministry. On both counts she saw him as being a highly desirable 'catch'. The fact that as students we were friends who never desired to progress beyond that, was a disappointment to her.

'There's nae shame in merryin yer kin,' she informed me dourly. 'Aabody dis it.'

Perhaps because my mother was so religious, I did develop an interest in matters spiritual, but not in the way she wanted. Our kirk was a dreich, grim, dreadful place of horse hair pew cushions and taloned mahogany eagle throttling plinths. I began to read about different religions in my early teens, and took to hiding in corners lighting candles and crossing myself, inventing Catholic rites. David Ogston's Aunt Daffy, a close family friend, found me at this pursuit and 'clyped' to my mother. They were extremely worried about my immortal soul, as everyone knows only Protestants go to heaven. Catholics, Hindus, Moslems, Buddhists, the whole shebang are damned.

'Yer tae stop this cairry on richt noo,' Daffy told me. 'Yer makkin yer mither nae weel wi this papacy.'

Like an Asda shopper seeking the best bargain I continued my spiritual window gazing. Finally, I discovered Buddhism, and it struck an instant chord of inner harmony. To this day, Buddhism has been my steadying influence and my refuge:

> The dew is on the lotus, rise great sun
> And lift my leaf and mix me with the wave
> Om mani padme hum, the sunrise comes
> The dewdrop slips into the shining sea.

I regularly go on retreat to Dhanakosa in Balquhidder, a meditation centre run by the Friends of the Western Buddhist order, and know of no greater joy on this earth than sitting amongst the hills above Loch Voile, breathing in a mixture of incense and wild flowers, contemplating the serenity of the enlightened Buddha.

My principal 'care-giver' as a child was my grandmother Lizzie. She was born on the Home Farm of Hopewell, by Corachree in Tarland, my maternal grandmother. As a child she attended Migvie School, and used to quote the Latin she learned there:

> Amo amas I luved a lass an she wis tall an slender
> Amas amat she caad me flat an dang me ower the fender

She was christened Lizzie Philip, daughter of George Philip (1857-1937) and Helen Craib (1862-1939), and was fond of saying she was the 'first ane born in wedlock'. The Craibs were a wealthy farming family, and the *Records of Aboyne* (1230-1681:309) explain how this Fleming family came to be connected with Deeside, specifically the area of Cromar. Johan Crab was originally a pirate, who so incensed the Count of Flanders that on November 1319 that nobleman threatened to break him on the wheel if he could have him apprehended. Crab was also a military engineer, who apparently designed a war machine which devastated the English troops during the siege of Berwick. The last reference to Crab, places him in Aberdeen, where he is disputing rights to land in Cults, Cromar. Over the centuries, the name Crab became Craib. Craibs were farming on Strathmore, Cromar, from the 1700s.

From her cousin Catherine, and her uncles Alexander and James, granny (who had never travelled furth of the North East) had acquired those wonderful oriental brass and ivory ornaments which made my childhood croup less troublesome. At night, after she had said her prayers, taken a small swig from a miniature bottle of whisky ('a wee drappie tae help me sleep, quinie'), she would poke the small fire to take the jeel off the room and retire for the night. The shadowy firelight played on brass bullocks and monkeys, on trumpeting elephants and a coal scuttle of palm trees and jungle creepers. I was always deliciously terrified by this, and seldom used 'the gizunder' to empty my bladder for fear that a crocodile might grab my leg.

Granny's trump card was the fact that she firmly believed (as did all the family) that her father, George Philip of Crathie (1857-1937) was of the blood royal, one of Edward VII's (1841-1910) many bastards. Crathie at that time was a core Gaelic-speaking area, indeed, shepherds around Crathie still spoke Gaelic till the 1920. The last time that Gaelic was used in Crathie church was said by a local man to be in 1922 'bit only a few auld shepherds doon frae the hills could spikk it.' Watson and Allan noted :

> …many names remained Gaelic but with Scotticised or Anglicised pronunciation; only a few old people still pronounce them according to the Deeside dialect of Gaelic. Others became translated or otherwise changed into Lowland Scots or English. Many Lowland Scots names have also altered to English ones. All three processes still continue as one can see by comparing how old and young people pronounce the same names. (Watson and Allan 1984: 180)

If George retained Gaelic he never spoke it. Presumably there was no Gaelic spoken in the Coull/ Tarland region where George eventually came to work, though Diack, collecting material on Deeside in the 1930s, found this local saying:

Theagamh gu faic mis' thu fhathasd an Turlann, is muc dhubh air do chroit:

I may see you yet in Tarland, with a black pig on your back (Diack 1944)

If his linguistic credentials are uncertain, his breeding was of the highest. Photographs of my great-grandfather bear an uncanny resemblance to the wayward Edward. The illegitimate boy from Crathie came to work as a young shepherd at Strathmore, where he quickly impressed Helen Craib, who bore their first child when she was fifteen years old. The Craib family held out against the marriage until the third child was on its way, as George had no money or prospects. Surprisingly, when he married Helen in 1878 he was given the tenancy of Hopewell and the stock to go with it. The owner of the Hopewell estate at that time was factor to Queen Victoria at Balmoral, fuelling suspicion that the money had come from that source.

George Philip farmed at Hopewell for 10 years and for 33 years at West Mains, Nethermuir, New Deer. One on occasion when the Middleton cousins crossed the moor at Coull to visit the Philips, chicken was served. 'Wull I carve this chucken the new-fanglit wye or the auld?' he asked. Chosing the old, he tore the meat into pieces with his hands.

Throughout his life he referred to his wife as his 'ither oxter', because she fitted neatly into his arm pit. She, in turn, likened herself to a 'brood soo', and said that her husband never tired of gingerbread and herself — a fair assessment as they had between them 10 children. Of these, young George emigrated to Medicine Hat in Canada, homesteading in Tilston, Manitoba in 1898. Patricia married a New Deer man and sailed for America on the White Line's 'Caledonia' to settle in Chicago. Her father stood at the quayside and waved till the ship was out of sight. Their brother William also emigrated to Chicago.

I have always been rather suspicious of America. Granny's brother William was shot and killed in a taxi there, an innocent victim of crossfire during Chicago's notorious gang wars. It was no surprise to me whilst I was performing on the Mall in 2003 with Stanley Robertson as guests of the Smithsonian Institute, when a paper cup that Stanley was drinking water from exploded in his hand, by a random bullet fired from the crowd. 'I dinna think they like traivellers,' was Stanley's sanguine response. My American relatives offered to pay my plane fare to Chicago, to meet up with them during that trip. I declined. The next bullet might have had my name on it.

The American emigrants frequently return to Scotland three generations on, and host their own 'Highland Games' in Manitoba. Patricia's grandchild, Hallie Lemon lectures in Journal Writing at the university of Western Illinois. Her mother Glenna wrote to give me the second part of a song my grandmother had taught me. The other half sailed to America with Patricia.

Takk the ribbons fae yer hair bonnie lassie-oh
Takk the ribbons fae yer hair bonnie lassie-oh
Takk the ribbons fae yer hair, life is nocht bit grief an care
Takk the ribbons fae yer hair bonnie lassie-oh

Philip, of course, was the surname of George's mother, and it is a long-standing belief that the original North East 'Philip' was one Juan Philippe, who swam ashore when the Spanish galleon the Santa Catarina sank in the bay of Saint Catherine's Dub off Collieston in 1588. A neighbour in Albert Terrace was convinced we were a family of Spaniards with our black hair and dark eyes. It may be no co-incidence that my brother Ian chose to emigrate to the Latin American country of Brazil.

The business of 'race' is a strange one. When I was Scots Writing Fellow at Aberdeen University's Elphinstone Institute a visiting Dutch PhD student was quite adamant that I was a Sephardic Jew, and flatly refused to believe otherwise! I had to tell her that the nearest I ever got to Jewry was a teenage crush I developed on Benjamin Disraeli. When other girls of my age adulated the Beatles, I adored Disraeli. I liked his style. He wasn't a team player, you see. I respect that. When Britain needed part ownership of Suez, he went out and got it. 'It is done, you have it Ma'am' he triumphantly told Queen Victoria. True, he dyed his hair, wore corsets and wrote abominable novels, but he was never boring. In his youth he resembled a male version of Shirley Temple. I assumed his mother made him curl his hair into ringlets like mine did. I think I could have married Disraeli, if time and circumstances had been changed.

So that's the myth of the set-in-stone North East family blown out of the water. Dr Robert Millar put it quite well when I interviewed him in the course of research into the linguistic and social changes in the North East:

> . . . I think too much is made of the North East of Scotland bein a static society, because it's never been static. The farming tradition seems bred intae the land, but maist o the North East o Scotland's maybe 250 year auld. (R.M./S.M. 7:12:99)

Before I leave my maternal roots, I should mention the Booth family. Patrick Morgan in the *North East annals of Woodside and Newhills* (1886) describes 'a worthy and well-known family of the name of Booth, farmers in the estate of Auchmill for nearly 200 years'. Here is an extract from my great-grandfather Matthew Booth's (1847-1922) obituary:

> Mr Matthew Booth, dairyman, 5 Desswood Place, was well known to the agricultural community over a wide district. He succeeded his father in the farm of Mastrick, and besides, Woodside, Stocket, he held the farm of Darrahill, Udny. . . . At various times he held public offices, being connected with Newhills Parish Council, the Udny Parish Council (of which he was chairman) & the school board of Udny. In 1886 he commenced the dairying business in Aberdeen. In this he was enterprising and progressive and the business increased until he had 6 shops and numerous carts retailing milk throughout the city. He was esteemed and respected in the dairying world and until recently was president of the Aberdeen Dairyman's Association. For many years he had been a Director at the Central Mart, Aberdeen . . . He was a devoted member and officer of the United Free Church.

Old Matthew is buried in the corner of St Machar Cathedral kirkyard. He had fathered 15 children and served as a JP. One of his sons, Douglas Booth (1874-1972) managed a rubber plantation in Kuala Lumper in Malay. One his daughters, Margaret, settled in Africa. Two of her gifts sat in the umbrella stand at Albert Terrace. There was a Zulu knob kiri, heavily stained. I was told the stains were from Zulu brains dashed out during a tribal conflict. There was also a Zulu war shield of zebra skin, which I liked slightly better, but neither object fired me with much desire to visit a place where skulls were cracked like walnuts at Xmas.

His son Matthew (1871-1923), my maternal grandfather, died the year after him. Of this grandfather I know little, other than the fact that he originally qualified as a ship's engineer, subsequently reverted to farming, married my grandmother and settled at Hillhead of Carnie, Skene. I know that he was a precentor at Kingswells United Free kirk, that he thrashed my uncle George for laughing while he was reading from the Family Bible, and that he would stay up all night in all weathers when his mares were foaling – a cross between 'A Man Called Horse;' and Calvin.

When grandfather died, my uncle George's ambitions died with him. George Booth was a dux bronze medallist in English and French, in the same year as John R. Allan at Robert Gordon's College. But my grandmother Lizzie needed him at home to help run the farm. When my uncle married his second cousin Isobel Craib of Tullyoch in Echt, my grandmother left Hillhead and moved to Aberdeen to live with my parents. Most Sundays we visited the farm, and I was turned out to roam the parks and woodlands and byres all afternoon.

Later, when I married a farmer's son from Tarland, we were cottared at the farm. My uncle, who was childless, offered to pass on the tenancy to myself and my husband, but my husband's family were beef and barley farmers, not dairymen, so he declined the offer. Now, with the town threatening to overwhelm it, I am glad of that.   My father's family are easier to track, as both his parents were Middletons. They are descended from Norman Scots, De Midletons. Humphrey De Midleton originally settled in Kincardineshire, but by 1623 the family had settled in Cromar in the parish of Coull by Tarland, on the farm of North Gellan. According to the records of the family genealogist & historian William Stewart (1872-1900), whose parents owned the Osbourne Hotel, Queen's Gardens Aberdeen, we are linked to John, first Earl of Middleton (1604-1674), the Covenanting General who later turned Royalist and led a revolt in the Highlands on behalf of Charles II in 1653. For a brief and ignoble time, he was Viceroy of Scotland on the restoration of the monarchy. A portrait of him hangs in the Courtauld Institute of Fine Arts, London, by the painter Jacob Huysmans. His brother was principal of King's College Aberdeen, which supposedly holds his portrait; but I have never succeeded in locating it.

Samuel Pepys described Middleton as 'a shrewd man but a drinking man as the world said, a man that had seen much of the world, and a Scot'. Sir Walter Scott features him in Wandering Willie's Tale as 'Bloody Middleton', the Deil's right hand man. William Stewart's family tree states that Patrick Middleton (in Coull, 1622) was a brother of Robert Middleton of Caldhame, father of John, first Earl of Middleton (1608-1674) though no mention of this appears in 'The Earls of Middleton, Lords of Clermont and Fettercairn & the Middleton family'. I like to think the connection existed. Today, I live on Montrose Drive, named after Montrose himself, overlooking the Auld Brig o Dee, where the Covenanters and Royalists once pounded each other with cannon.

After 1623, the kirkyard at Coull tells its own story, for all the Middletons who farmed North Gellan lie there. In 1696 the list of pollable persons within the shire of Aberdeen mentions in Meikle Gellan, Patrick Midletoune tenant there, and Alexander Midletoune, tenant there. Stewart's tree is detailed and complex. My great grandfather, John Middleton of North Gellan (1840-1919) married Sally Craib of Strathmore, the farm across the moor. My grandfather, Alexander Middleton (1877-1935) left North Gellan to farm at the Mains, a large farm in the grounds of Aboyne Castle. There, my father Charles was born (1907-1988). Granny Middleton was suckling her new-born son by the fire when a streak of lightening descended the lum and left through the door. In a deeply superstitious family, wondrous things were expected of father after this, a hard act to follow.

Grandfather, by all accounts, was something of a character. He moved to East Mains where he managed a croft, a haulage business and the Aboyne dairy. Lord and Lady Glentanar involved him in their Gilbert and Sullivan operettas. He fathered 12 children in wedlock, others out it. My father claimed to have been reared on a diet of 'tatties and pynt'. For years, I took this to mean the family sat round the table daily and got 'roarin fu' on potatoes and beer. Eventually it was explained to me that 'pynt' meant 'point', not 'pint'. Grandfather Middleton killed a pig once a year, salted it and hung it in the kitchen. For most of the year it hung there and was only pointed at, not eaten. The staple diet of the family was potatoes and poached salmon, deer, or trout, for my father like his brothers was a fine shot and fisherman with the Dee and the woods of Birse close by.

My grandfather was a grand master of the Aboyne Masonic Lodge, and was accorded a Masonic Funeral. Very handsome in youth, he followed the Middleton tendency to 'run to fat', was an asthmatic, alcoholic, village poet and writer and performer of cornkisters. Local lairds would invite him to sing at their soirees. When two of his nephews, David & John Middleton, were orphaned as a result of the Ballater flu epidemic of 1918, my grandfather fostered them until they were old enough to follow his Craib uncles out to Ceylon, to the Epalawae Estate in Kagale. I fondly imagined this was very charitable of him. 'Ay,' the boys' niece informed me dryly. 'Affa charitable. They'd tae wirk damned hard fur their keep!'

Every year, at the Aboyne Games the local travelling people would pitch their camp on grandfather's fields by Aboyne. If they refused to pay (or couldn't pay), one of their animals was confiscated to cover costs. Thus, grandfather acquired a white mule from Pinto's circus, a dour brute which refused to move. 'We lichtit a wee fire aneth it,' my father told me. 'It moved, syne.'

On market days, grandfather would vanish, sometimes for a week or more, touring his favourite hostelries and writing yet more songs — 'Bowties' at the foot of Morven, the Inver near Braemar, Coilacreich by Ballater and a small licensed grocer at the head of the Slack at the entry to the Howe o Cromar. He would stand at the market stance in Tarland, Cyard's Raw, and offer to thrash all comers. (Tarland down the centuries is noted for its 'hard man' image). He also had a fey sense of humour. During the Tarland Show when travellers camped yearly for the horse sales around the village, he crept up on a traveller sleeping off a drinking bout in a barn, and stuffed two brass balls down his trousers. When the man awoke, and reached down to relieve himself at the call of nature, he was horrified to feel two disembodied not to mention very heavy objects beside his manhood, and rushed off screaming 'ma baas his drapped aff.'

This was a very Tarland thing to do. My ex-husband, himself a Tarland man, was once chastised by his father, Rob, for sleeping in of a morning. He duly set off with some friends after a few drams, to climb the ruined church steeple to dislodge the kirk bell, bearing it back in triumph to his father's house. 'I winna sleep in noo,' he remarked.

Rob Blackhall once recited a piece of verse to me which he swore was by Burns:

> Far ben amang the widded trees
> I bent ma erse wi perfect ease
> An roon aboot did swarm the flees
> Tae hae a tasty denner.

One Hogmanay my husband Kenneth detached a dead sheep's head from its carcass, carrying it round the village and working its jaws like a ventriloquist's dummy, delivering a hell fire sermon as a first foot trick. Life in Cromar is always eventful. Every year at the summer solstice, the local farmers climb to the summit of Lochnagar to see in the dawn, as they have done since ancient times.

I had decided early on I would only marry a Deeside man and did so in 1972 at St Ninian's Church Aberdeen. My husband, Kenneth Blackhall, wore his corporal's uniform, as he was then serving with the RAF Regiment in Catterick. The Blackhall family had moved from Glenkindie to Tarland where Alexander Blackhall had married Catherine Coutts (1874-1967). My husband's uncle Alec was World Barley Champion seven times, travelling regularly to Canada to receive his prize. He was a county councillor and a playwright as well as a farmer. The Blackhall family farmed Melgum, Millhead and Barehillock in Cromar. Barehillock overlooked the fields and woods of Hopewell that my grandmother had loved so much as child. Once, when hairsting there, driving the tractor up and down the park gathering the bales, I could have sworn I saw her, a little girl dressed in a white lace smock and button boots smiling at me from the trees.

When Alec was off in Canada one year our elderly car expired. I wrote a poem which was published in the local Press and Journal bemoaning this. Alec was furious when he heard about it on his return. We were summoned to his house, where after an awkward exchange, he asked me to step out to an outhouse. He opened the doors to expose a Triumph car in immaculate condition aside from one or two hens' droppings on the bonnet. Without an other word, he handed me the keys.

'There noo. We'll hae nae mair bitties in the paper', he muttered. I know of no other Doric poet who was given a car because they'd written a poem.

My father, born in Aboyne, had none of his Tarland forebears wildness in him. He was a serious little boy, as anybody would be whose mother hit them over the head with a poker for allowing a small sibling to play in the coal scuttle. What he loved to do was sing, any and all of Burns and most of the 'weel kent' Scots and Irish ballads. There was always music in our house. His favourites were *Jock o Hazledean* and *Dark Lochnagar*, and when he sang he did so with a depth of feeling that could move the most hardened to tears. When my father was 8 years old he recalled sitting on a dyke at Aboyne where the Tarland Road meets the village, and watching his two young cousins William and John Middleton from Tarland march off with the Gordon Highlanders to fight in the First World War. Willie took off his watch, a gold hunter, and flung it over the dyke into the leaves, shouting out 'it's ower guid tae bladd, it'll bide here till I win back!'

The watch was never found. Willie never came back. John's name is on Le Touret Memorial in France, panel 39-41. Willie lies in the Highlander cemetery, Rollincourt, Plot 1 row A grave 15.

For the first 16 years of my life, my father worked at Ballater, leaving Albert Terrace early in the morning and not returning till late each evening. He was manager of the Deeside Omnibus service, owned by his widowed sister Mrs Helen Strachan, known locally as the 'Reid bussies'. Strachan's originally took over from the Royal mail horse bus which ran from the Bon Accord Hotel in Market Street to Blairs, the fleet growing to 14 buses at its peak. Strachan's ran its first bus from Blake's Station Garage, Rennie Wynd in 1925. The owner died young, killed at the wheel of his car in a smash that claimed the life of his brother in law Archie Middleton. Another brother in law, Ian Middleton, crawled two miles to raise the alarm despite serious internal injuries, for which he was presented with an award for bravery at the Victoria Hall, Aboyne.

'My faither didna ken foo tae help Ian fin he lay in the hospital,' my father told me, 'Sae he jist sang tae him.'

The company ran two services, one travelling the South Deeside Road from Aberdeen to Banchory, then via Ballater to Braemar on the North Road, while the second route went via Ballogie from Banchory up to Ballater. It ferried coffins, livestock, climbers, hikers, tourists. Under parcel regulations it stated that 'fragile parcels inadequately packed will be sent entirely at the sender' risk'. This may even have applied to a party of Canadian lumberjacks wanting to go to a local dance one wartime winter.With no room left on board, in blizzard conditions, they were invited (at their own risk) to step into the roomy boot. All arrived safely. There was an office in Langstane Place and a stance at Bon Accord Street in Aberdeen. This occasionally duplicated as a slaughterhouse when a deer was felled by a bus and smuggled in to be butchered and shared out amongst the drivers and conductresses. The main office, however, was Ballater and it was here that we stayed all summer, every summer, closing up the town house in Albert Terrace and occupying a property known as 'The Shack', a child's paradise, with Craigendarroch facing us from the front window and Craigcoilich looking in at the back window, with the Gairn, the Muick and the Dee, running between the hills and the tiny village.

When the business finally ran out of road, Pipe Major Norman Meldrum of Invercauld lead a procession of 40 cars and 200 people as the last of the red buses drove slowly out of Braemar. John Stammers of Birchwood said 'the old chaps who used to work for the firm were in tears. It really was something to remember.' Bob Webster, a member of Aberdeen's Transport Society spoke for many when he said 'Strachans ran such a unique service that inevitably the story of transport in the Dee Valley is the story of Strachan's. Tom Patey in 'One Man's Mountain', A Grampian Hairst' noted that 'The 3.15 from Bon Accord Square was a special bus tactfully set aside for climbers by Messrs Strachan'. This followed an incident in which old ladies had been isolated at the back of the bus by a mountain of rucksacks, only effecting an escape, several miles beyond their destinations by a desperate hand traverse.

For 16 years, as the manager's daughter and the owners' niece, I had the freedom of the roads from the city to the Braes o Mar. I could step on a bus anywhere on Deeside and jump off again, without paying a penny. I could change from the thin Scots speech of Aberdeen, to the braid Doric of Ballater in the space of an hour. I could stay weekends with my cousins, the McConnachs, who farmed at Drumneachie and Deerhillock in Birse. Dod McConnach had married my father's sister Mary, of whom I was greatly fond, and it was at Drumneachie that my cousins taught me to fish for eels, to hand milk a cow, to hand churn butter and to bigg the stooks at hairst time, though very little biggin o stooks was done with the Birse burn so close and the weather warm. Like Byron, who also holidayed on Upper Deeside, I more or less ran wild, exploring hills, cliffs glens, usually on my own, with a sketch pad.

I had wanted to be an artist from the time I first held a pencil in my hand. My father encouraged me, giving me cheap colouring pencils which transported me into realms of infinite delight. His cousin, Maudie Middleton, had studied Art at the Institute of Notre-Dame Aux Epines, Eecloo, near Brugge (Bruges) in Belgium. Maudie died of Hodgkin's disease aged 22 cutting short what should have been a distinguished art career.

When I had a sketch pad in my hand, I never needed friends, my imagination was friend enough. I always assumed that Glen Muick and Glen Gairn were pleased to see me when I visited, I thought of them as part of the family. I felt particularly close to Glen Muick. When I was 50 I discovered that I had an illegitimate brother in Oshawa, Ontario, Canada, Charles Middleton Ritchie, born in 1929, who had been partly raised in Glen Muick by an aunt at the Mill o Sterin. I grew up knowing nothing of his existence, not knowing that I had a brother in the Gordon Highlanders, who was serving variously in Germany, Korea, Hong Kong and Malaya. He emigrated to

Canada from Ballater in 1954 when I was seven. Ironically we were staying in the village when the piper played him off at Ballater Square. He died in the year 2000, but not before he had flown to Scotland to meet me, and I had crossed the Atlantic to meet his family. He was a great, warm bear of a Highlander, it was a great sadness to me that we discovered each other so late in life.

I have not, as yet, mentioned my other brother, Ian. Born in Aberdeen in 1940, he died in Buenos Aires aged 58, in 1999. He was seven years my senior. His one ambition was to be a concert pianist, but was advised to concentrate on becoming a chartered accountant which he did, eventually finding a post as manager of a merchant bank in Sao Paulo. He ferried a clavichord overseas, and frequently gave recitals in Sao Paulo of Jacobean and Elizabethan music. When I was small I could tell Ian's mood by the music he played. In a good mood, he played Bartok and Chopin. In a bad mood it was Beethoven, not played but pounded. I remember little of him other than his music, as we were never particularly close. When my father died, he sent a copy of Dante's *Inferno* in Portuguese to the family solicitor, who was as mystified as the rest of us. This brother was highly intelligent, with a biting wit, and a succession of Latin mistresses which my mother was always at a loss (on the few occasions he came home) as to how to introduce. 'Meet — Ian's intended,' she would say, not actually specifying what he intended. Before he emigrated to Brazil, he would supplement his income by giving organ recitals in Aberdeen. I remember once being dragged to St Machar's Cathedral to hear him perform by my mother. The recital seemed to last for an interminable time, but my mother was wearing her best hat, like a pigeon about to take flight, and was incandescent with pride throughout it all.

These, then, are the roots I draw poetic sustenance from, the nature, if you will. The 'nurture' aspect covers the educational system as it has coloured my writing, that and life events as they unfold. My first school was Mile End, a west end primary I was sent to as a result of failing my IQ test aged five. The entire test centred on identification of farm animals. The farms I had visited in my short life had REAL animals, DORIC animals. I had absolutely no idea what a 'hawss' was, as I had only ever heard such a creature called a shelt or a cuddy. 'A moron,' the tester at Aberdeen Girls High School attested. 'Not the sort we want here.'

Mother, was furious. When the eleven plus loomed, she crammed me and coached me every day for months. I scored the highest IQ in my class, thereby securing my place at the High School for Girls where I had failed to identify the 'hawss' six years before.

'I winna hae fowk sayin my bairns are feel,' my mother raged. 'They're maybe nae gweed, bit they're nae feel.'

There was some Scots at Mile End, Wee McGregor stories, and also the school choir run by Miss Auchinachie, who drilled 'Caller Herring' into us, not to mention the Gaelic 'Brochan Lom.' On the whole I liked Mile End, except when the head teacher Mr Ross fetched me a stinging wallop round the ear for changing tense in an essay.

Having passed my control exam, life at secondary school should have been reasonably smooth. However, when I was fifteen, I went, as they say, off the rails, like a runaway train. There was an incident of 'rough wooin' – a borderline date-rape – (an adolescent boy does not respond to the word 'no' after a certain point) and it affected me rather more deeply psychologically than physically. For a child brought up to think sex is sin, is dirty and unclean, emerging sexuality is confusing. Does this mean the child, too, is unclean? In an attempt to cleanse myself, after that particular trauma, I began to practise Yogic Basti. In Hatha Yoga the cleansing of the inner organs is achieved by drawing water up inside the body. Ironically, instead of cleansing the body, it had the opposite effect. To everyone's amazement I contracted jaundice, a severe case of it, turned bright yellow and was violently ill for some time. Naturally, I did not disclose how I'd come acquire a rather rare illness. Recovery was slow.

Two of my English teachers at the High School encouraged me to study poetry. Miss Dorothy Gordon was the sister of the Doric poet Donald Gordon, former ambassador to Vienna. In her class we learned the old Scots ballads and the usual set Scots poems for children 'The Puddock' etc. Miss Agnes Carnegie, my other English teacher was herself a poet, writer of 'The Timeless Flow'. Her favourite poets were Shelley and Keats, though of course Burns was studied too. My class report from her reads as follows: 'Sheena's work though interesting and showing signs of enterprising reading, is spoilt by irrelevance and inaccurate, often absurdly wrong, use of words.'

For reasons which I will not elaborate on, I did not greatly care for either teacher. The history class, however, was always inspired and inspiring. One day we would be taken to the city's Tolbooth to stand in the condemned cell. On another occasion we would be listening to Churchill's speech on record, feeling the shivers run down our spines as he intoned 'we will never surrender.' I had decided to leave school in fifth year. I had sufficient Highers to be admitted as an Art student at Gray's School of Art. I loathed school and wanted quit of it. I was to leave sooner than I had anticipated, however.

It was the beginning of Strachan's tourist season, the warm summer of

1964 and the city was in the grip of a typhoid epidemic. My mother shopped at William Lows', the supermarket which had imported the contaminated corned beef from the Argentine. I was off school with a splitting headache, which rapidly deteriorated into delirium. My mother immediately sent for the family GP, Dr Alistair Forbes. As a young Flight Lieutenant he had been captured by the Japanese at the fall of Singapore and held prisoner on the island of Hiroco between Java and New Guinea. He had stayed behind voluntarily to tend the sick and dying at the end of the war, when the death rate for dysentery was ten a day. He had seen typhoid first hand, had mixed his medicines in coconut shells till the fever abated. Now he was re-using those diagnostic skills. He sent me straight away by ambulance to the City Hospital, the town's official fever hospital, where I was locked into the male diabetic ward, quarantined with all other typhoid sufferers for the duration of the summer. As word spread that Strachan's manager's daughter had contracted the disease, tours were cancelled, profits plummeted. Next year, in February 1965, Strachan's ceased trading, and the long idyllic ties with Ballater were severed.

I never returned to the High School for Girls, I embarked on my career as an artist at Gray's, which at that time was situated in Schoolhill, next to the Art Gallery. I started to write poetry. But two years of jaundice and typhoid had taken their toll. I was too tired to attend classes regularly, was still on massive doses of antibiotics. I failed my first year at Grays. With three years left of a grant, I reluctantly went to Aberdeen College of Education to train as a primary teacher.

My Art master there was William Burns RSA (1921-1972) and my English lecturer was the poet Bill McCorkindale, who introduced me to modern Scottish poetry. My tutor was Ian S. Munro, the biographer of Lewis Grassic Gibbon (Robin Munro the poet, is his son). Munro encouraged me to write poetry. William Burns the Art master was a colourist, an abstract artist, whereas I was a detailed draughtsman, heavily influenced by Magritte, Dali and the Surrealists. One day when I had worked all through dinner at my easel, Ian Munro came into the art room to speak to Burns, carrying some of my poems. They stood behind the easel and discussed me as if I wasn't there.

'I wish she'd concentrate on her poetry, and spend less time on Art,' Munro whispered. 'So do I, oh so do I,' Burns groaned.

During this period, I was sent to a local primary school for teaching practice. I was slender then, and very nervous in a classroom situation. It was an inner city school, with the usual problems. One of the pupils had been partially strangled in a brutal murder case where another boy had died.

The survivor was highly disturbed and aggressive, but there was no place available for him at special school. A policy of containment was in force. His parents had sent him to judo classes to learn self defence. During one lesson, he was about to smash another child's model, I held his arm to restrain him. He countered by flinging me across a desk. I landed on the floor, to the delighted uproar of the class.

That night, I did not return immediately to Albert Terrace. I sat in a harbour bar quietly sipping whisky and deciding that if this was all life had to offer, I was better quit of it. I waited till my parents were in bed, returned home and swallowed a large quantity of pills. After the winding up of the bus company, to make ends meet my parents had started to take in student lodgers, and one of those, an English law student, arrived home late. He found me comatose and alerted the house. There was a car drive to Casualty where I had my stomach pumped. The duty doctor was finishing a long shift. 'I expect this one's pregnant,' he said as I vomited into a bucket. 'They usually are. No consideration for others, wasting everyone's time.'

My father brought fresh clothes to the ward, white faced and stunned. We never spoke of what had brought me to hospital. He seemed to have aged ten years. On Monday I was back at the same school as if nothing had happened. The lollipop man at the school, an old traveller called Johnny Stewart, noticed that things were amiss.

'Yer affa peely-wally quine,' he said. 'Tell me this, dae ye like singin? Wid ye like tae learn foo tae sing richt?'

I visited Johnny's house in Cotton Street for several months. Occasionally, Davie Ogston came with me. After much coaching, Johnny was finally satisfied that I had learned 'tae sing the auld ballads richt'. The travellers have always been kind to me. In later years at Aberdeen University, Stanley Robertson was equally generous, sharing his storytelling skills with me, and some of his vast store of traditional tales.

After the suicide attempt, Dr Forbes called at the house. 'Has she been doing anything unusual?' he asked.

'Oh ay, doctor, writing poetry and makkin Buddhist sculptures.' my mother confided. Both were evidently odd pursuits. I was told I would be 'seeing a counsellor for a few weeks.'

I had no idea I was regarded as mentally ill. I had no idea that counsellor is a euphemism for psychiatrist. I was fortunate, however, in the choice of physician. Dr J. D. Gomersall made a special study of poetry and was himself interested in Eastern philosophy. I gradually learned to trust and confide in him. I wrote prodigiously and began slowly to feel better.

No-one was more surprised than me when I qualified. For a time I taught in Easterhouse in Glasgow at Bishoploch Primary School, staying in a flat owned by the Glasgow singers Joe Gordon and Sally Logan. Then, I moved to Fraserburgh's Central School experiencing the Brethren at first hand, before returning to teach in the city's Inchgarth Primary. At this time, I married, and for a while settled in Middleton St George, near Darlington, teaching near to the RAF Regiment's married quarters. I was dreadfully homesick for the North East. On my husband's demob we returned to Aberdeenshire, and my uncle gave us his cotter house at Skene. It was within easy commuting distance of the city, and I taught at Beechwood Special school. Until then, we were childless. It was established that the fault was mine, and I was treated by Professor Arnold Klopper who pioneered infertility treatment in the North East. From no children, within five years I had four.

When my uncle rouped out from the farm we flitted to the Lyne of Skene, and from there to the Kirkton of Skene, where I stayed for ten years. Jessie Kesson was raised half a mile from our house, at Proctor's orphanage. The village was close to the Loch of Skene, and over the dyke in the old kirkyard we had an infamous warlock, the Wizard Laird of Skene, as a neighbour. All the while, I was writing, for the BBC, for the *Press and Journal*, for sheer survival.

My two closest friends were the critic and historian, Cuthbert Graham, and Dr J.D.Gomersall who had by now relocated to Sheffield's Centre for Psychotherapeutic Research. Due to Jim Gomersall's encouragement, I embarked on my psychology degree with the Open University, passing with Honours in 1995.

In 1987 for reasons which are not uncommon in Scots marriages I suffered a complete nervous breakdown. As my personal life descended into chaos, I became increasingly creative. For a period of about twelve weeks I rarely slept, sat up most of the night writing poetry, drew or painted Surrealist pictures and by day wrote stories. I had vowed that after the typhoid no-one would ever turn a key on me again. Under emergency section I was hospitalised, this time as an in-patient, for ten days assessment in a locked ward. I never returned to Skene. My husband was fighting his own demons.

When I left hospital, it was to return to Albert Terrace, this time with four young children in tow, to my elderly, disabled parents. My father was on suicide watch for some time. It took a long time to recover. The following year, I moved to Garthdee, where the painter, Mike Knowles, came to paint my portrait. The poet, Alastair Mackie, sent me a postcard, *Der Blaue Reiter* by Wassily Kandinsky. 'I trust you'll see its gay colours an earnest for the future,' he wrote.

I had been lucky professionally in having the friendship of Cuthbert

Graham, and through him that of Charles King, Advisor for English to the Region. For a time, Keith Murray published my work and for a long period after that I found that very artistic thing, a patron, my third cousin, Dr Gordon Booth, former Head Educational Psychologist for Grampian Region.

From 1984-2004, I published 37 collections of poetry, two Scots novellas and 10 short story collections, mainly in Scots. I exist in the world through the vehicle of words. I have known very few people in my life, despite being acquainted with many. The two poets I've felt closest to, were Angus Calder and Alastair Mackie. The longest correspondence I've had, has been with Cuthbert Graham, James Gomersall and Gordon Booth. Dr Gomersall and I had an arrangement.   He could use my dreams, drawings, and poems with his students, and in return he would suggest books for me to read or articles to study which would benefit me personally.

'A relationship's like a dance,' he wrote. 'If you're not enjoying it, you are allowed to stop, you know,'

When I read that I felt as if a huge stone had been lifted from me, permission to move on, to walk away, to leave my marriage behind.

I had always had a difficult relationship with my mother. I made her flesh creep, she would wince if I touched her. When she died, I worried that I might seem uncaring.

'You can mourn for what never was,' he wrote.

One of the hardest things for me during my time as Creative Writing Fellow in Scots at Aberdeen University's Elphinstone Institute was having to socialise with people, a skill I never learned or came to terms with. Social phobia is crippling and misunderstood. Once during a weekend of ballad workshops at the farm of Cullerlie organised by the Institute, I could feel my anxiety levels about to go through the roof and begged the farmer Tam Reid to let me stay in the pig shed for an hour or so. 'Michty ay,' came the amiable reply, 'bit dinna tell fowk or they'll aa wint tae bide wi my soos!'

When people ask which writers have influenced me, they expect me to say Charles Murray, Flora Garry, J.C.Milne. Not so. Dickens, Saki, Kipling, Bronte, Simenon, Calvino, Moravia, Maugham, Hughes and Heaney. Scottish artists, though, have affected me greatly, and Scots balladry, that fey and otherwordly zone of the weird and the supernatural.

Carl Rogers in his book A Way of Being wrote: 'Writing is my way of communicating with a world to which, in a very real sense, I do not quite belong . . . writing is the message I seal in the bottle and cast into the sea.' As a twentieth century child brought up speaking nineteenth century Scots, surrounded by ghosts from the past, I know exactly how he feels.

Alexander McCall Smith

Born Chipinga, Zimbabwe 24th August 1948

PROFESSOR OF MEDICAL LAW
AND NOVELIST

Slow Developer

How we end up where we are and what we are depends to some extent on what the philosophers call moral luck. Most of us would probably call it the luck of the draw, or more simply, plain chance. I am the sort of person I am, with my interests and views, not so much as a result of what I myself have done, but what has been done by others before me. This is nothing at all original: in fact, it is a truism. But it is worth reflecting, I believe, on the role of chance events in our lives. This reflection cuts us down to size and shows us what to regret and what to be thankful for.

In my case, the shape of my life was dictated by my paternal grandfather's decision to leave Scotland shortly before the outbreak of the First World War. He was a doctor, the son of a sheep farmer, who risked his professional and social reputation in an extra-matrimonial affair. He came under great pressure to leave the country, and he did so, ending up in New Zealand, where he played a major part in setting up a fine medical service for the Maori people in rural areas. He was something of a hero in New Zealand medical history, but his leaving split a family, and, by his departure, my father was deprived of ever knowing his own father. Had he remained in Scotland, then my father's life would have been different and he would not have ended up going off to what was then Southern Rhodesia in the early nineteen thirties. He served as an officer in the colonial police force and then ended up as a public prosecutor in Bulawayo. He was a kind and decent man. In Southern Rhodesia he met my mother, who had been orphaned at an early age. They married and my sisters and I were all born in that part of Africa, at a period when the British Empire was entering its final phase.

We lived in Bulawayo for much of my youth. This is a remarkable city — the city of the Matabele kings and of Cecil John Rhodes. We had a happy enough childhood, but it was an unusual one, given the circumstances of the country. I was educated at a smallish school for boys run by a Catholic teaching order (we were not Catholic, but there were a number of boys there who were not). The education was good in many respects; in others it was, by modern standards, perhaps too authoritarian. There was quite a bit of cruelty, although we did not always see it as that. After school, I spent a few months at the University in what was then called Salisbury and then went to Edinburgh as a student.

Everybody's upbringing leaves them with some burden or other. Our burden was that of having been brought up in a society in painful transition, with all the unhappiness that goes with that. We lived a privileged life and there was a great deal of unfairness and injustice, in which we participated. A fairer, moderate transition could have been negotiated earlier, and that would have been so much better. But the positive side of it is that I was exposed to Africa, and all that this means. It was only later in my life, as an adult, that I was able to see what this meant and to realise what a great thing it was to have that in one's background. Later on, I was also able to try to put something back in admittedly inadequate return for everything that had been taken.

My father had always hoped to retire to Scotland. He ended up in England. I, in the meantime, had completed my law degree and had started to study for a doctorate. I became a lecturer in law and finally a professor of Medical Law at the University of Edinburgh. But I always thought of myself as a writer, from an early age, and it was inevitable, I suppose, that I should eventually have decided to give more of my time to writing. Most writers will say the same thing: being a writer is a calling, a vocation. If you are called, you have to do it.

I had been much exposed to books in my childhood. My mother was a voracious reader and she encouraged us to read too. I devoured just about everything I could find, but my greatest treasure, as a boy, was a full set of Arthur Mee's Children's Encyclopaedia. This sprawling work devoted many pages to poetry, and I spent hours reading this. The literary style of the Children's Encyclopaedia was somewhat ornate, and high-minded. That fitted, I suppose, with some of the other things I was reading, particularly Kipling. And lest the modern reader finds it odd that I should have read such things, one should remember where we were living. Kipling wrote about cobras in gardens in that exciting story of his, Rikki Tikki Tavi. We *had* cobras in our garden. This, for me, was social realism!

At school we were obliged to learn screeds of poetry off-by-heart. A lot of it was of dubious value, but some of the poems in question were great poems and they gave me, I suspect, a fairly deeply-engrained respect for the poetic possibilities of language. We also learned great amounts of Latin and were taught how to parse sentences. I remain immensely grateful for all that.

As a young man I made up for the defects in my literary education. While a student at Edinburgh, I read a lot of fiction. I had periods of enthusiasm of the sort that young readers have: I thought D. H. Lawrence was marvellous; I thought Jack Kerouac was liberating; I was deeply impressed by contemporary "engaged" poetry of the sort which I would today, I fear, find very dull and pretentious. But I did read Scottish poetry and became very interested in it.

Then I went to live for a year in Belfast. I had been given my first academic post, which was a lectureship at the Queen's University, and I entered upon a year which was of fundamental importance for me. I was then twenty four, but I was a relatively immature twenty four and I needed to grow up. Being in Belfast at that time provided me with the opportunity to do so. I was exposed to a situation of great political and social complexity. I met marvellous friends. I loved the city, which I consider to be very beautiful, in spite of its bad image and its bad press. But I also made two discoveries: Irish literature, particularly the Irish short story, and the poetry of W. H. Auden.

I had heard of Auden, of course, and had read one or two of his poems in anthologies, but that was about the extent of my exposure to his work. Then one day I was browsing in the book stacks in the university library and I saw a collection of Auden's poems. I decided, on impulse, to borrow it and dip into it. I took it with me from the library to the university club and opened it while drinking a cup of coffee. And in this way there began my relationship with a poet to whose work has given me great pleasure and inspiration over the years. I saw Auden once, at a reading he gave in Edinburgh shortly before his death. He read in the George Square Lecture Theatre and I sat in the front row, hanging on every word. He was a marvellous, shabby figure, with his carpet slippers and, on this occasion, an unzipped fly. His suit and tie seemed stained with soup. But that wonderful voice, with its mid-Atlantic twang and curious half-flattened vowels was electric in its effect.

I became interested in Northern Irish writers, and took great pleasure in the works of Brian Moore, who in my view is a particularly skilled novelist, in a league with Graham Greene. I also explored some lesser known figures. Forest Reid is not talked about much today, but was a good writer. His difficulty was a personal demon which led him into sentimental forays into tales of boyhood in an Ulster Arcadia. Had his personal psychology not been thus directed I think that he could have been a more widely-read author. He certainly managed to convey a strong sense of the Ulster countryside.

I returned to Edinburgh and pursued an academic career at the University. In my spare time I became involved with publishing , in a small way. My friend, Peter Chiene, a man of great intellectual ability whose life was unfortunately marred by illness and who died too early, set up a small publishing company, of which I became a director. This company later became associated with Canongate Publishing, then run by that doyenne of Scottish publishing, Stephanie Wolfe Murray. I served for a time on the editorial board of Canongate, which gave me an abiding interesting in the mechanics of publishing.

I was doing a certain amount of writing in this period, but was publishing little, apart from the occasional magazine article. That was not because I was being thwarted; it was just that I was not then writing anything worth publishing. Then I entered in a literary competition run by Chambers, the Edinburgh publishers, best known for their dictionaries. Chambers decided to offer three prizes of one thousand pounds each – one for a novel, one for a children's book, and one for a work of non-fiction. I had embarked on the writing of a novel, which I completed in order to enter in the competition. For some reason I decided to try my hand at a children's story, which I duly wrote. Both manuscripts were entered.

I remember with great clarity the day that I received the letter from Chambers. It was in a registered envelope, and delivery of it had been taken by my flat-mate of the time, Dirk van Zyl Smit, a criminologist who was studying for a doctoral degree in Edinburgh. Dirk phoned me up and told me that the letter was waiting for me, and I made my way down the hill to Stockbridge more or less composing my acceptance speech in my head. I assumed it was the novel; it was not – it was the children's story, which had won the prize jointly with four others, the judges being unable to distinguish between them.

On the strength of this prize, I decided to find an agent. It was a premature move, but a good one, as it brought me to the doorstep of Gina Pollinger and her husband, Murray. Gina, who was considered to be the finest London agent for children's books, encouraged me to write more for children. Over the years that followed I wrote over thirty books for children. I was initially published by Hamish Hamilton, but I later had books with a wide range of publishers. These books were quite successful. One of them, *The Perfect Hamburger*, became reasonably well-known. It was translated into a number of languages and is still in print today, over twenty years on.

My life changed dramatically at the beginning of the nineteen eighties. I was due for sabbatical leave from the University and I decided to spend six months in Swaziland, a small southern African country. With the help of the British Council, I was appointed a visiting lecturer at the University College of Swaziland. I was given a house in the university grounds, and from the verandah of this house I had a magnificent view of the hills above to the north. I had a study at the back of the house, with a window surrounded by purple bougainvillea. That is where I wrote *The Perfect Hamburger*.

The important thing was that I was back in Africa. And, more importantly, I was back in Africa in a country that was at peace. I found the whole experience a very emotional one, and it enabled me to come to terms with that part of my past which I had effectively put out of my mind. While I was there, I drove over to Botswana on several occasions to visit an old friend of mine who worked as a doctor in a place called Mochudi, to the north of Gaborone. I stayed with this friend and his wife in their house next to the hospital, and this was my first proper introduction to a country with which I was later to have a prolonged love affair. I spent much of the following year in Botswana, seconded from the University of Edinburgh to help in the setting up of a new law school in Gaborone. Now that I lived there, I was able to get to know the country better, and, in common with so many other visitors to Botswana, I became intrigued by the features of this peacable republic. I realised that I was in a good country, in which a determined effort had been made to create a fine state in a troubled part of the world. The legacy of Seretse Khama, who was a man of peace and vision, was taken very seriously in Botswana, and it showed in everyday life.

I returned to Scotland somewhat reluctantly. I had been happy in Botswana and would have been content to remain there longer. But my roots were now in Scotland and I understood that Africa was really my past, not my present or future. Shortly after my return, I married and my wife and I started our life together living in Cumberland Street, at the bottom of the New Town.

I was at this stage still writing children's books. Sometimes I would publish three or more of these a year. This was, I suppose, a small measure of literary success, but my real desire was to write something more satisfying. I started to write more short stories, and these were broadcast by the BBC and published on occasion in the Scottish Short Stories collections which the Scottish Arts Council promoted along with Collins, the publishers.

In the middle of the 'eighties I embarked on a collection of African traditional stories. I had collected these in 1980, when I had been living in Swaziland and had visited Matabeleland, in the southern part of Zimbabwe. I had visited villages and, with the help of an interpreter, recorded stories told by old people and by children. I then retold these, using different language but trying to get something of the flavour of the original. I put these together into a collection which I called *Children of Wax*, which was published by Stephanie Wolfe Murray at Canongate. I received encouraging reviews and I decided that my next book would be a collection of thematically-linked short stories, set in a number of different countries. This was published as *Heavenly Date*, and was short-listed for the McVitties Award, but did not win. Canongate had by then been taken over by Jamie Byng and Hugh Andrew. Jamie was very helpful with *Heavenly Date* and I was most impressed with the way in which he was developing Canongate into an important publishing house with influence well beyond Scotland's borders.

Throughout the 'eighties and early 'nineties I had been continuing to visit Botswana virtually every year, now for shorter periods. I had a legal project in Lesotho, and sometimes went on to Botswana from there, but I was also involved in a writing a book on Botswana's criminal law with an old friend in Gaborone, Professor Kwame Frimpong. I thought that I might write something more general about Botswana, and in particular I wanted to write something about one of the enterprising Motswana women whose contribution to the country is so important. One evening I sat down and wrote a short story about a woman called Precious Ramotswe. Her father is dying and he summons her to his deathbed to tell her to sell the cattle and set up a business after he is gone. I paused – I had no idea what business she would start. And then it occurred to me that a detective agency would be a good idea. So I wrote the words "I shall start a detective agency" and with that my life changed utterly and completely, although I did not know it at that point.

I rather liked the character of Precious Ramotswe and so I decided to make the short story into something bigger. We went that year to spend a month in a small village outside Montpellier. The house in which we were staying was an old one, in the middle of the medieval village, and the study in this house looked out on to a private garden of crumbling stone and hard shadows. That is where I wrote much of *The No 1 Ladies' Detective Agency*.

Returning to Scotland, I offered the manuscript to Stephanie Wolfe Murray. She was the first person to read it, doing so on a lorry journey to the Balkans in the course of one of the supply trips she did for the charity which her sons set up. In the event, Canongate did not publish the book, although

Stephanie wished to do so. There were various reasons why they chose not do so, and I am sure that all of them were perfectly good ones. I was, of course, disappointed, but it did not discourage me from taking the manuscript to Marion Sinclair, who was then a commissioning editor at Polygon. Marion read the book and took a reader's report on it. She then put it to the publishing board of Edinburgh University Press, which controlled Polygon. They agreed to bring it out in a paperback edition, with a print run of fifteen hundred copies.

The critics were generous in their remarks and the book sold reasonably well by the standards of a small Edinburgh publisher. The book was reprinted and I was encouraged to write a sequel, which emerged as *Tears of the Giraffe*. This sold comfortably, and a third book in the series was commissioned. But my work was still not very well known in Scotland and I was completely unknown in the rest of the United Kingdom, other than as a children's author. I did not particularly mind this; I had achieved professional satisfaction in my academic career and I was involved with a number of public bodies and committees. I had a lot to do.

But something was about to happen. Edinburgh University Press had an arrangement with Columbia University Press under which each press distributed the books of the other. Columbia University Press usually restricted itself to the academic titles of Edinburgh University Press, but they decided that they might try importing into the United States a number of the Polygon books, including my own. They did this and at first the response was slight. Bookshops ordered a handful of copies. But suddenly they started to order more, and soon repeat orders were coming thick and fast. *The No 1 Ladies' Detective Agency* was suddenly becoming a word-of-mouth success in the United States — a cult book in certain circles. This was not happening in the United Kingdom, although there was now some interest being expressed in London. London publishers had consistently turned down these books when offered mass market paperbacks rights. Then Paul Barker, the former editor of *New Society*, came to see me in Edinburgh and wrote a large article in the *Telegraph Magazine* about my work and asked why it was being ignored. Round about the same time, the *New York Times* devoted a whole page to the books and the Random House group of publishers approached Polygon with a view to buying the rights to the series. We were then courted by a number of London publishers, and decided to sell the mass market paperback rights to Time Warner. I met and very much liked their publishing director, Richard Beswick, who is also the publisher of two other Scottish writers, my friend Ross Leckie and the inventive and amusing Christopher Brookmyre.

I remember the precise day that I realised that my literary life was going to change out of all recognition. I had gone to New York in July 2002 in order to meet my editor before the planned American launch of my books in September of that year. I had assumed that the meeting would be a brief one – perhaps a cup of coffee and a quick chat. I was completely wrong. I arrived at the Random House offices and was immediately taken in to meet all sorts of senior people. People came out of their offices to look at me in the corridor. I was taken to a grand lunch, for twenty people, in a specially hired room of a restaurant. And then, when I left their offices that afternoon, I walked out onto Park Avenue, where they then were, and looked about me. New York was bustling with activity. There was a narrow slice of sky between the towering buildings. The very air was charged with energy. My life was going to change. I did not want it to change, but it seemed inevitable.

Over the next two years I continued to write further novels in the series. I agreed to write eight in all, and I also signed a contract to write a series of four novels set in Edinburgh. This is the *Sunday Philosophy Club* series. The *No 1 Ladies' Detective Agency* series was published in New York and Toronto, and subsequently in mass-market paperback form in London. Foreign publishers then acquired my books, which are being published in thirty-five foreign languages, ranging from Chinese to Icelandic. I suddenly found myself one of the best-selling authors in the world. I hope that I do not say any of this in a boastful spirit; I am reporting what happened to me because it obviously affects my work and what I write. And I mention all this because it did change the conditions of my life, as I had expected it would. I could not continue with my career, and embarked on a three year unpaid leave of absence. Much of my time is now spent abroad, touring literary festivals and speaking to readers. I embark on regular tours of the United States, in particular, where the books seem to be especially popular.

To be favoured with success on this scale could well and truly turn one's head – and destroy one's life. I have tried to avoid this happening by reminding myself that the rewards of this world are very temporary, and nothing special. If my books have provided people with something for which they have been looking, then I am very happy that this is so. If I have managed, without setting out to do so, to convey to people a sense of the great human qualities of people in Africa, of their charm and generous-spiritedness, then I am pleased with that.

I remain rooted in Scotland. I love this country and I am proud of it. Although my books are now published all over the world, I am very keen that they continue to have a base in Scotland, with a Scottish publisher, before they are given wings elsewhere. For this reason, Polygon continues to publish every Mma Ramotswe novel before it goes to London and New York. For this reason, too, *44 Scotland Street*, my serial novel in *The Scotsman*, will be published here in Edinburgh before it has its London and New York publication.

People sometimes draw attention to the fact that my novels are very much concerned with moral issues. This is true. I am very interested in the whole question of how we are to respond to the moral challenges that beset our lives at every point. In the character of Mma Ramotswe I have created somebody who is a profoundly good woman; Isabel Dalhousie, the heroine of the *Sunday Philosophy Club* is a good person too, but in a different way. Some people may think, then, then that I am some sort of moralist (in the pejorative sense of the word). I am not. I am as weak and as flawed as the next person. I have manifested many failings in my life, and I do not find it easy to follow the advice of the characters I create. But I do find the whole business of how we might lead the good life an interesting and challenging one. If, as a writer, one can help in some way to show to those who read one's books the possibilities of forgiveness and love, then that is a great privilege, even if one has fallen short of those ideals in one's own life.

Joy Hendry

Born Perth 3rd February 1953

EDITOR AND POET

The Watergaw

One of my earliest memories, aged two or three, is standing in the front garden of the sub-police station in Letham council housing estate, Perth, pondering the nature of being. It was a sunny day, I remember the smellable green of the grass, the deep blue of the sky. My own consciousness was intriguing me. What was this strange thing, this sense of something located in my head?, this feeling that I was not like other people. There was a barrier between me and my parents and friends; what was flooding me then was unlikely to be shared, far less understood. Just having this 'experience' set me apart. I felt supremely alone, but not lonely.

I don't know how long I stood there, pondering, on the lawn. This was a 'thought' which could be never be had indoors, under my parents' 'umbrella'.

Neil Gunn's writing is a complex tapestry of "clifftop moments", glimpses of "delight". Everybody has them. What makes some people 'different'? "There is an ancient mariner, who stoppeth one of three . . . There's a chiel amang ye, takkin notes . . . there is the compulsion, the driving force to an unknowable destination. All life, from the most abstruse scientific insights to Biblical precepts, tells an intensely human story. I was stopped, on the Letham lawn, by the need to first live, and then tell, a story. This is the first time I've even tried to tell it, and I'm finding it very hard.

Starting: my parents were older, father and mother in their early 40s. I must have heard them, especially my father, railing against 'blacks' and people of a different-coloured skin. My father could sound like Alf Garnett without the laughs and the verbal exuberance. Enoch Powell was a hero — a man I admire, but for different reasons. "Rivers of blood" Never marry a black man, or a brown man, or a Catholic, Or I will disinherit you!! My mother held the same opinions, although more educatedly and politely.

One sunny afternoon, an African chief came as an 'official' visitor to the sub-police station. He sported the biggest, friendliest smile I'd ever seen, looked at me, took me by hands, and admired me from arms' length. He put his arm around me, enfolding me inside his Jacob-coloured cotton coat. I melted, overcome by the musky, dark smell of his body, and the frisson of delight at such an openly physical demonstration of affection (my parents undemonstrative), puzzled by how he could be so willingly received when his like were fundamentally unwelcome. Why was this man, of a kind presented to me as alien, even dangerous, so wonderfully warm and exciting?

My parents' influence was unintentionally malign and negative. Calvinism ruled the roost. It wasn't their fault. Their problem was frustration; their positive and creative natures had been dammed and twisted by events and the cultural mores of early 20th century Scotland, not to mention two World Wars, the first of which almost claimed both my grandfather, and my father. I rebelled from the start. Aged 18 months, my mother had me singing 'In a Contemplative Fashion', the quartet from *The Gondoliers*. I could get my toddler tongue round all of the big words except 'contemplative', which I would render as 'comtemplative. An engaging party trick, but also a mildly cruel exploitation, more of which later.

Ironically, their own marriage was about as mixed as you could get. (I'm sure there's 'tinker' blood' on the Hendry side). I derived satisfaction, and inspiration, from my father's background in the back-streets of Dundee, his family poor and very working class. My mother was upper-middle class, the Shepherds based in Forfar, the family stuffed full of doctors, ministers and other socially-successful types. Angus is a curiously individual county which even now throws up odd anomalies and people, and glories in its unique anarchism, Something in the water or the wind which makes them a breed on their own?

He by then was a policeman, she a staff-nurse, training for midwifery, both the youngest of their families: my father, William, had two older sisters Jessie and Jean, and a brother, David, my mother Janet, the youngest of five sisters. Both families were spread out — a 20 year gap between my mother and eldest sister, Agnes. This had a curious effect on them, as if they felt a lack of authority throughout their lives, however hard they might try to assume its mantle. As youngest siblings, both were maybe a bit spoiled, and rebelled against their respective 'regimes', or tried to, their most potent rebellion being their marriage to one another, opposed by both families. That lasting opposition damaged us all.

The Shepherds and the Hendrys were ruled by the Grannies. My maternal grandfather, a primary school headmaster (who taught Lord Ritchie Calder, father of Angus, now a close personal friend of many years), died not long after my parents married, in 1948; my paternal grandfather quitted the planet soon after my birth, his death prompting the second of two miscarriages. For most of the Hendry clan, now more comfortably off but still working-class close, my mother was a snob, a toffy-nosed clever-clever, to be kept at arms' length. On the Shepherd side, an uncle took my mother for a run in the car for a chat, begging her not to marry my father — she could do much better, pursue her nursing career, find somebody else more 'suitable'. But it WAS a love-match, and both rebellious and determined enough not to be deflected in their intent.

Poor things: they didn't have much of a chance. My maternal grandfather was renowned for strictness, but was a passionate educator who would do anything to 'bring someone on' — forcing after-school tuition on underachieving pupils — and a great believer in the belt. For family discipline, he would not beat, but instead mangle his knuckles into their spines, the pain excruciating. His son, first-born Michael, died in infancy of meningitis, and so he was left with only five women to fulfil his educational ideals. He sent Agnes to university to study medicine, and even set her up in practice; Margaret (Auntie Mac) went to finishing school in Switzerland, and then trained as a teacher, though, given half a chance, she would have been much more at home with Rowen Atikinson, using her verbal and pianist talents; Norah, second youngest, became a physiotherapist. The middle sister, Dibbie (Isabel), had her life ruined by my grandmother's 'physical breakdown' shortly after my mother's birth, and from age 11, Dibs ran the house, looked after my grandmother, had to turn down two rich, enticing suitors, a career, and neglect her wonderful bell-like singing voice. Waste, waste, waste!

My mother, stupid woman, developed the notion that the family needed her financial support, left school at 16 in spite of being, apparently, the brightest of five bright sisters, and worked in an office for 7/6 a week. Part of Granny Shepherd's 'breakdown' involved committing all available resources to the Jehovah's Witnesses and selling off all household 'goodies' to progress the cause. My grandfather knew this, and tried to deal with it in his will as best he could. The Grandmother lived on, dying grudgingly aged 97, having destroyed many lives in the process. I saw them both in their coffins: Granny Hendry a serene body, happy in the life she'd left behind her, despite all manner of tragedy; Grannie Shepherd, clutched and angry, grasping all available life to herself, even in death. But Dibbie was left, aged 70, with less freedom than a 17 year old could expect, even then, far less now. This makes me so angry, to this day, that I can hardly bear thinking about it.

During the war, Mother did a stint in a munitions factory in Birmingham – and, reading her sub-text, experienced freedom impossible at home. My father, typically, left school at 14 to become a chin-soaper in a barber's shop, and other sic-like 'jobs', eventually training as a plumber though his headmaster begged my grandmother not to allow him to leave school. Eventually he joined the police-force, but war intervened, and he enlisted as a commando, passing the entry test only by inventive duplicity, ingeniously masking the fact that he had already lost hearing in one ear through a botched mastoid operation, and was in trouble with the other.

Commando life suited him perfectly, but eventually his troop was captured. Six-foot three -and-a-half, hugely athletic and agile physically and mentally, he had anticipated trouble and hidden up a tree, but when his comrades were taken, he gave himself up and became prisoner of war for three years, latterly, and happily, on a small farm in Austria. Afterwards, he would only tell the funny stories. The 'bad bits' he kept to himself, showing themselves in occasional, frightening rages. I could match his rages, the result a thunderous impasse. I once saw him and my grandmother (same temperament we all share) caught in ossified lockjaw and black temper. Witnessing it was terrifying.

One problem of early years about which I have no distinct memory is the sibling jealously I felt at the arrival of my younger brother, Gary, with whom I am now very close. It was only after I had broken down at school, crying my eyes out into the teacher's lap and muttering incoherences like: "it's all about my little brother", and told my mother what had happened, that she finally admitted: "Yes, there has been a problem." The right word, two seconds speaking, could have saved years of pain.

So these two tried to stitch their lives together. Both were incredibly strong in disparate ways, and talented. My mother and her sisters were all 'intellectuals', all intensely musical, played the piano, sang beautifully – and very attractive women, though sexually repressed thanks to the narrow, strict Shepherd regime. My father, educated and unleashed into the pool of opportunity, could have done just about anything. And, but for the Roman, hooked nose, he looked like Clark Gable. And their two worlds clashed!

There was a constant battle of values and ideals, and it's a pity that my father bowed to my mother because of her 'superior intellect and education'. He repressed his own more volatile, open nature for her more socially-acceptable mores. He never used his Dundee dialect in the house, and determined that I should adopt my mother's educated 'proper' tones and social, cultural values. I didn't. I much preferred what he revealed to me of his own.

This all meant that we didn't belong anywhere. The Hendrys were always on best behaviour on our visits to Granny Hendry's tiny tenement flat. My oldest Hendry aunt, Jessie, a formidable woman, 20 stones heavy and addicted to confectionary, censored her rich, lively, seamy language when we were about. I feel cheated of the full blast of her culture, coarse tongue and personality. Some of that working class character inevitably, and thankfully, rubbed off on my brother and me, making us aliens in the Shepherd environment too.

Their marriage was a social disaster. My mother thought my father's friends 'common', disapproving of the occasional enthusiastic drinking (though at times she joined in); my father felt inadequate with my mother's. And she was snubbed by many (as was I, at the 'snob school') because her husband was "just a policeman". "I've got more breeding in my little finger," she would declare, defiantly thrusting her pinkie into the air, "than he has in his entire body!" So they became isolated, and worse, never quite understood or accepted each other, though they loved each other to bits. It used to drive me mad.

I have spent much of my life unpicking this morass of contradictions. Actually, I have inherited much from both, their rebelliousness, their strong, if thwarted individualities. They married late – aged 33. My mother had her ovaries removed shortly after, but the surgeon, who knew my mother as a nurse (and a good one) left in a bit in 'just in case' . . . The fragment did well – four children, the second me, the fourth my brother successfully launched into life, and two miscarriages. When my brother was born, they were both 42. Their strong but frustrated natures had by then calcified through lack of development, the result a restricted environment (especially for a girl). My brother, second-born and male, got off lightly – I never stopped "kicking over the traces" and he benefited from battles I'd already fought and won.

All this was hurtful, and I have always been hyper-sensitive, easily crushed and discouraged, but with a determination which, once activated, is virtually unstoppable. My brother and I knew they loved us deeply, and that knowledge let them off with a multitude of sins, to our disadvantage. I was incredibly hurt when my mother told me: "You were the apple of your father's eye – until he realised how difficult you were!" "Thanks," I thought, grimly, realising that I had been firmly rejected. They were bad at showing emotion, and terrified that I, especially, might get 'big ideas'. So whenever I succeeded at something, I got no praise, only a grudging – "well, you could do better" – this even if 'doing better' was impossible. Sometimes, involuntarily, an appreciation would erupt, but never directed at me. When I won the school trophy for all round excellence, she burst out "Oh, how lovely!" but negected to say "well done" to me.

School was torment. Determined that we should benefit from the education neither of them had, we were sent to the local grant-aided school, Perth Junior Academy. They were hard up, so this was a sacrifice, but not much of a blessing. It drove an impenetrable wedge with the pals in the housing scheme who went to the nearby state Goodlyburn school. Shortly before starting school, I broke my left ankle, and had my leg plastered to the hip. I was an enormous child, a foot taller than children of the same age, and also sticking out because I was 'different'. And I was clumsy and physically uncoordinated, wisely avoiding climbing trees which my friends did with ease and aplomb.

My father had befriended an old couple, the Flemings, who owned a farm at Burghmuir — now a private housing estate, and we frequently visited him. Just after my fifth birthday, we dropped in. Even then, I delighted in walks on my own, and, while my father and Old Man Fleming were chatting over tea and biscuits, I went for a walk in his field. At the end of this, I spotted a tree behind a fence. "It's not good enough," I thought, "that I'm scared of climbing trees. I'll climb this one now." I got as far as the top of the fence, unbalanced, and fell. Hence the broken leg.

And then there was the dog, Laddie. For as long as I can remember I'd wanted a dog, and finally got one, aged 8. We got him as a 4-month old pup already injured in a car accident, with a gammy leg as a result. We only had him another four months. He'd been injured in a car accident as a pup, had a gammie leg as a result. I remember my father holding out his collar, one Tuesday night after he collected me from the Brownies, he told me the dog was dead. Joke, he later had to admit. The dog hirpled up, wagging his tail.

I was a latch-key child at both ends of the day. My Father was often on night duty. An envelope arrived that I, aged 8, wrongly thought important. I woke him up to give it to him and was dismissed. But I locked the dog in the kitchen, forgetting that I had turned on the gas on the stove without lighting it, intending to make him breakfast. By lunchtime the dog was dead, and after I came back from the Brownies he had to tell me the dog was dead. I cried my eyes out for months afterwards. They tried to conceal the fact that I it was who had killed the dog. Two months later, they finally they had to tell me, hearing yet again my uncontrollable sobs late at night. Being told the truth at least began to lay the demons.

So I was different in just too many ways, and my classmates, led by one girl in particular, mounted a persecution campaign which continued for the first five years of school. They pleasured in reducing me to tears, or rage, excluding me from everything. I overcame it by forming friendships with girls 3-4 years older, demonstrating that I was better than most at almost everything. From age 6, I had been playing the piano, and swam, becoming proficient in both. When we were taken to the baths as a class, I told my 'friends' I could already swim. "Don't be stupid," they declared. "You can't swim. We know you can't swim". But they had to eat their words when they saw me in the pool. I also did well in class — never top, but narrowly missing proxime accessit of the school in final year. And I won the athletic trophy too. Faced with such evidence, the persecution diminished and eventually stopped. Secondary school was happier — especially the first three years. I enjoyed the work and better relationships. I stopped growing aged 10, reaching my adult 5 foot 10 ½ so the height-differential between me and others (not the boys!) narrowed, and, briefly, I fitted in better.

Aged about 11, I had started begging for a guitar. The initial response was 'no' — you don't practise your piano, so you're not getting a guitar. This wasn't true. My mother went back to nursing part-time when I was 8 and I used the solitude after school to play piano when nobody could hear, before my mother came home from work. I protested this, but wasn't believed. (A friend recently said, perspicaciously, that, like Cassandra, I had the doom of telling the truth, but never being believed!) They gave in, and I got a classical guitar from 'Santa'. But then I was next 'led astray' by an older friend who took me to Perth Folk Club to hear Billy Connolly, Hamish Imlach, Archie Fisher and others. (Being tall does have advantages – no questions in licensed premises, though bus-drivers were a torment from age 7). Soon I wanted an acoustic guitar, which parents refused to finance, so I saved up over 6 months out of my pittance of pocket-money by saving busfares etc. Once I'd saved £23, they coughed up the balance and I became the proud owner of a Levin guitar (the older, now much valued model). It wasn't long before its previous owner bitterly regretted selling it, since it was infinitely superior in tone and responsiveness to the expensive guitar he'd replaced it with. I treasure it to this day, but rarely touch it.

So I appeared regularly at folk clubs, forming genuine friendships with other singers, folkies, writers under the benignly eccentric patronage of the unforgettable Archie Gibson. My parents were not pleased: "We'd rather you didn't!" but they knew an outright ban would go unheeded. So I became a fixture at Perth Folk Club, mixing with people of whom my parents completely disapproved. What a relief — functioning in a world where I was inspired — and 'at home'. It hurt me greatly that my parents refused to come to hear me perform, but would happily get me to sing and play for visitors —

and even for the assembled throng at my father's retiral 'do', aged 15, in front of most of the Perth Police Force in licensed premises!

The same happened when I began to attend Perth Youth Theatre. Here too was a world which excited and stimulated me, — among my fellows Stuart Cosgrove — now Channel 4 Director of Nations and Regions, Ann Fleck, also Channel 4, and others who have distinguished themselves. Many were at Perth Academy, but we never mixed in the school environment. This was 1968. Perth Theatre had just suffered the loss of founder Marjory Dence, and Iain Cuthbertson had been appointed artistic director. He mounted challenging seasons of plays, including John Arden's *Live Like Pigs*, *Under Milk Wood*, Robert McLennan's *Toom Byres* — and allowed the Youth Theatre a whole week for our production *PPF* which was an incredible experience for all. Many lives were changed, but Perth Theatre sacked Iain as 'unsuitable'. In fact, he was using Perth as a rather dangerous vision for a Scottish National Theatre. That was not his remit as a theatre director; the vision was needed, for the benefit of those 'in the know' at the time. I was too young (15) to know what was going on in the political and cultural horticultures of this desert Scotland; I only knew that what Iain was trying to do was good, life-changing inspiring and we all loved it; Iain, a hero before whom the laurels should be raised.

The Youth Theatre now flourishes, but the entangled web of cultural complexity we were thrust into, throughout all those unthought-of battles, fought out by those who hadn't thought out the ground, far less the battles, and the fate of the 'also-rans'. It was VERY strange. I am only beginning to learn now, almost 40 years later, the reality of what I learned then! We all knew the truth, and all locked behind Iain and all he was trying to do, giving a commitment no modern establishment would think it proper to ask of any bunch of youngsters. We didn't' need to be asked; we were shouting the answer from the rooftops. The genuinely amazing thing is that NONE of us knew the battle were engaging in: the battle for Scottish theatre, poetry, language, you name it. But we ALL just did. Maybe it was in all of our bloods. We were about 60 in number, and I'm sure that while there may be Stuart Cosgrove, and Ann, and me, operating relatively 'in the public eye', all of us were changed.

We became the bête noires of the school, refusing any discipline we considered irrelevant, taking over school dances and transforming them from stiff formality into something much more lively and fun — pretty harmless stuff. We mounted school shows and concerts which, amongst other things, satirised the staff. Stuart and a friend wrote an alternative pantomime – *A*

Boot in the Puss!, whose fairy-tale plot was woven around a fantasy about St Johnstone winning the European Cup. I was Principal Boy, and Madelaine Taylor, now well known in folk circles, Principle Girl. Had my mother been dallying with the coalman— an unlikely but often-proffered explanation for my deviations?

Although I always did and still do suffer badly from nerves, I got involved in other projects and productions; the school opera *The Yeoman of the Guard* in which I played the formidable Dame Carruthers, a German operetta written by our head of German, George Donald, who went on to fame with *Scotland the What*, and other things, and also performing at Perth and other folk clubs.

I suddenly found science subjects, which I'd loved before, much more difficult — though all arts subjects held more attraction than ever. I packed in all 'proper' activities — playing hockey (only did it because I fancied a boy in the First XI anyway!), all involvement with guides and brownies, which I'd done since age 6. I baulked finally at the requirements for the Queen's Guide badge, but doing everything else, including being Pack Leader to the Junior Brownies. The change was noticed by the staff, who summoned my mother to tell her they were "worried about me", and that they feared I was "going off the rails". To my surprise and pleasure she defended me, insisting that I knew what I was doing.

Gossip was burgeoning. I had been seen, caught, doing dreadful things like walking solo along the Inch, singing to the river, going up Kinnoull Hill at dawn, not for sexual purposes, but to read poetry! Much worse than fornication!

By this time I was gasping to get away, dream destination Edinburgh University. I slaved (well, a bit) to gain university entrance qualifications in S5, so that I could leave Perth Academy, and my parents, who coped badly with their unusual, gangly, precocious 17-year-old. I was in fact extremely well behaved, but rebellion, and the determination to follow my own lights, created an impression of anarchic behaviour.

My social life was now firmly outside school, with people years older, involved with literature, music, or theatre. I had found a surrogate mother in poor emaciated Auntie Mac, and later Lucy Foston, mother of a 'boyfriend' (it never came to much), who understood all the aspects of my life and character which were anathema to my mother, and whose lifestyle and approach to life were positive and liberating. She had a 'reputation' and initially my parents wouldn't have anything to do with her. The menopause unleashed an unquenchable sexual appetite in her; she couldn't help but 'misbehave' — but eventually even they came to see her sterling qualities. Sadly, Lucy died of breast cancer in 1976. She, like my parents, had undeveloped talents, but had made the most of them and retained an indomitable, free spirit. Her nickname was 'Butterfly' – she used to call me "my rainbow Joy". I never had to explain anything to her. Her commitment to enhancing the human life and spirit survived undiminished until her painful, unnecessary death.

At the Youth Theatre, I made a close friendship with Gordon Stewart, then at Dundee Art College, with folk singers like Les Honeyman (now deceased), and others, and all my social life had nothing to do with school. Almost every evening, Gordon and I would chew over literature, philosophy, art, emotions . . . Young though I was, I realised he was gay, and he would talk endlessly about men he had crushes on, and his overwhelming feelings. Though he was six years older, I guided him through that process, until he moved from claustrophobic Perth to London to become an eminent stage designer, working on plays by John Byrne and many others. It was Gordon who rescued the infamous floor of the 1977 Edinburgh Festival production of *Carmen*. Once in London, he could participate in an open, gay scene. Inevitably we saw less of each other, and he died of Aids in 1989.

So I left school in June 1970. There had been endless rows about curfews, exacerbated by my falling in love with an Irish folk singer, participant in Perth Theatre's Summer Season – I was working evenings as an usherette.

The key thing, for me, was the word. I knew that my future lay in working with words in various ways, though not what exactly what might be in store. My compositions had been singled out in primary school as special. One English teacher pounced on me because, as she put it (unfortunately to the entire class,) that my writing had 'style'. I wrote my first poem aged 13, in half an hour before breakfast, having seen an ad for contributions to *The Young Barbarian*, the school magazine. It won the 'Light and Shade' prize – and I even illustrated it myself. However, later attempts to join the board of the magazine were rejected, and an application to be editor of the school French magazine also, because I was considered too radical and of "having too many ideas"! Between age 13 and leaving school, I probably wrote about 150 poems – mostly rambling personalia now mostly destroyed (wish I hadn't done that!). One teacher, Robert Hughes (sadly I was never in his class), a successful novelist, was one day overwhelmed when I presented him with an my entire folder poems, but he singled out a few to send to Robert Nye of *The Scotsman*. Kath Robbins' husband, playwright and novelist William Watson, also looked at it. Both set me on the road to concision and craft in writing. I had, and still have, a great deal to learn.

I dwell on my childhood and youth because of its tensions and contradictions and because, I still wonder how I managed to 'stick to my guns'. My parents wanted me have a career in law, teaching, some 'profession' or other — a 'proper job'. All my life so far I had been surrounded by 'should-have-beens' — talented people whose lives should have been very different. I was determined this was not to happen to me. Since those early moments of 'metaphysical consciousness', I've known that something ineluctable was driving me.

So, at last, Edinburgh University, a small bedsit in East Mayfield, and self-determination. Above all, I'd looked forward to immersing my life in words, music, theatre, art, meeting kindred spirits, and being myself, whatever that means. I remember in October, despite all above protestations, being desperately homesick.

University was a huge disappointment. With honourable exceptions like Colin Nicholson, most of the lecturers in the English department seemed devoid of anything like pleasure in good writing, or passion about literature. (I was studying English literature, British History, and Literature and Philosophy with a view to Honours in English Language and Literature) but found almost no kindred spirits — most seemed set on equipping themselves for a career and I found it hard even to talk to them. All the old gulfs loomed up, but worse, because I expected better. The same pattern emerged: I had nothing in common with people my own age, developed friendships with people now much older than myself — with a lovely Ethiopian town planner whose name now escapes me, Robin Thomson, 10 years older, mature student, actor, singer, and with Walter Perrie, whom I married in 1972.

I don't want to delve into detail about adult relationships — I'm still too young for that, and virtually all of these have been deep but troubled. My childhood left a deep-rooted lack of confidence in myself, especially as a woman. Because I was tall, the expectation was that I would become a 'big woman' in all respects (except mentally!) In the gospel according to my father, my doom was to become like all 20 stones of Auntie Jessie: "You'll never have a good figure," he said to me, aged about 13. "You're too big!" Wish he could see me now, aged 52! But my sexual confidence has always been poor; I found nothing in common with most men who might otherwise come 'a-courting' me. Most immediately got scared, and backed off. The most important relationships have always arisen through my work.

My lack of confidence usually doesn't show. I'm perceived as a strong woman, an Amazon, indeed. But, more worldly-wise and thick-skinned now, essentially I'm still hypersensitive, touchy, too sympatico for my own good — and still 'driven'. I have never shared most women's goals and ambitions. I was never interested in dancing, shopping — all that, and would rarely move the length of myself to 'net' a member of the opposite sex. My greatest pleasure was stimulating talk, music, reading, writing, singing, or wandering the environs of Perth, now Edinburgh, at all hours like "a trailing yowe", as my mother commented. I tramped the Perth streets in search of roses (used to pinch one or two from gardens), cherry blossom, vistas and sunsets, singing out loud, never quite understanding what drove me. I would have liked to have had children; think I would have been a superb, if rather odd mother. One teenage friend once said: "Your children will be materially destitute, but spiritually rich!"

I met Walter Perrie, through Robin Thomson. He already had a reputation as a poet, writing (pretentiously) as 'Patrick MacCrimmon'! When I met him six little issues of *The Chapman* had been produced, a project started not by Walter, but his friend, George Hardie. Walter liked my poems, (sleekit seduction move!) and took a couple for the next issue of what became *Chapman*. The six issues had been financed by the empty pockets of the editors,but the first issue of *Chapman* gifted £40 (in 1971) by an elderly lady, and a grant of £200 from the Scottish Arts Council. Walter also had his own work, *Ulysses*, which he wanted published, and I financed its printing out of my earnings from Marks & Spencers and Perth Theatre over the summer. £40.00. Lots of money then! Mug!

So it becomes clear that had I felt my parents didn't love me, things would have been easier. Walter has his own difficult history, and obvious physically disabilities — a hare lip and cleft palate, never mind the underlying mental scars. Having established a relationship, I would have been content to live with him, until such time as we had outlived our mutual usefulness, but 'moral' pressure dampened down the rebellion; I failed; cow-towed to conventional expectations, and announced him as my intended. The resultant row and its aftermath ruined our marriage, which unfortunately went ahead. My mother was not given to bitchiness, but she persecuted me over a period of almost a year about anything to do with our proposed wedding. Eventually I confronted her: if she didn't stop this, I would never see her again. She immediately deflated, with obvious relief, and thanked me for having the courage to face her. But it was too late: my father's irrational outburst had damaged us irreparably. My father also had deep jealousies over me, which he was never able to articulate and face. He went out of his way to alienate and destroy almost every man who came near me. Shades of Chris Guthrie. Enough said.

So Walter and I did all manner of silly things; and all manner of good things. An issue on Chinese art and culture had been planned, edited and printed. Having for this no SAC grant, we had to pay a printers' bill of £600. Walter's attempts to assemble a team of sellers hadn't worked, so I gave up work at Perth Royal Infirmary, to come to Edinburgh to do the selling myself – in pubs, university campuses, cafés, gardens – anywhere likely to yield up a sympathetic response – print run 3,000, cover price 30p. A month later we had enough money to pay the printer and another issue on the way, and were accumulating contacts with other writers and editors down south, including Richard Burns and William Oxley, then editor of *Littack*, which he eventually gave up, handing the mantle to his wife, Patricia, who began *Acumen* in its wake, which enriches our lives still. The drive then, and indeed still, is towards alternative visions, to provide a platform not sculpted and dictated by 'authorities' of one kind or another, and, to bring together people deeply at odds with currently literary fashion (the best, for the most part); those rare birds who cry in storm or desert, or shriek from mountaintops.

My relationship with Walter had to end, as it did, in 1976. It had become clear that if any money was to be earned, I was going to have to do it – which I didn't accept as my role in life. But we achieved a great deal together. With his friend, now one of my closest, Robert Calder, we produced several worthwhile issues of *Chapman*, especially those on theatre edited by Robert. And we had started a press, Lothlorien, publishing pamphlets by Richard Livermore, Walter himself, Donald Campbell and an interview with Hugh MacDiarmid. The interview was my idea, and I even compiled the list of questions, though, typically, Walter took all the credit.

Both these pamphlets, and *Chapman*, were appallingly produced: me on an electric typewriter, lots of cow-gum, doubled-edged selotape, medical scalpels and strips of cardboard to create binding. At one point we ran a printing business (which I eventually had to dismantle or Walter would have cracked up!), dealing with creditors and the like. We had had the printing machine in our spare bedroom in Spottiswoode Street. Our downstairs neighbour rang the doorbell one morning asking if he had actually heard a printing machine chunking away during the night – or was he going mad – a printer to trade. He was not mad. The printing machine was there, used, at very unsociable hours!

It was a nightmare. I remember working for 60 hours solid, without food or sleep, and crashing out over half a glass of sherry at the end of it all. Not to mention the hours trekking the pubs to find hapless customers for selling not just *Chapman*, but the eight magazines who were members of SCAMP, (Scottish Association of Magazine Publishers) – a joint distribution scheme set up in a mood of optimism by the Scottish Arts Council. In the end it was me, badly dressed and holes in the shoes, flogging the damned things hand to hand. Entry for the Guinness Book of Records 148 magazines in a day, at the Mod, Cumbernauld 1976. Anecdottle: met 2 civil servants from Centre One, well in their cups, in a hotel — gave them my P 60; they promised to get me my tax rebate real quick, and it was behind the door on my return to Edinburgh!) But SAC pulled the rug on funding for SCAMP shortly afterwards, with hindsight quite rightly. The problem of funding magazines is still a running sore.

But many good things emerged from it all. I had known almost nothing of Scottish literature before becoming involved with *Chapman*. Soon I had met Hugh MacDiarmid, Norman MacCaig, Sydney Goodsir Smith, Callum Macdonald, David Morrison, Tom Scott, Donald Campbell, William Neill, and many other younger writers, friends to this day, like George Gunn, Angus Calder — all men, you might notice — the women came later. In particular, Robert took me along to hear Sorley MacLean, with his electrifying delivery and disorganised presentation. On the strength of that, through poet and organiser Richard Burns, I was able, fighting Walter until the early hours about it, to secure his historic debut at the first Cambridge Poetry Festival, which established him as a player on the international stage.

Anecdottle: Walter and I met one night with Calum MacMillan, an old friend and co-performer from Perth Folk Club, in Sandy Bells, the famous Edinburgh folk pub. Calum is a brilliant guitarist, and has always led, shall we say, an 'alternative' life-style. In a fit of madness, probably my idea, we set sail for Skye, Calum driving, deftly dodging the deer in a January snow-beset landscape, starting about 10 pm at night, arriving on Sorley's doorsteps with two dogs and our three dishevelled selves, just after breakfast next morning. By this time Walter was losing interest in the magazine, and I was becoming more committed to it. Sorley was disconsolate about the fact that though English versions of the parts 1 and 2 of his long poem, 'The Cave of Gold' had appeared in English magazines, nobody would publish the Gaelic original. I immediately offered publication in *Chapman*. That earned me Sorley's life-long loyalty, and made many other things possible, such as the book *Sorley MacLean: Critical Essays*, co-edited with Raymond Ross and published by Scottish Academic Press. Out of madness comes forth a curious kind of sanity and, yes, rightness.

I was struggling to get a degree at all. The demands of *Chapman* and other things had forced me to leave university, and for 18 months I worked as an executive officer in the Registers of Scotland, selling magazines at night. Professor Peter Jones informed me when I told him that he too had spent time such 'time out' in the Civil Service which he found allowed great scope for reading. Indeed it was so. I found it good opportunity to improve my mind when no-one was looking, I managed to read a good deal of philosophy and much else, when officially employed to search writs – and turned in more than my quota too.

I stuck up for colleagues who were being victimised, asked awkward questions, sang around the place, and, again, just didn't fit – with the 'establishment' – so I think they heaved a sigh of relief when I left to return to university. (Once tried hard for a job with Marshall's Chunkie Chickens in Blantyre – but they saw through me straight away!) But in 'the working place' I did fit with my colleagues. I also chimed in with the women I worked in Woollies, M & S, the theatre kitchen, and the nurses, auxiliaries and cleaners in hospitals. Chip off the old block. My mother used to be upset when old pros and crones of Perth tapped my father for the price of a dram. He would always reach into his pocket, turn his hand backwards, and say: "Here you are, hen." My mother, indignant, defiantly middle class, skinny, stunning, and beautifully 'proper', would interrogate: "How do you know her!" But she also loved him for it.

Meanwhile, I'd wangled a flat in Heriot Row, no less, living there rent free on the basis that I'd six other rooms to let. Night after night we sang Schubert and Schumann lieder there, me on the piano, Robin, sometimes Robert, Walter (who thought himself Caruso resurrected) and I sang too, although it's difficult to do that and play complicated accompaniments) and anything else that took our fancy, until not so early in the morning. Our upstairs neighbour, friend to this day, patronised and indulged us. "Oh, I wear ear plugs," she said without a flicker of annoyance in her face. "The dawn chorus is so deafening!"

It was a wonderful, but horrible period. For me, a rebirth, the beginning of real education. Starting from a unionist point of view (both parents mostly voted Tory, although claiming to be floating voters). Working in literature began an awakening of a sense of Scottishness, a re-evaluation of all values, an abandoning of my Presbyterian upbringing in favour of a curious agnosticism, informed gladly by some of the intellectual rigours of Protestantism at its best.

On returning to university, my fellow students seemed even more mercenary than those of two academic years before – most set on a lucrative career in accountancy. Curiously, I didn't feel as out of place as before, and mothered most of them. But the demands of the magazine meant that attendance at classes was something of a luxury. To get my degree, I invited myself back to Perth, away from Walter and all pressures, getting through two years of study in six weeks. And I did get a degree, as good as could be expected in the circumstances — a 2/2, Honours in Mental Philosophy. I'd abandoned study of English Literature after second year because in comparison with the live participation in literature I was enjoying through the magazine, the way it was taught, and the general approach, seemed arid indeed.

I think I have been blessed and cursed by having too many talents. I am haunted by the poem by Joan Ure, published in 'Woven by Women', *Chapman* 27-8: "There was this little woman,/ and she had a tiny talent. She had this tiny talent that it was death to hide." Perhaps the 'answer' is in the way they all combine — which will probably always remain a mystery to me.

After all that is a very special period, during which, for many reasons, I had privileged access to many important figures in 'the Scottish Literary Renaissance'. Gradually I established myself as an editor, but not without difficulty. Having split up with Walter half way through a year at Moray House, I decided to finish the course. On my first day of teaching at Knox Academy, Haddington, a friend who had been charged with walking the dog, met me at lunchtime exuberantly waving a letter from the Scottish Arts Council. Sitting on the banks of the Tyne, in the August sunshine. Eagerly I opened it. It was a service of notice to quit. Despite the wonderful essays about their 'creative processes' from Norman, Sorley, George Mackay Brown, Kathleen Raine, Iain Crichton Smith and Tom Scott in *Chapman* 16, reprinted in *Chapman* 100-1, my short story issue, and the delights of the Children's Issue, my grant was to be withdrawn: the then literature committee had "doubts about my literary judgement". I had two issues to 'prove myself'. With support from Sorley, Norman and many others, I won that battle, but better not to have to fight it in the first place.

And, so, to another couple of relationships, another marriage to Ian Montgomery which has continued for 19 years, now 'on ice' — there comes a point at which none of it really matters. It has been my experience that I, and other 'strong' women known to me, fatefully (or maybe 'fatally') attract talented men, drawn to them by their energy and drive. Strong women are sexy, very sexy. Men drawn to them, strong though they might be, can quickly come to feel, or perhaps realise that they *are* inadequate, and begin to parasite on the woman's strength, while simultaneously trying to destroy it and restore the traditional status quo. I've seen this so often. I fervently hope that this is a generational phenomenon, which will disappear as 'new men' learn to be, truly, new men.

Patricia Oxley, editor of *Acumen* once described the nature of editing a magazine as "educating yourself in public". Wise words and true. Through editing *Chapman* I have become something of an authority on Scottish literature, tutored in the art of massaging the delicate egos of writers — an art, which being human, I can't always exercise. Over nearly 35 years now I have learned an enormous amount of all kinds of things, and got up to all manner of mischief — let me now indulge in a 'little list':

Chapman has done so much over the years I can barely bear to think about it. At least five issues have at least shaken up this little country we share, e.g. our Scots language issue (No 23-4) (the one which got us our grant back in 1979, after the episode on the Tyne); 'Woven by Women', the first publication (1980) to give credence to the notion that women have actually made a contribution over the centuries and decades to Scottish culture. Our 'Predicament of the Scottish Writer' issue (35-6) fairly set an argy-bargy going and elicited from cultural protagonists, unanimously and unprovoked, a statement that we needed the autonomy to look after our own affairs and culture (thereby hangs another couple of tails for the future!); 'Scottish Theatre' issue (43-4) helped secure a revenue client status for Communicado, and forced the SAC to review its policy towards new theatre and writing for the theatre. And we are still committed to causing trouble when necessary.

Despite huge pressures to the contrary, to do the 'male' thing and take sides, I resolved long ago to have none of all that. I viewed with sinking despair the feuds between so many writers, and so many magazines, during the 70s, and learned about previous carnapcious abysses in the past. Obviously, over such a long period, there have been some writers I've been very close to: Norman, Iain Crichton Smith, Tom Scott, George Bruce and others — not to mention Jessie Kesson and Kathleen Raine, both of became another surrogate mother.

It's been necessary to get involved in many enterprises, almost too numerous even to mention, including The Committee for the Advancement of Scottish Literature in Schools (CASLS), ASLS. Then there was the very creative AdCAS, the Advisory Council for the Arts in Scotland, with brave campaigners like Bert Davis and Paul Scott, both unlikely-looking rebels. They jumped on the Theatre Issue, which had caused something of a steer, organised a conference, subsequently written up in *Chapman* 49, and stirred up a debate resulting in various campaigns for a National Theatre and, very ironically, my serving on SAC's drama panel for 6 years.

Then there was the Campaign for a Scottish Assembly, out of which came the committee which produced *A Claim of Right for Scotland* and led to the Scottish Constitutional Convention, Artists for Independence, trying to develop another joint magazine initiative, now called SLAM, participating in the Literature Forum for Scotland — all kinds of malecho and mischief. I organised events, launches, poetry reading, including major ones like 'birthdays' for Norman MacCaig, Sorley MacLean and Hamish Henderson, involving many performers and hundreds of spectators initially egged on by the irrepressible and much-missed Morris Blythman and the John Maclean Society . Norman's 80th in the Queen's Hall is still recorded in Scotland: the Facts as the biggest poetry reading held in Scotland, attended by 850 people. It was more than that. I was 'ensuring entrance' to about 100 people over and above, many friends of Norman's who hadn't secured tickets in time!

One great highlight has been my work on Perth poet William Soutar. It started with a commission from *The Scots Magazine* to write an article about the man seen through the eyes of Perth people. One thing led to another out of that — the refurbishment of Soutar Hoose and the establishing of a Writers Fellowship. Then there was my play about Soutar for Perth Theatre (1990), *Gang Doun wi a Sang*, and then a 90-minute play *The Waa at the World's End*, for Radio 3. Working with actors and directors was tremendous. I've always hoped to write another play, but not so far. This is probably the most notable example of the curious serendipity which seems to govern my life.

Working as a journalist, I was able to do much which fitted my 'programme', and get paid for it! For example, *The Sympathetic Imagination*, about Scottish Poets of World War Two, refused by Radio Scotland, was scooped up eagerly by Radio 3 — including interviews with Sorley, Hamish Henderson and even Norman MacCaig, who really suffered as a 'conscie'. But it was Radio Scotland who commissioned me to do a 3-part 'report' on Scots language, in 1993, in the course of which I got the opportunity to stitch up a willing and eager Robbie Robertson (now deceased and much missed) to commit the Scottish Office to provide real resources for teachers to teach Scots in schools. Result: *The Scots Kist* — a resource still not properly used.

And there has been rescuing writers in distress. Answering the doorbell at midnight to a writer or artist who might have stayed too long in Edinburgh and imbibed too much, requiring to be taken in at night, and ushered out in the morning furnished with bacon roll and the rail-fare home. And much worse than that!

I have to face, with considerable difficulty, the notion that *Chapman*, and myself as an individual, may be perceived as 'establishment' now. It certainly doesn't feel like that. A new generation may even perceive me now as part of an 'old guard', needing broomed away. All's fair in . . .

So what has my life been about? Certainly key was the discovery of Scotland, and its diminished state, politically, culturally, in virtually every respect. Editing *Chapman* as an arrogant youngster exploded a bomb under almost everything I had already worked hard to define. I vowed to do whatever was in my power to change the fabric and supporting structure of Scotland, in literature and language, theatre and the arts, education, to ensure that future generations would not be so cheated of their own inheritance. Seeing promising writers disappear in frustration about never getting that first book (or succeeding ones) published, I started the *Chapman* New Writing Series. I realised that the cultural desert Scotland had become was death, in fact to many. Of the writers we have published over the years, two had untimely deaths: Ian Abbot's *Avoiding the Gods* we published in 1988; six months later he was dead; of Colin Mackay, his book, *Red Ice*, was his, and our first book, and 10 years later *Cold Night Lullaby* about his tragic experiences in Bosnia. He committed suicide in 2003. A more hospitable, sympathetic Scotland could have saved both these lives, and those of Giles Gordon, Neil MacCallum and recently Sandy Craigie, who topped herself in a telephone booth.

Not just Scotland, but the UK in general, must wake up to the necessity of treating our creative people better. Attending a European convention of magazine editors in 1998 provided me with the unenviable knowledge that we treat not just writers, but editors of magazines such as *Chapman* with unbelievable neglect. Even the then East/Middle European magazines, and even those from war zones like Serbia, had better provision and resources than we do in the UK, and in particular in Scotland. Much has been done to rectify the treatment of writers, but less than nothing to address the plight of magazines. For many years I have been doing at least two full time jobs simultaneously in order to live, since *Chapman* can afford a 'salary' considerably below subsistence level, but is certainly a full time job. So first I taught, then dropping that in 1984, journoed away in broadcasting, and as a reviewer on cultural aspects until the Chronic Fatigue Syndrome put a stop to all that. Another fatal casualty in the last couple of years was William Cookson, the redoubtable editor of *Agenda*, who went under because of lack of financial support, in spite of efforts by many, including Harold Pinter, who valued his work. Why does it have to be like this!

And, maybe finally, there is what has happened to me over the last ten years. After a trip to Bangladesh in 1993, a nasty dose of food-poisoning crippled me on the journey back, and for some days afterwards, I suddenly found myself with severe energy problems. Immune system blighted, I began to go downhill. Suddenly I had to put myself to bed three times a day, on bad days, through sheer exhaustion. I tried to rehabilitate myself in all manner of ways, but to no avail. 1996 was a good year, including presenting a four-part series for BBC Science Unit on Radio 4 on memory, *A Many Faceted Thing*, but that was only a temporary upwards blip. Sorley's death, and other things in my private life were dragging me ever-downwards. The medically inexplicable Chronic Fatigue Syndrome set it.

From 1997 on, I was beset by a series of illnesses, cold, flues, until 1999, when I was ill for almost a year. Many's the afternoon I've lain in bed, quoting desperately to myself, often in tears: "A terrible thing is happening to me" — *pace* Arthur Miller — feeling powerless to do anything to stop it. Depression set in good-style. I remember it taking me four days to put an empty packet of cigarettes in the bin — three days to think about it, and the climax day four, when I managed it. Not funny. You learn to welcome these small successes.

Turn-around began in 2000. I started teaching/lecturing at Queen Margaret University College and Napier University in drama and periodical journalism respectively, which gave me real social contact with good students, a different challenge, and all manner of other stimulations. I developed and accepted, much against my temperament which is, shall we say, naturally 'lively' — a regime of accepting a restricted, disciplined life, governed by regular food and exercise, and gradually clawed my life back. Not much help is possible from medical authorities in such complex situations. In the end, you have to heal yourself. But the problem about 'getting well' after a prolonged spell of debility, is that you are forced to live in the past, catching up, dealing with things you simply can't do when you were ill. Roll on the present.

Flotsam from that period afflicts me to this day, but gradually it diminishes, in quantity as well as force of impact. Things which would have floored me two or three years ago, I can now slough off with a shrug. More times than I can count, I've hit what I thought was rock-bottom, but something deep within will not let me stay there. Commando's daughter. Survivor.

I've had to reinvent myself several times over, and that has involved examining my old passions: Scotland, poetry, literature, theatre — everything. There have been so many times when everything (and I mean everything) has seemed quite pointless. It has not been easy.

One recent bombshell was being awarded an Honorary Doctorate of Letters from the University of Edinburgh, which was strange, disconcerting, terrifying — and incongruous given the odd circumstances of my life. I haven't got used to my new 'elevated' status yet!' But it has given me more confidence, and a renewed sense of commitment and responsibility.

I've served a long, hard apprenticeship, and know a lot. Writing this essay has made me realise that there are several books in me I didn't know I had. And as to the future? Who knows?

Ronald Frame

Born Glasgow, 23rd May 1953

NOVELIST, SHORT-STORY WRITER
AND DRAMATIST

Saltire Book of the Year, The Lantern Bearers, 2000

Ghost City

We were known by the blazers of our schools; grey, navy blue, Prussian blue, marine blue, leaf green, bottle green, purple, lilac, navy and moss green, chocolate-brown and gold, beige. In the suburbs of Glasgow, as of Edinburgh, the vital question was "Which school do you go to?" Always single-sex, quite naturally. The Academy, Kelvinside, Boys' High, Girls' High, Laurel Bank, Westbourne, Park, Hutchie Boys, Hutchie Girls, Belmont House, Craigholme, Drewsteighnton.

The sixties were still the days of precedent of fathers' sons and mothers' daughters, of professionals. Trade already had a foot in the door, and probably paid the fees more promptly than others. But we were brought up with the psychotic Scottish attitude to money: respect for those who make it off their own bat, and a deeper sense that it is a vulgar matter and ought to be beneath regard.

The appearance of our suburb was a schizophrenic mixture of Scottishness and Englishness. Sandstone villas, of red or grey, and a somewhat gaunt style of architecture: sash windows with the lower panes plain glass, and the upper stained, oblong fan lights of enchased or frosted glass, tiled vestibules, the largest houses equipped with an ornately skylit billiard room in the attic.

I have a persistent memory of polished granite curling stones set on front steps, and the names on gates and gateposts, like a litany – 'Brora', 'Loch Fannich', 'Raasay', 'Beinn Dearg', 'Glenquoich', 'Kinlocheil', 'Schiehallion', 'Ardnish. Another type of domestic building was a pure and unadulterated import from England: white walls or pebbledash and small-paned windows, rain barrels, oak front doors, red rosemary roof tiles, and names evocative of their foreignness: 'Walberswick', 'Lyndfield', 'Staplehurst', 'Hurstpierpoint', 'Penwithick'.

We could never be quite sure where we belonged, to ourselves or as northern vassals of a southern imperial power. (After I was born there was a debate as to which I should be called: 'Ranald' or 'Ronald'. The Scottish lobby lost out, and I was given to the mainstream, to what was thought to represent convention even with its Sassenach cast.)

One of the two principal sports in our suburb was tennis — my coach, a cruel look-alike for Simone Signoret in her last days, would wearily remind us as we panted after lost balls about a handful of past (long past) pupils who had played Junior Wimbledon — and the two rival clubs with their lists of rules and their cindertracks and Balmoral bicycles thrown down under the straggly rhododendrons returning to wildness could (more or less) have been in any of the Home Counties.

The other sport was skiing, a more risqué pastime. The organisers put their faith in the blasting cold Grampian air and the hot alcohol-purged punches at the obligatory ceilidh, that those — and the terror of all that unmitigated distance of purple heather — would add up to good clean living of the *White Heather Club* variety.

Roman Catholics were virtually beyond our ken, and a coloured face would have been an event — if we'd ever encountered one. Most of us had parents who went to church — Church of Scotland, of course — and their choice of which one, like school, was carefully made. If, as an adult member, you missed more than two Communion Services in a row, you were drummed out, for life and eternity.

The miniscule Episcopal Church — hassocks, cassocks and choirboys — was straight out of 'Dad's Army' and treated by the rest of us as a bit of a joke. Somehow, the Presbyterians' dreary décor and twenty-minute sermons — very pussy-footing reflections on our modern consuming world — and the bossy, trilling voices in the choir and the frequently fluffed organ anthems were all supposed to bring you closer to God. Jesus Christ, one was constantly reminded, was *only* a carpenter's son. You could never have pictured Him — even wearing a cap — going to the right school, or making it to the Nazareth equivalent of tennis-fours, which caused you to wonder if everything had turned out so gloriously by God's say-so after all.

Some random memories. As a boy, I apparently had a predilection for undoing latch gates, running up pathways and ringing doorbells — and then running off again and away before the door was opened behind me.

Another incident, which still haunts me. I was ten and after school I was running for an orange-and-yellow bus picking up at a stop: the one, just by Wyllie's book and pen shop on Sauchiehall Street. I sprinted out from behind a lorry; a car's brakes screamed, it's tyres burned rubber on the road – and I found myself no more than two inches from its front chrome bumper. It shouldn't have happened – the alertness of the driver's reactions, the instantaneous effectiveness of the shoe on the pedal on the brake pads – but it did, and I owe my life to somebody I know nothing about, appearance or name.

The viciousness of our Latin classes at ten and eleven years old, having the language thrashed into us by a man who had been tortured by the Gestapo in his youth. Nothing, even chemistry, could ever be so bad after that. We even survived two years of Cicero, and our reward was blood and guts in Virgil and Tacitus.

Greek by comparison was tourist stuff: from "The sailors are in the market-place", "The teeth of the lion are large and sharp", to Homer's purplish travelogues and the Swann – Hellenic lectures of Thucydides – or as we called him "Thucky-die-daze". I was better at Latin. Fear and trembling did the trick, having the rudiments – literally enough – impressed upon us by our tormentor as our corrected ink exercises were hurled across the room at us, or a grammar book was slammed down on a thick, unreceptive skull.

But when our form-mistress, Miss Lightbody, returned to us after our regular beating sessions, she was all sweetness and coy smiles to the man. When he'd made his theatrical exit with cloak flying and leather tawse secured beneath his jacket, sensually laid over his thin shoulder, her face immediately fell. As the resounding steel tips of his shoes grew fainter, she gave us her sourest expression and put a curious degree of pity into her voice. "Boys". Her accent was Kelvinside genteel, but not quite so super-genteel as the best front-of-shop one she reserved for parents and the senior heads of department. (Miss Lightbody instructed us in elocution, not southern received pronunciation, but that unique, strangulated version of long, distorted vowels, believed to be the mark of true home-bred gentility.) "– boys, *why* do you have to be making such heavy weather of this?" Sometimes her hands shook, and her breath smelt of the tobacco that stained her index finger, because she had been up in the eyrie of a staff room, terrified to think of the sneering, sarcastic jokes and the flashing strap of leather.

She wanted to cry for us, perhaps, but she couldn't allow herself to. At ten and eleven we were being propelled into the adult world, hurled in at the deep, deep end.   Three years later, still approaching the prime which Miss Jean Brodie on the east coast had luxuriated in, Miss Lightbody died — quite unfairly — of lung cancer.   Such redoubtable women.

Between the ages of nine and thirteen we were theirs, and as Miss Brodie would have claimed we were theirs for life.   They taught us what couldn't be learned again: taking personal pride in self-discipline and hard graft (being able to shut yourself in a room for a couple of hours or however long it might take to tackle a specific piece of work), practising good manners and quiet courtesies as an instinct.   Even the elocution.   Perhaps the price of such tight control was a certain uniformity, and not a little dullness.   But in their spinsterly way they knew the supreme value of self-dependence.

Every Friday morning there was a test over three periods of what we'd learned in the week, and once every month a more searching super-test which lasted all five periods of the morning, until the lunch break.

At the age of nine I could cross the length of Glasgow on a succession of buses, wearing regulation garter-topped stockings and compulsory cap and — if I'd done well enough to earn the honour in the last week's test — with a First Work War medal on a stripped ribbon pinned to my brown blazer.   I must have looked like a chocolate soldier.   At the time, however, I thought nothing of it, and no harm ever came to me; if you have the courage of yourself, the dangers fall away, like the temptations of Vanity Fair.

During the same interlude, between the ages of nine and thirteen, the history we were being taught was European and Scottish: the Armada, the Black Death, and the six King James's, Kings Malcolm I-IV, Alexander I-III, Margaret of Denmark, The Maid of Norway.   We concerned ourselves with English history only obliquely.

Likewise in geography periods we celebrated the existence of all the red countries in the atlas: the *British* Commonwealth, that is to say, and preferably those corners colonised by Scottish adventurers and missionaries.

A quarter of my own school were Jewish — shul-boys, so to speak — and their spiritual home was two and a half thousand miles away.   During the '67 War they spoke with tears in their eyes of going out to fight to the death in the Sinai heat.

Home-readers included *Kidnapped* and an interminable Neil Munro novel about the 1745 rebellion, set among heather hills and gurgling burns.   What persuaded me I wanted to write one day was hidden away in another textbook.   *The World's Classics Scottish Short Stories*, with a green, white and black synthetic 'tartan' paper cover.

The story was by Dorothy K. Haynes, about the busy tedium of one day in the life of a quarryman's wife in a fifties tenement — doing the wash in the wash-house, whitewashing the bed recess, eating a mutton pie with ketchup for lunch, flicking through old magazines, papering the walls of their one cramped livingroom with a pattern of rosebuds over the old one of peacocks and pagodas: a simple, dignified, affecting story about memories and surviving dreams in Mrs McCallum's head, which make life unaccountably shine for her, in the quiet sifting of sunlight through summer dust, and to the floating tones of a belfry bell.

For ten years I went to piano lessons. I don't think I'm a very musical person, and the Theory quite defeated me, but I had a freak aptitude for Debussy and Ravel. It was heady music, and evocative, and faintly decadent: playing it, one should have been able to be *impressionistic*, that is not too accurate, but in fact it was perilous to lose a single second's concentration, so tightly was the business constructed — one hand playing against the other, each at their own tempi. It has to be as meticulously disciplined as jazz.

Two Saturday evenings per term there would be a "hooley", as it was called, at Miss Mac, the piano teacher's house, "Oronsay", in Hyndland, where we went for our lessons. We were divided into two camps, the Picts and the Scots. Only grave illness or a rugby international in Edinburgh, at Murrayfield, was an excuse for non-attendance. The evenings took three forms. First, the table tennis duels, my especial dread, which were performed in front of the mustered howling Picts and Scots with raquets you drew lots for. Each raquet had been sawn into a ludicrous shape — the stave of a question mark, a circle with three smaller circles cut out, a triangle to paddle the air with. Then there were sit-down games evenings. Divided up into groups of four, we rotated round the tartan-carpeted room, from baize card-table to baize card-table, playing more and more aggressive games with ever keener rivalry.

In one mindless exercise you had to pick up plastic straws from a heap with a little curved brass hook and not disturb the pile; in another you had to guide with a steady hand a closed metal hoop along — God help us — a switchback of electrically charged wire.

Finally, there were the infamous stramash evenings. We all perched on children's folding canvas camp-stools, behind music stands at their lowest settings, and played a variety of percussion instruments — gongs, cymbals, drums, tambourines, triangles, and some fiendish dulcimers — while Miss Mac played 'Bluebells of Scotland' and Gilbert and Sullivan and the 'Gay Gordons' on the piano, shrieking out the bar numbers as we reached the point — vaguely — in our accompaniment: "Thirty two!", "Fifty nine!", "Eighty six!" The windows ran with condensation, our armpits ran with perspiration; knees cracked, there were glimpses of lilac school knicker, and even a drooping gusset of the black tights, de rigeur for uniform now as then. Some unfortunates had pimples that had popped or were about to, others blackheads and sheeny grease slides on the wings of their noses; hair hung lankly or was too soft to comb, freckles joined together to map a cheek with its own little Sicily or Madagascar; there were teeth braces, and incipient moustaches in male and female, and both sexes of ankle hanging from the backs of shoes during another epidemic of athlete's foot. There really must be a hell, because at the hooleys in Hyndland we had our first intimation of it.

Sundays in my teens were spent on homework: from 8 am until at least 8 pm, with stoppages to be fed and watered. I was carrying up to ten subjects simultaneously. Even applying myself the round of the clock or longer — sometimes I wasn't finished until midnight, and Saturdays always included an amount of preparatory work — each subject was only cursorily treated: I timed them by the watch on my wrist. Greek, I've been told, has always been indifferently taught in Scotland. Why? Do we not truly believe in it? All those tenses and implied choices, aorist/preterite and the optative to complement subjunctive and future perfect — are they all too wishy-washy and indecisive for a traditionally black-and-white intellect?

But by another reading, we Scots should have been receptive to these subtlest nuances in the distinction between tenses in the Ancient Greeks' language. Who more practised than ourselves at the *might-have-been*, after all? We relive our past, not quite truthfully, in a purple alpenglow of possibility. *Might have, could have, would have* . . .

For all the evidence of a national adventuring spirit, we live also with the consciousness of failure: four, five, six hundred miles from London and the South, on a cold wet edge of Europe.

With the example of precedent, we have a right to suppose the worst, and so we anticipate it: defensiveness becomes what it has to but ought not to, wee censorious mouths and that awful smugness, the inward-turning, the struggle for faith in ourselves, the "wha's like us?" battle-cry which repetition renders as full of thunder as a pea-rattle in a drum.

Glasgow — as Philip Prowse of the Citizen's Theatre has observed — has the feel of a north European sea city: of Hamburg, of Amsterdam, of Gothenburg. On its hills it bears a distinct resemblance to Genoa, or to Turin; the Victorians built their warehouses as Italian palazzi, lived in colonnaded villas, and worshipped in churches of an angular, mythically antique style devised by "Greek" Thomson.

And I've never responded to American taste, East Coast literary or Hollywood cinematic. In my late teens when essential tastes were formed, I went to see sub-titled European films in the Cosmo cinema during its last days. (and where better to watch Visconti for one, than surrounded by so much slightly tatty operatic Art Deco maroon plush?) The books I read were European, black-spined Penguin Classics, or grey-spined Modern Classics I bought from the sliding wallracks in Wyllie's.

I read and read, even travelling home on the 'Blue Train', on that colourful-sounding excursion to the suburbs. Restaurants called 'The Blue Train' exist in Paris and Manhattan, and that's why I can believe that, try as you will, the past is only lying in wait in gleaming new circumstances, ready to haul you all that long, long way back.

Cafes and wine bars in Glasgow, as in Edinburgh, masquerade now under Parisian and Milanese names, and it's said to be a revival. But new money has no memory. There was real style before them, an informed opulence, but it has disappeared: there is a ghost city, and I can remember it – just – from my childhood and early schooldays.

Older people refer to shops and restaurants and hotels that didn't survive the fifties and sixties, pummelled to rubble as successive labour-dominated councils raized despised Victoriana – just as the Victorians in prior turn had done away with medieval Glasgow.

The memories recede yearly beneath copper-tinted money towers, in the wide-eyed stares of seamless plate glass. Simpson Hunter, Rowan's, MacDonald's, Copland & Lyle, Manson's, the North British Hotel, Forsyth's, Jackson's, Pettigrew & Stephen, Daly's, Wyllie Hill's, Wyllie & Lochhead, Sorley's the St Enoch Hotel, Lyons, the Grosvenor, the Berkeley, Ferrari's, One-to-One, the Clyde Model Dockyard. Nostalgia is a vast temptation, and one which the race is prone to. Perhaps it's the citified variant of the Celtic supernatural third eye which is our national legacy: the recognition and articulation of those phases of time running parallel to the meagre living one, currents pulling beneath the surface of the stream.

It was Edinburgh, not Glasgow, which had the tradition of split psyche: Deacon Brodie, Burke and Hare, Jekyll and Hyde, Major Weir, one (respectable) man by day and another (a brigand) by night. Or Robert Louis Stevenson walking at nightfall from the genteel New Town to the Old Town of low dens and dives. A city of Election and Damnation, of long shadows in Close walls, echoing footsteps in the steep, staired vennels between the nine-storey tenement-lands like cliffs.

But today it's Glasgow that has the split psyche. There's the proletariat

Glasgow of cliché, strident and complaining and unforgiving, and there's the ritzy, glitzy, revamped new version, packaged with glib ad-slogans. A surface place – but what if it's appearance *is* it's reality? Does it have an intellectual structure? The much-hyped paintings of the New Glasgow Boys – and Girls – borrow weighty references, they're clad in other artists' names and styles.

Shopping malls are fashion cat-walks, where the emperors parade their new clothes, and the indoors air has a fusty, manufactured taste.

And somewhere else, out of the reckoning, is Another Glasgow, the one in which I and all my sort were brought up.

Edmund White has spoken of the significance of social dislocation in the shaping of American creative mind – a sideways or, more likely, downwards slide on the social scale. I didn't slide but a sense of precariousness seems to me essential to do the thing that I do, which is writing stories and novels. You're holding on to the old beatitudes, be they personal (parents, a remembered history) or more general (a shared milieu – the customs and roles of a certain caste in the community). It's an emotional and social impairment: nothing is ever as good as . . .

So says memory, as it has done in all the ages of history, but it's compounded now by the speed of vertical (up-and-down) social movement.

There's an element of resentment, of course, which has to do with others having showy money: *I* at least, I need to believe, have the gifts of undemonstrative education and infallible courtesy, which *their* money is too sticky-new to buy. And I also have some measure of talent, some small considerations of class, profession, income. Thus – I can persuade myself – I make myself immune, to a degree, from categorisation. Well, maybe . . .

The British middle class define themselves by their appearances but somehow it's more extreme with the Scots: complicated by our self-righteous Calvinism, the difference is more pronounced between who we appear to be and who we really are. Falls from public grace are bloodier, even more vituperative affairs in the north than in the south.

It's a situation made to be written about. Yet the writing involves flouting all the rules which were dinned into you as you grew up: all disposing to the same end, namely, our commonly abiding by the social (sectarian and attitudinal) status quo, not drawing attention to yourself. The writing act each time is one of the grossest treachery, not of individuals – you learn to cover your tracks – but betrayal of your background. A felt-tip pen is a Kalashnaykov.

So much has disappeared. At thirty-seven I'm already a ghost. Writing fiction, they say, is like making maps, like trying to trace your way back to a certain place; in my own case to a city, one far from perfect but quite complete, one that can never be so whole again.

In one of the great Glasgow department stores we would sometimes meet up after school to have afternoon tea — my mother, my sister and I — while mannequins walked between the tables and a small orchestra played.

Women then had a *sound*: silky, sheeny, slithery. The models wafted perfume behind them, scissor-striding. Sometimes they smiled, but sparely. They never spoke, so you didn't know to hear whether or not they were "ordinaire", as people called the condition in our neck of the woods. I wondered how on earth you could hold them, these aloof paragons of elegance, how to stop them from walking away from you.

At seventeen I started to rush-write stories. They appeared in Scottish newspapers. Everyone we knew read them, and I saw them reconsidering me in a new, not very favourable light. I was giving too much of myself away. They might have been reading my diary. I had power for the first time in my life — to demand time, to occupy people's thoughts for however long a short story took to read — but the having of that power frightened me. I stopped; I didn't write another story for the next ten years. When I was ready again, it just boiled up out of me, all my piety and my rage.

I have to warn you — I've been immersed in fiction-writing for the last decade. Even the facts have started to recede. This isn't 'my' story any more than it is several thousand others'. Novelists are notoriously unreliable chroniclers. If I *am* a kind of ghost, then the past is already suspended between what may have been the truth and the fable it's already turning into.

EPILOGUE, October 2004

Ghost City was broadcast first on BBC Radio Scotland, then on Radio 4. It was later made into a television film, broadcast nationally on BBC 2.

The bald facts about my career can be found in reference books. I'm not convinced that much 'happens' to a fiction writer beyond the age of, say, seventeen: which was when I had my first short stories published (in a Scottish daily newspaper). I subsequently read a great deal. I continued to look at the films of the great European directors of that time, who might equally well have been writers — until, for some mysterious reason, I started to lose interest in the moving image.

I was really writing from the time I was in my pram, in the sense that I observed everything that was going in around me – and maybe too much (all my life I've seen into rooms before doors quite closed shut).   I remember what I've seen, and heard, and smelt.   I have a vein of melancholy, I realise now — an instinct for *what was passing*.

Russian literature, I once read a famous poet claim, began with Pushkin and his like, who believed that the old ways were being done away with. Change is entirely natural — but is forgetfulness? *They* became recorders. I feel there was also a way of life here which — to judge from its neglect — might never have been.   I became a recorder too.

For 'thirty-seven years old' in *Ghost City*, please read fifty-one.   Am I too hard in what follows on the Church of Scotland? — I would distinguish between the stuffy institution and those folk who do their good works in its name.

I was dealing with suburbia, but my existence actually began in East Kilbride, one of the post-War new towns.   They were exciting places to be in the early days, with an interesting mix of young hopefuls embarking on adult life.   I remember our very white interior walls and sleek Scandinavian furniture; I remember poring over copies of *Design* as well as *Look and Learn*, and thinking, *yes*, I *shall* be an architect (school of the Brazilian Oscar Niemeyer) when it's time to choose a job.   (Alas, notwithstanding some blood link with (Logarithms) Napier, I proved to be no whiz at maths.)

POSTSCRIPT

Not so long ago I was walking across a road bridge with a burn in spate beneath it.   A rustbucket of a car chanced to go past at the same moment, sputtering exhaust fumes.   The combination of the two — the heavy wateriness in the air, and the reek of petrol and oil — was instantly evocative: I was standing on board one of the redoubtable paddle-steamers which used to ply up and down the Clyde.   I hadn't made that journey for at least thirty-five years.

Writing fiction is of the same order: finding the connections — often quite random — to summon up an experience, to make it believable, and somehow to place it beyond time.

Jamie Reid Baxter

Born Buckie, 16th July 1954

HISTORIAN, POET, PERFORMER

"Preclaro Domino Davido Lyndsay de Monte, Scocie defensori"

> The land ye loed wi hert an harns is hyne.
> Hir gloir is dungen doun til dirt an glaur:
> Her mervells aa bot memoreis oot of mynd,
> Wicht wyne til watter wersch aa went, or waur,
> That ance did fill wi flammand dremes an fyre
> Hir sons' sweit sangs, quha eirar daith wald daur
> Tae live at libertie, nor menseless myre
> Thair saulls in saikless swouns an doutis dire
> Anent thair richt tae breathe, be blythe an ring
> In this loed land that did your spreit inspyre:
> Clene gane is graice an growth an coort an king.
>> Yit Lyoun, ye dwall aye apone the heichts,
>> An your guid werks sall yit set aa tae richts.

Speaking to the Living

Growing up in Banffshire in the 1950s and 60s — mostly on the coast, apart from four years inland, in the foothills of the Cairngorms, until my sixth birthday — I was always aware of something bigger than me, something that was omnipresent and yet very mysterious. Not the sea, strangely enough, though I enjoyed playing on the magnificent beach of golden sand, or scrambling around on the rocks looking for crabs under stones. Nor the hills, though I loved them more than the sea, and still do; singing the opening lines of Ps. 121 in kirk was always a great moment. But the vast presence was not God, either, sending his aid from the hills. It was the past. I really wanted to know what had been there before me. My father, a science teacher at Keith Grammar, and then rector of Macduff High, had an insatiable interest in just about everything, and he it was who encouraged my infant interest in what was basically archaeology for the very, very wee. Bits of porcelain, rusty nails, broken clay pipes dug up in the garden fascinated me. These were fragments of a meaningful whole. As I grew a bit bigger, more impressive manifestations of the past impinged on me: the glorious Baroque pile of William Adams's (never finished) Duff House at Banff, on the other side of the Deveron, and on the Plainstones at Banff, outside the Townhous, a captured Crimean War canon. To the east of Macduff, there was Gamrie with its thousand year old kirk where the skulls of defeated Vikings had been kept for centuries, and an ancient settlement at Cullykhan, above the wonderful cave called Hell's Lum. And at home, we had (heaven knows where from) a beautiful stone axe head. Beaker People, the Bronze Age and the Iron Age actually meant something to me, as a child, on the basis of the heaven, or Eden, that lay about me not only in my infancy but right through my youth.

Most potent of all was the spell cast by 'ancient ruins', which my childish imagination longed to see un-ruined and alive – Inchdrewer, Boyndie, Findlater castles, and the tower house actually called Eden, were all pleasurably accessible by bike in those distant days of very little traffic. And inland, towards the Cairngorms, there were massive Auchindoun and Balvenie, which I visited on an overnight trip with my father when very small, and just over the border into Aberdeenshire, Huntly Castle in all its ruined glory. Slightly further afield were the ruins of Elgin Cathedral, its religious significance entirely escaped me as a kirkgoing presbyterian bairn: I merely regretted the fact it was in ruins. Travelling further west still – for our family holidays (I have two younger brothers) generally took us west, into the Highlands – Castle Urquhart at Loch Ness. Other family holidays took us down the east coast to Fife to visit my grannie in Cowdenbeath. The vast outline of Dunottar on its promontory over the sea haunted me, but the one time I was allowed to go off to explore it, the place was closed and I returned defeated. In Fife, there was Macduff's Castle, and much more memorably, Aberdour Castle, complete with echoes of 'Sir Patrick Spens'; and Inchcolm Abbey, reached by crossing the (worryingly choppy) waters of the Forth from Aberdour in a fairly small open boat. I vividly recall my disappointment that there was no castle in Dunfermline, where the king had sat drinking the blood red wine, but the towering nave of the Abbey impressed me no end. Decades later, in August 1992, I had my heart in my throat as that nave resounded to the processional chant for St Andrew, in a performance of *The*

Passioun o Sanct Andraa, a 'kirk sangspiel' to words I had written in 1986, with music by Dafydd Bullock. Edinburgh Castle was far too big to take in for a primary school bairn from Banffshire, though Mons Meg was memorable. But the model of James IV's 'Great Michael' in the Royal Scottish Museum, now, that was something else. Perhaps my seafaring maternal ancestry made this ship, the largest of its age, bristling with saltires and lions rampant, particularly significant to me as a child. Many, many years later, the 'Great Michael' would sail majestically back into my life on an ocean of sound, as it were, in the music of Robert Carver's 1506 Mass for St Michael's Day, *Dum sacrum mysterium*, for 10 part choir.

It is strange to think that none of these manifestations of the past had very much of a context. We did get mediaeval Scottish history at primary school – tofts and spiders and kings and heroic Scots hidden in hay carts – which meant that Kildrummy Castle had some specific associations for me. But it was childish stuff, and my own conscious interests, even by primary seven, were elsewhere: Ancient Mesopotamia, Egypt and Meso-America, and – of all things – nineteenth century Central Europe. I liked the idea of the ramshackle Austro-Hungarian Empire, with its multiple nationalities and cultures; I had been introduced to it by Strauss's 'Radetzky March', which I simply loved. As I did the idea of a double-headed eagle. Little did I think, at the age of eleven in the schoolhouse of Macduff, as I avidly read (with how much understanding, I cannot now say) about the Fall of the House of Habsburg, that twenty years later I would be sitting in a canteen having Otto von Habsburg, MEP, pointed out to me in the coffee queue. But the Habsburgs had long ceased to interest me. From age eighteen, Scotland had intervened. And though I would study modern languages, found the international Havergal Brian Society for the promotion of the work of that ʿ(then virtually unknown) English composer, become a lifelong member of the Orthodox Church, live in Spain, Germany and Colombia, write a PhD about a Cuban Marxist novelist and musicologist, and end up spending the last eighteen years and more being based in Luxembourg, working as a translator and participating in Luxembourg City's remarkably international and polyglot society, yet Scotland has never ceased to be – under God, as folk used to say – the central focus. Scotland's past: where Scotland comes from.

My eighteenth year, 1972, was decisive. First, there was the last summer before going up to Aberdeen. A magical summer of high hills at Kylesku, Torridon and Glencoe, ending with weeks working as a grousebeater at Tomintoul, surrounded by the mountains. And there I read not only *War and*

Peace for the second time, and *Le Rouge et le Noir* for the first, but also, and with far more longterm effect, Nigel Tranter's *Robert the Bruce Trilogy*. The reader can smile indulgently or contemptuously *ad lib*, but Tranter's work had an enormous and entirely positive revelatory impact on me and several of my companions from other parts of Scotland. The SNP was in the news, and we were newly eighteen and surrounded by the glory of the Cairngorms. Tranter's gripping Trilogy was a heady experience. It made me aware, for the first time, of how unbelievably little I knew about my own country. It was a great moment, nearly thirty years later, in 2001, when I found myself in the pulpit-canopy over the king's tomb in Dunfermline Abbey , declaiming John Barbour's *Brus* amid mediaeval Scottish and French vocal music as part of a Cappella Nova concert celebrating Bruce.

The second decisive encounter in 1972-73 was with the thinking of the composer Ronald Stevenson – whose name I already knew as that of an authority on Havergal Brian. I had read several articles by Stevenson in *The Listener*, which Banff Academy took. Listening to Stevenson on the radio speaking about why there was no Scottish music made me sit bolt upright. Since about the age of 10, I suppose it was, I had been besotted with orchestral and choral music, and Smetana's *Vltava* had been one of my first favourites; my father had introduced me to it, and taken me through the programme. I had latterly become passionate about the 'nationalist' music of Sibelius, Dvořák, Nielsen, Bartók, Mussorgsky – and Vaughan Williams, whose centenary year was that of that unforgettable summer before going up to Aberdeen.

The exact date of this broadcast is unknown to me. But in the late summer of 1973, on Radio 4 Scotland, I heard parts of a big 'Music of Scotland' series, which further underlined the point that I had been living in utter ignorance of the fact my own country had 'classical' music of its own. There is no small irony in the fact that from April to June 1973, there had been seven programmes devoted to Early Scottish Music, the field to which I would devote myself from 1982 onwards. I had not heard a single one of those broadcasts. After all, I listened to Radio Three, since, in all my adolescent arrogance, I knew there was there was no 'culture' to be had on Radio 4 Scotland. But now I became a devoted follower of 'The Musician in Scotland', those 30 minutes a week on Sunday evening, which is all Radio 4 Scotland devoted to classical music. There were, of course, virtually no gramophone recordings of any Scottish music at all, nor was it exactly easy to find out anything about the subject. And perplexed though I was by this bizarre situation, I did not know to how rectify even my own ignorance. After all, I was busy studying French, German and Spanish and elementary Gaelic (not that I ever really mastered it; but as to so many Scots, Gaelic matters to me, and my deep friendship with Meg Bateman since 1983 means Gaelic poetry has a vital personal place in my life); immersing myself in Thomas Mann; setting up the international Havergal Brian Society with the encouragement of Tom Hubbard (future co-founder of the Scottish Poetry Library), a lifelong friend made my first days at Aberdeen. Och, I was awfy busy with being a confused young man with far too many diverse and unfocussed concerns.

Things became slightly less unfocused after a visit to the USSR in July 1973, which caused me to lose my faith (aesthetical and immature) in Nietzschean atheism. This had replaced my childish, dutiful and utterly un-numinous attendance at kirk and Sunday school. With hindsight I can see that there was always a thirst for some spiritual truth, for a greater vision, behind my impatience with the kirk. There was my dabbling, while still at Banff Academy, in the Prophetic Books of William Blake, and my wonderment at the intensely religious closing scene of Goethe's *Faust II*, as set to music by Gustav Mahler — indeed, a schoolfriend and I read the whole of Faust in an attempt to understand what Goethe meant by 'das Ewig-Weibliche'. We had never heard of 'secondary literature', so we simply tackled the primary text, with great delight, even though in 1971 we never did find out what the word meant. That same year I encountered the Book of Revelation in Vaughan Williams' oratorio *Sancta Civitas*, and was immediately gripped by the Biblical text, going as far as to borrow a commentary from the minister. Things dinna come muckle mair visionary nor the Apocalypse of St John the Divine; and just after this, I encountered Franz Schmidt's oratorio of 1937, *Das Buch mit sieben Siegeln*, which sets a great deal more of the text than the Vaughan Williams does, and contains music at least as powerful and evocative of realities behind reality. And then, there was my unconditional love of the music of the Catholic mystics Anton Bruckner and Olivier Messiaen, which also spoke (almost exclusively) about the reality of the Beyond, the *au delà*. Messiaen's *Quartet for the End of Time*, particularly, was another direct encouragement to study the Apolcalypse. — purely as a work of literature, of course. I didn't believe in God!

By the end of July 1973, I did. The two week visit to the USSR had itself come about through music too. It was a schools essay competition prize, which I had won, for a wonder, with an essay on Shostakovitch and Prokofiev and the advantages, for the average listener, of a doctrine like Socialist Realism which meant that composers were not allowed to write uncommunicatively abstruse, 'alienated' music for tiny coteries of the initiated. Well, I was young and very naive. The Soviet authorities, who paid for the trip, I imagine, must have liked my defence of the indefensible. I have never ceased to think that art ought to communicate, if it is to have any validity or 'use' (*pace* Oscar Wilde!), but the idea that a government or anyone else has the right to tell artists what they should be creating was one that I dropped as direct result of my visit to the Soviet Union. For that trip, whatever the Soviet authorities saw its purpose as being, resulted in my conversion to Christianity – on my first morning in Moscow, a Saturday, when I walked into a funeral service at the Novodevichii Convent; not in the cathedral, of course, which was a museum at that time, but in the 'working church' in the former refectory of the monastery. From one second to the next, the atheism had evaporated in the face of the palpable reality of the Holy Spirit speaking to the living, something I had never encountered before. Here was living Christianity in a form that I instinctively recognised. As for so many other converts to Orthodoxy, it felt exactly like 'coming home'.

For the rest of my fortnight, I could not keep out of churches, and the church would not stay out of my head after I came back, either. 'Try the spirits, whether they be of God': there was a lot of reading to be done about comparative religion, and then the history of the Christian church, with the conclusion that the 'original' church is the Orthodox Church. Westerners are very unclear about this term, but all Orthodox Churches confess one faith. The adjective Greek, Russian or whatever merely reflects the use of the vernacular in Orthodox worship. I wanted to be Orthodox, not to become a pseudo-Russian. God's grace provided the means for this: less than a year after my experience in the Novodechii Convent, I was baptised in London, in an English-speaking parish within the Russian archdiocese. I still belong to that 'parish community', as well as to the Edinburgh parish of St Andrew of Scotland, Greece and Russia – which did not really exist at all in 1973, hence my being directed to London. Being Orthodox has profoundly affected the way I experience all sorts of things, starting with Western Christianity and everything that has arisen out of it, i.e. Western 'civilisation'. The differences are very deep. Orthodoxy does not teach 'Original Sin', the dreadful Augustinian doctrine which has had such incalculable consequences for the Western mind. But at the same time, my Orthodoxy also provides me with a real sense of identity with the old 'Orthodox West' before 1054, when the growing apart of East and West became formalised. So there is a living link with Saint Columba, Saint Ninian, and all the many other early saints of Scotland and the British Islands. And there was much indeed in pre-Reformation Roman worship and practice that I can also relate to, as I discovered when, from 1982 onward, I began actively to promote Scottish Early Music.

Back in the 1970s, however, I found myself regularly combining trips to London for the Great Feasts and some parish life with modern English music, in the shape of meetings of the committee of the Havergal Brian Society. Eventually, with the centenary of that composer's birth in 1976, some friends and I set up the sonorously named Aberdeen University Havergal Brian and British Music Society (hereinafter HBS), which went on until 1981. Thanks to the enterprise and commitment of those, particularly real practising musicians, whom I managed to infect with my enthusiasm, we presented many public concerts of seldom heard, neglected, or even brand new music. Sometimes we had visiting guest professionals, sometimes we used local professionals, but mostly we drew on the real pool of talent available amongst the student body. Like everything I have ever 'catalysed', if that is the word, it was an entirely collaborative effort. I take no credit whatever for it: had other people, so many other people, not been willing to make my ideas into tangible realities, none of it would have happened. I personally believe that this is always the case: none of us, as individuals, can achieve anything. All is collaboration: we are all dependent on each other, and nobody should ever be taken for granted. All of those other people whose friendship, collaboration and sheer kindess have blessed my life deserve to be mentioned by name here, from active 'fellowfechtars in the guid caus', to my teachers and tutors – everyone, including cheerful porters and security men who provided keys for rehearsal rooms or found missing 'feeties' for pianos.

It was after my first, pre-Orthodox trip to London, to attend BBC rehearsals and recordings of three Havergal Brian symphonies, that I wrote my first letter to Ronald Stevenson, encouraged by a fellow-Scot, the musicologist Malcolm Macdonald. It elicited a beautifully calligraphed reply, which spoke of my beloved Havergal Brian and William Blake as 'blood brothers'. The foundations were thus laid of a friendship that has been perhaps the greatest single (secular) influence on my life. Stevenson did not only open up for me a hitherto unsuspected Scotland. He also made it impossible for me to see it except in terms of his own universalist nationalism, his pacifism, his clear-eyed view of the tragedy of man's inhumanity to man, and the need to speak out against it at all times. I fear that as with everything I have tried to do in my life, so with the richness of what the Stevensons (for Ronald is unthinkable without his wife Marjory) have set before me in terms of humanity: I have been but a poor pupil, but that is no reflection on the greatness of the spirit of the teaching on offer.

In academic terms, however, I was a good pupil. I loved studying, and particularly liked exams; the challenge of having to distill a lot of information onto paper, coherently, in a given space of time was something I found satisfying. I did not strain myself; French and German were fine, but I abandoned my original intention to study Russian, in which I had only an O Grade, as soon as I discovered how challenging the course was. I changed over to Spanish as my subsidiary third subject and unwittingly determined a great part of my future. We were almost immediately introduced to contemporary Latin American fiction, and I liked this new world so much I carried on with Spanish in second year as well, greatly encouraged by having met a family from Algeciras in Macduff (jings!) on my return from the USSR. They were to become 'my Spanish family': a year later, immediately after my Orthodox baptism, I went to spend three months with them, as I would continue to do for years to come (thus providing one at least of the boys with a distinct Scottish accent and turn of phrase to his English, as well as an undying enthusiasm for Tolkien and Havergal Brian). French I had decided to drop after two years, because I was still quite uninterested in the Middle Ages, and my Orthodoxy was so out of sympathy with the spirit of Descartes and the whole subsequent French Enlightenment. Further study of German, most unexpectedly, lost all its interest after a year at university in Kiel which showed me that modern Germany was, even then, profoundly Americanised and not at all the *Kulturnation* I had fondly imagined. Hitler's ghastly legacy includes having left modern Germans seriously and increasingly alienated from their own cultural heritage and even their own language.

But Spanish was not, in any sense, what I did my degree in *faute de mieux*: it was a real love affair with a hitherto entirely unknown universe. What made me continue with a PhD course at Aberdeen, however, was not just a wish to become a Hispanist in a university somewhere, but a more immediate wish to continue working with the HBS on promoting Scottish culture, in the shape of music by an Aberdeenshire composer I had discovered: Ronald Center (1913-73), thanks to being put in touch with his widow by the Invernessshire composer Willliam Wordsworth. Here, at last, was somebody writing 'modern' Scottish music before Ronald Stevenson. Before we began work on Center, though, we organised a visit by Stevenson, who gave not one but two recitals in two days. The first included some Francis George Scott premieres, and the second was Stevenson's own 80 minute long *Passacaglia on DSCH* . Both recitals were greeted, predictably, with rapturous enthusiasm. This was mind-opening creative art. But the discovery of Center, a real local composer, was important too: I was almost the only 'local' boy involved in the Society, but Aberdeen University in those days, when it was small enough still to create a sense of intimacy and shared identity, inspired a lot of students to be 'north east' by association. I was far from alone in my enthusiasm for Center, and the HBS performed a lot of his music in 1977 and 1978. Absolutely no Scottish music of any kind, was taught or even mentioned in the Music Department; and indeed, on expressing an interest in writing a thesis about Center, the student who conducted the world premiere of Center's moving *Lacrimae* for Strings, and his even more affecting pacifist cantata *Dona nobis pacem* in King's Chapel in March 1978, was firmly dissuaded from such parochialism, and told to write about 18th century Austrian parish church music instead. Plus ça change . . . Nonetheless, in 1985, the HBS's edition of Center's *Dona nobis* was on the first ever commercial recording of Ronald Center, with Stevenson as solo pianist, made in Aberdeen's Cowdray Hall. At the launch, I gave a lecture highlighting Center's awareness, in quiet rural Huntly, of the fragility of human existence in the post-Hiroshima age.

In 1977-78, there was so much going on musically in my life, that very little work got done on my PhD. A lot of reading of Latin American novels, certainly, since I had opted for an area that looked as if it would be growing in importance, and hence more likely to get me a university post in the future. Apart from organising concerts with the HBS, I did a lot of listening to music, as I had been doing assiduously since age 12 or so. Radio Three (as it was then, not what it is now) was an amazing resource to have available in my life, and was another of the major influences in my development. It provided a very specific turning point with a broadcast of a reconstruction of High Mass for St Michael the Archangel on Michaelmas Day, 29 September 1978. It was part of a series of 'liturgical reconstructions' of mediaeval church services. Liturgy already fascinated me, for Orthodoxy is a very liturgy-based faith; all the services are chanted and sung, speech being used only for the sermon and certain prayers. The first of the BBC broadcasts had left me stunned by a richness, comparable in my experience, only to Orthodox worship. And at the end of the programme, the announcer had specifically stated that the next programme in the series would be on Michaelmas, featuring the 10 part mass *Dum sacrum mysterium* by 'Robert Carver, canon of the Augustinian Abbey of Scone in Scotland'. I made sure I would be able to tape the broadcast.

The BBC introduction explained that *Dum sacrum mysterium* was directly linked with Revelations and the Last Trumpet, and that the ten voices of the polyphony represented the Nine Orders of Angels joined by the voice of mankind. After the long opening stretch of plainsong (processional hymns, triple introit, ninefold Kyrie) the first few bars of Carver's setting of the "Gloria" were indeed a Johannine revelation. Here were the shimmering colours described in the Apocalypse, here were the voices of angels, 'many thousand times thousand', here was the 'voice of many waters, and as the voice of a great thunder', here was the Angel standing in the sun crying 'There shall be time no longer'. I had never, for all my wide ranging exploration of 19th and 20th century music, heard anything remotely like this lambent ten part polyphony. And it was Scottish. James IV's 'Great Michael' suddenly had a context, and the ruins of Elgin Cathedral had suddenly reassembled themselves to stand shining, complete, perfect, and self-explanatory. 'Behold, a door was opened in heaven', indeed.

Only two weeks before this revelation of the unknown Scotland, I had hitch hiked (my favourite form of travel for many years) down to West Linton overnight from my last season grouse beating at Strathavon Lodge to go with Ronald Stevenson to Hugh MacDiarmid's funeral in Langholm. It was Stevenson, a close friend of the poet's from the 1950s onwards, who had made MacDiarmid such a living force in my life; the actual visit to Brownsbank was just an added bonus. The funeral and the wake were unforgettable, with the Communist Party there in force, and the Labour Party resoundingly absent as one would only expect, though not the well-represented SNP which MacDiarmid had mercilessly pilloried so often in his writing. Norman MacCaig delivered an extempore oration over the open grave that made an indelible impact but was unfortunately not recorded. I was so moved that I stayed behind after the other mourners had moved off, and was thus perhaps the only witness to Valda Grieve's going up, looking down at the coffin, and saying 'Well, goodbye Chris. I've brought you some flowers. They aren't roses, but at least they are white" as she threw them in. As the leader writer in the Scotsman had written, 'Scotland seems a colder and a quieter place since C M Grieve died in the early hours of this morning', going on to say that while his work would stand forever, the country needed his irritating, critical presence. McCaig, in his oration, spoke of MacDiarmid 'coming into my mind like a torch bearer, no, a whole army of torchbearers, lighting up all sorts of things, including many things I did not want to know were there.' Nobody seems ever to have made anything of the fact that the poet, surely quite deliberately, kept himself alive in hospital to die on 9th September, the anniversary of Flodden. Robert Carver, whose music's splendour embodies all the boundless self confidence of James IV's Scotland, entered my life at an apposite moment.

However, I was going to Latin America in January 1979 for a year on a scholarship. Just before I left, the HBS presented the world premiere of Center's Piano Sonata as part of an extraordinary recital (Schumann, Beethoven, Havergal Brian, Busoni, Isidore Philippe, Maurice Emmanuel, Satie and John Foulds) given by Ronald Stevenson on 20 January 1979. At the reception afterwards, in his home, Ronald's friend Charlie King presented me with a viaticum, as he said, for my foreign travels: his own *Twelve Modern Scottish Poets*, which is still a superb anthology today, and a locally produced paperback, *The North East Muse*. Two days later I had left Scotland for Colombia and a year at university in Bogotá on a Rotary International Fellowship. At twenty-four, life seemed full and exciting, not least because I fully thought I would be returning to a country with an autonomous Assembly and a new political, and hence, I naively believed, cultural future. I went to Colombia to do fieldwork for my PhD, which at that point was focussed on two Caribbean Marxist novelists: The Colombian Gabriel García Márquez is pretty well known in the English speaking world, the Cuban Alejo Carpentier, very much less so. My deeply anti-Communist Orthodoxy did not in the least blind me to the towering greatness of their humanism. Indeed, my intention was to show that they both used that traditionally bourgeois (and even escapist) form, the novel, in a consciously Brechtian manner, confronting readers with situations which the novel does not resolve within itself, thus — with any luck — forcing readers themselves to find a solution in the real world.

The experience of living in a Latin American country, in what was probably the best year of my entire life, catalysed a deep but at first unnoticed shift to the left in my thinking: never had I encountered the existence of poverty and utter destitution, cheek by jowl with inconceivable wealth. I was far too busy being busy to see the way that this screaming injustice affected me — going to classes, and keeping Orthodox Lent and going to Panama for Holy Week, inter alia. But also singing in a choir, sitting on the board of the Orquesta Sinfónica Juvenil de Colombia, going around with my unforgettable Colombian friends, including a very informative anthrolopologist, reading a great deal, writing hopelessly amateurish music, and, inspired by my two Scottish poetry anthologies, learning how to write in Scots by plaguing my parents with weekly letters in that language. It was a strange year: on the one hand, it made me feel far more consciously Scottish, and European, than I had ever felt, and I expended a great deal of energy on promoting Scotland (which was part of my Rotary Club remit, in any case), and on the other, I felt more and more Colombian as the year went on and I adjusted to a place and society utterly unlike anything I had ever known. In Bogotá and elsewhere, in those days before the drugs and the cocaine cartels, I never felt remotely threatened or even uneasy. So much did I like it, that I very nearly stayed on into 1980, after the big 10-concert "Festival Escocés" I organised in November with the National Youth Orchestra, two choirs I was linked with, and lots of young soloists I knew personally. It also featured some 12 short films about Scotland, and a poetry reading by myself with extemporised translations.

Such a Festival — all the music was by Ronald Center — would have been utterly unthinkable in Scotland, then as now. But in Bogotá in 1979, anything seemed possible if the determination were there. The Colombians said 'This is good music: let's do it'. And they came to listen to it, too. Scotland was less than attractive, that December, seen from sunlit Bogotá, or indeed Cartagena de Indias on the Caribbean. After all, the referendum catastrophe and the election of Thatcher made the incredible vibrancy and youthfulness of Colombian culture particularly attractive. Had I accepted a friend's invitation to go cattle ranching (partly by helicopter, imagine) in the eastern plains in January 1980, I might never have come back to Scotland. None of us knew then what unspeakable tragedy would engulf Colombia only a few years later, a horror that has not abated one whit today, whatever the pro-USA media may report.

Coming back to the dismal cold of Thatcher's first winter, it took a very long time, perhaps years, to readjust to Scotland. One of the things that drew me home was my desire to try to do something about the music of Robert Carver, but first I had to convince people in Aberdeen that it was worth it. And there was other music to be performed and explored. Many of the stalwarts of the HBS were coming up for graduation and departure, but 1980 saw some great concerts, inluding a recital by Richard Deering of mostly Scottish music, with seven of the eight composers represented in the audience, in a celebration of the new Society of Scottish Composers (in whose founding I was, somewhat improbably, involved, as I would be – equally improbably – with that of the Scottish Poetry Library). This was when I came to know Thomas Wilson, regularly staying at his house. My long conversations about music and religion with that quiet man were a true privilege, as were his discussions of his own scores with me. Like all Scottish composers except James MacMillan, Wilson has not had a fraction of the recognition he deserves. Though CDs have made available a wealth of Scottish music I could only have dreamed of in 1980, let alone in Macduff in 1973, a shockingly small amount of it makes its way into live performances or regular broadcasts, and hence, into the awareness of the Scottish public. As Ronald Stevenson once said on the radio in answer to a question about his advocacy of neglected composers, 'It's not a question of neglected composers. It's the public that's being neglected, when it's deprived of such wonderful music'.

A new activity, on my return to Scotland, was drama, with which I had never had any contact except as set texts. Aberdeen University Theatre (AUT) was a very lively body, and at the Edinburgh Fringe 1980, I performed a chunk of the opening of MacDiarmid's *Drunk Man*. I purchased the two volume *Collected Poems* for the purpose, and thus entered an Aladdin's Cave of Gold whose treasures have never ceased to amaze me. Also in 1980, I made a breakthrough with Carver. My HBSoc friend James Ross, who had become a passionate enthusiast for Early Music, was dismissive of my claims about Carver, voicing the all too familiar sentiments: "if I have never heard of him, he canna be ony guid, and that'll be because he's Scottish". Once I finally forced James to sit and listen listen to my recording of that BBC broadcast of the 10 Part Mass, he changed his mind completely. Carver would turn our friendship into a collaboration of kindred spirits that continues to be the richest of my collaboration-rich life. In November 1980 James put on a concert of Scottish Early Music in King's Chapel, including the 'Gloria' of Carver's four part *Missa L'Homme armé*. That year, however, I was thoroughly focussed on drama. I persuaded AUT to let me direct something rather unusual for Aberdeen: *The Magus*, a verse translation of Calderon's 1664 Faust play, *El mágico prodigioso*, in St Machar's Cathedral. It had a remarkably stellar cast, in terms of the later commercial success some of the actors have met with. Still resolutely anti-Communist, I shifted the play's depiction of the persecution and martyrdom of Christians from Antioch under the Romans to an unidentified modern Baltic seaport, complete with Russian soldiers, and lots of Orthodox church music. We took *The Magus* to the Fringe that summer. Just as I had made lifelong friends through my musical involvements, so too through this amateur involvement with drama, above all the poet Ken Cockburn, and the writer and artist John MacWilliam. My life has been blessed with many friendships, but each friend is unique, and John's untimely death in April 1999 has left me, cruelly conscious of the force of the last lines of Miguel Hernández's lament for his friend Ramón Sijé: 'tenemos que hablar de muchas cosas / compañero del alma, compañero'.

Drama and music were all very well, but in 1981 my PhD grant was coming to an end, and I still had a thesis to write. After radically rethinking its shape and scope, I discovered my investigation of the musical symbolism and content of Carpentier's novel of the Cuban Revolution, *La consagración de la primavera*, required a research trip to Havana in July to consult otherwise inaccessible early journalism by Carpentier. And the Fringe production of *The Magus* it was the day of reckoning, as my father made very plain. All of Carpentier's work and life is pervaded by music; he was a self-proclaimed *musicien manqué*. He wrote a superlative history of Cuban music, a huge amount of very fine musical criticism, and a great deal of other journalism too; and in that of the 1920s and 30s, I everywhere found startling parallels with the prose polemics of Hugh MacDiarmid: here was the same struggle to create a sense of respect for autochthonous, home grown culture in two small countries labouring a massive deadweight of colonial values. My thesis quoted MacDiarmid with some frequency, including on the title page: 'Unconscious goal o' history, dimly seen . . .' As a young man, in Havana and Paris, Carpentier had organised or brought about many concerts of native Cuban music, and written texts for composers who were his friends, an activity he placed firmly under a Blakean quotation from Miguel de Unamuno: 'It is within, and not outside, that we must seek for Man: the universal in the very heart of what is local and lies around us, and the eternal in this moment of passing time'. Exactly the understanding of Scotland that Ronald Stevenson had instilled in me. The visit to Cuba contextualised my Colombian experiences of 1979: in Havana there were no beggars, no street children, no sign of rickets or other disease, books were cheap, chemist's shops were open 24 hours and medicine was free. I was extremely impressed, despite all the anti-Communist prejudice with which I had arrived. The actual writing of the thesis crystallised the shift in my political perspective, and I found myself struggling to reconcile Orthodoxy and my desire for cataclysmic social change: the Thatcher regime was in full swing, and unemployment was soaring. On top of this, for the first time in my life, I was also in love. Like all of my infatuations, it came to nothing, but it did make the last six months of 1981 and the whole of 1982 incredibly intense: a PhD to write (and it was done, in all essentials, in three weeks in early spring 1982), entirely unfamiliar hurricanes of emotion to cope with, and . . . a live performance of a Robert Carver Mass to promote, at last.

In late 1981, James Ross wrote to me asking me to reconstruct a liturgical framework for a complete Carver Mass, which he intended to perform in Aberdeen at Easter 1982. He wanted me to chant the epistle and gospel readings, too. This was all quite uncharted territory for me, but Aberdeen University Library had the wherewithal, in the 'stacks' of less consulted material. I loved the research, since it let to audible results: from 1982 until 1989, Eastertide saw Old Aberdeen's mediaeval precincts filled with the celestial sound of Carver's music, framed in pre-Reformation plainsong. This was when I realised that music, far more than literature, has the power to transcend the centuries. There are no apparent barriers, whereas even educated people nowadays claim to find Chaucer, say, incomprehensible. Music's immediacy as living sound seems to bring even the distant past shiningly alive in our own time, even when we make all necessary allowances for the fact that we cannot possibly be perceiving Early Music the way previous ages did. But those performing it can try to achieve a small measure of 'authenticity', and our 'liturgical reconstructions' restored something of the original impact (and spiritual context) of the glowing, variegated colours of polyphonic music. Thrown into high relief by the surrounding plainchant, prayers and Scripture readings, it blazes out like a stained glass window, flooded with light, in a great edifice of stone.

The impact that first Carver concert had on its hearers (and even its perfomers) was palpable, that sunny evening of Low Saturday (i.e. first after Easter), 17 April 1982. It was, though we did not realise it, the beginning of the "Carver Crusade", an ongoing tradition of actually singing this music which has ensured that Carver's name now appears in the index to many a book about Scotland and Scottish history. We were lucky that we started singing Carver in the 1980s; it would scarcely be possible to publicise such events in the resolutely anti-intellectual and populist Scottish 'national' media of today, but our efforts in Old Aberdeen regularly got Carver's name into 'Good Morning Scotland', as well as Grampian TV and the then Press and Journal, (a real newspaper, unrecognisably different from what it is today.) In that same year, 1982, the interest in performing Carver spread down the coast to St Andrews, where the 'Renaissance Group' would consistently perform (and record) Carver, taking his music, in fullscale musical re-enactments of early 16th century Chapel Royal services, to the official Edinburgh Festival between 1987 and 1991, where the audiences started in the four hundreds, rising to over nine hundred by 1990. That was possible only because Frank Dunlop, the Festival Director, had decided to involve the Saltire Society in the official Festival, thus guaranteeing an unprecedented amount of Scottish content for the only time ever in the Festival's history.

Thinking back today on all the emotional and intellectual intensity of 1982, it is clear that only the Carver mass in St Machar's Cathedral led anywhere. Nothing grew from the furious passion of being in love. Nor from the furious work on the PhD: though it eventually contributed hitherto unknown material to Malcolm MacDonald's recent book on Edgar Varèse, it did not get me a job. The Carver concert committed me to a course to which

I have held ever since: the promotion of earlier Scottish culture, looking 'within and not outside' for the universal, in artefacts produced when Scotland was an independent, European kingdom that did not need endlessly to explain and apologise for its right to be part of humankind. The old lies about the cultural poverty of mediaeval and Renaissance Scotland really are lies. And so much of this European-Scottish culture is still there to be experienced, despite all the colossal vandalism of the English invasions of the 1540s, the "reforming" mobs of 1560, the Covenanters of 1638, and Cromwell and his troops. Until I did the research to prepare for that concert in 1982, I had no idea of the richness of earlier Scottish culture; I had studied no Scottish literature, ancient or modern, during my secondary education, and then I had studied foreign languages. Carver changed all that. The very next year, after the Carver concert on Low Saturday, St Machar's Cathedral was the setting for my staging of George Buchanan's *Jephthes sive Votum*, originally written in Latin c.1540; the verse translation used was one I cobbled together myself, as the actors baulked at using the splendid Scots version by Robert Garioch. The play itself is a masterpiece, which deeply affected the audiences, but for all its merits, and its sheer importance in the development of Renaissance drama, there has been no performance of it since. In 1983, too, I bought my first Scottish Text Society volume in a second hand shop, the *Poems* of Alexander Scott, court makar to Mary of Guise and Mary Queen of Scots. Jewelled, cuttingly ironic lyrics – with music extant for some of them. This led on to the discovery of the poetry of Alexander Montgomerie, the dazzling "maister poet" of the court of the young James VI, for whose lyrics many musical settings are still extant. Kenneth Elliott had edited a whole large volume of *Music of Scotland 1500-1700* as long ago as 1957, and we devoured its contents.

And far more importantly, we performed them: James Ross put on a whole concert of early Scottish secular music in St Machar's in June 1984, combining, as we did for the Carver concerts, Aberdeen-based musicians with James's own resources in the Inverness area. People really liked this music. Friends married in 1986 had Andro Blackhall's 1573 setting of Ps.128 sung at their wedding, as well as walking out of the chapel to the sound of 'Lyk as the dum solsequium', the catchiest of all the Montgomerie songs. Our sense that Renaissance Scotland was a cause really worth fighting for was heightened by seeing Tom Fleming's Edinburgh Festival production of *Ane Satyre of the Thrie Estaitis* in August 1984; the glory of the production contrasted sharply with the feeble and inauthentic musical accompaniment. The real music of the period existed!

We did not limit ourselves to Old Aberdeen. In 1985 – a year which also saw the professional ensemble Cappella Nova, founded in 1982, really get into gear with their own crusade for Carver – our Aberdeen group went to Inverness and to the ancient Norman kirk of St Athernase in Leuchars, with Carver's five part mass *Fera pessima*, framed in the plainsong liturgy for St Andrew of Scotland. In 1986 we gave the first modern performance of the six part mass on the Feast of Pentecost, in King's College Chapel. And, the PhD long since submitted and awarded, I was reading Scottish literature of all kinds, and even lecturing on it to student poetry circles in St Andrews, where I had developed yet another circle of fellow enthusiasts and friends. After all, I was unemployed most of the time, with the odd commercial translation bringing in some supplementary income. Not one job application secured even a request for references, let alone an interview. There was a brief flash of hope in summer 1985, when I obtained a short term contract with British Airways Helicopters at Dyce, to act as an interpreter for a mission to Colombia. It was genuinely moving to be back there, and see my old friends, but BA's requirements in terms of safety guarantees were too high for Occidental Oil (Piper Alpha was but a few years in the future): and the prospect of some years back in Colombia evaporated as suddenly as it had arisen. These were difficult years, psychologically. Unemployment is a dreadful scourge; what is amazing is how understanding people were about it, how unrejectingly they behaved towards me. Human society is a priceless thing, *pace* Thatcher's monstrous proclamation that 'There's no such thing as society; there is only the individual and the family'.

Until summer 1986, many of my musical collaborators and other friends were still students in Aberdeen (and St Andrews, the source of many of my happiest memories), and their comradeship provided a kind of false security. My real situation of longterm unemployment needed to be faced, and I took a conscious decision to force myself to face it. I moved to Alyth in Perthshire, at the kind invitation of an old, old friend from my very first day at Aberdeen University. In Alyth I wrote an opera libretto in Scots at the request of the poet Peter Davidson, a spang new friend. *The Passioun o Sanct Andraa*, set in Kinloss Abbey on 30 November 1559, includes all the plainsong 'propers' for the Feast of St Andrew, and Carver's brief, beautiful mass setting *Pater Creator Omnium*. And I had not one but two job interviews, at last. One was a minimally paid job creation scheme activity with a body within Edinburgh University called 'Scotland's Cultural Heritage'; the other was for a tenured job as an institutional translator, based in Luxembourg. During my brief months with the former, helping prepare their Tercentenary Exhibition about

Lord Provost George Drummond, on behalf of the Royal Bank of Scotland, I managed to organise a commercial recording celebrating the rich musical life of the capital in the 18th century; *Music of Classical Edinburgh* was possible, as always, only thanks to collaboration, in this case with the (too little) acknowledged expert in the field, the composer David Johnson.

And then it was off to mainland Europe in January 1987, to Luxembourg, where I have been based ever since. In June that year, my emotional frame of reference, the way of understanding and misunderstanding myself and the world that I had grown up with, was shattered by the unexpected death of my father, before he had even retired. We had had an unequal parent-child relationship for far too long, but my finally having obtained gainful employment had changed many things, liberating my father from his longstanding concern about my future. This meant that he had reliquished his longstanding contempt for my efforts at writing poetry, and also his suspicion of my involvement in the arts, which he saw as evading the need to face up to reality (he may have been a pantheist, but Calvinism had left deep scars in his psyche). He had been moved to tears by an extempore recital, in the kitchen in Macduff, of my text for *The Passioun*, and in May, for the first time ever, he, with my mother and youngest brother, attended one of 'my' public performances: the Eastertide Carver mass at King's College, this time the five part *Fera Pessima*, performed by the St Andrews University Renaissance Group under my dear friend, the late Professor Douglas J Gifford, of the Spanish Department. Again, my father was deeply moved and congratulated me on what I had done to bring Carver alive in this way; he observed of the tremendous 'dona nobis pacem' of this mass, one of the world's great expressions of man's longing for peace, that those who had lived through wars ' really knew what peace was about'. At the end of August, Douglas Gifford directed Carver's *Fera Pessima* mass in St Giles as part of the Festival, to be followed by all the other masses over the next four years. I wrote the programme notes, as for the HBS concerts, for what were thilling and also rather nerve wracking concerts – I chanted the part of the celebrant, and though I was very used to public speaking, and indeed, to singing Orthodox services, using my singing voice in front of hundreds of people in a concert context was rather a different matter. Yet these Edinburgh Festival Carver masses were, as more than one member of the audience pointed out, 'much more than concerts'; they were genuinely spiritual occasions, thanks no doubt to the radiant, earthy spirituality of Douglas himself, a non-stipendiary Episcopal priest.

Since going to live in Luxembourg, I have never ceased to work with perfomers in Scotland, both amateur and professional : whether as organiser and/or participant, pre-performance speaker, adviser or even just translator. But always in direct connection with live performance. To me, music, drama or poetry are only truly experienced in live performance, as 'living sound', preferably in historic settings whose past life they can restore with incomparable immediacy. The combination of music and words is particularly potent. I deplore the way that poetry and music have become separated in the modern mind, particularly the academic mind; doubtless, my experience of sung and chanted Orthodox worship has greatly heightened my awarenss of how much they belong together. In the Renaissance, the two arts still went hand in hand. To hear Alexander Montgomerie sung is to acquire a very different perspective on that master's poetry. But he also declaims most effectively, as do all the earlier Scots poets. The poetry of Scotland's sixteenth century golden age is not difficult to put across to audiences at all. Indeed, Barbour's *Brus* (c.1360) is no problem, as I was able to confirm when performing it with Cappella Nova in 2000, and, in a very different programme of my own devising, with the Dunedin Consort in 2003. Even more effective for reaching audiences than individual poems, however, is drama. Having used me to recite Dunbar *et al* in concerts in Nairn, James Ross went on to produce *Ane Satyre of the Thrie Estaitis*, using only eight actors, with his own Early Music consort, Coronach, in costume on stage. I played King Humanitie, and the Pardoner, and Foly (who was entirely lacking from the Kemp edition used in Edinburgh). This was performed both in various Northern venues and in the Spiegeltent at the Edinburgh Fringe. Then in 1995, James came up with a second text, using 'all the good bits' that had been left out of the first version. Here, I played Humanity, the Soutar, and . . Foly again, complete with a prominent pillie. As my mother said after the Brodie Castle performance, "good clean dirt". We also presented this show in Glasgow, at the huge European Society for the Study of English (ESSE) Conference in 1995, at which I incidentally presented my first academic paper, on the anonymous comedy *Philotus*. The Scotsoun company filmed the Glasgow *Satyre* on video, an invaluable teaching aid – as is their video of the 1997 Biggar Theatre production of my edition of *Philotus*, a wonderful little Renaissance comedy on which I have now published two essays. In Biggar, we followed James Ross's lead, and had a live Renaissance band, in costume, on stage. The previous year, in Oxford, I had produced the entirely unknown tragi-comedy *Pamphilus, speakand of Lufe* (1590), by the Edinburgh merchant burgess John Burel. Admittedly, the audience was the 8th Triennial

International Scottish Mediaeval and Renaissance Language and Literature Conference, but the actors were English and coped perfectly with a wordy script in Middle Scots.

The success of these productions, not least the Glasgow *Satyre*, performed to a largely non-British audience, makes nonsense of claims that Middle Scots "needs to be put into English so Scottish people can understand it". The Welsh composer Dafydd Bullock, who teaches in Luxembourg, was so struck with the sheer sound of a densely Scots poem of mine (about Carver), that he spontaneously set it to music, even though he knew Ronald Stevenson had already set it for 12 part choir, for Cappella Nova. He liked the language so much, in fact, that he went on to set *The Passioun o Sanct Andraa*, which had been languishing since 1986. Premiered and then recorded in Luxembourg, we brought it to the 1992 Festival Fringe. Only two of the singers were Scots; but none of the English heroes who sang the work ever complained about linguistic difficulties (and this despite my stringent demands as regarded the pronunciation of my text: naething deaves my lug mair nor Scottish (sic) professional singers merrily failing to rhyme "die" with "thee", or Burns Supper speakers misrhyming English "sow" with spew). The current attitude of hopeless passivity in the face of the ever faster marginalisation of Scots is an indefensible disgrace; and these two very different dramatic works are ideal for using (and even producing) in Scottish schools. It is up to teachers themselves, of course; a 'Scottish' Executive which removes Scottish literature from the core curriculum is by definition not going to be doing anything to encourage any sense of Scottish identity. The reason is so simple and so terrifying that Scotland's establishment-friendly media are extremely reluctant to discuss it : nuclear weapons and nuclear waste. English voters would not stand for any new nuclear waste storage facilities, and no English port or naval facility would house the real weapons of mass destruction that Scotland, unlike Iraq, is involuntary home to. A Scotland aware of its own identity, and hence demanding real autonomy or even independence, would be a disaster for London's pitiful delusions of being a great world power. So the establishment steadfastly maintains a situation described by Edwin Muir over sixty years ago, in his poem 'Scotland's Winter', with its heartbreaking ending: 'The people of Scotland, content/ with their poor frozen life and shallow banishment'.

At the academic level, curiously enough, the picture has changed dramatically. Scottish history and Scottish literature are studied at university. Many, many scholarly books on 'earlier Scotland' have appeared in the last thirty years, including, in 1993, one to which I contributed, James Ross's

Musick Fyne, about Robert Carver. It is a source of the keenest satisfaction to me that I am now an honorary research fellow in Scottish History at Glasgow University, and that though I have yet to publish a word about Alejo Carpentier or any other Spanish language writer, I have now a modest but respectable list of published essays on 16th century Scotland, and preparing the *Collected Poems of John Burel* for the Scottish Text Society. I have even managed to make a genuine minor discovery or two (after all, the fields are all white and the reapers have been very few until recently). And perhaps even a quasi-major discovery, namely a great body of verse written by a woman in the late 1590s and early 1600s. The Calvinist poetry of Elizabeth Melville, Lady Culross, declaims well, and some of was written to be sung – so a presentation in words and music duly took place in Culross Abbey itself in April 2004, with audience participation in the metrical psalms (sung in Scots, of course) that closed both halves. I believe in this kind of event, bringing these historic glories into the living present, out of the scholar's study and the pages of scholarly books. Scottish people are interested in these things, however much the media pretend otherwise. Michael Lynch's Rhind Lectures 2004, on the emergence of Edinburgh as a capital city in the late 16th century, packed the large lecture theatre at the Royal Museum of Scotland for two whole days.

Oh but, but, but, the cry goes up, you need money to do these things. Ay weel nae necessarily. Even CD recordings can be sponsored for surprisingly little (and I have sponsored four). A few hundred quid can make marvels available to many. Oh but but but, they say, clinging on to their cash, does anyone under the age of forty want serious art these days anyway? Well it is perfectly true that the whole 'First World' establishment is now enslaved to the cult of 'anti-elitist' philistinism, post-modernist decentered meaninglessness and generalised endorsement of 'anything goes', as long as it does not upset the financial markets or stop illegal invasions of countries with natural resources. It is not politically correct to impose 'canons' of 'great art' on the minds of the young. After all, an awareness of the heights the human spirit can aspire to might, just might make them pause long enough to stop spending quite so much money in frenzied pursuit of momentary gratification, and that would be very bad news for consumerist economies. So of course it is not self-evident in 2005 that Muir's 'people of Scotland' care whether their lives are impoverished and frozen. Even so, when it proves possible to publicise events involving live presentation of earlier Scottish culture, audiences appear. When in February 1998, working with the Noel O'Regan's Edinburgh University Renaissance Singers, I managed to bring a long cherished dream to fruition and put on a programme of post-Reformation Scottish kirk music in St Giles on the anniversary of the funeral of the Regent Moray, a great number of folk turned up, and joined in singing Ps.43, 'Judge and revenge my cause, O Lord' to its own, forgotten melody from the 1564 Scottish Psalter. It was one of those timeless, universal, local moments when the past really was speaking to the living.

Janice Galloway

Born Saltcoats, 2nd December 1956

WRITER

Saltire Book of the Year, Clara, 2002

Showing Off

This piece is an extended version of an article written for the Edinburgh International Book Festival publication, republished in A Scottish Childhood, *1998.*

When I was very wee I didn't read at all. I listened. My mother sang Elvis and Peggy Lee songs, the odd Rolling Stones hit as they appeared. These gave me a notion of how relationships between the sexes were conducted (there were no men in our house), the meaning of LURV (ie sexual attraction and not LOVE which was something in English war-time films that involved crying); a sprinkling of Americanisms (to help conceal/ sophisticate the accent I had been born into and which my mother assured me was ignorant and common) and a basic grounding in ATTITUDE (known locally as LIP). This last, was the most useful one. In fact, the only useful one. The words to BLUE SUEDE SHOES are carved on my heart.

I was reading by the time I went to primary school. I know because I got a row for it. Reading before educationally permissible was pronounced SERIOUSLY DETRIMENTAL TO HER IN CLASS. This was true because I had to do it again their way, with JANET and JOHN and The DOG with the RED BALL. Books were read round class ie too slow, and you got the belt if you got carried away and keeked at the next page before you were allowed by the teacher. WHO DO YOU THINK YOU ARE? she'd roar, SOMEBODY SPECIAL? Dulling enthusiasm, or at least not showing it, became an intrinsic part of my education. This did not trouble me. I was a biddable child. Most are.

At home, I read OOR WULLIE and THE BROONS, the BEANO and BUNTY. BUNTY was best because it had girls in it. There was Wee Slavey (the maid with the heart of gold) and the Four Marys (who went to boarding school) amongst others. They had spunk. Only the former seemed a role model, however. I also read Enid Blyton *Fairy Tales* and *Folk Tales of Many Lands*, a whole set in the local library. When the Folk Tales were finished, I began fingering the Mythology Religion books on the adult shelves whereupon the librarian (Defender of Books from the inquiry of Grubby People and Children) smacked my hands and told me I wasn't allowed those ones: I would neither like nor understand them and was only SHOWING OFF. This was another lesson in the wisdom of hiding natural enthusiasm because it sometimes annoyed people in authority. I ran errands to the same library for my nineteen-years-older sister who read six books a week and hit me (literally) if I brought back books by women authors. WOMEN CANNY WRITE, she'd say: CAN YOU NOT BLOODY LEARN? She was afraid, I think, of Romance. Other hitting offences included asking to watch *A Midsummer Night's Dream*, keeping a diary and, mysteriously, "reading too much". Words, it seemed, carried pain, traps, bombs and codes. They were also, alas, addictive. Nursing bruises, welts and the odd black eye, I blamed myself. Earlier than I learned to do the same thing with sex, I learned to look as though I wasn't doing it at all and became devious as hell.

Thrillers, adventures and war stories caused no ructions. They were the things my sister liked. My mother read too, mostly biographies of film stars, to learn how they'd escaped, I suppose. She also read the odd novel from a stack on top of the cupboard shelf which I could not reach, books that had pictures of women with their frocks falling off on the covers and the name ANGELIQUE featured on the spines. I knew enough to understand, however, that she was not the author. My father had apparently been a reader but he'd been dead for ages and not around much before that either. His books — from a club — were stacked at the bottom of a cupboard. The only one that had jokes was a big black tome with gold letters on the side: THE COMPLETE PLAYS of BERNARD SHAW. Without understanding much, I read it anyway. At ten or eleven, I accidentally wrote a novel in blue biro and pencil. My mother found it but didn't tell my sister. She lit the fire with it.

Secondary school proved my sister uncannily perceptive. Women couldny write. There were none, not one, not even safely dead ones like Jane Austen, as class texts. On the plus side, they encouraged reading, largely on the grounds you could pass exams with it. You could only pass exams, though, with books from the school store, which meant the aforementioned no women and not much that was Scottish save Burns who had the added benefit of being useful for school suppers which girls might attend if they served the food. This troubled me a bit, but not oppressively. I was good at exams. I passed everything, though what to do then seemed a mystery to all, especially Head of Girls who told me I'd never get far with an accent like mine, and why I wanted to go to University was anybody's guess. Actually it was the Head of Music's idea. With treacherous speed, I fell away from books and fell in love with MUSIC because nobody had told me (not yet anyway) that women canny compose. The Head of Music became my Bodyguard and my sister and the Head of Girls couldn't say boo because he was a teacher. He taught me MOZART was pronounced MOTZART and not as spelled on the biscuit tin at home. He taught me lots of things. Through third to sixth year, I hoovered up Purcell and Byrd, Britten, Warlock and Gesualdo (my sister's example meant I wanted nothing to do with something called Romantic music, even if it was by men) and sang folk songs. These were not pop songs. They had better words and led me by a sneaky route to Opera. Opera! It was unbelievable! In my final year, the Head of Music gave me a copy of *The Prime of Miss Jean Brodie*, my first book by a living Scottish author. Read, he said. Learn. And he talked my mother, mortified in her school dinner lady overall, into letting me fill in the Uni forms. The day I left, I turned up at school in trousers and got sent home. This did not trouble me. I was taking the music and getting out. I visited Hillhead, peering out the filthy windows of a 59 bus without apology or concealment. At last, I would revel in Great Works of Music and Profound Literary Texts without shame or concealment. I couldn't wait.

In three years of MA I read less than two Scottish authors and two women, all dead. My music list seemed not to know women or Scotland existed at all. There were no folk songs. In my third year, I cried a lot and everyone was very nice. They let me have a year out. I was, I realised with intense embarrassment, suffering from a broken heart. I went back and finished the fastest degree they had only because someone called the Student Advisor said, GIRLS OFTEN GIVE UP, IT'S NOTHING TO BE ASHAMED OF. Books were bastards. I could no longer listen to music. There was only one thing for it. Teaching.

On teaching practice, I turned up at school in trousers and was sent home. This troubled me a bit but it wasn't new. I could handle it. Eager as a squirrel, I taught happily for ten years. I got into trouble for not taking my register seriously enough and teaching stuff outside the syllabus to the "wrong" age group sometimes, but the children were very forbearing. I was a good teacher, the Head informed me one day, but not promotion material. He wasn't sure why. Maybe I needed my wings clipped. I thought he had a point. I wanted to stick with this job. I enjoyed the children, their enthusiasm and inventive cheek. I did not like the book shortages but teaching was fine. I still cried off and on and took to writing the odd poem, but wary I was heading down the primrose path of SHOWING OFF all over again, concealed them as much as I could. Occasionally I caught myself gazing down the stairwell, at the bland, blank walls. One day, a propos of nothing, I caught myself glaring at a child. WHO DO YOU THINK YOU ARE? a voice roared, terrifying from the back of the classroom. SOMEBODY SPECIAL? And the voice was mine. This troubled me a lot.

Bizarrely, it led me to reading. I re-read the curious woman who had written the equally curious BRODIE, then everything else I could run to ground. I read Carver and Kafka. I read Duras and Carter. I read Machado da Assis and Mansfield and Carswell and Barges and Woolf and chewed up national anthologies of stories — any country's — whole. I fell over Gray's big book about Glasgow that is also a big book about everywhere, and something clicked, not just from Alasdair's work but from everybody's. It was the click of the heretofore unnoticed nose I'd just found on my own face. It was astounding, a revelation. For the first time since I learned how to pronounce MOZART, I realised Something Big. I had the right to know things. Me. I had the right to listen, to think; even godhelpus to *join in.* A tentative glimmer of freedom started squirming around beneath the sea of routine shame and I remembered being another way. I remembered being wee. I remembered the Saltcoats Library and the living room fireplace. I remembered Elvis. And I knew three things. I knew:

a) that all Art is an act of resistance;

b) that the fear of SHOWING OFF would kill me if I let it; and

c) the words WHO DO YOU THINK YOU ARE? stunk like a month-old kipper.

My mother was dead.

I had not seen my sister for years.

Reader, I started writing.

Alan Riach

Born Airdrie, 1st August 1957

POET AND PROFESSOR
OF SCOTTISH LITERATURE

The View from the South Pacific

*An expanded version of an essay which appeared
in* In Scotland *No 4, Summer 2001.*

> Success? I never had to worry about success.
> Coming from where I come from,
> You were a success the minute you left town.
>
> *Edward Dorn*

When I left Scotland for the first time I was 4 and didn't have much choice. My father was a merchant seaman and he wanted a shore job to be closer to my mother and me, so he became a Trinity House Pilot and we moved from Lanarkshire to Gravesend, in Kent. Gravesend is where Conrad's *Heart of Darkness* begins — and ends. There's a story that when Burns was working as an exciseman he confiscated two cannon and sent them off to the French Revolution with his compliments — but they were stopped at Gravesend. The Indian princess Pocahontas is buried in Gravesend. There's another story that the place got its name because it marked the furthest extent of the burial grounds after the great plague and fire of London. Whatever the apocrypha, you get a sense that the place had a terminal aspect. That was magnified by childhood and made Scotland all the more deeply home. We went back in school holidays, to family and friends, Lanarkshire and Glasgow. I counted the days.

School, a first degree in English at Cambridge, then back to Scotland for the PhD, in the Department of Scottish Literature at the University of Glasgow. Exile may be the mother of nationalism but Scotland was always more than a memory. Scottish literature is surely even now one of the most under-researched areas in professional scholarship. It was important to do the work I wanted in the Department best able to foster it and, after meeting him in 1976, Edwin Morgan was a constant source of knowledge and encouragement. Family and friends kept doors open into different realms of the social spectrum, from darkly sectarian nodes of increasingly post-industrial Lanarkshire to Glasgow at its brightest and most brilliant. Then the inevitable spell of various kinds of job beyond part-time teaching took me into driving and warehouse work in Glasgow, surveying for a roof-repair firm, and unemployment, with the usual moonlight sonatas.

When I left Scotland for the second time, I was 28. I had no greater wish to go than when I was 4 but there was more necessity. This was what the American poet Edward Dorn termed the Rawhide Era, what Liz Lochhead called the Thatcher Monster was swinging the scythe. As the Miners' Strike was broken, the nuclear clouds of Chernobyl drifted west and the technology of arms shadowed us all, I found the job I wanted to do.

The University of Waikato, in Hamilton, in the middle of the North Island of New Zealand, offered me a fellowship for one or three years. I chose one — three, I figured, would be too long. It was 14 years before I came back.

It wasn't an escape. I went not knowing anyone, a deep-end dive from the highboard. Walking around Auckland Harbour soon after I arrived, I remember seeing the Greenpeace ship, the *Rainbow Warrior*, crippled at her moorings. A few months before, she'd been blown up by the French after the Greenpeace protests against nuclear tests in the South Pacific. New Zealand was central. The then prime minister David Lange was telling the nuclear management to keep out and most New Zealanders thought he was right. Most of us in Scotland had felt that way too, but had had no voice to say so. That's the value of the definite article. Nations need to be states to make statements like that take effect.

Some years later I was commissioned to write a poem for a book published in protest against continued French testing at Moruroa. Quotations came in from Walter Benjamin, Tacitus's *Agricola* and Hugh MacDiarmid. The poem wrote itself:

THE CORAL ISLAND

'Even the dead will not be safe from this enemy,
if he wins.'

The border was there. We had been protected.
Today the shield is broken. Nothing but waves, and rocks,

and Empire's bleak intentions to englut: an ocean
breaking past us, on our sense of what should be.
                    Justice
is for everyone, and anyone to see; but judgement now is
                    singular, and
all last things are lonely.

The ocean that surrounds our isolation
                        is unpredicted element.
We trust to its encircling and resounding;
we are committed to it,
                in the end.

The fleet is our example: set sail, set
                    keel to current cross-wise
                    with wreckage to fear, brave hearted,
women and men with knowledge of
                    the consequence most likely:
Casualties of war, the wrong end of empire,
                    stupidity of suits, the fluency of lies.
A struggle that always continues, in words and in
                these human lives.

This, not Ralph nor Peterkin, prevails
day after day, night after night, calling out for freedom from
the wrong that is as one with empire's name.

These people are pledged:
their grasp is all the world, and they are strange,
for they will attack the poor as violently as the rich.
'Theft, destruction, rape, these liars name Empire.
They make a desert, and they call it peace.'

In spite of their kind, 'some elements of worth
With difficulty persist, here and there on the earth.'

There was finding out about the place itself, and finding out what it was
I was away from, and then there was finding a way to get back.

At the northernmost coast of the North Island is a place called Spirits
Bay, at Cape Reinga, from where the spirits of the Tangata Whenua, the
people of the land, the Maori dead, are said to depart on their long journey
back to Hawai'iki, their ancestral home. Scotland was further. I travelled

around on a tour with a tough wee Welshman in a transit van with the words 'Discover New Zealand' painted on the sides. In Northland, one night, we were having a beer in a rough bar, full of unemployed people, locals, and a big Maori man comes in and says in a big challenging voice, 'Who owns that van out there with "Discover New Zealand" on the side?' And my pal says, diffidently, 'Ah . . . I do.' The Maori guy beams, booms out: 'Well — you found it then!'

I found it. A poem followed, 'At Spirits Bay, the Empty Sea' and it was published in the New Zealand journal *Landfall* and simultaneously in the anthology *New Writing Scotland*. A New Zealand reviewer of the magazine singled it out for comment, saying, 'Only a Scot could have written this.' A Scottish reviewer of the anthology suggested that only a New Zealander could understand it.

There was plenty to wonder at. The Coromandel peninsula in the North Island is one of earth's most beautiful parts. The Southern Alps are spectacular. Seen from close up in the starry night sky, they're so high they seem to curve over you like claws, ice-sharp, unlike anything in Europe — talons, stretched straight up from the Antarctic. It's supposed that the central crater which cradles Lake Taupo, in the middle of the North Island, was formed by the meteor whose dustcloud caused the sky to go dark at the time of the crucifixion. The timing would be almost exact: it connects.

There was the weather, of course. The Waikato has long hot summers and never any snow. So I missed the theatre of seasons and landscapes, people, climates of language and humour and silence. Qualities of quietness were different. In a country bigger than Britain with a population of only just over 3 million, believe me you could hear it. I liked it in a way, even if it wasn't home. The human terrain was different. I was curious. I explored. But it was lonely. 'The Blues' is a not entirely serious kind of love poem:

THE BLUES

The lights are on all over Hamilton.
The sky is dark, blue
as a stained glass window in an unfreqented church
say, by Chagall, with grand and glorious chinks
of pinks and purples,
glittering jewels on those glass fronted buildings
where the lifts are all descending
and the doors are
being closed.

You're out there somewhere,
going to a concert in wide company or maybe
sitting somewhere weaving a carpet
like a giant tapestry, coloured grey,
pale brown, weaving the wool
back in at the edges of the frame, your
fingers deft as they turn the wool in tight and
gentle curves.
           Or somewhere else.
           What do I do
           except imagine you?
           The river I keep crossing
           keeps going north. The trains
           in the night cross it too.
           Their silver carriages are blue.

I remember writing to a friend about things I missed, and got caught in the flow, letting myself carry on past places and people, to Scotch pies, Irn Bru, Tunnock's Marshmallow Teacakes, Lees's macaroon bars, ice cream oysters. And the reply, 'Alan, I've always admired your insistence on including the ugly along with the bad and the good, but which category Tunnock's Marshmallow Teacakes come into I'll never know!'

I was wrong about the seasons too. They changed. The high adventures of the Academy at its best became waterlogged with management and jargon, swamped and vandalised. The first lessons, the Hippocratic oaths that poetry insists you take, the need people have of the arts, all seemed awfully vulnerable in a world thoroughly sold out to commercialism. It seemed to me that even in Thatcher's Britain, certain structures withstood the onslaught; some, in despite, got stronger. After all, the 1980s also saw Troy Kennedy Martin's *Edge of Darkness*. But even the strongest warnings fail. A kind of Kiwi Thatcherism swept New Zealand — beginning, in fact, from Lange's government itself and economic policies brought in by Roger Douglas – 'Rogernomics' they were called. Lange resigned. I felt nostalgia for moments ago.

There was one time I got on a plane in Auckland and got off in London and the Berlin Wall had come down. It wasn't the Europe I'd left. It wasn't the Scotland I'd left either — but we'll come to that. There was a weird disorientation. And then, after reading newspapers and listening to the radio, I found that in the 24 hours after I'd arrived, the first old lady of the season had died of hypothermia, police were riding students down on Westminster Bridge, and two Conservative Party politicians were drinking tumblers of irradiated water at Dungeness Power Station and telling you it was good for you. Home?

But there was another home. No. Two other homes: professional and private, and they could never be entirely separate. And two things came slowly into focus: the centrality of Scottish literature in the work I was most concerned with, and the writing of my own I couldn't give up.

I had left my poems behind in a box by a desk in my parents' home in Kent. Either abandon it now, I figured, or decide you need them and work to make them publishable. It took two months. I phoned and asked my parents and they sent them out. At the end of my first sojourn, Auckland University Press published the first book, *This Folding Map*, and Oxford U.P. published it in Britain. That was followed quickly by *An Open Return*, a book-length sequence of poems and notes from my first year in New Zealand, and then in 1995, *First & Last Songs*, co-published by A.U.P. and Chapman, Edinburgh. The title is a simple code for love songs and elegies, but it's also a pun: songs, music, words that make music, poetry, first and last — what else might connect love and death at either end of the world?

DONA NOBIS PACEM

You had no wish to leave this world and time
or us, but knew that in the way of things you would.
Without the indulgence of fancy, allow us to let you
go with the innumerable angels.

Not everyone can hear the things they need to
most, or tell them. I never had the chance
to tell you what I'd learned of Robert Carver —
voices in the vault of God, lifting, turning as a
film will take your eyes round corners
unsuspected, into naves and arches, liberated texts
of stone, cavernous cathedral space, pillars of sound supporting
the weight, rivers of voice, carrying rafts of us onward, on
parabolas of song: registers of penitence,
humility, and faith.

This morning at eight I heard you had died in the night,
at four. The lowest segment of the clock
closed in; night filled it, carried

the news to me, waking to the winter dawn.
At ten I played the six-part mass
and listened to it for you,
soaring, ascending, leaving us
things that are living
always so easily hurt.

The deaths of older family and friends in Scotland coincided with love and new family in New Zealand. I was lucky. I went into the University library looking for an obscure Scottish novel of 1944 (*Soon Bright Day* by Mary Baird Aitken) and started talking to a bright librarian who got the book and married me. The love poems started to appear in anthologies both in New Zealand and Scotland. If home is something you leave it's also something you make.

Then there was the professional home we made, with good colleagues and professional friends, introducing new courses and new ways of teaching – I mean the old ways, of course, but always freshened, always applying Pound's advice to Hemingway, 'Go in fear of abstractions.' Distrust adjectives as you will learn to distrust certain people you cannot rely on. Use everything available: technology, music, slides, film, all the arts are part of the story. What seemed like old and outworn truths acquired a practical application that remains a deep lesson: you have to tell the story first, and you have to tell it in ways that keep it up for discussion, tense, fresh, not to let it sag or slip. You have to start out of particulars – William Carlos Williams's advice – make a start out of particulars, beginning from where you are. And remember that sometimes it's good to look good. These days, we all need to be a lot smarter in our packaging.

It was salutary to be reminded that you have to ask yourself these questions sometimes: why should you take it for granted that your students will know of Ulysses? Or the Clearances? What if they have different traditions of voyaging, warfare, leadership, other historical tragedies or metaphors of dispossession? Perhaps it was wiser to start without baggage, light as I arrived, with a suitcase – though mainly of books (MacDiarmid, Olson) – and a shoulder bag (toothbrush, change of clothing, duty free, passport). After the immersion in the work of one man – MacDiarmid – for the doctorate, it was wonderful to have the chance to be teaching the whole scene again, the big boogaloo, to lecture on *King Lear* here, on Joseph Conrad there, on George Eliot, and the Americans: Twain, Frost, Eliot, Pound. Being in New Zealand afforded me the chance to cross America, on my way there from Scotland, more than once, and to touch down for visits on my way back, to Singapore or Hong Kong: the world, literally, circled.

Then there was the construction of the first courses in Scottish literature – the first full courses on the subject in New Zealand – which became increasingly popular, both because of students' interest in where they'd come from and a curiosity about an accessible non-mainstream 'English' literature. One Maori student came up to me after a showing of 7:84's *The Cheviot, the Stag and the Black, Black Oil* and said, 'But that's my story – that's my story too!' Year after year, by word of mouth, Lewis Grassic Gibbon's New Zealand reputation grew. Students were sitting in cafés, hurrying to read to the end of the trilogy, holding back tears, before rushing into the lectures. Edwin Morgan, Hugh MacDairmid, Liz Lochhead, Tom Leonard: voices were heard in the Waikato that hadn't been heard there before. This was internationalising Scottish literature in ways rarely dreamed about and not often seen.

And it made you especially curious about those aspects of Scottish literature off the beaten track, the visitors, the travellers, the unrecognised or marginal. These writers remain important even if they are out of the mainstream: Veronica Forrest-Thomson, John Henry Mackay, Poe and Mary Shelley in Scotland – and Melville, that Pacific man, what had driven him to try to find an answer to the question of family and home, in Scotland?

MELVILLE IN GLASGOW

Consider it a sketch: charcoal on grain, white paper, black ash,
clouds and the Necropolis, the perfect size and shape of that Cathedral,
to see it from the south side of the Clyde and think of modesty
and reach, the country all around; to think of what was there, and what
that man was looking for, a past that might say more than all the risk
he'd known before he stepped up on that quay: what did he want?
A family? A line? A net? A country? A link in a chain he couldn't put down,
to haul up something far too deeply rusted out of sight; yet not too far:
he knew it was there, went looking for it, crossed the country, walked and rode and
came back in to Glasgow: his place, his port. The first and last he saw, of something then he must have thought ancestral, real as all the things he knew had
                                                                                happened
to him, in the South Pacific, visceral, in blood and muscle, yielding to delight,
yet also always fictional: build on that. On what? Where was he then?
What strength and what uncertainty, and what desire to know, dared push
                                                                                that pen?

And yet, the point of departure was always reliable. What do you think of when you think of 'Scotland'? The answers came out with surprisingly lusty glee: the usual clichés. Haggis tartan heather whisky mountains and the Loch Ness Monster. And of 'Glasgow'? Gorbals gangs, Billy Connolly and *Taggart*. The kitsch mingled with real history and another lesson started to come through. Even Tunnock's Teacakes do look different from a distance. Taggart: 'Sorry, Jean. I can't come out tonight. [Sigh] There's been another murder.' The humour began to toughen out of marshmallow nostalgia into a sense of no going back, only *through*, whatever way there is. To begin with the clichés was not to accede to them but to recolonise the colonisers, to take up the humour and flype it inside out, to use it to get back. Glamour, glitz, colour and fun aren't foreign — what's foreign anymore anyway? — why not take and turn them back into smart packaging? The dour, recalcitrant, glum-mute Scot, bred for the rifle and service, the Scot of the John Brown glare and the tree-sized kilt, images that were still dependably recognisable in New Zealand as in America, all over — the trick was not to waste time opposing them but to turn them to our advantage, to find a way of making them open the door on the whole range of our expressive possibilities, instead of keeping it shut.

Ireland set an example — the Irish women presidents, the Irish cultural policies for arts and education, the sheer delight in the arts, the brio and fun of the Irish visitors, despite, or maybe fuelled by, their disagreements. If Ireland, why not New Zealand? Why not Scotland?

Our own visitors were far enough removed from the clichés — John Purser toured New Zealand with a message about Scotland's music and the value of republicanism that was reported widely; Angus Calder arrived to work with me editing MacDiarmid's revolutionary prose; Edwin Morgan read at the Wellington International Festival and accepted an honorary doctorate from the University of Waikato. After Morgan's reading to the class of 200 first-year students, the Vice-Chancellor, Wilfred Malcolm, turned to me and said, 'It's *that* that makes all the work of running a university worthwhile!'

There was progress, there were friends and there was, it became clear, the enemy. The enemy in general was the sense that Scottish literature was competing — either against po-faced, long-bearded, blue-stockinged, shrill-minded, so-called 'traditionalists' (so often, alas, Oxbridge-impaired!) or against other incipient developments in colonial or 'post-colonial' literatures or New Zealand literature itself. It's true you can only do so much, but the gauge should never ignore quality and there's always something to learn from what students demand.

The danger is universal. There's always someone out there trying to colonise you. But the change was happening internationally too. The initiatives we'd set up in New Zealand were running alongside and linking up with similar things in Scotland: the development of research into Irish and Scottish cultural relations, the establishment of inter-disciplinary study of national artistic traditions, the sense that whatever the attractions of getting into the esoteric upper reaches of research were, it was worthwhile trying to get back and tell the story.

Maybe that was the lesson: don't take it for granted. Read it again. And act on it. People were acting on it in Scotland. Over the time I was in New Zealand, the major 20th century critical overhaul of the country's artistic and cultural history was taking place. It had started with Hugh MacDiarmid's Scottish Renaissance in the 1920s, a movement MacDiarmid himself defined as 'a propaganda of ideas' – that is, once the ideas are out, just leave them to work. In the 1980s and 1990s they were working coherently. There was Roderick Watson's *The Literature of Scotland* (1984), Cairns Craig's 4-volume *History of Scottish Literature* (1987-88), Duncan MacMillan's *Scottish Art 1460-1990* (1990), John Purser's *Scotland's Music* (1992), Paul Scott's *Scotland: A Concise Cultural History* (1993), and Douglas Gifford and Dorothy McMillan's *History of Scottish Women's Writing* (1997). From New Zealand, Marshall Walker's *Scottish Literature Since 1707* was published in 1996, I was editing the *Collected Works* of Hugh MacDiarmid, putting MacDiarmid firmly into history, from 1992 on, and Jan Pilditch began work on Catherine Carswell, breaking ground to produce not only a full-scale biography but also the possibility of a socio-cultural history of the Scottish Renaissance. The nation's cultural redefinition and assertion of self-definition – the end MacDiarmid had fought so hard to begin — was established more comprehensively than ever before.

The view from Waikato was long-distance enough for us to be critical of certain things, tendencies that seemed to us cripplingly unquestioned. So much of Scotland comes out of the 19th century that a kind of Victorian sluggishness too frequently seems normal. That's one reason why Edwin Morgan's space-age speed stays fresh. There's a Scottish nouveau-kitsch about that needs a handy scalpel. Pieties, correctnesses, the legacies of lickspittle are as evident here as anywhere, so there's no need to idealise. The distance allowed you to see the terrain in a longer perspective, to be certain, for example, that some things are dispensable and some things are not. It also allowed us to work undisturbed on Scottish literature in ways that might otherwise have been pretty brutally interrupted by controversy and disagreement. There are some things we are agreed on, aren't there? We must never give in to the angels.

The distance also conferred a certain authority on your judgement about what is worth keeping in mind. The referendum of 1999 and the establishment of the resumed Scottish Parliament is far more important than anything the daily press and news programmes report about it. Media is clearly just that – *between* the people and the event. The crucial fact of the new parliament is that it initiates the possibility of international recognition of cultural identity in a new way. It opened with two acts unimaginable in Westminster: a singing of Burns's 'Is there, for honest poverty . . . ?' so full-throated that the too-complacent rich then present began to squirm, and a reading of a new poem by Iain Crichton Smith, a hope for the future. These were exemplary acts. What's worth remembering is what brings you back in the end. The poem says it better:

CLEARANCES

The clouds go over
singly, or in fleets, trailing
raggedly back, against a sky
where looming vaults of rain
come over too. Then the sky lets loose:
the shades of grey become uncountable,
the rain comes down on everything, diagonal, banks:
the windows, roof, the wooden deck,
the trees around, the green slopes run
with mud, the fields below are soaked and fill;
the road becomes a grey and moving river.

The baby hasn't heard this sound before: the heavy rain
on the iron roof, and cries himself
to sleep, at last, as the downpour
eases off. It must be time to leave.
The weather is an actual farewell.

I used to think the old Gaels of Ireland,
or the west of Scotland, knew
so little of our modern world.
It seemed they were a pastoral people
and burdened with a culture of conservatism.
But clearances are always strong in the mind,
the images recurrent, the rubble of the ruined homes,
the ghosts of children, animals, and men
and women helpless in the face of the event.

Farewells and birth, there are some things
no clues or forms of knowledge alter
in themselves. I won't say they can't help.
They knew about departure, those old people,
and the kinds of life we deal with here
require that inherited wisdom. Now
the heavy showers have passed, but different shades of grey
reflect, refract unnumbered tones of light.
It's time to pack what we have and can carry.
It's time to take what we can, and go. The boy
will not remember this, the landscape
of his parents, unless we do.

                                        (Coromandel, 25/9/94)

It is 1st January 2001. I am returning to begin work in the Department of Scottish Literature at the University of Glasgow. Now with my wife and two boys – the oldest the baby mentioned in 'Clearances' — without hesitation, I'm back.

It isn't long before I hear the mortmain tone of cynicism: 'Home?' — the voice sarcastic — 'Just you wait till the winter! Ye'll be aff again to sunnier climes!'

When I get on the bus from Ayr to Glasgow one freezing January morning, 7.00 am, pitch black, the driver says, 'Ye're on the wrong bus, pal. The university bus is that one behind us...' and as we look round, the second bus is overtaking us and driving away. My driver says, 'It's okay pal, don't worry — sit doon — we'll catch 'im!' and we're off like Speed, like Arnold Schwarzaneggplant, racing through the empty streets. And my bus cuts in diagonally and brakes in front of the next bus-stop, blocking the university bus off completely. 'There ye are now,' says my driver, nodding, satisfied: 'On ye go. He's no' gonny get oot o' that!'

Home!

'You know,' I tell my father, 'even when the novelty wears off, there'll still be so much to take pleasure in, daily . . . '

'No,' he shakes his head sternly. 'You're wrong, Alan. The novelty will never wear off.'

He's right. It's 1st August 2005 and no sign of it yet. There's a lot more damage to do.

There's an Elle Macpherson advert which shows the model in a tartan bra and underpants turning defiantly to two burly-looking men who seem a little threatening. The words at the top of the advert read: 'It's Macpherson

Clan tartan – who wants to know?'

I described this to a friend of mine and suggested, gently, that it displayed a note of self-determination that signalled a common cause shared by the discourse of nationalism and the discourse of feminism.

My friend said he thought there was a slight problem there because it also invoked the discourse of capitalism and took place entirely within it.

'Yes,' I said. 'Which proves my final point: that even within ideologies that seem inescapable, we may find the strategies of our own liberation.'

LANARKSHIRE, JANUARY

low sun —
        late winter afternoon —
the shadows stroll and stretch themselves across
                the green fields and the iron earth —
the widescreen light is cold and clarifies on paths white with frost, all
the lengthening day,
        from Loudon Hill to Tinto
from Darvel to Drumclog.
The spires of village churches sharpen
themselves, pointing up. Branches click like blades
or needles in the breeze.

Covenanter land: a hard terrain
of outdoor congregations, sheer
determination, beliefs you'd stand and die with,
live for in commitment, be
determined by.
           The bare trees
strain the sunlight in the sky.

James Robertson

Born Sevenoaks, 14th March 1958

POET AND NOVELIST

Saltire Book of the Year, Joseph Knight, 2003

Becoming a Writer

When I was five and at my first school, I wrote a poem about a dog and a cow. It went like this:

> My little dog went out to play
> Over the hills and far away.
> He met a cow
> That said "Bow-Wow".
> "All right," said the dog, "then I'll eat hay,"
> And that was the end of the dog that day.

My teacher, no doubt trying to be helpful, and failing to appreciate the subtlety of the role reversal, altered it so that when it was printed in the school magazine it read:

> My little dog went out to play
> Over the hills and far away.
> He met a cow
> And said "Bow-Wow".
> "All right," said the cow, "then I'll eat hay,"
> And that was the end of the dog that day.

This editorial interference completely destroyed the point of the poem. It might also have been a fatal blow to my literary career, but I rose above it. Perhaps even then I was determined to be a published writer whatever the obstacles. Certainly, by the time I was seven or eight, I knew that that was what I wanted to be. I do not know where this notion came from, but it lodged in my brain very early on. Naïvely, I thought I might achieve my aim by the time I was about twelve. But then I was a very naïve child in most respects.

I was born in 1958, in Sevenoaks, Kent. My older sister and brother and both my parents were born in England too. Yet by the time I was conscious of any kind of nationality, I felt Scottish. My mother's parents and my father's father were Scottish, although they had all moved south decades before. When in 1964 my father announced that we were going to live in Scotland — he explained to us with the aid of an atlas just how far away it was — it seemed absolutely the right thing to be doing. It seemed (or maybe we were told) that we were going *back*. I remember singing the words of 'Loch Lomond', about taking the low road as opposed to the high road, and thinking they really applied to us, although when the time came we actually took the sleeper.

The poet Carol Ann Duffy, who was born in Glasgow but moved to England when she was about the same age I was when I moved to Scotland, has a poem in which someone asks "Where do you come from? Originally?" In the poem, the narrator hesitates, unsure of the answer, or perhaps of the question. For me, I don't think there was ever much doubt. Originally, I came from a country I did not set foot in until I was six years old.

Identity is such a tricky matter. Culture, place, class, family, history, politics all play a part in determining one's identity. Had I remained in the south of England I would have grown up to be English. I would have been a different person: the same flesh and blood, but a different person. But the possibility of that particular different person ended when I was six. I find this an interesting proposition, both sobering and exciting. We all have the stories and endings of various different people in us, but we have very little conscious control over which ones finally emerge.

My father had taken a job as general sales manager for John G. Stein, a firm manufacturing refractory bricks for lining furnaces, mainly in the steel industry. Later he became sales director. In 1964 central Scotland was still a land of heavy industry: on wet days the whole country from Fife to Ayrshire seemed to smell of coal. John G. Stein had plants at Bonnybridge, Castlecary and Linlithgow, but we settled at the other end of Stirlingshire, in the well-to-do village of Bridge of Allan. Bridge of Allan was so posh and rural it was almost in Perthshire. Older residents who stayed down near the river referred to it as "the Brig o Allan" but up on the hill, where we were, the designation had long been anglicised — rather as the name of the road that led to the upper part of the village had itself both an official (English) and a colloquial (Scots) title. The sign said "Well Road", but it was commonly referred to as "the U.P. Brae", because the United Presbyterian kirk once stood at its foot. But in the 1960s, the kirk was demolished and replaced by public toilets, an early sign that times were changing.

Bridge of Allan was separated from Causewayhead, the northern extreme of Stirling, by a mile or so of road with Graham's dairy park on one side and the grounds of Airthrey Castle estate on the other. If you went the back road into Stirling, after a similar distance you crossed the railway before passing through the council schemes of Cornton. Quiet and leafy and slightly aloof, Bridge of Allan was very much a village with its own character.

Some of the shopkeepers might have stepped out of a novel by J. M. Barrie. There was Mr Scobie the ironmonger, who was also, I think, the provost: posters bearing his name would appear in shop windows before public holidays, which were strictly enforced so that no shop should have an unfair advantage over the others. Such regulations were in disuse by the 1970s, by which time Graham's the dairy had opened a self-service supermarket across the street from the old-fashioned grocer's, D. & J. McEwan. McEwan's were renowned for quality, and also had shops in Stirling, Crieff and Callander, but gradually their trade shrank in the face of modernity and eventually they closed altogether. Next to Scobie's was the butcher's: the floor was covered in sawdust and great sides of beef hung on hooks in a row. M. & K. Ritchie's was the newsagent where I used to buy comics and my first long-playing records — which, I'm embarrassed to confess, far from being at the cutting-edge of contemporary music were *Music for Pleasure* albums of Western movie themes. At the far end of Henderson Street, the main street, was the Allan Water Café, run by the Tognieri family. Their fish and chips were excellent, as was their ice-cream. Two scoops of vanilla between two nougat sliders, a treat so delicious it was almost indecent, went by the now politically incorrect title of a "double black man". There were also numerous pubs and hotels, but a decade would pass before I entered any of these.

We stayed in a big stone house set in a huge garden full of beautiful trees. Opposite us was the manse, occupied by the Reverend William MacDonald and his two unmarried sisters. Every year before Christmas my sister, brother and I were summoned to the manse. Once we had passed a quarter of an hour in conversation, we were rewarded with a box of chocolates, usually rather tired as if they had been stored since the previous Christmas. Mr MacDonald, or Willie Mac as he was nicknamed, was a kindly soul with an evangelical, sing-song way of preaching that held your attention even if you didn't fathom everything he was saying. It was not until years later that I learned more about him. According to the *Dictionary of Scottish Church History and Theology*, he had "conducted one of the most distinguished of Scotland's twentieth-century pulpit ministries" at Palmerston Place in Edinburgh for twenty-five years, "from which he removed through ill-health to Chalmers, Bridge of Allan", in 1952. When he finally retired in 1975, at the age of eighty-four, he had been a minister for fifty-six years.

The village roads were quiet and safe in the 1960s, so that, during school holidays, from the age of about eight I was allowed to spend all day cycling around, usually going the few hundred yards to my best friend's house, but sometimes pedalling the country roads of the Carse or those that led up through the glen to Dunblane and to Sheriffmuir. I knew every path and feature of the Coppermine and Airthrey woods, and of the walk along the Allan Water. At weekends our whole family, with dog, might tramp around the Cocksburn reservoir by Pendreich, where a pair of swans always glided and which, each spring, was the breeding-ground for thousands of frogs. The nine-hole golf course might have been a mountainous challenge for golfers, but when it snowed the fifth hole, known as The Hollow, was a fabulous venue for sledging. Every first weekend in August the Strathallan Highland Games were held, accompanied by one of the biggest funfairs in Scotland. It is, I know, a trick of memory to have such a nostalgic view, but it does seem, looking back, that Bridge of Allan was an idyllic place to grow up.

Another writer had also loved his childhood days in the same haunts. "I shall never forget some of the days at the Bridge of Allan," Robert Louis Stevenson wrote. "They were one golden dream." He came on many occasions as a boy, with his mother or both parents, to get away from the unhealthy air of Edinburgh. For the Victorians, Bridge of Allan was the "queen of Scottish spas": it boasted scores of lodging houses and several large hotels, to which ailing visitors came in droves to take the waters enriched by minerals from the disused mines. Stevenson seems to have loved the open air, and especially walks along the Allan Water and excursions to Dumyat in the Ochil Hills.

There was a cave known as Stevenson's Cave, down by the river, which apparently was the model for Ben Gunn's cave in *Treasure Island*. As a young man he describes it like this:

> A large broken branch hung down over the mouth of it, and it was all cased in perfect ice. Every dock-leaf and long grass, too, was bearded with a shining icicle. And all the icicles kept dropping, and dropping and dropping, and had made another little forest of clear ice among the grasses and fallen branches and dockens below them. I picked up one of these branches and threw it on the ground; and all the crystal broke with a little tinkle, and behold! a damp stick.

A century on, that cave was still giving its ice performances. In spite of its association it was rather disappointing — dark and dripping for most of the year; the icicles of winter were the best thing about it. I think I must have thought that Stevenson sat and wrote in it, which didn't seem very appealing. Other places — islands in the river, and certain houses and hostelries in the village — have their Stevenson associations. He still haunts Bridge of Allan and, to a lesser extent, he haunted my childhood. Later, I came to love his work and to empathise with his strange half-dreaming, half-awake, never quite grown-up relationship with the world.

But though Stevenson was part of the history of the place, he was only a small part. Vital and decisive chunks of Scottish history were played out in the area around Stirling. One of my favourite views is from the top of Drumbrae, the hill at the back of Bridge of Allan which in the 1980s my father, as a community councillor, fought to preserve from being covered in houses. From here you can see the flat expanse of the Carse, the mountains rising in the north-west, the start of the Ochils to the east, the Campsie Fells to the south-west, the meeting of Forth, Teith and Allan Water below you; Stirling Castle is on its rock and beyond it is the Gillies Hill from which Bruce's "second army" of camp followers descended on the English at Banockburn; nearer to hand is the Abbey Craig on which stands the Victorian monument to William Wallace. Behind, out of sight but a reminder of how quickly one can pass from built-up into wild Scotland, lies the great waste of Sheriffmuir, where yet another battle was once fought. You can see the truth of the 19th-century writer Alexander Smith's remark that "Stirling, like a huge brooch, clasps Highlands and Lowlands together". Often when we had visitors, and sometimes when we did not, we climbed the two hundred and forty-six steps of the Wallace Monument, counting them all, and stared out over this landscape. How could it not stir deep emotions in any child with an imagination?

Our large Victorian house had three storeys, the third — which was where I spent most of my time — being an attic space accessed by a steep staircase. Up there were four wood-panelled rooms with coombed ceilings, three with skylights and one with a dormer window. My brother had his electric train set in one of these rooms, and I played with my toy soldiers in another. The third contained the cold water tank and was used for storage. The fourth, the one with the dormer, I eventually took over as my bedroom, when my brother and I exhausted our tolerance of sharing a room. From this eyrie I could look out on the surrounding houses and gardens, play music at whatever volume I wanted, read books and hammer away at my typewriter without disturbance. Summoning me to meals stretched the vocal chords and the patience of other family members. I was, in effect, away in another world.

Throughout my childhood Bridge of Allan's separateness, its uniqueness, was gradually being eroded. New housing estates were built; the University of Stirling opened in Airthrey's grounds in 1967; the M9 motorway bypassing the old A9 north through Stirling and Bridge of Allan was constructed across the Carse between 1969 and 1974; Cornton Vale prison was completed in 1975; local government reorganisation in 1973-4 centralised council powers in Stirling. This process of change was not new: the village's growth in the 19th century — before which, according to Miller's *Handbook of Central Scotland*, "a narrow hump-backed bridge, an old-fashioned mill and kiln, a wayside inn, a smithy, with a few hovel-looking huts constituted the sum and substance of the place" — was far more extensive; but each generation thinks its experience unlike anything that has gone before, and that nothing will ever be the same again. Which of course is true. My parents moved away from Bridge of Allan in the Thatcherite 1980s, when it became even wealthier than it ever had been, and on the odd occasion when I pass through now, it does seem very altered, and nothing much to do with me any more.

In the 1960s and 1970s something like four per cent of the Scottish population were educated at private schools. The percentage of the Bridge of Allan population must have been substantially higher: many of the sons and daughters of my parents' friends went to private schools or to grant-aided ones like Dollar Academy. My sister went to a girls' school called The Beacon, a few hundred yards down our road. My brother and I went to Hurst Grange, a prep school in Stirling. Hurst Grange, which took in about a hundred boys, occupied three or four houses in Victoria Place overlooking the King's Park, joined into one complex warren of corridors, basements, dormitories and classrooms. I was there from the age of six to thirteen, and probably got the best of my education there.

The headmaster was a man called Tim Brown, who ruled with iron authority and who discouraged, in fact forbade, parents from entering the premises unless they had made an appointment to see him. He was nicknamed "the Boss" and it was a very brave or foolish boy who crossed him. While he could be kind and entertaining, he was also capable of terrifying outbursts of temper, and was intolerant of boys who failed to come up to his exacting academic standards. He taught Latin, which we all took from the age of nine, and these classes were nerve-racking ordeals if you were unsure of your conjugations or the construction of an ablative absolute. Physical violence used by adults on children in the classroom was not, of course, restricted to private schools in the 1960s, but it was fairly widespread at Hurst Grange. In one of the Molesworth books by Geoffrey Willans and Ronald Searle, those hilarious, frighteningly accurate portraits of prep school life, there is a "table of grips and tortures for masters", including "the side hair tweak", "the headshave with ruler" and "the plain blip for numskulls". All of these and others were in use at Hurst Grange. The Boss's heavy hand hovering above your head ready to strike while you declined a Latin noun is not easily forgotten.

But I was lucky, because I was academically inclined. There were others who suffered far more than I ever did. Minor misdemeanours could lead to detention, lines, or a "black mark" entered on the school notice-board: serious offences, or the acquisition of three black marks, resulted in a beating with a gym-shoe in the Boss's study. "Six of the best": that phrase, once ironical, now sounds rather sordid. There was also a kind of Old Testament moral code whereby the entire school would suffer for the malefactions of one or two. For example, there was an allowance of three sweets a day handed out to boarders, but if Brown found three dropped sweet papers the ration would be stopped for everybody for a week. One year, the annual Halloween party, one of the great events of the school calendar, was cancelled because of some lapse in behaviour of which we were all, apparently, guilty. We railed against the unfairness of this blanket dispensation of justice and against other kinds of intimidation, but we were generally a polite, orderly and litter-conscious set of children.

Religion of a traditional Presbyterian variety underpinned the ethos of the school. Brown also taught Scripture, and he led the daily morning assembly which included a hymn, Bible reading and prayers. For boarders – I was a boarder for my last two years there, as this was considered necessary preparation for public school – there was an additional evening service of about fifteen minutes before tea, and on Sundays we went to the local church in the morning and had a school service in the late afternoon. There were other activities like Scripture Union and the Scouts where Christian moral values were taught. I was a very holy boy so long as I was at that school, and although I have long since ceased to attend church or to hold, in any formal sense, religious beliefs, I am grateful for the fact that the education I received there gave me a thorough grounding in the Christian heritage, without which so much classic literature must remain half a mystery. I am also well aware that, whatever kind of agnostic or atheist I may be, I am first and foremost a Presbyterian one. The democratic and egalitarian aspects of Presbyterianism also, without question, informed my political views.

The other subject that Tim Brown taught, to Form Six, the most senior class, was English, and for that I owe him a great debt. He was incredibly encouraging to those of us with any talent for writing; he built into the school week a lot of time for reading and being read to, and he was excellent at giving us a taste of a wide range of English literature. (Scottish literature, except for a bit of Burns, didn't exist.) He could have been dismissive of my attempts to write a Western, but he wasn't. Again, though, I was lucky: poor spellers, or boys who simply could not grasp the workings of English grammar, received little mercy from him.

He died in May 2004, at the age of ninety, having been retired in Gargunnock for the better part of thirty years. In September, the *Daily Record* ran a story headed 'Teacher's Millions Stun Pals'. It turned out that he had amassed a small fortune of £2.2 million. Most of it went to charity, including the Scripture Union and Gargunnock Parish Church. He was a major influence on me, one way and another.

He did not, however, have any role in feeding my infatuation with the American West. I don't know where this came from, but "cowboys and Indians" were a fairly prominent part of popular culture then, in comics, novels, films and TV shows, and I was fascinated from about the age of five. There was, in particular, something exotic and wild about American Indians that intrigued and excited me. As I read and learned more about them, I developed a sense of outrage that they had, for the most part, been grossly mistreated and crushed by an overwhelmingly more powerful civilisation. I found that, in history, I usually took the side of people who had opposed the high and mighty. There was an Italian tribe called the Samnites who humiliated a Roman army at a narrow pass called the Caudine Forks, making the Romans pass under a yoke of three spears in token of their defeat. I liked the Samnites for this, although they paid for it later. Likewise, the Zulus, the Maoris, the Sioux, the Modocs and the Apaches all got my vote. I always wanted people to win who, in reality, had generally lost. Is there some Scottish connection here? What Scottish patriot, however much they may be grateful to Robert the Bruce for winning at Bannockburn, does not feel a closer kinship with William Wallace?

History informed my imagination from the beginning. I started writing creatively almost as soon as I could write physically, and usually wrote about the past. There were always books in the house, but why I should have decided so early that I wanted to write them as well as read them I have no idea. Certainly by the time I was eight or nine I was writing stories, drawing cartoons and planning a multi-volume saga set, I think, in a U.S. cavalry outpost in Arizona. When I was ten my parents gave me a portable typewriter for Christmas, an Imperial Good Companion which I still have even though I've long since abandoned working on it in favour of computer. It was small but robust, which was just as well for on it I battered out a history of the Plains Indian wars of the 19th century and many, many pages of fiction. By the time I was sixteen I had started many books and actually completed two, both of which I had tried — and failed — to get published. It was quite an isolated apprenticeship, but I improved at each attempt.

Round about then my attention was diverted from Westerns by the paintings of Rene Magritte, Paul Delvaux and Salvador Dali, and by the idea of automatic writing and delving into the subconscious for subject matter. I tracked down an edition of Lautreamont's *Chants de Maldoror* and was thrilled by descriptions of God staggering around drunk and by the phrase which the Surrealist movement took as a motif, "beautiful as the chance encounter of a sewing machine and an umbrella on a dissecting table". I wrote a collection of very odd short stories, which again, luckily, never found a sympathetic publisher. I assumed I was Bridge of Allan's only surrealist, but there were probably several others, concealing their bizarre imaginary lives behind conventional, plooky facades.

A new library had opened in Bridge of Allan in 1971, with an extensive stock, and during the holidays I used to cycle down the hill at least once a week to hunt through the shelves. I had tickets for the main library in Stirling too, and W & R Holmes had a bookshop on Barnton Street where I spent many hours browsing: I read everything from Louis L'Amour to Flann O' Brien, George Eliot, P.G. Wodehouse, Thomas Hardy, Thomas Berger, Richard Brautigan, Jane Austen, Roald Dahl and very early Ian McEwan. Books have always been hugely important to me, a kind of backdrop against which the rest of my life has played out.

At thirteen I had left prep school and gone to Trinity College, Glenalmond. If Hurst Grange was, in many ways, a thoroughly Scottish school, Glenalmond was a little island of Englishness in the middle of Perthshire. It was a hellish place for anybody who was not a survivor, which fortunately I was. There were pupils there who were turned into emotional basket-cases by the isolation, the snobbery, the archaic traditions and rules, the emphasis on sports, the absence of home comforts and the ruthlessness of teenage boys in packs. Some of the teaching, particularly in the sciences, was of a truly appalling standard. Again, I was lucky: there were some very good teachers of English and History, the subjects I was best at. I can't say that I hated

Glenalmond at the time: I did well in class, I enjoyed rugby and the other outdoor activities, and I had friends. But I knew all along that I was in a very privileged and unusual place, and that not only was the rest of the world not like it, but that there was something fundamentally unjust and shameful about its exclusivity. As soon as I left I joined reality, and within a year had lost contact not only with the school but with almost all of my fellow-pupils, including all those I called my friends. Ideologically, ever since, I have been opposed to private education. The parts of my secondary education that were probably better than the education I might have got at a state school related to smaller class sizes and access to better extra-curricular facilities. Money was what made these things possible, and money would or could make them available to every child. Everything else that Glenalmond stood for — excessive wealth, a post-Empire imperial mindset and an ethos of acquisitive selfishness — I rejected. Quite apart from anything else, why was I always hungry there, and why did I reach the age of seventeen with virtually no notion of how to communicate with women?

But even as I ended my last term there, something happened that enabled me to break away from the expectations the school had of me. Having sat the Oxbridge entrance exam I journeyed to Cambridge to be interviewed for a place, to read History, at Downing College. My father and uncles had been there after the war. But a day and a night were enough to make me realise that Cambridge would be too much like Glenalmond for my liking — more cloisters and public schoolboys and, perhaps, more networks of snobbery and élitism. The dons who interviewed me told me that my papers had not been as good as they might have been. I was a borderline case: why had I picked Downing anyway? Only because my father and uncles had been there, I said innocently. Eyebrows were raised. Oh, well, we'd better find room for you then, was their reply. A few days later, back home, I duly received an offer of a place. Disgusted, I wrote back to say that I had decided to go to Edinburgh instead, where my brother had gone. I still have the two-line response that this impertinence generated. You can feel the outrage coming off the letter, which begins "Dear Robertson" and is unsigned. I am grateful for that letter. It always reminds me that I made the right decision.

Before I went to Edinburgh I spent six months working in the Safari Park at Blairdrummond. Many of the workers there were from the Raploch, a housing scheme in Stirling which, though only three miles from Bridge of Allan, might as well have been on another planet. As for Glenalmond, my workmates had never even heard of it. I went back to the Park for two subsequent summers, and it gave me at least as good an education as boarding-school. The hours were long and the pay poor, but the experience was invaluable. I saved up enough money to buy a small motorbike, and in October, considerably better attuned to reality than I had been a year before, I went to Edinburgh to be a student.

By this time my political opinions had formed into a socialism coloured by a strong infusion of nationalism. The next twenty years would see many people in Scotland, including myself, having to rethink not only the balance between these –isms, but the entire ideological basis of their political beliefs, in the light of the failed attempt to gain devolution in the 1970s, the triumph of Thatcherism, the collapse of the Soviet Union and the rise of single-issue politics. As an undergraduate, I was interested in radical politics but I never engaged with the various left-wing groups in the student body. I've always been shy of political posturing, of which there was a great deal, and I've always guarded my independence. I was also, to be honest, having too much of a good time to become seriously involved in political activity.

In 1978-9, I took part in an exchange scheme between the Universities of Edinburgh and Pennsylvania. I spent a year in Philadelphia, the first time — apart from a family holiday in Connemara in the west of Ireland ten years before — I had ever been out of the United Kingdom. There is no space here to describe the many ways that year opened my mind to the wider world, but it affected me profoundly. Not only did I inhabit another culture, and see places and landscapes of astonishing variety, but, having stepped outside Scotland, I saw my own country in a different light. I don't think I had ever seen the *possibilities* of Scotland so well before: in spite of my attachment to it, its limitations had always seemed greater. I had left not long after the agonising farce of the World Cup campaign in Argentina; while I was away, the confidence-sapping 1979 referendum on devolution took place, and then Margaret Thatcher came to power. The 1980s were to be a decade of government-inspired nastiness, and Scotland would enter a long and gloomy phase of self-reappraisal; but it is clear to me now that this was a necessary process, and that Thatcher, that arch-Unionist, did at least as much for the cause of Scottish self-government as any Scottish Nationalist.

In the same month of September that I went to Philadelphia, a poet died whose name meant almost nothing to me. Nevertheless, something in the obituaries of Hugh MacDiarmid, and the reviews of his posthumously published *Complete Poems*, made me sit up and take notice. I knew very little about Scottish literature, past or present, but MacDiarmid's fiery public persona, his linguistic and political extremism, excited me. I read what I could of his work in America, and on my return bought the *Complete Poems* and immersed myself in his poetry and his ideas. He unlocked thoughts and feelings in me as he did in many others. MacDiarmid never reached, and never will reach, a mass audience, but his effect on those whom his poetry does reach is incredible. It's not even a question of *liking* everything he wrote: one is simply overwhelmed by the beauty of some of his work, and by the audacity and scale and challenge of the rest. Some years later I wrote this:

> I came to poetry, and another view of Scotland
> Through MacDiarmid in the year he died.
> Pushing twenty-one, I became aware of motion,
> Mysteriously familiar, something lumbering through the mists
> Beyond mastodon and mammoth, and possibilities in waves
> Rolled in, their distant clashes flooding out
> The tannoyed voice announcing his departure.
> With a jolt I started, struck by the sudden staring sight
> Of my reflected ignorance, idle on the line,
> Sitting late and bland and patient in a standing train.
> A new-found anger knotted at the neck of my exclusive education
> And I began to deconstruct and reconstrue.

There is no doubt that MacDiarmid started a revolution in my head. I saw that all my writing and political thinking up to that point had hardly been writing and thinking at all, but marking time. From beyond the grave, this flawed but immense intellect started giving me lessons in everything. I began to read other Scottish literature, of every kind and from every era – a literature that nobody had told me even existed. I had not written much for several years, but now I began to write poetry, and to write, rather self-consciously and imitatively, in Scots – not the language of my upbringing, certainly not the language of my schooling, but a language that had been going on all around me, and that in some deep way I had tuned into, for years. It was curious that I should have wanted and needed to write in Scots. It was not my first tongue, yet somehow it enabled me to explore ideas that I could not reach, and to say things that I could not say, in any other way. "Names for nameless things" is a phrase in MacDiarmid's manifesto poem 'Gairmscoile' that comes to mind, yet my experience of the liberating attributes of writing in Scots was quite different from his, as his was quite different from that of other writers who, when they used Scots, were naming *familiar* things. The many different routes by which writers have come, and continue to come, to write in Scots, and in many varieties of Scots – despite all the pressures to write only in English – continue to prove that Scots is not just a spoken language but a living, developing and essential literary language too.

After university I went travelling again, to Australia and New Zealand. I worked my way around Australia, picking up jobs whenever the money ran low, then spent two months hitchhiking through New Zealand, which reminded me often of home. When I returned, it was to a dis-United Kingdom in the grip of recession, with unemployment rife and the Falklands war in the offing. I could not find a permanent job for more than a year, during which time I wrote another novel, again never published, before landing a job as a publisher's sales representative. I sold Berlitz pocket travel guides all over Scotland and the North of England for eighteen months, then I went back to Edinburgh University to do a PhD on aspects of the writings of Walter Scott. At this time I became politically active, mainly through my involvement in the magazine *Radical Scotland*, which sought to build bridges between nationalists, socialists, liberals, greens, feminists and others in the revitalised campaign for a form of self-government. The 1980s were years of frustration, despair and anger, but they were also, gradually, years of hope, determination and renewal.

I worked part-time and, once I had finished my PhD, full-time, in the first Waterstone's bookshop to open outside London, in Edinburgh's George Street. It was an exciting place to be, with readings and launches happening two or three times a week. Through these I met some of the old guard of Scottish poetry, men like Norman MacCaig, Sorley MacLean and Iain Crichton Smith, all of whom would die in the 1990s. In 1989 I transferred to Waterstone's Union Street branch in Glasgow. I had been having poems published in those literary magazines, like *Chapman* and *Cencrastus*, that played so important a part in revitalising Scottish cultural life in the 1980s, but by now I was writing fiction again. I put together a book of short stories, *Close*, and in 1991 the Edinburgh publisher B&W Publishing, then in its infancy, published it as a paperback in a print-run of a thousand copies. It did surprisingly well.

I have said almost nothing here about my personal life — about my family, friends and lovers: that would be a different exercise from this one. When I thought about what I would say in this essay, I imagined a trajectory that would describe my development as a writer, and that is what I have tried to keep foremost in mind. Obviously, one aspect of life can never be kept in isolation from all other aspects. Nevertheless, whatever else has happened to me, I have always managed to keep imagining myself as a writer, and that writer has, to some extent, remained a separate being. To maintain that separate, perhaps selfish space has been very important to me, and perhaps in late 1992 it asserted itself most strongly. I was still turning out stories, but I was the deputy manager of the bookshop, and my time for writing was limited to days off and sessions stretching into the small hours. I was also in a marriage that was unhappy and without hope. Something had to change.

Some time before I had seen an advertisement for a writer-in-residence post to be based at Brownsbank Cottage, near Biggar in Lanarkshire. Brownsbank was where MacDiarmid had settled in the 1950s, and where he had lived until his death in 1978. His widow Valda had stayed there alone for eleven more years until her own death in 1989. (I met her briefly, the year before her death, when she came to the Edinburgh branch of Waterstone's for the riotous, drunken launch of Alan Bold's biography of MacDiarmid.) The cottage had subsequently been bought and restored by the local museum, and preserved as a monument to the most significant Scottish writer of the 20th century. The advertisement was seeking a writer to live at Brownsbank and do creative work in the community as well as having time for his or her own writing. I assumed that this post would go to some well-known and well-established literary figure, but then I heard through another source that the Biggar Museum people were still looking for candidates, and that they, bearing in mind MacDiarmid's perpetual struggle for recognition and against poverty, were keen to encourage little-known writers to apply for the job. I phoned up for details, was encouraged by the positive response, and sent in an application. The interviews took place one January afternoon in 1993, and shortly after I got back to Glasgow that evening the phone rang, and I was offered the Brownsbank Fellowship.

If there has been one pivotal moment in my writing life more significant than any other, it was the day I arrived at Brownsbank in February 1993 to begin a two-year residency there. I was going to live and work in the tiny cottage, full of MacDiarmid memorabilia, in which the writer who had most heavily influenced me had once lived and worked. I drove down in a newly purchased, very used Volkswagen Polo (the first car I'd ever owned), a confusion of emotions raging through my mind. It was cold and wet that night, and the cottage too was cold and damp. I lay in my sleeping-bag on what had been Valda's bed, listening to mice scurrying around in the roof-space above me, and wondering what on earth I was doing there. But, really, I knew what I was doing. I was a month short of my thirty-fifth birthday, and I was making a new beginning. I was finally about to be what I had, from the age of seven or eight, always intended to be: I was about to be a writer.

Alexander Stoddart

Born Edinburgh, 30th May 1959

SCULPTOR

Looking for Silence : How I discovered Thorvaldsen

It is as though the vast and the unexpected had a purpose, and that purpose were the showing to mankind in rare glimpses what places are designed for the soul — those ultimate places where things common become shadows and fail, and the divine part in us, which adores and desires, breathes its own air, and is at last alive.

Hilaire Belloc — *The Inn of the Margeride*

I wish in this essay to give the gist of a particularly tatty period in my career, when hopelessness of any future as an artist opened up for me an unimpaired vision of what I should be as an artist. This unhappy spell ended in my arrival at a certain door, in a certain European city, with my pride in ruins around me and my clothes in no better condition.

With no prospects ahead, and no real achievement behind me, I found myself in Kensington Gardens in London upon a fearsomely cold winter's morning in 1981 with my friend Tom McEwan. We had been at the Glasgow School of Art together, and he had come south shortly after our leaving in 1980, to learn how to be a brass engraver in an Eastend workshop. Tom came from Dalry in Ayrshire and had an entirely rural outlook on life.

He had taken lodgings in a single room in a very drab commercial hotel in the Baker Street area of the city. I was visiting for a few days and illegally sleeping on the floor, quite unpadded, with only a coat for a cover. There was just enough floor-space between his bed and the wardrobe to let me stretch out and the temperature was so low that there was little washing or changing. We didn't hang about in the mornings, but checking the coast, smuggled me out into the blasting six o'clock proto-dawn to find a cup of coffee. He was off to Braham's workshop for his early start; the trades all start early. I would wait for the libraries to open at their convenience. I was booked in at the Royal Academy to go through the archive of the 19th century sculptor Sir Francis Chantrey. There was lots of time to kill, chittering on doorsteps, studying the masonry detailing.

Then came a morning, colder than ever, when Tom had the day off, so we headed out at the usual hour for Kensington Gardens to do something before the museums opened. We were going to see a specific work of sculpture, situated at the intersection of two paths above a broad sweep of grass. There, in the sounding park and the half light, rose the equestrian statue known as "Physical Energy", the brazen titan by George Frederic Watts, about which we had read a good deal, but of which we had seen, really, nothing. We kicked about the base of the structure for a while, inspecting from all angles. One of us (I don't know which) then came out with it; the usual, tired old stock response to any sight of this preternatural object. If you see a painting by Lucian Freud then you ought at some point to recite the following words; "I really love the way he paints *flesh!*" So it is that when you see "Physical Energy" you are obliged to make the observation that no horse ever stands like that, except if it is urinating. This fact told, you will find yourself liberated from the spell of the statue and safely transported back to the land of the living.

People have been making the urination comment about "Physical Energy" for over a hundred years. Only last week, here in 2004, I had it rehearsed yet again to me over the 'phone by a truly great architectural historian. So no matter who or what you are, stripling youth or sage veteran, the remark is viable. I had the suspicion back in '81 that saying this about the horse was saying something about the nature of this kind of work *itself;* a measure taken to protect oneself against this *kind* of work. I still believe that today. The comment is the sound of the world guarding itself against the threat of ideal art. The horse's posture is no real occasion for mirth — rather it is a superb piece of sculptural composition — but the rider's face has an undoubtedly terrible, aesthetical aspect and because of this we reach for our toilet-talismans. Tom and I followed suit and had our wee nervous laugh.

I had struggled through art school in Glasgow much against the general drift. The sculpture department was in a low state of morale and, knowing this, I'd elected to go there in order to pursue a radically avant-garde programme of "art-making" as some contemporists still describe it. I needed a weak context in which to try out my notions. I greatly admired the autodestructive artist Yves Klein, often looking with admiration at a photograph I had of that unfortunate man hurling himself off a wall in a suburb of Paris. I, of course, could not do this, but I did throw a sculptural experiment made of very heavy cardboard tubing off a fire-escape at the back of the first-year building. It landed in the lane off Bath Street, a matter of inches from a parked car. Astonishingly I had not checked to see how the land lay down there prior to my art-deed. My heart thrilled and my limbs weakened. Conveniently, a rubbish skip lay a few paces off. No camera recorded this event, but about a year later another student tried something similar. He squirted same paint out of a window and spattered a passing lady's tights. She complained to the school authorities. He had to recompense and write a sorry-note. So much for the cutting edge.

By the time I got into the sculpture department I was near insane with the effort of sustaining such stupidity. So I swung in another direction to follow a brutalist/formalist path, much in favour in sculpture in those days. You found a railway sleeper, preferably one rather the worse for wear, then wrapped it in a coil of barbed wire. Onto the barbs you hung a series of, say, smoked mackerel — the better through which to appreciate the "spatial relationships inherent in the intervals between wood, tar, and metal." The impaled fish would introduce an element of pathos about which you would rather keep quiet; compassion was not in favour. But you were expected to march against Nazis. You wore a waistcoat, smoked a pipe and drank lots of beer. I looked like a child extra from Oliver!

We were never taken on any official tour of an art gallery or museum, but did get bussed down to Port Glasgow to see a ship-yard in operation. *The* ship-yard, I suppose. We glumly looked at a propeller and fancied we saw sculptural potential there. As far as I know no team of naval architects ever visited the GSA Sculpture Department in an equal quest for enlightenment as to the "way forward" for shipbuilding. The girls seemed to specialise in sticking twigs together with rat-spit.

I remember hearing in panic that one couldn't pass into the third year without having done some welding — and I'd done none. So I welded two five-inch rods of mild steel together at the last minute, and secured my mortal fate. Of course, not one jot of life drawing was required, nor the slightest morsel of clay modelling.

I often notice how glamorous welding seems to careless and impressionable people, especially those who make up the ranks of the modem art mandarin class. They pay no attention to the great big neoclassical sculptures I make, and base no respect for me upon that foundation; but once they see me welding everything changes. Somewhere along the way they think that this semi-skill proves me a "man of the people", rather than an aesthete fixated on Ludwig II of Bavaria. They can "relate" to me as a constructivist. Next they are observing how the rough welded armature has "a sculptural identity of its own", which is only a last minute plea to me to stop right there.

I'd done a pop-riveted construction which had been a hit at a tutorial. On leaving the Macintosh building that night, I passed the plaster cast of the Apollo Belvedere which still stood in the foyer of the School at that time. I knew nothing about the resounding culture lurking behind this stalking figure; it was simply a form which belonged to that category of shapes which I was rapidly learning were irrelevant, reactionary and Aryanist. It was a great comfort to be gathering the knowledge of exactly how reprehensible such items of antique art were. Imagine if, on the contrary, these objects represented a paradigm of goodness! What a pickle we would all be in, for they would be so hard to emulate and deeply troublesome to make. Thankfully, we were certain that culture-free constructivism on the one hand, object-free conceptualism on the other, and an all-round embrace of the pig-ugly was the route-royal to the moral high ground. There was almost a curricular duty upon us to ridicule the fragmentary remains of the masterpieces of antiquity. Has anyone ever done a study of the pyschological imperative that makes young men, especially at art-school in the 1970s, draw on the nipples, eyes and pudenda of plaster-casts?

Praise to the god! Hot and smug from my recent pop-rivet triumph, yet I was quite arrested by a sudden intimation, upon sight of the Apollo, that it was certainly — absolutely undoubtedly — a perfect fraud and outright lie that I had done anything of even the slightest worth. In later times, when describing this epiphany for purposes of teaching, I have illustrated the intimation in verbal terms: "The god said to me, etc . . . " The great truth, which I'll disclose here, is that of course the message was given precisely without speech, and that this is of the utmost importance, this speechlessness, in the later unfolding of my headlong career.

It was all in the sight of it; purely in the percept. The concept of admiring this cast of the Apollo lagged far behind the roaring imperative of the knowledge-free percept laid plainly before me. They say that Socrates, having been seduced by a flow of argument, found himself speaking against Love and that, upon crossing a brook he had been rebuked for it by his *deamon* - his personal genius; what we would now call conscience. He had been provoked by his accomplishments into riding roughshod over the name of a god. It is so often our accomplishments that bring us to iniquity; our knacks and talents; our sophistries. A later philosopher, Chrysippus the Stoic, warns us that these accomplishments are like wayside inns into which we are in danger of falling, forgetting the road to our homes, our fatherlands and our families in the general carousing. So it was only a kind of accomplishment that earned me a good criticism for my little metal construction. What I was experiencing before the image of the god on the other hand (and do not forget that in paganism the image *is* the god) was in fact a glorious dissolution of all my skills and talents, a banishment of my dialectical ingenuity; a non-participation, an obliteration.

What the statue made me understand above all was that I was not needed. We used to tell young men this important information in all sort of ways, until quite recently. Structures of mortification existed in military service, apprenticeships and in bureaucratic postings where the central message given to the young man was that the older he became the more he would be respected and "empowered". Seniority was the thing. Thus he learned to imitate his elders, which was only in fact to rehearse his own self of the future. In this way he was taken out of his self of the present – his contemporary self. He gained practical experience of an actual selflessness, which made him able to apply this frame of mind to his social conduct. Society was made better. Modernism, the rump end of which I was suffering at art school, made contrary injunctions. You were encouraged to do your own thing, and to value it as your own. And the problem of young men, which is the big problem in all societies, was diverted in a gender consciousness which needlessly incorporated the female into the crisis. In truth, society is never in any danger from women, no matter how many of them fancy they might have a viable trouble-making role. Strife is only fomented authentically by the male youth; to stamp on him is precisely the role of the patriarchy. Many years later I discovered that the Apollo Belvedere has in its mythological sources a relation to the question of the patriarchy; how it arrived, and under what divine aegis. For it is a *sauroctonos*; a lizard-slayer, or a serpent-killer.

Now, I trundled along on a Rodinesque ticket for the remainder of my time at art school. It was a stop-gap measure. You couldn't attempt the Belvedere for fear of your miserable little qualification, and there was no tutor to assist the young student who aimed for the traditions of the Occident. But Rodin was a possibility; gestural, kind of rough and incompetent, carnal, on the cusp of modernism and above all fragmentary. The instinct to throw objects from high places still prevailed.

Nowadays in architecture schools there is a tacit policy to fail all students who attempt classical design. You are instantly marked down in a draconianism typical of those regimes who hungrily search out evidence of artistic degeneracy. But in the late 1970s the idea that any art student would be looking towards the grand tradition in a non-ironic, quite sincere way was so outlandish that no serious structures of prevention were yet in place, in the way they are today. I slipped through, largely because of the lack of vigilance, the basic decency and kindness of my tutors; their existential simplicity. They were all great admirers of tools and materials, and drawing was a matter of "mark-making". They were, in fact, the very ones who used to be artists before the Enlightenment put the injunction upon us all to be philosophers too.

There is a kind of sunshine that pours up Bath Street in Glasgow in the mid afternoon in the summer. It seems to rest in the dust that gathers in the corners between the free-stone verticals of the buildings and the pitted concrete horizontals of the pavements. The dust and the wan glory mix to give remnant form to the 19th century. All has strengthened and declined. A man might scoop up some of this powder and fancy he holds in his hands relic evidence of Israel in Egypt. Faith of the Patriarchs, rule of the elders; this light and remnant masonry are the substances of the Presbytery. They are recorded in the paintings of Roberts and McCulloch and Hill, and the stuff can still be seen today in pockets around that deserted area down from Blytheswood Square. I was crouching there with my fingers in the dust, leaning my head on my arm against the church wall, giggling and distraught. The notice in the art school corridor had listed my name against a BA 1st class Honours designation. I was one of the elect. I walked some more, then ran a little, turning and turning, and tittering. By no stretch of the imagination had this been a Degree, first class or otherwise. It was only a devalued Diploma, as Art School Degrees still are to this day. Had it been a Diploma, in the old DA style, then I should have failed; an untutored, undisciplined rascal. I decided to go and get a degree, at University.

I made an appointment to speak to the Head of the Department of Fine Art at the University of Glasgow, Professor Ronald Pickvance. He had a look of Henley and wore white gloves for a skin condition, so it was said. He was very friendly and told me that I wasn't allowed to be an Undergraduate again, and that I'd only be admitted into the University as a Post-Graduate. Then I could get a grant. My degree was very good and I shouldn't disregard what I had managed so far. My final year dissertation (a very primitive study of the 19th century Glasgow sculptor John Mossman) had been highly regarded, and this would be enough to let me enter Post-Graduate studies at the level of M. Lit. So here is the comic thing; I entered Glasgow University with the Art School behind me, crowing about having had a student go on to University from an Art School degree, while that student himself had approached the

University precisely to gain that level of primary scholarship which the Art School had failed to insist upon. Yet flattery opens a wide and ceremonial portal in the youthful conscience, so in I swept to the vale of tears known as "Post-Graduate Research".

They gave me a room in University Gardens where I sat in misery for nearly three years. Being upgraded to Ph.D studies only depressed and emburdened me the more. I adored and rejoiced in the works of the Victorian sculptors I was set to study, and felt myself charged to bring forward their forgotten names: but this was all I wanted to do; to sit in their company, solitary in the gathering dust of the Necropolis of Glasgow, or under the *telamones* that bear up the lintel of the old St. Andrew's Halls. I devoured archive material concerning the struggles and tragedies, as well as the local triumphs, of these sound and accomplished men and read far into the night in the Mitchell Library. Sometimes I would unearth a photograph of one of them, dead a hundred years and more. There was James Fillans, with his daughter Wilhelmina. She had had a fine medallion hand. Her father never failed in a bust. Old John Henning, stooping beside a metope from the Parthenon, exhausted after those years of tortuous reconstruction in terrific miniature of the Frieze from Athens. Pirate-copied throughout Europe, his intaglios brought him no fortune and he died in London in that increasingly familiar poverty that seemed to conclude so many of the biographies I learnt by heart. William Behnes literally found dead in a gutter somewhere near the Middlesex Hospital, threepence in his pocket. For every successful John Mossman there was always a tragic brother George; the latter a still uncounted member of that elusive body of sculptors who can be associated with the Pre-Raphaelite movement; he had been at the Royal Academy when the tyros of The Brotherhood were exchanging red painting grounds for white and sniping at the regime of Sir "Sloshua" Reynolds. He died in Glasgow aged forty. The merchants of the city scraped together a relief fund for his wife and children.

Here was a photograph of one John Steell in ardent youth, beardless and lean, with thick curls and no knighthood. There was a look of radical Europe in the picture, and more yet in the same photographer's account of the outstanding Edinburgh architectural sculptor Alexander Handyside Ritchie from whom my thoughts are still never far. In the backgrounds of these photographs I could sense the nation of Scotland staggering from some recent upheaval. As the subjects themselves had been woken up to the understanding that, while once they were just masons, now they could be true artists with the remit to monumentalise cities, so the background air in the pictures seemed "charged" with the consciousness of morning. I was looking, in my long days of idle study, into the rooms and darknesses of post-Disruption Scotland; the devastation after the storm.

I still find it hard to fathom how it can be that the Scots know so little about the single most important event for them in the 19th century, the Great Disruption of the Church of Scotland in 1843. The twentieth century was pretty keen on revolutions, but they had to be secular for the lefty little Scots. Being "out in the '43" was equivalent to mounting a barricade in Dresden against Prussia acting for the Palatinate, or stirring up the kind of turmoil that necessitated some serious city re-planning by the Baron Hausmann in Paris, but it cut no ice with the inheritors of revolution in 1980s Scotland.

The Disruption was necessitated by the overwhelming desire, particularly in rural Scotland, to end the rule of patronage, where the laird chose the minister of the parish. Reacting against this, the "evangelicals" proposed an out-and-out Presbyterianism. The word derives from the Greek for "old man", so this revolution advocated that the elders of the parish should choose the minister. This was an extremely radical proposal, and not exactly the sort of insurrectionary programme to be run to the sound of Jimmy Somerville. But in the Tanfield Hall in Edinburgh, after the 470 ministers had marched out of the General Assembly to organise themselves into "the First General Assembly of the Free Church of Scotland", whereby they did "separate from and abandon the present subsisting ecclesiastical Establishment in Scotland, and renounce all rights and emoluments pertaining to them in virtue thereof," were not the voices of Chalmers and Welsh drowned in the general tumult? Were not the names of Wallace and Bruce heard shouted above the din? Was the nation not, quite simply, beside itself?

Most revolutions are grubby, optimistic, money-grabbing affairs; personal advancement "by other means". The Disruption, however, settled itself in the lonely and untended churches we see all around the country today. Scotland had gone on to double its stock of ecclesiastical architecture and, by virtue of the appeal of the evangelicals to religious antiquity, so the antique style of building (Grecian for building, Hebrew for faith) survived later in Scotland than in England. Yes, we built in Gothic too, but the need for the temple and for the austerity of the Doric order continued. We had confirmed our national style. This is why I do deplore the common use today of the expression "cultural Presbyterian". When I think of Presbyterianism I think of Hugh Millar, McCosh of Princeton University and the classical philologists of mid-19th century Edinburgh. Looking further I see the quest to recover the lost Semitic order in Greek Thomson's St. Vincent Street Church as related to that glorious sunburst of continent, reasonable religiosity. I see the Disruption in our garden cemeteries and in every edifice erected by the Glasgow City Improvement Trust towards the end of the 19th century. The very stones seem to be hewn by cultivated, god-fearing hands. So it must be wrong to use the words "cultural" or "Presbyterian" to describe the grinning philistines we mean. For me, Edinburgh's Calton Hill, sometimes positively opalescent in the light of evening, is the very image of Cultural Presbyterianism. Donald Dewar is quite another thing.

The stones of Glasgow had whispered to me their fatal national date; 1843. By its lead I would be taken away from my contemporary times for ever and be alerted to the necessity to act upon conscience, *renouncing all rights and emoluments*. In a roundabout way this date would also take me to the geographical destination of this story.

At last the Royal Academy opened its doors. In under ten minutes, I suppose, I had found all I needed to know from Chantrey's archive. All that waiting and freezing. My glasses had hardly de-misted when it was time to put my notebook back in my schoolbag, get back into my soaking coat, and face teeming old Piccadilly once more. I would go to an art gallery - again. Tom would be finished by six o'clock, so that just left eight hours to burn away. There was always the Royal Artillery Memorial. My days were spent in the shelter of monuments.

Back in Glasgow I had to report to my supervisor Dr Alan Tait. I was very afraid of this man, for I found I could not write for him. I think I could not write anyway, but for him I felt especially illiterate. I did not write for him in the same way as I could not practise for my piano teacher. Come to think of it, one bore a striking resemblance to the other. Standing outside Tait's office, bottling up to knock, I found my face so cold and the skin stretched so tightly across it, that I paused a moment to rub and exercise the mouth and eye regions. Shutting my eyes I mouthed some wide, gaping facial gestures; oohs and eehs performed silently, and lots of brow-puckering and gurning. This would flex the musculature and aid my performance before my inquisitor whom I found, upon opening my eyes, to be standing directly in front of me in his doorway. He was pausing. Then he battered past me to speak at the department secretary. I drifted into his office thinking that things had gone far enough. Looking out of his window onto University Avenue I saw happy students meeting each other, clutching bundles of notes and planning their lunchbreaks; the very undergraduates I had wanted to be among. I was the guy with the steamed-up glasses, the steaming coat, the master of the near-empty note-book (I had tens of them), the solitary face-contortionist with no class-mates. Time to chuck it.

But of course I didn't have the nerve, and instead sprang into action upon Tait's return to tell him I had dug up an "interesting lead" and was sure there was documentary evidence in Copenhagen concerning Handyside Ritchie's youthful sojourn as a student of sculpture in Rome. I should cross the very North Sea to spend a further ten minutes before some letter or other, in some grim archive. I called it devotion, but wasn't it all really simple avoidance? In any case, Tait agreed I might go and told me to "run along".

I took a route that put crossing the North Sea to the end of my trip. In fact I arrived in Copenhagen via London, Paris, Milan, Florence, Pisa, Munich and Hannover. Crossing the Brenner Pass on the way north again, and having no seat on the train, I found myself in the night-long company of a Viennese fellow in the gangway, next to a toilet that had being acting above and beyond the call of duty since Naples. My companion was some kind of ticketless criminal with a pile of car number-plates tightly tied together and hung over his shoulder like a mercenary's gun. He was always looking up and down the interior of the train, anticipating the arrival of the ticket inspector. Mercifully the train was going slowly on the upward trudge over the Alps when this desperate individual suddenly opened the window and disappeared into the night, his number-plates clanking after him. Aghast, I turned to see the ticket inspector open the door to our gangway and ask to see my ticket. Something stopped me from crying "man overboard!"

In a few moments the window was opened again, and in came our now rather windswept bravo. He pulled the trick again, soon after, when the inspector was on his way back down the train. Somehow he knew how to cling onto the outside of a moving train. I thought that to save on expenses some people will go to any lengths. Yet he must have an exciting life, I mused, as the train lumbered onwards, and upwards, towards Ritchie's letter in Copenhagen. Perhaps it would be a letter. Or maybe just a receipt.

I had only a small foil-wrapped piece of Parmesan cheese to eat on the Hannover-to Copenhagen leg of my journey. The skies were brightening and the land flattening, and my new companions in the Pullman carriage were agreeably self-contained — each with a valid ticket and as chatty as an Edinburger. I drifted in and out of sleep.

At a port north of Lubeck the train stopped to be loaded in total onto a ferry. Out came the passengers to mingle on the decks. Now the air was truly delightful and the sun burst out over the stretch of Baltic between Germany and Demnark, the low-profiled island of Lolland before us. When I think back to that crossing I feel returning to me the same strange sense of deep gratitude and overwhelming felicity. Perhaps it is only my subsequent returning and returning to Copenhagen that enchants my recollections and reforms my memories. But no; I maintain I felt a blessing put upon me as the happy land of the Danes approached.

And so I came to Copenhagen's famous train station which everyone who goes there admires. An undercroft of steel trusses and concrete, like a sight of the Occupation still available, opens to a superstructure, in a National style, of stone and mighty wood. There I found accommodation in a suburb, but not to waste the afternoon (and now to placate a certain sense of urgency building around my errand) I set off in the direction of the Christiansborg Palace in the warm afternoon through the quiet streets. Before that edifice, as though protected by the State and Monarchy of Denmark, insulated from the city itself by a redundant canal, I first saw Thorvaldsen's Museum. In those days the front door, in the middle of the facade, was the way in. I mean, the entrance was the entrance. Now the side door is the entrance, in the peculiar way that progress seems to demand. It's a most divine side door, I hasten to mention, and always a pleasure to use, but what is wrong with the front door? I am saying that I entered the Thorvaldsen Museum "on the axis". I could have changed my name to Paul.

Bertel Thorvaldsen died in 1844, the most famous artist (not just sculptor) alive. Before him the most famous artist in the world had been Antonio Canova, another sculptor. He had died in 1822. For about half a century in Europe art had meant above all *sculpture*. After Thorvaldsen, art would turn to music (in my view a logical and philosophically sound recourse), but what "condition of music" could be found in the saved plaster models, studies and colossi of Denmark's national hero! Late in his life the Danes sent a frigate, the *Rota*, to Italy to collect the man himself and all his studio effects and bring them back to Denmark so that the sculptor might die on Danish soil. They commissioned a young architect named Bindesboll to design a museum for the original models and collected marbles, and sited it in the bosom of the capital's city-plan. "It's more your museum than mine," grumbled the old sculptor to the young architect, but nobody was really complaining. If you look at the paintings of Denmark's "Golden Age of Art" you'll soon see how friendly everybody was.

The *Rota* was carrying Thorvaldsen's personal stuff too. Today his coat and top hat can be seen on display beside his medicine chest (glass phials containing crystals and powders; one marked *cannabis*), and his canes and sashes and badges of honour. There lies the emblazon of his Papal Knighthood — and him brought up a Lutheran, and never a convert, and indeed not a believer in any solid sense. His letters came to Copenhagen too, and amongst them I found the one I wanted. It was from Ritchie to Thorvaldsen, starting "Caro Cavaliere Alberto . . . " (Dear Sir Bertel). Ritchie had gone to Thorvaldsen for tuition as a matter of course; there was thought to be something properly "Presbyterian" in the old sculptor's style, with its appeal to the archaic and its eschewal of glorious polish, such as is found in Canova. I found a photograph of Thorvaldsen, making the sign of the Evil Eye at the camera, in the year of his death. How could he have known that the camera would be the death of modern art?

I cannot remember a word of Ritchie's letter. The truth is that I was in no state to read or understand anything, for the second instance of form overwhelming the conceptual faculty was upon me. So I spent the next five days starving from lack of money, dumbstruck in the Thorvaldsen Museum before the same thing as I had seen in the foyer of the Glasgow School of Art. What is it? Words cannot tell, for they are too crude an instrument.

One thing was for certain. I must leave words and try to become a perceptual (not merely conceptual) artist. I returned home from Esbjerg to Hull, and then - not to Glasgow, for my research was from that moment doomed - but to Paisley where I had always lived and in which I would attempt my career. There I received a letter from the poet Ian Hamilton Finlay. Words again. So I set what I had seen in the Foyer, and in Kensington Gardens and in Copenhagen aside once more, and trucked again with the modern, contingent world, reviving the worst parts of my character for the purpose. A five-year indenture to Little Sparta and the charms of post-modern referencing almost brought me to self-destruction. My work was only saved, some years later, by the appearance at my studio of a kind modernist architect called David Page. By then, of course, my actual life had been saved by a girl. She had held on to me throughout the years with Finlay, gripping tight though I turned into a scorpion, a torrent, a mad dog, a thundercloud and a hot coal. Was it Voltaire who said "We are always poor executants of other people's ideas"? Undoubtedly it causes terrible spasms.

We live lives of fantastic counterpoint. In this story I've sung only one voice of an infinitely more complex fugue, and only over a short passage. Centrally, the theme is the telling of how a young man, posing as an artist, removed himself from the temptations of conceptual contemporism through the sight of certain works of sculpture: *The Apollo Belvedere*, a Roman copy of a Greek original of the fifth century BC; *Physical Energy*, a bronze equestrian made between c. 1870 and 1904 by the English painter George Frederic Watts (1817-1904); the 1801 study for an unexecuted statue of Achilles and Penthesilea by Bertel Thorvaldsen (1770-1844), and the Jason and the Adonis by that same sculptor. Before all these works, and many more in the same class, I still find myself silent. I have even made one myself before which I dare not speak.

The French Symbolist Odilon Redon believed that recourse to language in art was always undertaken in the context of some "plastic failure". His address was to "those who yield, quietly and without the assistance of sterile explanations, to the secret and mysterious laws of the sensibility of the heart." We find it hard to yield, and harder still to shut up. And I believe that the modern — the "contemporary" — Scot, perhaps above all national types, lives in perfect terror of the secret and the mysterious, and wages ceaseless mental fight against any sensibility of the heart. My struggle with that very Scot (the Scot of modern power) is the subject of another story.

Jackie Kay

Born Edinburgh, 9th November 1961

POET AND WRITER OF SHORT STORIES

Saltire First Book of the Year, The Adoption Papers, *1992*

A Dance with Fate

These poems were provoked and inspired by finding my birth father and going to visit him in Nigeria. He was a leading ethnobotanist which made me think a lot about trees and roots. But he was also a born again Christian and insisted on praying for me for a full two hours. The whole experience made me think again about what is real and what is received, what is truth and what is fiction. It seemed to me that life is a long dance with fate, fact and fiction. These poems form part of a sequence in my new collection *Life Mask.* I was interested in writing about what we conceal and what we reveal. Oscar Wilde said 'A mask tells us more than a face'.

A WHITE AFRICAN DRESS

Yesterday, as I thought about what my father wore
That Sunday in Abuja when we first met,
A huge heron lit up my path through the woods
Far from the river bank where the proud bird
Usually stood, grave as a prayer.

It flew ahead of me away from the water —
Its huge wings hesitating like a heavy heart —
Through gold leaves fluttering from the bright trees.
He was dressed all in white, my father;
A long white African dress, ornate like lace,

Repeating its pattern of intricate stitching.
The bright white lit up his black face.
My father chanted and ranted and prayed at my feet
creating wings with his hands; *Oh God Almighty*,
My hands, clasped tightly, nursed on my lap.

He held a black bible and waved it about
As he sang and danced around the hotel room
Until the Holy book opened its paper aeroplane wings
And my father flew off, his white dress trailing
Like smoke in the sky, all the lovely stitches, dropping

Dropping like silver threads on the dark red land.

GEORGE SQUARE

My seventy seven year old father
Put his reading glasses on
To help my mother do the buttons
On the back of her dress.
'What a pair the two of us are!'
my mother said, 'Me with my sore wrist,
you with your bad eyes, your soft thumbs!'

And off they went, my two parents
To march against the war in Iraq,
Him with his plastic hips, her with her arthritis
To congregate at George Square where the banners
Waved at each other like old friends, flapping,
Where'd they'd met for so many marches over their years,
For peace on earth, for pity's sake, for peace, for peace.

I KIN SEE RICHT THRU MY MITHER

My mother always said you could see right through me,
And on winter days she was the first to notice
If I was peally wally, when I looked like her father's
peeweet, his miner's singlet, the colour of lapwing's wings.
My voice plummeting or flying too high was picked up,
If I was peesie-weesie or perskeet, she'd remember
The names of the girls in her class and recite them
Like a lovely kirk service, how those eight tight friends

Played peever, and how my mother's hair back then
Travelled the length of her back, thick-thick
Until it had to be shaved off, Oh god, bloody awful.
On days when my wings were grey and still,

My mother's stories of herself as a girl flew around
Our house like Uncle Wullie's, from Lochgelly, birds
In his home made aviary, such pretty colours, chests puffed
As Aunt Ag's puff pastry, my mother brought the colour back,

To my winter face. Stories of mine shafts and pewter tubs,
The long lengths of miners' backs washed for a penny;
The days when the past was so dreamy it seemed it was lived
By somebody else; the days we savoured her past like ghosts.

THE WOOD FATHER

His hands were bark; his hair was leaves
He stood tall and dark amongst the trees.
His arms waved in the wind, hello, goodbye;
Words fluttered like birds from his eaves.

I couldn't tell if he loved me or not.
His eyes were darker than his barking hands,
Nor if he wanted to meet again
In the dark forest, in the old red land.

His daughters, his sons, he would not name
Or speak of them or anything they had done.
And when the rain fell down in the rainy season
He got up and moved across the forest floor

Like a tree from Shakespeare; dragging his roots
All the way from Abuja to Enugu,
In the dead of night into the red of dawn.
Before he left, he gave me a name — Umeoja;

And I didn't point a twig or a finger.

THINGS FALL APART

My birth father lifted his hands above his head
And put the white mask of God on his handsome face.

A born-again man now, gone were the old tribal ways,
The ancestral village — African chiefs nonsense, he says.

I could see his eyes behind the hard alabaster.
A father, no more real, still less real — not Wole Soyinka.

Less flesh than dark earth; less blood than red dust.
Less bone than Kano camels; less like me than Chinua Achebe.

Christianity had scrubbed his black face with a hard brush.
'You are my past sin, let us deliberate on new birth.'

The sun slips and slides and finally sinks
Into the swimming pool, in Nico hotel, Abuja; lonely pinks.

I knock back my dry spritzer, take in the songs
Of African birds. I think he had my hands, my father.